WINGS
OF FAME™

CW01648748

Aerospace Publishing Ltd
AIRtime Publishing Inc.

Published quarterly by
Aerospace Publishing Ltd
179 Dalling Road
London W5 0ES
UK

Copyright © Aerospace Publishing Ltd
1998

ISSN 1361-2034

Aerospace ISBN 1 86184 013 6
(softback)
1 86184 014 4
(hardback)
AIRtime ISBN 1-880588-23-4

Published under licence in USA and
Canada by AIRtime Publishing Inc.,
10 Bay Street, Westport,
CT 06880, USA

Editorial Offices:
WINGS OF FAME™
Aerospace Publishing Ltd
3A Brackenbury Road
London W6 0BE UK
E-mail: info@aerospacepbl.co.uk

Publisher: Stan Morse
Managing Editor: David Donald
Editors: Jim Winchester
John Heathcott
David Donald

Sub Editor: Karen Leverington
Editorial Assistant: Tim Senior
US Correspondent: Robert F. Dorr

Artists: Mike Badrocke
Chris Davey
Keith Fretwell
Tim Maunder
Mark Rolfe
Mark Styling
John Weal
Origination by
Chroma Graphics, Singapore
Printed by
Officine Grafiche DeAgostini,
Novara, Italy

All rights reserved. No part of this publication may be reproduced, stored in a retrieval system or transmitted, in any form or by any means, electronic, mechanical, photocopying, recording or otherwise, without the permission of the publishers and copyright holders.

The editors of WINGS OF FAME™ welcome photographs for possible publication, but cannot accept any responsibility for loss or damage to unsolicited material.

The publishers gratefully acknowledge the assistance given by the following people:

Forward air controllers Thomas E. Cleland, Chuck Corley, Bob Kirkwood, Robert C. Mikesh and Darrel Whitcomb, and forward air navigator Dale Kingsbury for their help with the FAC article

For their help with the Sabre article the author would like to thank the following: David Menard, a long time friend and Air Force historian, Robert F. Dorr, Marty Isham aka "Mr Air Defense Command", Ed Horkey, 'Mac' Blair, and John Henderson of North American Aviation, Bob Ashcraft, Dee Harper and the rest of the F-86 Sabre Pilots Association, and finally Mr. Gene Boswell – the original North American Archives master.

For subscription information and details of other products, visit the new *Wings of Fame* web site
http://www.wingsoffame.com

Wings of Fame™ is a registered trademark in the United States of America of AIRtime Publishing Inc.

Wings of Fame™ is published quarterly and is available by subscription and from many fine book and hobby stores.

SUBSCRIPTION AND BACK NUMBERS:

UK and World (except USA and Canada) write to:
Aerospace Publishing Ltd
FREEPOST
PO Box 2822
London
W6 0BR
UK

(No stamp required if posted in the UK)

USA and Canada, write to:
AIRtime Publishing Inc.
Subscription Dept
10 Bay Street
Westport
CT 06880, USA
(203) 838-7979
Toll-free order number in USA:
1 800 359-3003

Prevailing subscription rates are as follows:
Softbound edition for 1 year:
$59.95
Softbound edition for 2 years:
$112.00
Softbound back numbers (subject to availability) are $16.00 each, plus shipping and handling. All rates are for delivery within mainland USA, Alaska and Hawaii. Canadian and overseas prices available upon request. American Express, Discover Card, MasterCard and Visa accepted. When ordering please include card number, expiration date and signature.

U.S. Publisher:
Mel Williams
Subscriptions Director:
Linda DeAngelis
Charter Member Services Manager:
Janie Munroe
Retail Sales Director: Jill Brooks
Shipping Manager: E. Rex Anku

WINGS OF FAME™

CONTENTS

Volume 10

Air Combat

Air War over the Desert

The Allied air forces in North Africa, 1940–43

One of the most recognisable images of the North African campaign was the Tomahawks and Kittyhawks of No. 112 Sqn, RAF, famously adorned with shark-mouths.

The war fought in North Africa between 1940 and 1943 was neither foreseen nor planned for by Adolf Hitler when he embarked on his campaign for European dominance in the mid-1930s. Italy, after its entry into World War II, promised to secure access to the Suez Canal without German assistance. Having regard for Britain's thinly deployed forces throughout the Middle East, such a promise seemed not to be a flight of fancy. Two circumstances, however, conspired to frustrate Italian objectives and turn what so easily could have been a quick and profitable campaign into a long-drawn-out slogging match that sapped the resources of the two European Axis partners. They were Italy's adventures in the Balkans, and an underestimation of Britain's determination to rush reinforcements (and its ability to do so) to Egypt – even when the war in northern Europe had turned so dangerously against Britain.

Italian entry into World War II was signalled by Mussolini's determination to scrape some territory from his old French enemy by marching into the south of France while Hitler's Panzers were engulfing the north. Embarking on this opportunist gesture, however, also clarified the situation throughout the Mediterranean and, by implication, throughout North and East Africa and, indeed, the Middle East. The Suez Canal, Alexandria and Malta would be directly threatened by the overt alignment of the Italian land, sea and air forces. On paper, at least, they could have been formidable; for instance, the RAF fielded squadrons of aircraft largely responsible and trained for local policing duties in Palestine and Iraq, with but a token strength to protect the Canal Zone, and therefore equipped with largely obsolescent aircraft, whereas Italy's Regia Aeronautica could deploy its main strength, which comprised modern if not particularly impressive aircraft.

For Britain, the term 'Middle East' embraced an area covering more than 4 million sq miles (10.4 km^2), from the Balkans in the north to British East Africa in the south, and from Malta in the west to Iraq in the east. In 1940, the commander of all forces in this huge area was General Sir Archibald Wavell, and to protect it in the air Air Chief Marshal Sir Arthur Longmore, CinC RAF Middle East, could field just 29 squadrons with about 300 aircraft. Nineteen of these squadrons were equipped

General Sir Archibald Wavell (right), the British Army C-in-C Middle East, meets with Air Commodore Raymond Collishaw (second from right), commander of No. 202 Group, RAF, sometime during the 1940 campaign. No. 202 Gp was responsible for applying pressure on the seemingly unprepared Italian forces in Cyrenaica.

No. 33 Squadron, RAF undertook some of the first patrols over Cyrenaica after Italy declared war in June 1940. The unit was equipped with Gladiators until 26 October, when conversion to Hurricanes was completed.

Sand was not only an uncomfortable fact of life for servicemen in the desert, it also played havoc with machinery. Aircraft suffered major serviceability problems before the advent of adequate air filter systems. This Wellington Mk IC shares space on a Libyan landing ground with, among other types, a Bristol Bombay.

Below: Having returned from a 'met' flight over the Western Desert, a Gladiator pilot prepares to climb into a staff car for the trip to his unit's meteorological office for debriefing.

with Blenheims, Gladiators, Lysanders and Sunderlands, and the remaining 10 with a hotchpotch of Bombays, Valentias, Wellesleys, Vincents, Audaxes, Battles, Hardys, Harts, Hartebeests and Londons. Among the bombers, only the Blenheims could be regarded as 'modern', and the only fighters immediately available were five squadrons of Gladiator biplanes.

Against them was available a total of nearly

It was not all sand in North Africa. Rain brought mud and equally difficult operating conditions. These Hurricanes are seen on an 'airfield near Algiers', probably Maison Blanche. One of the aircraft carries the 'GZ' codes of No. 32 Squadron, based at the airstrip in early 1943.

Nos 33, 80 and 112 Squadrons were equipped with Gladiators when fighting with Italian forces began. By November, Nos 33 and 80 had been transferred to Greece.

1,700 Italian aircraft, the great majority of which were held in Italy and Sicily, but, with a little effort, they could be deployed in Africa, the Near East or simply used to attack Malta. However, all was not gloom, for on closer inspection the principal Italian fighter, the Fiat CR.42, was roughly equal in performance to that of the Gladiator, while the best Italian bomber, the Savoia Marchetti S.M.79, was of similar vintage to the Blenheim, though possessed of more muscle and range. By August 1940 the Regia Aeronautica could field some 600 aircraft based in Tripolitania and Cyrenaica.

Italian campaigns

Apart from the ill-conducted French adventure, the Italians embarked on three other campaigns, beginning with a poorly thought-out offensive across the Libyan border with Egypt. Fortunately, with the strategically vital Suez Canal the most obvious British asset, Longmore had deployed his strongest air forces in Egypt, and the early air battles fought by the Gladiators and Blenheim fighters showed that the RAF pilots, strengthened by South Africans, were more than able to hold their own against the somewhat nervous Italians, while even the lumbering Lysanders, doing their utmost to support the ground forces, proved effective while operating under a token fighter protection. After a masterly blocking campaign by Lieutenant General O'Connor, accompanied by bombing attacks on Tobruk, Bardia and other Italian supply ports, the Italian army was allowed to make

No. 33 Squadron's famous hart's head and 'Loyalty' motto are prominent on the tail of this aircraft. K8013 was one of a number of Gladiators transferred to the Royal Hellenic Air Force in 1940.

Having received Hurricanes in November 1940, No. 33 Squadron passed its Gladiator Mk IIs to No. 3 Squadron, RAAF. A number of these aircraft are seen still carrying No. 33 Squadron's 'NW' codes, after transfer to the RAAF, at Gerawala in November.

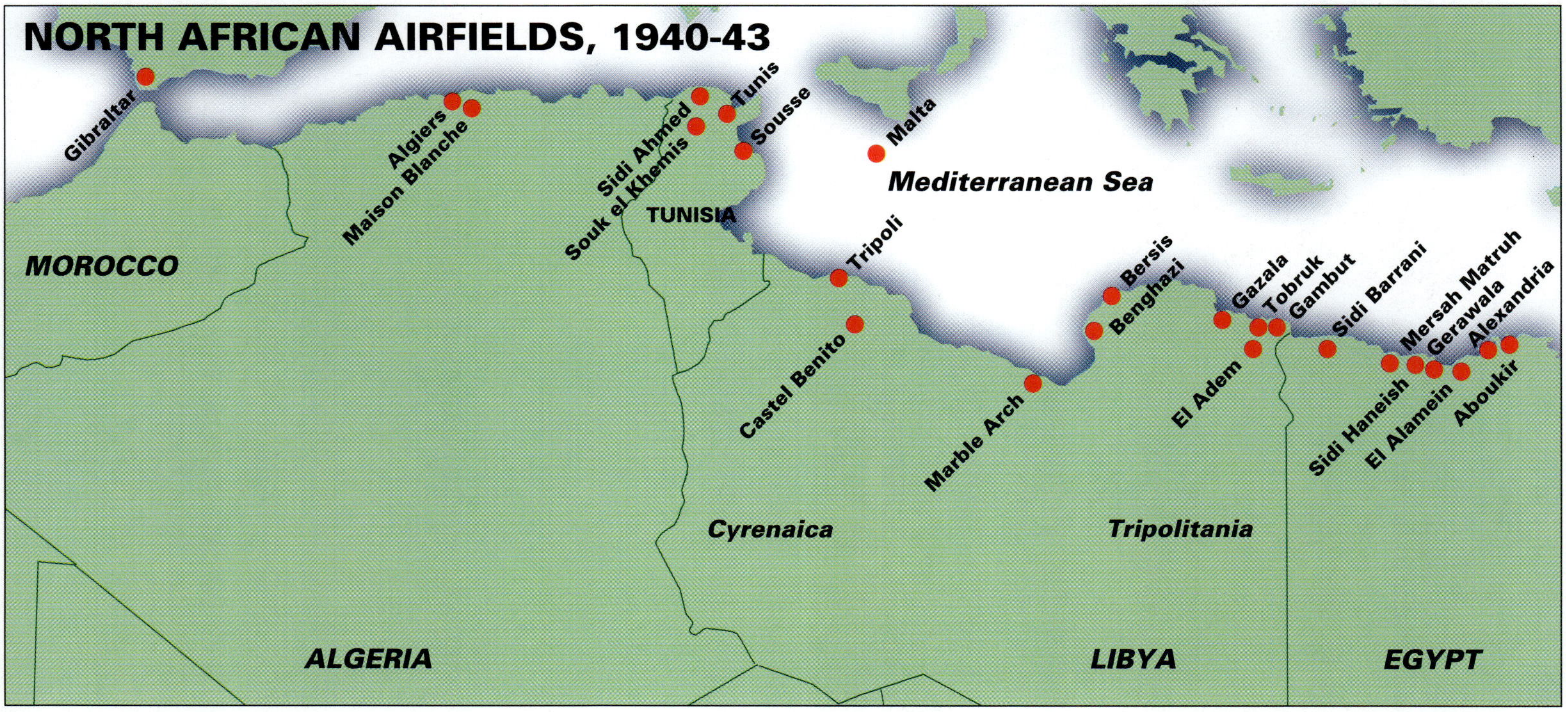

Nos 70 and 216 Squadrons, both bomber-transport units, flew their faithful Vickers Valentias into late 1940. In fact, the latter's examples were in service as late as October 1941. In this, possibly pre-war, photograph, a No. 216 Squadron Valentia is seen at Lydda, Palestine with a number of Blenheim Mk Is. From 1941, No. 216 was engaged exclusively in transport and airborne support duties.

Above: Though the Gladiator was a more common type in North Africa, a few examples of the earlier Gauntlet soldiered on into 1941. This aircraft, fitted with a Vokes air filter, was one of six to serve with No. 3 Squadron, RAAF between September 1940 and February 1941. Alongside the unit's Gladiators they provided escort for tactical reconnaissance Lysanders and saw service in the dive-bombing role in December 1940.

a small advance, but in effect advanced into an easily containable and heavily mined salient, where they stalled. Now, unwilling to extend his supply lines any further, the Italian Marshal Graziani halted. To compound the Italian uncertainty, Mussolini, impatient to demonstrate military successes, on 28 October attacked Greece through Albania, but soon found that progress was slow. With some misgivings by both Longmore in Egypt, and the Greeks themselves, it was decided (in London) to send forces from Egypt to assist the Greeks, and three Blenheim squadrons (Nos 30, 84 and 211) and two of Gladiators (Nos 80 and 112, the latter with orders to hand over its aircraft to the Greek Air Force) were despatched. In a campaign which began with some promise, as the Gladiators – usually outnumbered but flown with great determination – built up an impressive score of Italian aircraft destroyed, the ground battle degenerated into stalemate.

The winter weather during 1940-41 brought the campaign to a virtual halt, while the poorly drained Greek airfields allowed little in the way of bombing operations. Infuriated by the delay in clearing his southern flank for his forthcoming attack on the Soviet Union, Hitler decided to take a hand, and German forces invaded south into Macedonia, making rapid progress towards the Greek capital. The campaign ended swiftly at the end of April as the British forces sought to extricate themselves by sea and air either to Crete or, where possible, to Egypt. It was the final days of April before the Germans entered the Greek capital. The newly-appointed CO of No. 33 Squadron, the South African Squadron Leader M. T. St J. Pattle, was shot down and killed while protecting Piraeus; with well over 40 confirmed air combat victories gained in little more than six months, he was by a wide margin the highest-scoring RAF fighter pilot of World War II, and many of his victims fell to the guns of his Gladiator.

By the time the last Allied forces left Greece, Generalleutnant Hans Geiseler's X.Fliegerkorps was fully committed to operations in the Mediterranean theatre, with elements of three Geschwader deployed or deploying in Cyrenaica, including Junkers Ju 52/3ms of KGzbV 1 and 9, Messerschmitt Bf 110Cs of III/ZG 76, and Junkers Ju 87Rs of StG 1 and 2, already deployed in Africa.

Egyptian build-up completed

When the winter-enforced standstill in Greece had begun, General Wavell and Air Marshal Longmore had almost completed a remarkable build-up of forces in Egypt with scarcely any interference from the Italian air force. In the air, the transformation had been extraordinary, following the realisation by the Air Ministry that, come what may, the Middle East Air Force had to be reinforced, and quickly. Even at the height of the Battle of Britain, Hurricanes and Blenheims had been flown out from Britain in small numbers, a few of them arriving in Malta within days of Italy's entry into the war. Shortly after, during August 1940, the island was reinforced by a small number of Hurricanes flown off the carrier *Argus*, which had entered the Mediterranean at Gibraltar and reached a point from which the fighters could complete their journey by air. Two more con-

Left: This pair of Italian fighter-bomber aircraft (Fiat CR.32 and Breda Ba 65) was flown by the Regia Aeronautica's 50º Stormo Assalto, based at Sorman, near Tripoli. Despite its apparent modernity, the Ba 65 served only briefly in Libya; comparatively slow with its single engine, it suffered at the hands of RAF Hurricanes.

Left: In the hands of an experienced pilot, the excellent Fiat CR.42 was more than a match for the Gladiator in terms of speed, and could out-turn a Hurricane. However, with just two 12.7-mm machine-guns, it was short on firepower.

Above: Savoia-Marchetti's S.M.79 Sparviero bomber was marginally slower than a Blenheim, but was both offensively and defensively better armed. It also had a better range performance and equipped four Stormi in Libya in 1940. These two carry the markings of 10ª Squadriglia, Regia Aeronautica.

Old timer

Vickers Valentia Mk I
Essentially a strengthened Vickers Victoria re-engined with Bristol Pegasus radials in place of Napier Lions, the Valentia served the RAF from 1934. In all, 28 were built, another 54 being converted from Victorias. This aircraft was in service with No. 216 Squadron, RAF and undertook night bombing alongside the unit's Bristol Bombays. The 'VT' codes were applied at the time of the Munich crisis and were eventually replaced by 'SH' upon the outbreak of war.

signments of Hurricanes were shipped out before the end of the year. By then, another air route to the Middle East had been opened. Carriers and other vessels from Britain were sailing with crated Blenheims and Hurricanes to the port of Takoradi in West Africa; these aircraft were disembarked and assembled before making the long flight across the continent to airfields in Egypt. By December 1940, Hurricanes were arriving in a steady trickle – sufficient to equip three squadrons by the time Wavell was ready to strike west across the desert. By then, two squadrons of Wellingtons were lending their weight to raids being made on the enemy supply ports of Benghazi and Tobruk.

Operation Compass

On 9 December 1940 General Wavell's ground forces opened an attack (Operation Compass) with full air cover by eight squadrons of Hurricanes, Gladiators, Blenheims and Lysanders. The Italian forces in Sidi Barani surrendered the same day, and Sollum on the border with Cyrenaica fell on 3/4 January 1941, Tobruk less than three weeks later, and Benghazi on 6/7 February. It was at this point that the Luftwaffe intervened. Becoming frustrated by the Italians' unwillingness to move in Egypt, Hitler had ordered large elements of three Luftwaffe Geschwader to Africa, enumerated above – amounting in effect to 50 Messerschmitt fighters, and about 150 bombers, dive-bombers and transports, as well as some 50 Hs 126 and Fi 156 ground liaison aircraft. Before British ground forces reached the border between Cyrenaica and Tripolitania at El Agheila on 8 February (the limit of the advance), the German aircraft were landing in Libya. It was also at this moment that Longmore was ordered to send further aircraft to Greece, this time some of his most valuable Hurricane fighters. It was no better on the ground, for the total British forces now halted in Cyrenaica comprised no more than an armoured brigade and a half-trained Australian infantry division. To provide air cover,

Above: A formation of Blenheims Mk Is, believed to be of No. 30 Squadron, overflies the sandy wastes of the Western Desert. No. 30 was one of those units sent as reinforcement to Greece after the Italian invasion.

Right: Armourers bomb up a No. 113 Squadron Blenheim Mk I in Egypt, 1940. Not only were the RAF's aircraft in the Middle East outmoded, but the facilities available for their operation were equally as primitive.

Above: Blenheim Mk Is and crews of No. 113 Squadron rest between sorties. No. 113 claimed to be the second RAF unit to bomb the Italians (No. 45 Squadron being the first) on 11 June 1940 and was active throughout the first Libyan campaign, before being transferred to Greece in March 1941.

This circa May 1941 photograph depicts a No. 216 Squadron Bristol Bombay with the unit's 'SH' codes applied. By this stage the type was employed purely as a transport. Black undersurfaces were applied for night bombing sorties carried out during 1940.

This early batch of Hurricane Mk Is is seen on the Takoradi run circa *October 1940. All have yet to be fitted with Vokes filters; the nearest aircraft has exhaust glare shields, suggesting that it may have served as a night-fighter earlier in the war. Discernible on the rudder and wing of the lead aircraft are chalked serial numbers, applied to avoid mixing up components during assembly at Takoradi.*

Above: The overland route to Egypt from Takoradi, on the Gold Coast, was one of two primary reinforcement routes for forces in the Western Desert (the other being via the Mediterranean). Hurricanes were among the aircraft shipped to Takoradi and assembled before the 4,000-mile (6437-km) flight to Khartoum and north to Abu Sueir.

Above: This is the only known photograph of **Collie's Battleship**, *Hurricane Mk I L1669. Shipped to the Middle East in 1940, the aircraft had a desert camouflage scheme applied locally and is believed to have been flown by No. 274 Squadron. It was distinguished by its 'squared-off' radio mast and had a yellow nose-band, indicating that no guns were fitted.*

Left: Regia Aeronautica-style 'sand and spaghetti' camouflage was applied to Hurricane TacR.Mk Is operated by Nos 208 in Libya in early 1941. They were converted by the RAF's No. 103 Maintenance Unit at Aboukir and had an F.24 camera fitted in the rear fuselage.

Longmore's forces had shrunk to one squadron each of Gladiators, Hurricanes and Lysanders, and a bomber-reconnaissance squadron (of Bombays).

The situation could not have been more promising for the Axis forces in Libya. The British had advanced some 500 miles (800 km) in little over three months; they were obviously tired, their supplies had a long, hot and tortuous journey to reach them, and they had very little air cover. The new Afrika Korps was as yet unblooded, but its supply routes were short, and it had a small but well-trained and well-equipped air force for cover. The next move was inevitable: the German general, Erwin Rommel, attacked the British at El Agheila towards the end of March 1941, recaptured Benghazi within four days and reached Tobruk in less than 10. The RAF had managed to provide some cover, its losses being light for the simple reason that there were relatively few aircraft to lose.

Before going on to deal with the next phase of the desert war, it is necessary to look briefly at the third of Italy's grandiose campaigns in prospect some six months earlier. Once again a cursory glance of the military balance sheet in Italian East Africa gave a misleading picture. For the Italians to reinforce their empire in East Africa from Libya was tricky but not impossible; for the British, it was the small Italian naval presence in the Red Sea and around Aden which made the Italian empire in the Horn of Africa an embarrassment, for it represented a significant threat to troop and supply convoys forced to take the Cape route from Britain to Egypt with the effective closure of the Mediterranean. The first move was made by the Italians during August 1940 by forcing the small British contingent out of British Somaliland, but then appeared to sit back and await events. A number of bombers were flown into Eritrea from Libya, but little was done to strengthen the fighters squadrons, some of which were equipped with Fiat CR.32s – a generation older even than the CR.42s. The RAF, on the other hand, had a squadron of Gladiators, some Blenheims and a few Vincents at Aden, as well as some Wellesleys in the Sudan and an increasing number of Hurricanes coming up the Takoradi route, a few of which were already operating from bases in the Sudan.

Eritrea attacked

As the Italians sat tight and waited, General Platt attacked into Eritrea in January, covered by Hurricanes and Gladiators, and with Blenheims and Wellesleys ranging further afield, striking at Italian fuel dumps. In the Red Sea the RAF sank three Italian destroyers, and the Fleet Air Arm another, while two more ran aground or scuttled themselves. A brand-new Italian submarine was sighted by a Gladiator pilot on the surface near Aden, was bombed by a Vincent and finally sunk by a Blenheim.

In fact, Platt's campaign in the north was but one arm of a huge pincer movement, as General Cunningham's three divisions from Kenya advanced from the south, supported by slender air resources, comprising mainly two squadrons of ancient Hardy and Hartebeest biplanes, half of them flown by South Africans.

In the early months of the Libyan campaign the tactical reconnaissance burden was carried by No. 208 Squadron's Westland Lysander Mk Is, in service with the unit since January 1939. Here, three of the unit's aircraft are seen over the Suez Canal, near Ismailia.

While the RAF employed its Marylands in the reconnaissance role, those with SAAF units were engaged in light bombing. Between March and November 1941 Maryland Mk IIs equipped No. 24 Squadron. These aircraft initially flew with dark earth/dark green camouflage, with sky blue undersides. Visible on the nose of this aircraft is the unit's badge, while the dorsal turret has been modified locally with a pair of Vickers 'K' gas-operated machine-guns added to its defensive capabilities.

RAF fighters encountered little opposition, and much of their time was spent attacking Italian aircraft stranded on their bases without the fuel to fly. When Mogadishu, in Italian Somaliland, fell on 25 February 1941, there had been no opposition from the air, but the wrecks of 21 aircraft on the nearby airfield told their own story.

Iraqi rebellion

Apart from the capture of more than 200,000 Italians, the British Commonwealth success in the Horn of Africa freed airmen and other resources to help bolster defences at other danger spots in the Middle East, not least in Iraq where, following a seizure of power by an Iraqi politician, Rashid Ali – with Axis collusion – the very large RAF base at Habbaniya was immediately threatened, and with it the resident No. 4 Flying Training School. At the same time, the RAF suddenly had to undertake the evacuation of some 250 British subjects from Baghdad. Faced with a menacing ring of hostile artillery on the perimeter of the air base, No. 4 FTS set about adapting about 70 Oxford and Audax trainers to carry light bombs; the biplanes could just manage a pair of 250-pounders, but the Oxfords only eight 20-pounders. On 2 May 1941 the battle of Habbaniya opened as instructors and student airmen went into action against the Iraqi guns. A few aircraft of the Iraqi air force put in an appearance but their gunnery aim was as weak as their resolve, and after some visiting Gladiators had shot down two Iraqi Audaxes, the rest made off and did not return. The battle went on all day. Some Wellingtons arrived during the night from Shaibah, and joined the fighting; by the second evening the Habbaniya 'wing' had flown 193 sorties for the loss of five aircraft and 20 damaged. By then, more Gladiators, another flight of Wellingtons and some Blenheims had also arrived.

When some transport aircraft of No. 31 Squadron delivered men of the King's Own Royal Regiment to join a company already on the base, the night forays against the Iraqi gunners were stepped up, as were the air attacks by day, encouraging the Iraqis to limber up their remaining guns and disappear into the night on 5/6 May. Although the Germans made some efforts to support Rashid Ali's revolt by sending some military aircraft (including He 111s and Bf 110s) via Syria to airfields in northern Iraq, around Kirkuk, this effort collapsed when the German commander of the force was killed in an accident while landing at Baghdad during the revolt.

Control of Syria

After securing Allied interests in Iraq (by the despatch of military forces from Habbaniya to Baghdad by road), it was next the turn of Syria to be brought into the Allied sphere of influence, this time by wresting control of the country from a pro-Vichy administration – which had permitted the passage of German aircraft through its airfields to Iraq. A brief but strenuously opposed campaign, heavily supported by the RAF and Fleet Air Arm squadrons, was successfully concluded in July 1941, thereby securing the northern flank of the forces in Egypt and therefore of the Canal Zone.

Thus ended the first phase of the war in the Middle East. The Balkans and Crete had been lost, and the German Afrika Korps was established in the Western Desert, as was a growing Luftwaffe presence. In that first year the RAF's strength and quality of equipment had been

Below: The Free French Cross of Lorraine adorns the fuselage of this Potez 29/2 casualty evacuation and liaison aircraft, one of 120 built for the Aéronautique Militaire in the early 1930s. At least one example was impressed into RAF service in the Middle East.

Below: Operated by the Vichy French forces from Morocco in 1942, this Amiot 143M bomber was employed as a transport by either GT I/15 or II/15. As well as yellow/red Vichy markings, the aircraft also carries the white fuselage stripe and roundel surround originally applied to Vichy machines.

Below: By April 1940, 215 Martin 167-F1s and -F2s had been delivered to the Armée de l'Air in Morocco. Known to French pilots as 'Glenn Martins', or simply 'Glenns', a few were ordered to the French mainland after the German invasion, though most remained in North Africa. After the French capitulation, the 167 fleet was split between Vichy and Free French forces. Other 167-F3s and -F4s on order were shipped to Egypt for use by the RAF, entering service as the Baltimore Mk I and II, respectively.

Above: From early 1941, yellow and red striping on tails and engine nacelles (seen here on a Dewoitine D.520) distinguished Vichy aircraft in North Africa from similar types flown by Free French units. D.520s remained in limited production by the Vichy French and by November 1942 equipped six units of the Armée de l'Air.

Above: During 1940, at least 22 ex-RAF Lysander Mk IIs were transferred to the Free French forces. A number served as support aircraft for General Leclerc's ground forces in the Sahara, 1941-42.

Above: Two Potez 63.11s tactical reconnaissance and army co-operation aircraft are known to have been impressed by the RAF in the Middle East. This aircraft, seen in Egypt in 1941, appears to carry a serial number in the 'AX' range.

***Left:** As in every other theatre, USAAF and RAF C-47s transported stores, food, ammunition and casualties for the advancing Allied armies in North Africa. The first RAF Dakotas arrived in the theatre in June 1943, for service with No. 117 Squadron, which had formed in 1941 and trained on impressed DC-2Ks.*

***Below:** Lockheed A-28As, like this one, were a rarity in USAAF service, as most were delivered to the RAF and Commonwealth air forces as Hudson maritime patrol aircraft. A number of the latter, designated Hudson Mk VIs, served as transports (with their turrets removed) during the closing months of the war in the Middle East.*

***Below:** Another Lockheed product, the Model 14 Super Electra (from which the A-28/Hudson was derived) found its way into Middle Eastern service as a staff transport. Two examples were acquired from British Airways and a third from the US for use by the RAF. This unidentified aircraft is probably one of the former.*

increased, largely owing to an infrastructure that had been created over two decades and which could be expanded with little difficulty once the problems of reinforcement and training had been overcome. Much had already been learned about the behaviour and serviceability of aircraft operating in high temperatures and pervading dust – in a nutshell, a demanding environment. For more than 20 years the RAF in the Middle East had made do with a single aircraft depot (at Aboukir) for all salvage, repair, rebuilding and second-line maintenance of aircraft in the theatre; in the first year of the desert war, half a dozen autonomous maintenance units had been created out of the Aboukir depot and had coped admirably with the demands of five campaigns so that, apart from the problems encountered in Greece, all losses suffered by the operational squadrons had been quickly made good.

Before returning to the fortunes enjoyed and misfortunes suffered in the Western Desert, it is essential to outline the part already being played by the tiny island of Malta. The sheer willpower displayed by its people, combined with the British (and later American) determination to sustain the island with food, fuel and weapons at almost any cost, played an extraordinary part in the operations to disrupt the flow of essential supplies to the Axis armies and air forces in North Africa.

Malta

When Italy entered the war it was possible to consider Malta as much an asset as a liability. It lays roughly halfway between Gibraltar and Alexandria, and therefore was not only an important facility with some docking accommodation and a base from which medium-sized warships could operate across Italian routes to and from Libya, but it could refuel long-range aircraft en route to and from either ends of the Mediterranean. The island had never seriously been considered as a base for aircraft to attack Italy, Sicily or North Africa. Common sense seemed to suggest that in such circumstances it would be impossibly vulnerable to air attack. There is a favourite myth that in the opening stages of the war with Italy, the defence of Malta depended for several months upon a trio of Sea Gladiators. In fact, on the day that Italy entered the war, Hurricanes were already flying to Malta, via the south of France. True, hardly any of them survived the long and difficult flight, but others set out at intervals of about a fortnight until, by the end of June, something like a dozen Hurricanes and a handful of Blenheims had arrived. Nor were the Italians greatly anxious to test the island's defences in the first three or four weeks, with seldom more than half a dozen sorties being flown against the island on any day. A few fighters appeared, but were generally ignored, while most of the other sorties were flown by reconnaissance aircraft, two or three of which were shot down.

In truth, Italy's entry into the war convinced the Air Ministry, if not the Admiralty, that, as a staging post for air reinforcements to the

***Above:** Three of No. 37 Squadron's Wellingtons are seen here, airborne over the desert. A common modification made to Wellingtons in North Africa was the removal of the nose turret, which was largely redundant given the type's night bombing role and comparative lack of fighter opposition.*

***Right:** Seen here during January 1941 when the unit was flying night bombing missions in support of the capture of Tobruk, Wellington Mk IC T2508 of No. 37 Squadron carried interesting nose art in the form of a crest representing the crew, including the pilot, one Flt Lt 'Cheese' Lemon. The crest included the Latin motto 'Defaecamus Luces Purpuras', suggesting a certain human function conducted from a great height.*

Desert 'Wimpey'

Vickers Wellington Mk I
Wellingtons were among the new types committed to the desert soon after fighting began in 1940, to bolster the RAF's otherwise meagre force. No. 37 Sqn was among the first units to employ the type in the Middle East. Arriving in Egypt in November 1940, No. 37 later served in Libya and Tunisia, forming No. 202 Group with Nos 38 and 70 Squadrons.

Above: Abandoned on an airstrip now in Allied hands, this Bf 110 was among a number of Bf 110C-4/B and Bf 110D-2 fighter-bombers able to carry two 250-kg or 500-kg bombs with which to harass Allied ground forces.

Above: Hurricane Mk I V7670 was originally abandoned by the RAF in Cyrenaica during the first Allied retreat of 1941. Having apparently been flown by the Luftwaffe, it was recaptured later in the year, during Operation Crusader.

Middle East, Malta was of the utmost importance if modern bombers were to be sent out from Britain. And, during those early weeks of hesitation by the Italians, Wellingtons passed through Malta in growing numbers. During the campaign in Greece, the opportunity was taken more than once to carry out raids on Italian forces in Albania and northern Greece before continuing on their way to Egypt. They were not the only operations undertaken by aircraft from Malta in those early weeks: a Sunderland crew sunk two Italian submarines in quick succession, while No. 830 Squadron of the Fleet Air Arm flew its Swordfish on wide-ranging patrols to keep a watch for Italian supply vessels making for Tripoli and Benghazi. Early in August, 12 Hurricanes were flown off the carrier *Argus* and arrived safely on the island. Three Marylands were flown from Britain in September to form the nucleus of a reconnaissance Flight, No. 431.

The next batch of Hurricanes due to arrive from the *Argus* was launched at too great a distance from the island, the ship's navigating officer having made an error in estimating the Hurricanes' cruising range, with the result that only four of the 12 despatched reached the island safely. (The same calculations had been made on the previous delivery, but the mistake was spotted by one of the pilots, and the carrier sailed a further 150 miles/240 km closer to Malta.)

A dramatic demonstration of Malta's vital position in the Mediterranean was provided by a Maryland of No. 431 Flight flown by Flying Officer Adrian Warburton on 10 November 1940, ordered to report on the dispositions of Italian warships at Taranto in southern Italy. After flying round the harbour three times in the face of intense flak to ensure that the exact positions of every ship had been recorded, Warburton returned to Malta where his records and photos, showing the location of five battleships, 14 cruisers and 27 destroyers, were passed to the carrier *Illustrious* . On the evening of 11 November the carrier launched 24 Swordfish armed with bombs and torpedoes of Nos 813, 815 and 819 Squadrons of the Fleet Air Arm, led by Lieutenant Commander K. Williamson. In the ensuing attack, for the loss of two of the old biplanes, one battleship was beached and abandoned, never to sail again, two others were sufficiently badly damaged to keep them in port for six months, and two cruisers and two fleet auxiliaries had been sunk in shallow water. At a stroke, half the Italian fleet had been immobilised, and the balance of naval superiority redressed in Britain's favour, if only for a few months. Those months were to be vital for Malta's survival.

Cyrenaican offensive

The great efforts made – via Malta and Takoradi – in the second half of 1940 to improve the RAF's strength in the Middle East, though misinterpreted by the Air Ministry (and Prime Minister Winston Churchill), were adequate to launch the first offensive into Cyrenaica in 1941, only to come to nothing with the stiffening of the Axis forces in Libya and the effective wastage of half a dozen squadrons of Hurricanes and Blenheims during the campaigns in Greece and Crete.

Before and during Rommel's build-up in Africa, it was necessary for the Germans to join in the attacks on Malta so as to ensure that there was no interruption in the flow of men and war

Above: Fire erupts from the starboard engine of a Luftwaffe Ju 52/3m as it comes under Allied attack from the air.

Above: Bearing the RAF serial HK827, this captured Ju 87B was apparently made airworthy and flown by No. 39 Squadron, a Maryland unit based in Malta and North Africa during 1941.

Above: Between November 1941 and April 1942, Free French unit GB 1 'Lorraine' (the product of the amalgamation of GRB 1 and EB 2) operated 21 Blenheim Mk IVs in the Western Desert. After a stint in Syria, the unit's personnel were shipped to Britain where they formed No. 342 (French) Squadron, RAF and re-equipped with Bostons for service over northern Europe.

Blenheim Mk IVs entered service in the Middle East in March 1940 when they replaced Mk Is based at Heliopolis. Eventually eight squadrons were equipped, the type making a useful contribution during Operation Crusader. Here an unidentified and somewhat weatherbeaten example awaits repair on a waterlogged airstrip.

Escorted by RAF Kittyhawks, tropicalised Blenheim Mk IVs (the nearest of which has a single fixed Browning machine-gun fitted under its nose) display No. 14 Squadron's distinctive fuselage marking.

Above: One of No. 112 Squadron's Tomahawk Mk IIBs is run up at Sidi Haneish, not long after the unit became the first unit with Tomahawks in June 1941. The shark-mouth marking is reputed to have been the idea of a flight commander with No. 112, D. F. 'Jerry' Westenra, a New Zealander who went on to lead No. 65 Squadron during the Normandy campaign. Photographs of these fiercely painted aircraft, published in the **Illustrated London News*****, inspired the American Volunteer Group in China (the 'Flying Tigers') to similarly decorate their aircraft in 1941/42.***

Above: Tomahawk deliveries were made via Takoradi, where the aircraft were assembled before being flown to Egypt. This aircraft and its personnel belong to No. 3 Squadron, RAAF. Formed in Egypt in August 1940 as a tactical reconnaissance unit with Gladiators and Lysanders, No. 3 became a fighter unit with Hurricanes the following March. Within two months it converted to Tomahawks Mk IIBs.

Below: Having formed in South Africa in May, No. 5 Squadron, SAAF arrived in Egypt in December 1941. By the following February the unit was operational with Tomahawk Mk IIBs, undertaking fighter sweeps and bomber escort duties over the Western Desert. By June its Libyan airfields had been over-run, No. 5 retreating to Egypt for a five-month stint and re-equipment with Kittyhawk Mk IIIs. 1943 was spent making fighter sweeps behind enemy lines in support of the Eighth Army.

materiel across the narrow waist of the Mediterranean. To this end, X.Fliegerkorps, established in Sicily, opened up a bombardment of the island, using Ju 87s and Ju 88s in January 1941. A convoy, sailing from Gibraltar to Malta, was heavily attacked by Ju 87s and He 111s, scoring six direct hits on, but not sinking, the carrier *Illustrious*, sinking the cruiser *Southampton* and damaging another, the *Gloucester*. As the British advanced through Cyrenaica, the opportunity was taken to fly in more aircraft from the African mainland, including 27 Hurricanes which had recently arrived up the Takoradi route, among them the first Mk II aircraft with the slightly improved performance and increased armament. Having regard for the calls from Greece for more fighters and the gradual sapping of the RAF's strength in the desert, this was a bold step.

The subsequent loss of Greece and the British retreat to Tobruk were not only morale-sapping setbacks, but had been caused by the intervention of German forces which were now established much closer to the Suez Canal than a year earlier. It was, however, in April and May 1941 that Hitler began his preparations in earnest for his great assault on the Soviet Union, and they included redeploying his air forces from western and southern Europe to what would soon become the Eastern Front. Rommel felt it unwise to push further east than the Egyptian frontier – bypassing Tobruk – so long as his supply lines across the Mediterranean from Sicily could not be protected after the departure of X.Fliegerkorps for the east. Moreover, the Allied ground and air forces in Egypt were being strengthened continually. By May the RAF first-line strength comprised five Hurricane squadrons, five of Wellingtons, three of Blenheims, one of Marylands, a transport

No. 112 Squadron Hawks

Curtiss Tomahawk Mk IIB
AN413 *Nan* was based at Sidi Haneish, Egypt during the autumn of 1941 as part of No. 258 Wing at the time of the Operation Crusader offensive. Most of the RAF and Commonwealth Tomahawks in North Africa were Mk IIBs (Model H81-A2/A3s) and were broadly equivalent to the USAAF's P-40B Warhawk variant.

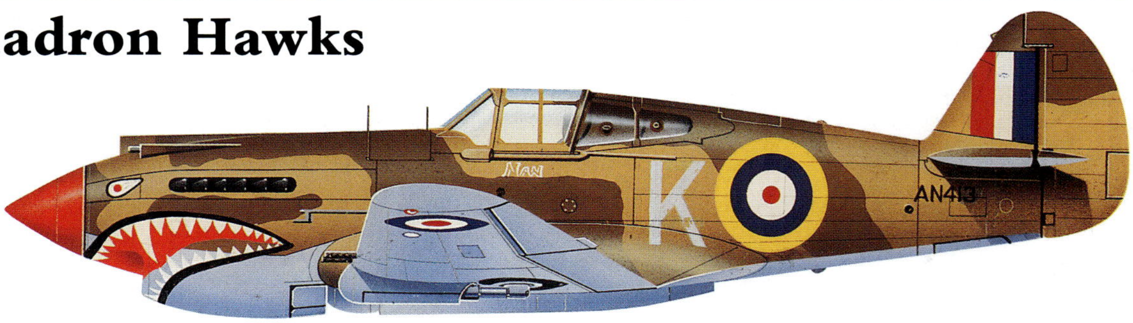

Curtiss Kittyhawk Mk I
The RAF's first Kittyhawks were 560 Model A87-A2s (P-40Ds), the first of which were delivered in late 1941. They differed from the Tomahawk in having a more powerful Allison engine installed in a redesigned forward fuselage. Armament was limited to four wing-mounted 0.5-in (12.7-mm) machine-guns. Many were fitted with a centreline bomb rack for a 250-lb (113-kg) bomb. The serial number's olive drab background indicates that the aircraft was delivered from the US with this colour applied, the desert colour scheme being applied upon arrival.

AK578 was flown by Flg Off Neville Duke from LG 91, south of Alexandria, in September 1942. Duke had recently converted from flying Kittyhawks and his kill tally stood at two. However, he was to finish the war as a squadron leader with the RAF's top score in the Mediterranean theatre – 26 victories. Post-war, Duke became Hawker's chief test pilot and held the world air speed record.

Despite its greater power, the Martin Baltimore was not as popular with crews as its predecessor, the Maryland. It was a comparatively heavy aircraft and its Wright engines proved unreliable in desert conditions.

No. 55 Squadron operated various Baltimore marks between 1942 and 1944. The unit followed the Eighth Army to Tunisia before moving to Italy, where it converted to Bostons.

Nos 252 and 272 Squadrons introduced the Beaufighter in the desert in 1941, initially in the long-range day-fighter role. A welcome addition to the Desert Air Force inventory, Mk IF (and later Mk VIC) aircraft undertook convoy escort, anti-shipping and ground-attack duties. During 1942, Beaufighter-equipped night-fighter units were deployed to the theatre.

Right: Believed to have been attached to a maintenance unit at the time, this Beaufighter Mk I is seen being run up at Ismailia, in the Canal Zone, sometime in 1942. A USAAF P-40 and B-25, and an RAF Wellington, may be discerned in the background.

squadron of Bombays, two equipped with Sunderlands and one with Lysanders. About to be withdrawn from Crete were three Blenheim squadrons and No. 33 Squadron with Hurricanes, all by now much below strength and in need of a rest. Elsewhere in the Middle East were three Blenheim squadrons, and one each of Gladiators and Tomahawks. Surprisingly, this total was two squadrons fewer that the total a year previously; now, however, all but one were at least equipped with monoplanes.

Among the German air units becoming established in Cyrenaica was a Gruppe of JG 27, equipped with between 40 and 50 Bf 109Es, fighters which possessed more than an edge over the Hurricane Is which still constituted the bulk of the RAF's desert fighter squadrons. Although these fighters had fought each other during the Battle of Britain, the Hurricane, through necessity, had been fitted with a large air filter over its carburettor intake, and this reduced the fighter's performance by some eight per cent (or 25 mph; 40 km/h), whereas the German filter, fitted for the same purpose, penalised its speed performance by slightly less than five per cent. Thus, whereas the Bf 109E's maximum speed had fallen to about 340 mph (545 km/h) at 15,000 ft (4572 m), that of the Hurricane at the same altitude was scarcely over 310 mph (500 km/h) – a substantial margin. (Care should be taken when quoting or comparing maximum speeds of fighters, particularly those serving in the tropics, and few official sources take account of the 'desert air filters'.) The German Messerschmitt was therefore to become a real thorn in the RAF's side during the coming months.

Curtiss Tomahawks

Unfortunately, Spitfires were still a year away from the Middle East, and had not yet even undergone tropical trials. American Tomahawks were already arriving at RAF maintenance units to be prepared for issue to fighter squadrons, but this fighter proved to be little better than the old Hurricane Mk I.

It was upon newer versions of this sturdy British Hurricane fighter that so much was to depend during the next decisive year in the Western Desert.

On 1 June 1941 Air Chief Marshal Sir Arthur Tedder was appointed Commander-in-Chief, Middle East Command, his brief being to build up the Desert Air Force without delay, so as to be ready to support the next major offensive into Cyrenaica. Having regard for much criticism by the ground forces of the RAF's inability to provide adequate air cover during the retreat from Cyrenaica during the spring (which, as has been explained, had been largely due to the whittling away of resources to support the Greek campaign), it was clear that the entire gamut of 'Army Co-operation' tactics would have to be revised. Aircraft like the Lysander were adequate as long as enemy fighters were not in the neighbourhood; if they were, the Lysanders had to be escorted the whole time – an unacceptable waste of fighter aircraft. The answer, which had been recognised by the Luftwaffe from its very beginnings, was to have fighter aircraft supporting the ground forces (such a stratagem was entirely logical to the Germans, as the Luftwaffe had been conceived, built and staffed by army officers; it was the very *raison d'être* of the German air force in the context of Blitzkrieg).

Fortunately, the Hurricane had already been developed as a fighter-bomber in Britain and

Among the varied collection of second-line types to serve in the Western Desert were de Havilland DH.86/86Bs impressed in Australia by the RAAF. A number served with the No. 1 Air Ambulance Unit which arrived in Egypt in July 1941. At least one of the unit's aircraft was shot down by the Luftwaffe, replacements coming from among impressed BOAC aircraft.

Left: Serialled HK832 and carrying the name **Wings of Mercy*****, this Fairchild 91 was originally delivered to Panair do Brasil. Acquired by the British-American Ambulance Corps, it was delivered to the Air-Sea Rescue Flight in November 1941. Following service along the North African coast, it sank in May 1943 after hitting a submerged object off Benghazi.***

Below: Evidently captured in one piece and made airworthy, this Junkers Ju 52/3m was a useful addition to the assets of an unknown transport unit somewhere in the Western Desert.

Boston Mk IIIs arrived in the desert in April 1943. No. 12 Squadron, SAAF (coded 'VL') was equipped with the type between March 1942 and December 1943, undertaking tactical bombing until the end of the campaign. These No. 12 Sqn aircraft fly in tight formation to provide maximum protection from fighter attack.

Right: This is an unidentified RAF or SAAF Boston Mk III in the process of being bombed-up somewhere in the desert. These Bostons were able to lift a 2,000-lb (907-kg)bomb load, while the four nose-mounted 0.303-in (7.62-mm) Brownings were useful for ground strafing.

A South African air gunner relaxes with his pipe and two 0.303-in (7.62-mm) machine-guns aboard a No. 12 Squadron, SAAF Boston Mk III prior to another mission. Boston units in the desert (Nos 18 and 114 Squadrons, RAF plus Nos 12 and 24 Squadrons, SAAF) experienced heavy losses during early unescorted operations. Airfields and harbour installations were typical targets, against which Boston crews enjoyed considerably more success once an escort was supplied to keep Luftwaffe Bf 109Fs at bay.

was just coming into service at home; Hurricane IIBs and IICs were also starting to arrive in the Middle East, and their squadrons immediately began training in the close support role. In the more specialised role of fighter reconnaissance, Hurricanes were modified in the Canal Zone to carry a fan of cameras in the centre fuselage (this version being referred to as the TacR.Mk I or II). Initially, the Tomahawk was confined to the fighter role.

In the medium and light bombing role, the Blenheim was being joined by American-built Marylands and Bostons, while the Wellingtons (six squadrons of them) continued to ply back and forth over the desert, and into and out of Malta. In the anti-shipping role, two squadrons of Beauforts were in the Middle East to complement the Fleet Air Arms's Swordfish and Albacores. Photo-reconnaissance (PR), which had not existed in the RAF before the war, was now an essential element of warfare, particularly over the very large war theatre of the Middle East. Thus far, all available air photography had been undertaken by Blenheims and Marylands, but now specially-prepared Hurricanes and Beaufighters were being flown by No. 2 PRU, based in the Canal Zone.

Operation Brevity

The first British counter-offensive, Operation Brevity, was launched on 15 May 1941, but was limited in its objectives, largely owing to a short-term dearth of fully operational RAF squadrons and a need for the Eighth Army to consolidate its forward defences and supply routes. At first the operation seemed to be succeeding, as Sollum and Capuzzo were captured, but Rommel recaptured Halfaya Pass. In the air, the RAF Hurricanes and Tomahawks gave a good account of themselves, largely owing to the majority of air combats taking place well below the Bf 109E's rated altitude, so that it was more closely matched by the Hurricane and Tomahawk; by the same token, the British and American fighters were able to reach the vulnerable Ju 87 dive-bomber formations before their Messerschmitt escort could react from above. In an effort to regain air superiority, I/JG 27's Bf 109Es were joined by the Bf 109Fs of Joachim Müncheberg's 7./JG 26. There was a pause in the ground fighting as both sides prepared for what each perceived as the decisive attack.

'Battleaxe'

On 14 June the British launched Operation Battleaxe, intended to relieve Tobruk and recapture the whole of Cyrenaica. In the past

Air-to-ground Hurricanes

Hawker Hurricane Mk IIB
No. 73 Squadron was well known for its unofficial use of this pre-war fuselage marking. Uncertainty exists as to the colour of the central stripe; some sources suggest it should be blue. From early 1941, the unit flew defensive patrols over ships supplying Tobruk, and later undertook night patrols and ground-attack missions.

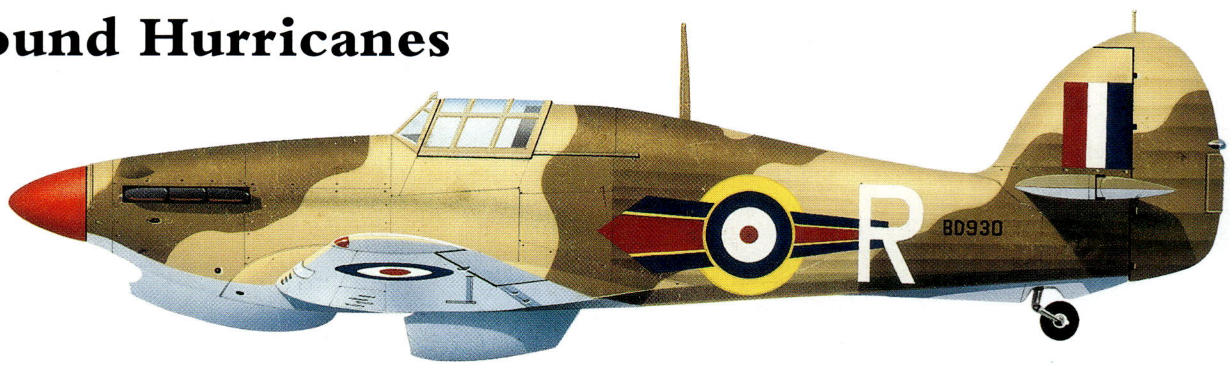

Hawker Hurricane Mk IID
No. 6 Squadron, RAF was the first unit to fly this variant of the Hurricane, equipped with two 40-mm Vickers 'S' cannon for use against armoured vehicles. This aircraft, BP188/*Z-Zebra* of 'B' Flight, No. 6 Squadron was among the second batch of Mk IIDs delivered to the unit in July 1942. Though the unit achieved notable successes, especially during the Battle of Alamein, it suffered heavy casualties due to flak.

Right: Two Spitfire Mk VCs of a section of No. 417 Squadron, RCAF are run up prior to another escort sortie. No. 417 had flown Spitfires while based in England, but upon arrival in Egypt in June 1942 was without aircraft until Hurricanes were issued in September. Conversion to Spitfires Mk Vs was not completed until the following January, after which the unit moved west to support the Allied advance into Tunisia.

Right: Of this formation of Hurricane Mk IICs of No. 94 Squadron, seen in mid-1942, the furthest three aircraft are those presented by Lady Rachel MacRobert of Douneside and Cromar, in memory of her three sons who were all killed in the RAF in the early years of the war. Note that the first, third and fourth aircraft also appear to have had a pair of their 20-mm cannon removed as a weight-saving measure.

Above: As part of No. 244 Wing, No. 601 (County of London) Squadron's Spitfire Mk VBs were engaged in armed reconnaissance from late 1942, during the break-out from Alamein. Once re-equipped with Mk VCs in 1943, the unit was able to add bombing to its repertoire. Here, an unidentified Mk V, coded 'UF-?', lands at a forward airstrip.

Order of Battle

ALLIED AIR FORCES – WESTERN DESERT

El Alamein, October 1942

Headquarters, RAF Middle East

No. 2 Photographic Reconnaissance Unit	Spitfire (11), Hurricane (8), Beaufighter, (5)
No. 60 Sqn, SAAF Detachment	Maryland (8)
No. 162 Sqn, RAF	Lodestar (1), Wellington (8)

Air Headquarters, Egypt

No. 13 (Dutch) Sqn, RAF	Blenheim (10)
No. 46 Sqn, RAF	Beaufighter (12)
No. 47 Sqn, RAF (Detachment)	Blenheim (7)
No. 89 Sqn, RAF	Beaufighter (14)
No. 94 Sqn, RAF	Hurricane (12), Spitfire (8)
No. 417 Sqn, RCAF	Hurricane (11), Spitfire (9)

No. 201 Group

No. 15 Sqn, SAAF	Blenheim (13)
No. 38 Sqn, RAF	Wellington (16)
No. 39 Sqn, RAF	Beaufort (14)
No. 47 Sqn, RAF	Beaufort (16)
No. 203 Sqn, RAF	Blenheim (11), Baltimore (10), Maryland (11)
No. 221 Sqn, RAF	Wellington (20)
No. 230 Sqn, RAF	Sunderland (7), Dornier 22 (1)
No. 252 Sqn, RAF	Beaufighter (11)
No. 272 Sqn, RAF	Beaufighter (15)
No. 458 Sqn, RAAF	Wellington (19)
No. 459 Sqn, RAAF	Hudson (23)
No. 701 Sqn, FAA	Walrus (5)
No. 821 Sqn, FAA	Albacore (13)
No. 815 Sqn, FAA	Swordfish (11)
No. 826 Sqn, FAA	Albacore (14)
No. 889 Sqn, FAA	Fulmar (6), Hurricane (9)
No. 1 General Reconnaissance Unit	Wellington (9)
Sea Rescue Flight	Wellington, etc. (10
No. 1435 Flt	Spitfire (5)
No. 1412 Flt (Met)	Gladiator (5)

No. 205 Group

No. 14 Sqn, RAF	Marauder (15), Boston (13)
No. 37 Sqn, RAF	Wellington (18)
No. 40 Sqn, RAF	Wellington (15)
No. 70 Sqn, RAF	Wellington (17)
No. 104 Sqn, RAF	Wellington (15)
No. 108 Sqn, RAF	Wellington (15)
No. 147 Sqn, RAF	Liberator (13)
No. 148 Sqn, RAF	Wellington (18)
No. 160 Sqn, RAF	Liberator (16)
No. 227 Sqn, RAF (Detachment)	Halifax (8)
No. 462 Sqn, RAAF	Halifax (13)
Special Liberator Flight	Liberator (5)

No. 207 Group

No. 16 Sqn, SAAF	Beaufort (14), Maryland (10)
No. 34 Flt, SAAF	Anson (7)
No. 35 Flt, SAAF	Blenheim (6)
No. 41 Sqn, SAAF	Hartebeest (7), Hurricane (8)
No. 209 Sqn, RAF	Catalina (11)
No. 321 (Dutch) Sqn, RAF	Catalina (9)
No. 1414 Flt, RAF	Gladiator (6)
No. 1443 Flt, RAF	Lysander (5)

United States Army Air Force

1st Bombardment Group (Provisional)

9th Squadron	B-17E Fortress (11)
Halverson Squadron	B-24D Liberator (12)

98th Bombardment Group

343rd Squadron	B-24D Liberator (17)
344th Squadron	B-24D Liberator (16)
345th Squadron	B-24D Liberator (16)
415th Squadron	B-24D Liberator (12)

Air Headquarters, Western Desert

No. 1 Air Ambulance Unit	DH.86 (3)
No. 12 Sqn, SAAF	Boston (14)
No. 21 Sqn, SAAF	Baltimore (17)
No. 24 Sqn, SAAF	Boston (16)
No. 40 Sqn, SAAF	Hurricane (21)
No. 55 Sqn, RAF	Baltimore (14)
No. 60 Sqn, SAAF	Baltimore (15)
No. 208 Sqn, RAF	Hurricane (20)
No. 223 Sqn, RAF	Baltimore (13)
No. 1437 Strategic Reconnaissance Flt	Baltimore (7)
No. 2 Photographic Reconnaissance Unit	various (8)

US 12th Bombardment Group

81st Squadron	B-25 Mitchell (?)
82nd Squadron	B-25 Mitchell (?)
83rd Squadron	B-25 Mitchell (?)
434th Squadron	B-25 Mitchell (?)

No. 211 Group

No. 2 Sqn, SAAF	Kittyhawk (15)
No. 3 Sqn, RAAF	Kittyhawk (14)
No. 4 Sqn, SAAF	Kittyhawk (16)
No. 5 Sqn, SAAF	Tomahawk (18)
No. 6 Sqn, RAF	Hurricane (13)
No. 7 Sqn, SAAF	Hurricane (15)
No. 73 Sqn, RAF	Hurricane (18)
No. 92 Sqn, RAF	Spitfire (10)
No. 112 Sqn, RAF	Kittyhawk (15)
No. 145 Sqn, RAF	Spitfire (12)
No. 250 Sqn, RAF	Kittyhawk (16)
No. 260 Sqn, RAF	Kittyhawk (14)
No. 450 Sqn, RAAF	Kittyhawk (17)
No. 601 Sqn, RAF	Spitfire (13)

US 57th Fighter Group

64th Fighter Squadron	P-40 Warhawk (18)
65th Fighter Squadron	P-40 Warhawk (19)
66th Fighter Squadron	P-40 Warhawk (18)

No. 212 Group

No. 1 Sqn, SAAF	Hurricane (23)
No. 33 Sqn, RAF	Hurricane (17)
No. 80 Sqn, RAF	Hurricane (19)
No. 127 Sqn, RAF	Hurricane (17)
No. 213 Sqn, RAF	Hurricane (18)
No. 238 Sqn, RAF	Hurricane (19)
No. 274 Sqn, RAF	Hurricane (15)
No. 335 (Greek) Sqn, RAF	Hurricane (12)

(Approximate number of serviceable aircraft in brackets)

Above: An unusual aerial view of Kittyhawk Mk Is of No. 2 Squadron, South African Air Force assembled on an unidentified LG (landing ground) between operations. In July 1943 this squadron moved to Italy and re-equipped with Spitfire Mk Vs which it employed, as it had the Kittyhawks, in the ground-attack role.

Above left: Kittyhawk Mk IIIs of No. 260 Sqn, RAF get airborne from a landing ground (possibly Castel Benito) in 1943. They are short-fuselage Mk IIIs (equivalent to the P-40K-1) with the dorsal fin extension to improve directional stability. The nearest aircraft has a USAAF serial number on its rudder, but no RAF identity.

Below: Bearing traces of the olive drab camouflage in which they were delivered, these Kittyhawks are coded for No. 3 Squadron, RAAF. The second aircraft seems to be finished in USAAF-style 'desert pink', while the third machine ('CV-V') appears to be one of the few Mk IAs which served briefly alongside the unit's Packard Merlin-engined Mk IIs during November and December 1942.

Above: This machine, one of the RAF's first batch of 300 Kittyhawk Mk Is (P-40Ds), appears to have seen little service before being flipped on its back in a landing accident. The Mk I was lightly armed, with just four 0.5-in (12.7-mm) Brownings.

four weeks the RAF had been strengthened by the arrival of two further Tomahawk and two Hurricanes squadrons, and the losses were made good, but recent casualties among the Blenheims had not been replaced. On the second day of the attack, the Afrika Korps counter-attacked and a fierce tank battle followed, in which the Eighth Army was forced back to the Egyptian frontier. In the air, a total of 116 RAF fighters had faced a slightly larger number of Bf 109s and Bf 110s but, in one month's fighting, the RAF lost 33 fighters and five bombers, compared to 10 German aircraft of all types. Tedder was uncompromising in his verdict – the Allied pilots lacked the skill and experience of their Luftwaffe opponents, and the British and American aircraft were markedly inferior to those of the German air force, and little better than the Italian Fiat G.50s and Macchi MC.200s. The Blenheim Mk IV light bomber was hopelessly vulnerable in air combat, and the Maryland (previously criticised and shunned by Bomber Command in Britain) was now seen to be superior, more reliable and better able to withstand battle damage than the Blenheim.

In May 1941, when the desert front stabilised, Tedder had no more than 200 aircraft of all types serviceable for operations. By the start of the next offensive, Operation Crusader – which opened in November that year – the figure had grown to 600, even though both sides engaged in operations, with occasional German and Italian air attacks on Cairo, Alexandria, Port Said and some of the RAF stations in the Canal Zone. For the RAF, the Wellingtons kept up the pressure on enemy ports and airfields, mainly at night. However, as the recently named Eighth Army made its final preparations for Operation Crusader, with the approach of the Russian winter X.Fliegerkorps return to the Mediterranean.

The principal objects of Crusader were the relief of the Tobruk garrison and the reconquest of Cyrenaica, preparatory to an invasion of Tripolitania. To begin with all went well, Tobruk was relieved and, such was the measure of air superiority gained by the RAF and SAAF, that the new ground support tactics succeeded beyond expectation. Once more the desert army swept forward into Cyrenaica, but this time its opponents were made of sterner stuff. Occasionally, the Germans made a stand but, now able to call in fighter-bombers, Tedder's new air force took a considerable toll of enemy vehicles and guns. The German dive-bombers put in several appearances early in the campaign but were withdrawn after suffering losses that could not be sustained. In one respect, the Luftwaffe maintained its superiority, as adequate Bf 109Fs arrived to re-equip two Gruppen of JG 27, and III/JG 53 'Pik As' spent a short detachment at Tmimi in Libya.

Hans-Joachim Marseille

It was at this time that a young German pilot of JG 27 sprang into prominence in the Luftwaffe. Hans-Joachim Marseille, between April 1941 and September 1942, destroyed no fewer than 151 Allied aircraft in North Africa (all of which were confirmed) before being killed while baling out of his Bf 109 after engine failure. By far the highest-scoring pilot of the desert war, Marseille was awarded the Diamonds to the Knight's Cross, only the fourth German pilot to be so decorated.

When the British Commonwealth forces again entered Benghazi, they were able to see at first hand the effects of the Wellingtons' numerous raids on the port, with sunken vessels everywhere and tremendous damage to jetties and port buildings and other facilities.

Left: The most famous of the RAF's desert Kittyhawk units was No. 112 Squadron. This example of one of its Mk III aircraft carries a 250-lb (113-kg) bomb on its centreline.

Right: No. 250 Squadron flew Kittyhawk Mk Is for about six months during 1942. This example (AK919) carries a non-standard drop tank on the centreline. Note the arrow marking surrounding the exhausts.

A detachment of No. 76 Sqn undertook the first overseas deployment of four-engined RAF bombers when it arrived in Aqir, Palestine in July 1942. In the weeks that followed it made attacks on Tobruk and in August moved to Egypt. The following month it was absorbed into the new No. 462 Sqn, RAAF. Here, Halifax B.Mk II W7755 'MP-A' is seen on an unknown airstrip in 1942.

No. 462 Squadron, Royal Australian Air Force was formed in September 1942 from detachments of Nos 10, 76 and 227 Squadrons, flying Halifax B.Mk IIs. This was to be the only full squadron of four-engined bombers deployed to North Africa and initially made raids on ports and bases in Libya, though it later struck targets in Tunisia, Italy and Greece.

Elsewhere, dotted about on a dozen enemy airfields, a total of 458 Axis aircraft lay crippled or burnt out as evidence of the RAF's new ground attack tactics – as well as the attention of Bostons and the other medium bombers.

Hurricanes diverted

Once more the tide of circumstances flowed in Axis favour. Not only was Malta subjected to the most serious of all the island's raids by German and Italian bombers, forcing most of the Wellingtons and other aircraft to leave Malta, but the entry of Japan into the war in the Far East caused three Hurricane squadrons and one Blenheim squadron, already en route for Cairo, to be diverted to Singapore. With no means available to attack German and Italian air bases in the central Mediterranean, it was impossible to keep Malta regularly supplied by sea.

Sustained by a flow of men and supplied with little interference from Malta (except by ships of the Royal Navy), Rommel regained the initiative once more on 21 January 1942 – aided by a flooded forward airfield at Antelat (south of Benghazi) which had kept RAF photo-reconnaissance aircraft grounded. Only the most strenuous efforts by ground crews made it possible for almost all the aircraft to be flown out on a small make-shift section of the runway, with the airfield under fire from German tanks as the last aircraft took off.

The retreat finally halted well west of the Egyptian frontier; Tobruk was still in British hands, as were a number of enemy airfields well inside Cyrenaica. With a period of relative calm prevailing, it now proved possible to sail a number of much needed convoys to Malta, where starvation had been calculated as being only weeks, rather than months, away. The Luftwaffe continued its attacks on the island, with an ever-mounting tonnage of bombs falling on the rubble of Takali and Hal Far airfields. In February 1942 alone, almost 1,000 tons of bombs were dropped on the island. However, on 7 March, Malta was given a new weapon, for on that day 15 Spitfires flew in from carriers – the first such fighters to arrive in the Middle East. In the desert, the Hurricanes and Tomahawks (now joined by the much improved Kittyhawk), although outnumbering German fighters by almost three to one, were still outclassed by the Bf 109s.

The final chapter

As the final chapter in the desert war approached, the 8th Army faced one final crisis, to a considerable extent abetted by the tremendous bombardment launched against the tiny island of Malta. Between 24 March and 12

Below: Orange replaced red in the roundels and fin flashes applied to the aircraft of No. 40 Squadron, SAAF. This Spitfire Mk VB also sports No. 40's distinctive red/white unit code letters, an Aboukir dust filter under its nose and a red spinner. The latter was adopted by RAF/ Commonwealth and USAAF units in North Africa as a theatre marking.

Above: As the Marauder was unable to carry a torpedo internally, the weapon was mounted on the centreline between the tandem pairs of bomb bay doors. Here the installation is seen on a No. 14 Squadron aircraft.

Under Lend-Lease, 522 Marauders were handed over to the RAF and SAAF and served exclusively in the Mediterranean. Marauder Mk IA (B-26B) FK375 Dominion Revenge *of No. 14 Squadron leads a flight of other No. 14 Squadron aircraft. This was the first RAF unit to employ the Marauder, reconnaissance operations with the type beginning in October 1942. No. 14's primary role – torpedo bombing – commenced in December and from January the unit came under the control of the North African Coastal Air Force as it provided indirect support for ground forces by attacking shipping in the Mediterranean. FK375 was one of the unit's first Marauders, and on 28 December 1942 attempted No. 14 Squadron's first torpedo-reconnaissance mission. This was abandoned due to bad weather, the aircraft being forced to return to its base at Fayid, Egypt.*

Above: *Some of the less well-known tasks performed by the FAA's Fairey Albacores were those carried out by shore-based aircraft in North Africa. These Albacore Mk Is of No. 826 Squadron were employed as 'pathfinders', dropping flares to illuminate coastal targets during night bombardment by the 7th Cruiser Squadron. Such was the success of these operations that pathfinding for army and air force units was added to No. 826's repertoire.*

Left: Still carrying its US Navy BuAer. serial number (3876), this No. 805 Squadron Martlet Mk I is seen on an LG somewhere in the Western Desert, between mid-1941 and mid-1942, while serving with the RN Fighter Unit. In August 1942, No. 805 moved to the Canal Zone for shipping protection, disbanding in Kenya in 1943. Coded 'H', the aircraft is believed to have been allotted the FAA serial number AX746.

Right: This Fairey Fulmar Mk I (the seventh production aircraft, N1860) was dismantled and shipped to Takoradi, where it was reassembled in March 1941, for use by No. 806 Squadron, FAA. Its history while in the Middle East is unclear; No. 806 was nominally equipped with Hurricanes while based ashore.

FAA Martlets ashore

Grumman Martlet Mk III

Flown by Sub-Lt W. M. Walsh, RN, AX733 was among the aircraft of No. 805 Squadron, FAA that, with Hurricane squadrons Nos 803 and 806, made up the RN Fighter Unit. This operated alongside RAF squadrons in the Western Desert during 1941 and 1942. Sub-Lt Walsh downed a Fiat G.50 in this aircraft, one of five victories scored by No. 805's aircraft during this period. Originally finished in all-over azure blue, the unit's Martlets were soon resprayed middle stone.

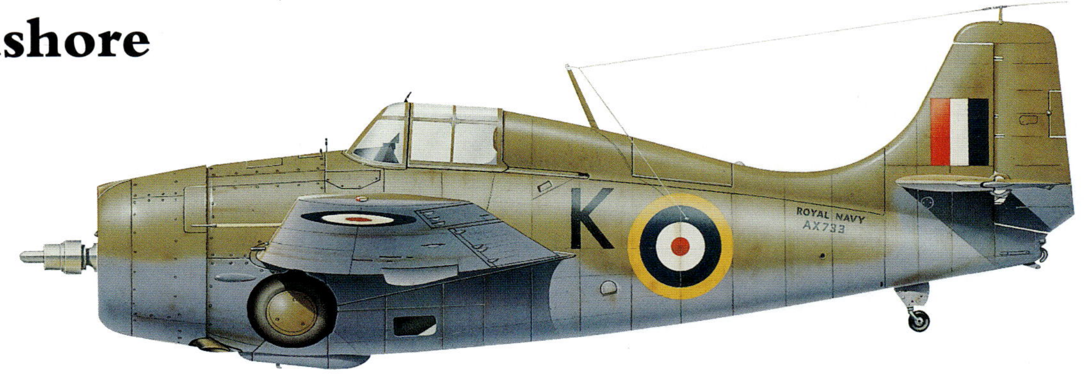

April 1942, II.Fliegerkorps flew no fewer than 2,100 bomber sorties against the docks, airfields and radar stations, so damaging the runways that it was as hazardous for the Hurricanes and Spitfires to take off and land as it was to meet the enemy in combat. Raids launched on 7 and 8 April were carried out by more than 250 aircraft on each occasion. Faced with total destruction of the island as a base for ships and aircraft, a determined effort was made to fly in 47 Spitfire Mk Vs from the American carrier USS *Wasp* on 21 April, and all but one reached their destination. However, after only two days of furious raids by the Luftwaffe, just 11 of the Spitfires were airworthy. Nothing daunted, in Operation Bowery, carried out by USS *Wasp* and HMS *Eagle* on 9 May, 64 more Spitfires were flown off and reached the island. When the German raiders appeared about three hours later, about half the new arrivals were ready and were scrambled to intercept, as were 13 Hurricanes. During the fighting that day the defenders claimed the destruction of 23 German aircraft. These losses had their effect on the morale of the German and Italian aircrews, coming as they did after weeks of continuous battles, and at once the tempo of raids slowed. Within a fortnight, elements of Loerzer's II.Fliegerkorps were withdrawn for despatch to the Eastern Front, where their presence was now seen as being of higher priority than casting down bombs on an apparently indestructible island.

Nevertheless, Malta's ordeal had effectively prevented any interference with the flow of men and war materiel to Rommel's Afrika Korps. As those last Spitfires were landing safely on Malta, the Germans were seen to be making preparations for a large-scale assault on the

Above: These Packard Merlin-engined P-40F-20s were repossessed by the USAAF from Kittyhawk Mk II production intended for the RAF, a number equipping the 33rd and 325th Fighter Groups, 12th Air Force. Here a number of aircraft from the latter unit are seen about to leave the carrier USS Ranger, *en route to Casablanca in January 1943. The leading aircraft is 41-19952* Bastard Blaster.

Above: Along with three other aircraft-carriers, USS Ranger, *the US Navy's first purpose-built carrier, was a vital asset during Operation Torch. As two US Army Piper L-4 Cub spotter aircraft cruise overhead, a VF-41 F4F-4 prepares to roar down* Ranger*'s deck and into the air. The carrier had 54 Wildcats aboard during Torch, but lost almost a quarter of them to ground fire and enemy aircraft. Among other aircraft deployed from* Ranger *during Operation Torch were SBD-3 Dauntlesses of VS-41. This was the only operation outside the Pacific in which the SBD saw service.*

Torch Wildcats

Grumman F4F-4 Wildcat
Lt Cdr John Raby of VF-9 aboard USS *Ranger* flew this aircraft during Operation Torch. Standard US Navy markings of the period are carried, with the exception of the yellow ring around the national marking. Though Raby himself downed a LeO 45 and a Curtiss Hawk, many of Raby's pilots were inexperienced. Torch proved a relatively inexpensive training ground for them, VF-9's pilots coming up against experienced Vichy French crews, some of whom were aces from the Battle of France. The Hawk 75 was more agile than the F4F and French pilots had the advantage of flying over friendly territory.

Grumman Martlet Mk II
FN112 was flown by Lt Dennis Mayvore Jeram, RN, of No. 888 Squadron, Fleet Air Arm from aboard HMS *Formidable*, during Operation Torch, 9 November 1942. Though he was not a top-scoring Martlet pilot, Jeram was the only FAA ace to fly the type. He added two Martlet kills to four kills scored while seconded to No. 213 Squadron (a Hurricane unit) during the Battle of Britain. Flying near Algeria during Torch, he claimed a Vichy Bloch MB.174 and a share in a Luftwaffe Ju 88. With its No. 888 badge applied over the fin flash, FN112 carries a US-style roundel over its roundel and a 'U.S. NAVY' legend.

Eighth Army's positions to the west and south-west of Tobruk. The German plan was to throw four Italian divisions against the northern flank of the British line, while moving one light and two Panzer divisions in a wide sweep round the southern flank, which was anchored on the Free French Brigade at Bir Hakim. The plan was successful, but only up to a point. The frontal attacks failed to penetrate in the north, but such was the determined resistance of the defenders at Bir Hakim that time was bought in which to prepare screens of armour which allowed time for the greater part of the Eighth Army to withdraw without suffering disastrous losses. The 90th Light Panzer Division was held at El Adem, and the Panzers were held at Knightsbridge, 15 miles (24 km) short of closing the trap.

Air superiority

In the air, Tedder's squadrons had one aim – that of gaining air superiority over the battle area – and this was achieved by elements of the first four Spitfire squadrons to arrive in the desert and by the new Kittyhawk fighter-bombers, not to mention the constant raids by Bostons, Baltimores and Wellingtons, which kept up unrelenting attacks on the Axis ports, airfields, and troop and armour concentrations. And a new weapon was introduced, the anti-tank Hurricane IID. No. 6 Squadron was flying the first of these aircraft, armed with a pair of 40-mm guns (the same calibre as a Bofors gun), and these weapons were found to be most effective against all but the heaviest German tanks, apart from destroying scores of thin-skinned troop-carrying vehicles.

As the Eighth Army fell back over the Egyptian border, Rommel pressed on without

A 97th Bomb Squadron, 47th Bomb Group A-20 Havoc is seen buzzing a camel train in the Kasserine Pass.

Sweet Sue, a B-26B Marauder of an unknown unit, is seen at Hergla, Tunisia in July 1943. The 319th Bomb Group introduced USAAF B-26s to the MTO in November 1942, as part of the 12th AF, and were joined later by the 17th BG (in December) and the 320th BG, in April 1943.

Below: P-38G Lightning* Beantown Boys *was the mount of 1st Lt Daniel Kennedy, a pilot with the 27th Fighter Squadron, 1st Fighter Group when the group arrived in Northwest Africa in November 1942. The 1st FG was followed by the 82nd FG and two squadrons of the 14th FG before the end of the year.

This Sea Hurricane Mk IIC (converted from a Canadian-built, 12-gun Hurricane Mk XII JS327) of No. 804 Squadron, FAA was mistakenly shot down by friendly French forces near Oran, Algeria on or about 8 November 1942. The aircraft was among six Hurricanes with the unit aboard HMS* Dasher*, providing escort during the Torch landings. Ironically, it carries the American star marking applied to aid 'friendly' identification.

Above: These A-20B Havocs are believed to be of the 97th Squadron, 47th Bomb Group, 12th AF. They entered service in North Africa from November 1942 and were later joined by A-20s of the 68th Observation Group and the 15th Bomb Squadron. Seen here in March 1943, both these aircraft carry variations on a special Northwest African camouflage applied in the field. Gasoline was used as the paint solvent.

***Above and below:* The 57th arrived in North Africa (aboard USS *Ranger*) in July 1942, training with the RAF in Palestine before beginning operations in October. The 79th and 324th FGs joined them in the MTO at the end of the year, the three groups serving under US command but RAF control as part of the Western Desert Air Force supporting the Eighth Army. After participating in the Battle of El Alamein, all three groups moved west and were in Tunisia by the end of the year. These P-40Fs are 57th FG machines.**

***Above left:* Crewmen of Seven-Oh-Seven, B-25D 41-29707 of the 12th Bomb Group, arrive at their aircraft for another mission. In the background, tent accommodation can be seen.**

***Above:* Mitchells of the 487th Bomb Squadron, 340th Bomb Group get airborne from Sousse, Tunisia. These aircraft were finished in an all-over coat of sand paint. Also known as aircraft sand or desert sand, this shade became bleached in the harsh desert sun and took on a pink hue, resulting in the common nicknames of 'desert pink' or 'tittie pink'. The RAF fin flash, seen here, was applied to all USAAF aircraft during Torch and was used until well into 1943.**

making any serious attempt to capture Tobruk, which was cut off once more. Now, though, it was Rommel's turn to suffer the problems of long supply routes. The Eighth Army halted its retreat at a prepared line of defence based on a small dot on the map called El Alamein.

While the land battle was being fought on the Gazala line, an elaborate plan was unfolding to carry relief to Malta once more. This time a convoy sailed from Alexandria in the east at the same time that a convoy sailed from Gibraltar in the west, the object being to split the enemy air and naval forces, thereby allowing a greater chance of more supply ships getting through to the beleaguered island. Another important aim of sending such valuable convoys to sea was to tempt the Italian fleet to put to sea and be brought to battle. Between them, the convoys comprised some 24 merchant ships with heavy escort provided by cruisers and destroyers. Preceding the 'western' convoy, HMS *Eagle* had flown off 63 more Spitfires, of which 59 reached Malta safely.

Both convoys were sailing towards Malta by 14 June, and both were soon detected by the Germans and Italians. That in the east quickly came under air attack from bases in Crete and Cyrenaica and was forced to turn back when it was discovered that the Italian fleet, including two battleships and four cruisers, had put to sea from Taranto as the convoy itself came under concerted attack by U-boats and E-boats.

Wellingtons and Beauforts from Malta, as well as Liberators and Beauforts from Egyptian bases, carried out attacks on the Italian warships, the Beauforts scoring torpedo hits on both Italian battleships, putting one out of action for many months. A cruiser was sunk and several other warships badly damaged.

With air attacks now centred on the convoy approaching Malta from the west, the merchant ships suffered heavily in raids launched from Sardinia and Sicily, until only two merchantmen were left. An enemy minefield had claimed two ships and a cruiser, and when an

Based in Tunisia, 1943

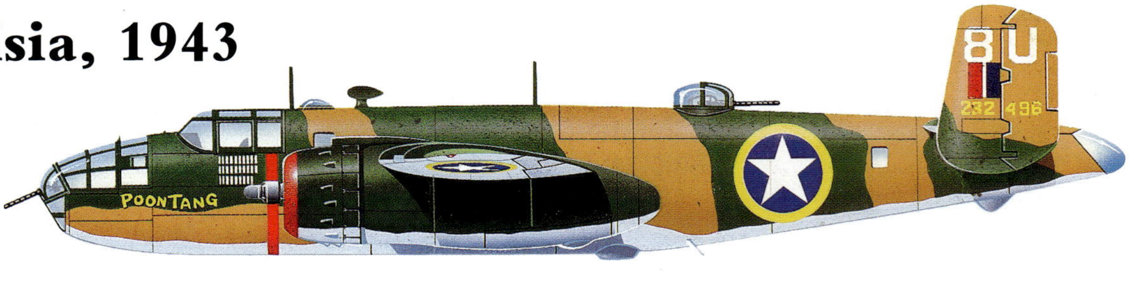

North American B-25C Mitchell
Poontang was a B-25C-15 (42-32496) of the 488th Bomb Squadron, 340th Bomb Group based at Sfax, Tunisia in April 1943. The group had arrived in the Mediterranean the previous month in support of the 9th AF's other medium bomb group, the 12th BG. Notable is the disruptive pattern of olive drab paint applied over the basic desert sand scheme. Use of an RAF fin flash was peculiar to 9th Air Force aircraft.

Curtiss P-40L Warhawk
Lt Col Gordon H. Austin flew *Lighthouse Louie* with HQ Flight, 325th FG, in Tunisia, 1943. The black-and-yellow chequered tail was 'standardised' by the 325th FG from July 1943. The P-40L was, like the F model, a Packard Merlin-powered aircraft, indicated by the deletion of the air scoop seen on Allison-engined aircraft, above the engine. P-40Ls also sported the 20-in (50.8-cm) fuselage extension, as applied to all but the first 699 P-40Fs.

Rarely seen after the end of November 1942, the 'Old Glory' flag decal was applied to a number of fighter, reconnaissance and medium bomber types for Operation Torch. A number of the aircraft types involved in Torch were new to the MTO and carried an unfamiliar star marking; the flag decal provided an extra form of identification for AA gunners. This was especially important for the Mustang, given its resemblance to the Bf 109. This aircraft, 41-37328 of the 154th OS, 68th OG, had the distinction of flying the first USAAF Mustang mission of the war, a reconnaissance of Kairouan airfield, Tunisia.

Italian cruiser force put to sea from Palermo it was attacked by Swordfish and Beauforts from Malta itself. As the last two supply ships struggled on, the Spitfires from Malta took off and formed a protective canopy to ensure that the vital supplies, such as they were, reached their destination. The cost of getting those two merchantmen to Malta had been a cruiser, five destroyers, two minesweepers and six merchantmen sunk; the other supply ships had been badly damaged and forced to turn back. With Malta now able to put up almost 100 Spitfires – not to mention two squadrons of Wellingtons, two of Beauforts, one of Beaufighters, and two of Hurricanes – the island could now play a vital part in disrupting enemy supply lines in the coming decisive battle in the Western Desert.

The Battle of El Alamein opened on the

Right: USAAF P-39 Airacobras based in Tunisia flew reconnaissance and ground-strafing missions from late 1942. Able to withstand considerable flak damage, they gained the nickname 'Baby B-17'. The 81st and 350th Fighter Groups and two squadrons of the 68th Observation Group flew various P-39 variants (some with cameras fitted), as well as a few ex-RAF P-400s. Named **The Pantie Bandit*****, P-39L 42-4558 is seen at Sousse, Tunisia in July 1943, while assigned to the 91st Fighter Squadron, 81st FG.***

Seen at Hergla, Tunisia, in mid-June 1943, this A-36A Apache carries the markings of the 27th Fighter-Bomber Group, 12th AF. The 'A' code letter is believed to indicate the 324th FBS. Along with the 86th FBG, the 27th operated the Apache in the dive-bomber role; one of the aircraft's dive brakes is visible on the top surface of the wing, straddled by the yellow theatre stripe marking.

With a USAAF star and unit codes (of a squadron in the 79th Fighter Group) applied over RAF desert camouflage, this P-40F-1-CU is a repossessed Kittyhawk Mk II.

TacR Mustangs

North American P-51 (F-6A) Mustang
Mah Sweet Eva Lee was the third production Mustang and among the 35 shipped to North Africa in the spring of 1943. They were the first USAAF Mustangs to enter service and were equipped with two K.24 cameras behind the cockpit. Also known as F-6As, these aircraft flew hundreds of missions with the 154th and 111st Observation Squadrons of the 68th Observation Group. This aircraft (41-37322) was flown by Lt N. F. Bush of the 154th and carries an 'Old Glory' applied during Operation Torch.

North American P-51 (F-6A) Mustang
Finished in RAF desert camouflage (dark earth/middle stone/azure blue), this aircraft was one of four Mustangs (41-137361, 41-137366, 41-137424 and 41-137428) borrowed from the USAAF for use by No. 225 Squadron, RAF from Souk el Khemis during the Tunisian campaign from April 1943. Another four aircraft are believed to have served with No. 14 Squadron, in the reconnaissance and escort roles.

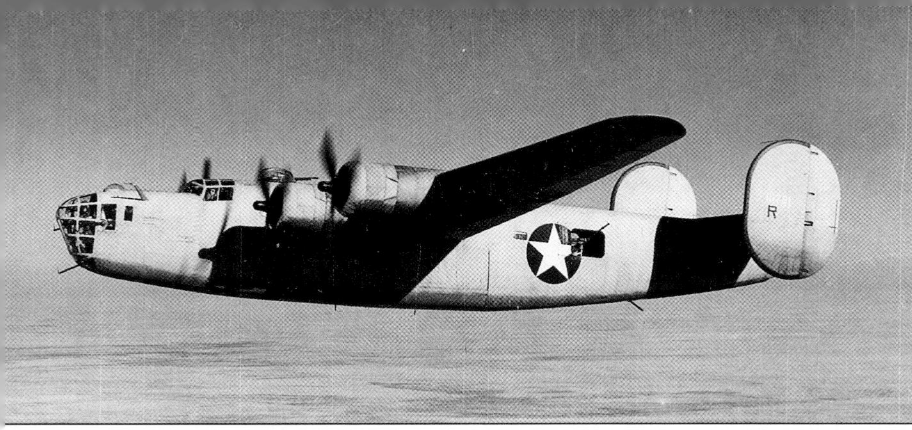

One of the 98th Bomb Group's 'desert pink' B-24Ds cruises over the desert. From August 1942 the 98th was operational from bases in Palestine, Egypt and, eventually, Libya. The first B-24s in the MTO arrived in Egypt in June to join the 1st Provisional Group, diverted from a batch of aircraft bound for China and a planned attack on Japan. From Fayid these aircraft made the first raid on the Ploesti oil refineries in Romania. The 98th BG arrived in August and were followed by the 376th BG (which absorbed remnants of the 1st PG) in October. These Liberators were engaged in bombing Rommel's supply lines for the rest of the North African campaign. During Torch a detachment of the 93rd BG arrived in Northwest Africa in support; this was the last B-24 deployment until mid-1943. RAF use of the Liberator in the theatre was confined to Nos 159 and 160 Squadrons, which between them served in the Middle East for about a year from mid-1942. Targets included Tobruk, Benghazi, Tripoli and points in Italy.

Douglas Aircraft ran Gura Air Depot, Eritrea for the USAAF as a repair and modification facility. Desert sand/neutral grey B-24Ds are seen being serviced at Gura; the mainplanes in the foreground appear to be for RAF Kittyhawks.

Among the more unusual aircraft flown by the USAAF in North Africa was this Potez 540, employed as a flying darkroom by the 15th Photo Mapping Squadron, 3rd Photo Group in January 1943. Although US markings were added under the wings and crossed national flags applied to the fuselage, the aircraft's French markings were retained, as the Army Air Force was anxious not to convey the impression that the aircraft was a war prize.

night of 23/24 October with 'the loudest noise ever heard in Africa', as more than 1,000 British guns saturated the Axis lines which extended some 30 miles (50 km) south from the shores of the Mediterranean. In addition, six squadrons of Wellingtons added a welter of explosive; at daybreak, the attack was taken up by 14 squadrons of Hurricanes, Kittyhawks and Spitfires of the RAF and SAAF, the Hurricanes now being confined to bombing and strafing (and shelling) the enemy positions and supply roads. Fifteen squadrons of Baltimores, Marylands, Blenheims, Beauforts, Bostons and Mitchells of the RAF and SAAF flew a total of 700 sorties over the area immediately behind the German and Italian fronts, and in the course of doing so detonated three large dumps of tank and artillery ammunition. There were reports of large numbers of enemy troops simply downing arms and walking over to the British lines, declaring that they could endure no more. There could be no question of a slogging match developing, and on 3/4 November reconnaissance reports came in that the German and Italian troops were taking to the roads and streaming westwards, while the artillery gave what cover it could. The success of the Allied air forces in preventing any significant interference by the Axis air forces in the land battle had been of paramount importance. As Erwin Rommel was to report to Berlin, "British air superiority threw to the winds all our operational and tactical rules. The strength of the Anglo-American Air Forces was, in all the battles to come, the deciding factor."

Personnel of the 43rd Service Group refuel B-17F 42-5782 **High Tension** ***of the 429th Bomb Squadron, 2nd Bomb Group, on an airfield near Benghazi, Cyrenaica towards the end of the North African campaign in mid-1943. B-17Es were first sent to the MTO in mid-1942 from the Far East. Forming the 513th BS, 1st Provisional Group, these aircraft bombed ports and other facilities until the end of the year, when they transferred to Algeria and the 12th AF. The 97th and 301st BGs were moved from England in time for Torch, followed by the 99th BG (with B-17Fs) in March 1943 and the 2nd BG in April.***

Operation Torch

If any doubt remained in Axis minds as to the strength of Allied determination to rid North Africa of the Germans and Italian forces, it would have been dispelled by the events of 8 November 1942, when predominantly British and American forces landed on the coasts of Algeria and Morocco with the support of substantial Allied naval and air forces not previously committed to the North African campaign.

The success of these landings, despite some spirited opposition by Imperial Vichy French forces and a furious reaction by Sicily- and Italy-based German forces, represented as decisive an action as that of the battle of El Alamein, but presented the Allies with a number of disagreeable but foreseeable circumstances which had to be eliminated if the clearance of German forces in the desert was to be exploited quickly. For one thing, the Torch landings enabled German forces to occupy

Below left: The P-38F was first deployed to North Africa in support of Operation Torch in November 1942, diverted from the 8th AF in Britain. The 1st and 14th FGs were operational from British bases before moving south; the third group, the 82nd FG, flew its aircraft to Algeria without seeing action, though it encountered and downed two Ju 88s over the Bay of Biscay en route. Against the German and Italian defenders losses were comparatively high, but, as the tide of the battle began to turn in the spring of 1943, Lightnings did much to eventually establish air superiority in Northwest Africa. Lightning reconnaissance variants (the F-4 and F-5) were also employed by the 12th AF from late 1942. The 5th and 12th Photographic Reconnaissance Squadrons flew the former type, while two units of the 3rd PRG operated F-5s. In 1943, the 154th RS obtained camera-equipped Lightnings by modifying P-38Fs. F-5s, like this F-5A of the 3rd PRG, were often finished in 'haze' or 'synthetic haze' – the standard USAAF high-altitude photo-reconnaissance camouflage.

Ex-USAAF P-40F transferred to Free French unit GC II/5 'Lafayette' are seen here during formal handover ceremonies at Algiers, 9 January 1943. These aircraft were flown by ex-Vichy personnel, GC II/5 being attached to the 33rd FG at Thelepte, Tunisia in January 1943. This period saw considerable re-equipment of French forces in Africa. Other aircraft made available were 165 P-39N and Q Airacobras.

Tunisia and exploit the proximity of Sicily to Tunis itself, shortening the eventual evacuation passage of the enemy ground forces from Africa. This in itself placed Malta in an even more exposed position for air attack, as well as providing a much longer enemy-held African coastline on which supplies might be landed.

Nevertheless, it was the very strength of the Allied air forces which now entered the North African campaign that became the telling factor in all future campaigns in the central Mediterranean theatre. As Montgomery's Eighth Army fought to keep the pressure on the retreating Afrika Korps and Italian forces right through Cyrenaica and then Tripolitania, the scale of air reinforcement that flowed into Algeria along routes almost entirely beyond the reach of any enemy air opposition was prodigious. By the end of March 1943 the British First Army, together with the American II Corps fighting its way into Tunisia from the west, had linked up with the British Eighth Army fighting its way into southern Tunisia from the east.

Stiffening opposition

In the air, stiffening opposition was offered by the Luftwaffe – now being frantically reinforced by aircraft and airmen formerly hardened by combat and conditions on the Eastern Front. Messerschmitt Bf 109Gs became commonplace, and were joined by Focke-Wulf Fw 190 fighter-bombers, as well as Junkers Ju 188s and Henschel Hs 129 anti-tank aircraft.

Spitfires were quickly assuming a predominant part in the fighting as no fewer than 11 squadrons arrived in Africa in four months. Yet, in just that one role remaining to the Hurricane, No. 6 Squadron was taking an astonishing toll of enemy armour and troop-carrying vehicles. The efforts of the RAF fighters and fighter-bombers prevented the Afrika Korps from establishing a powerful barrier against the Eighth Army at Mareth where, by a skillful flanking movement, the British Army got among the rear echelons of the Axis forces, only to find that the Hurricanes had scattered enemy armoured concentrations to such an extent that the enemy had little or no time to create an effective defence line. There were set-backs in this final phase of the campaign, such as the forlorn low-level attack on an enemy airfield at Chouigui by 11 Blenheim Mk Vs (Bisleys) of No. 18 Squadron. As the attack went in, the escort of Spitfires was engaged high up and was unable to protect the bombers from German fighters, which set upon the Blenheims and destroyed every one. The CO of No. 18 Squadron, Wing Commander H. G. Malcolm, was among the last to succumb, and was awarded a posthumous Victoria Cross.

Evacuation

By 1 May the Axis forces had been squeezed into an area about 60 by 80 miles (95 by 130 km) around the port of Tunis. Some 300,000 German and Italian troops were hemmed in, awaiting evacuation that, for many, could never materialise. The Luftwaffe made desperate attempts at evacuation by air, using fleets of Ju 52/3ms and a score of huge Messerschmitt Me 323 transports, bringing fuel from Sicily to Tunis and carrying back as many men as could be jammed into the aircraft. The RAF and USAAF took every available opportunity to attack these vulnerable transports, destroying many on the ground and others struggling to maintain height over the Sicilian narrows. And all the while, the American P-38s and P-51s, and the RAF's Spitfires, Kittyhawks, Hurricanes and Fleet Air Arm fighters, kept up their vicious attacks on the dwindling airfields still in enemy hands. Rommel himself was evacuated safely, leaving General von Arnim to sign over the surrender of 250,000 men, some 70,000 others having been killed in the final murderous battles of the Western Desert. The war in North Africa ended on 13 May 1943.

Francis K. Mason

Finished in RAF desert colours, this GC II/5 aircraft was among those attached to the 33rd FG. After a couple of early defections by ex-Vichy pilots, GC II/5 suffered heavy losses in its first three months of operation, but managed to claim seven victories before being rested in March 1943.

This Lioré et Olivier 451 was believed to have been used for the evacuation of Tunisia in May 1943, when it served with the Luftwaffe, coded OK+ZD. Once the USAAF had captured Sicily, the 57th FG commandeered the aircraft and applied 12th AF fin flashes.

***B-25 Desert Warrior** returned home to the North American factory after 73 missions in the MTO. It was decorated with a detailed map showing the group's travels during combat in North Africa and Italy, and its crew represented the four squadrons of the 12th BG ('Earthquakers').*

Beyond the Frontiers

Sud-Ouest Trident

Mixed-powerplant fighter

The destruction wrought during World War II by RAF and USAAF heavy bombers over Germany, and by B-29s over Japan, left no-one in any doubt as to the value of the strategic bomber, and the difficulties faced in defending home skies against such an onslaught. In Germany (and elsewhere) rocket-powered fighters were seen as one answer for the rapid-reaction point-defence mission, and much effort was expended on their development. While rocket power provided the necessary performance, range was severely limited, due in part to the major expenditure of energy required to get the aircraft off the ground. A mixed powerplant, combining rockets and turbojets, appeared to be an elegant solution to the problem. By using the turbojets for take-off and cruise, the endurance of the fighter could be dramatically extended.

The first Trident (note nose badge) is shown in its initial guise, which was distinguished by the unusual intake arrangement of the Marboré II engine pods. The nose-mounted air data probe was a constant feature of the SO.9000.

As the Cold War intensified, the need for a rapid-reaction fighter increased dramatically. The distances from NATO bases in Western Europe to the borders with Soviet-occupied territory were such that there would be little warning of a nuclear attack, while a new generation of Soviet bombers was under development that would be much higher- and faster-flying than the aircraft of World War II.

There was never any doubt that any new rocket fighter would be small and light to maximise its performance. This was initially a function of the available power from contemporary jets and rockets, but was a view reinforced by US experience in Korea from late 1950 onwards. The 'official' lesson learned in Korea (later shown to be seriously flawed) was that the fighter's traditional attribute of agility should be sacrificed for outright speed/altitude performance, while aircraft size should be kept to a minimum. The ultimate expression of this philosophy was the Lockheed F-104 Starfighter, while it heavily influenced many other projects on Western drawing boards.

Right: The SO.9000's first public appearance, at the 1953 Salon du Bourget, was less than impressive as the aircraft had not then used its rockets. Two years later the machine gave an astonishing rocket-augmented performance.

One of these projects was the Trident, a lightweight high-performance fighter under development by the Société Nationale de Construction Aéronautique du Sud-Ouest. SNCASO was a major player in the reborn French aviation industry. Much of France's design and manufacturing capacity had been retained intact during the war and used to augment German efforts, while secretly developing its own projects. Thus much of the infrastructure was already in place to begin a vigorous post-war rebirth.

Servanty's project

SNCASO's design office was located at Courbevoie, and was divided into two departments. One, under Charles Parot, was working on the SO.4000, which would mature as the Vautour bomber. The other was headed by Lucien Servanty, and in the late 1940s had a number of diverse projects, including the SO.6000 Triton, which was the first jet-powered French aircraft (first flight 11 November 1946), the SO.6020 Espadon fighter and the SO.10000 rocket-powered aircraft.

Proposals for what became the SO.9000 Trident date to 1948, at which time the Triton was well into its experimental test programme; it was also the year in which the Espadon first flew. The SO.9000 was based structurally and

Right: The lighting of one rocket chamber gave the SO.9000 a sparkling take-off performance, although the Marborés struggled by themselves to get the aircraft off the ground with any margin of safety. Note the turbine exhaust in the lower fuselage.

Building upon German research from World War II, France became a pioneer of mixed rocket/jet-powered fighters in the 1950s. Leading the way was Sud-Ouest and its extraordinary Trident fighter. This was designed as a fast-climbing point-defence bomber-destroyer, and harnessed the power of the SEPR's rocket motors to provide outstanding speed, altitude and climb performance. The Trident nearly saw service, but in the event was overtaken by the considerable advances achieved by conventional turbojets, and the move away from strictly single-role aircraft.

With the SNCASO badge emblazoned on its tail, the prototype Trident demonstrates a take-off with one of its three rocket chambers lit, the thrust more than compensating for the woefully inadequate output of the wingtip-mounted Marboré II jets. Easily visible is the joint immediately aft of the cockpit where the nose could be severed in the event of an emergency. A feature of the SO.9000 was the fitment of bumpers on the tailplane tips to avoid damage on over-rotation.

Sud-Ouest Trident

Espadon testbeds

The redundant Espadon fighter prototypes proved invaluable for testing the new SEPR rockets, although only single-chamber motors could be fitted. Other Trident systems tested on the Espadon were the tip-mounted jets, and the flight control system and its Jacottet-Leduc irreversible servos.

The SO.6025 was the SO.6020-03 fitted with an SEPR-25 in an underfuselage fairing.

The second Espadon prototype was converted to SO.6026 standard with an SEPR-251 under the tail. The rocket was coupled to the turbojet, which provided power for the turbopumps.

Marboré II testing was conducted by the first Espadon modified with engines in the wingtip pods. The test programme also encompassed the use of afterburners, and later saw the fitment of Gabizo engines.

These three views show the SO.9000-01 after re-engining with the Viper turbojet, distinguished by the redesigned intakes. This powerplant had been acquired for licence production by Dassault for the MD.550 Mystère Delta (later Mirage) and at the time was the only lightweight turbojet available which offered sufficient power for the Trident. With Vipers the SO.9000-01 achieved Mach 1.53, and for a time in 1955 it was the fastest piloted aircraft in Europe before being pipped by the Fairey FD.2.

aerodynamically on the SO.10000 project, featuring a very thin, streamlined fuselage and thin taperless wings. The cockpit would have only a small canopy, to preserve as near as possible the elongated bullet shape, while the thin wings meant that the undercarriage would have to be accommodated within the fuselage, all units retracting forwards. Like the SO.10000, the SO.9000 had its rocket powerplant in the rear fuselage, but added turbojets in wingtip pods.

This proposal was officially presented on 7 July 1950, and was rewarded by a study contract for an aircraft with a 5000-kg (11,023-lb) take-off weight, powered by three SEPR rockets and two Aspin II jets, able to carry a 250-kg (551-lb) load of air-to-air rockets and AI radar, and to have a performance encompassing a speed of more than Mach 1.6 for two minutes at altitudes between 15000 and 18000 m (49,210 and 59,055 ft). In addition to variations on the basic layout described above, SNCASO also investigated swept-wing and tailed-delta designs, but eventually settled on the straight-wing aircraft for its final proposal, presented on 3 August 1951. Servanty's team had no access to supersonic wind tunnels.

Two prototypes for experimental purposes were subsequently ordered, with provisional flight dates of 1 April 1953 and 1 November 1953. SNCASO's was not the only supersonic interceptor programme in France: SNCASE, Arsenal and Leduc also had proposals, but the SO.9000 was the only programme to receive a contract.

Flight profile

The SO.9000 was intended to follow this basic mission profile: take-off on jet power alone and climb to 11000 m (36,090 ft), acceleration to supersonic speed and climb to 18000 m (59,055 ft) using all three rocket chambers and both jets, followed by a reduction to one or two rocket chambers to sustain at least two minutes of flight at Mach 1.8. In the event, the rocket motor would also be used for take-off and climb to decrease reaction time against high-flying targets.

Technically, the most interesting feature of the SO.9000 was naturally its mixed powerplant. In the rear fuselage was the SEPR (Société d'Etudes pour la Propulsion à Réaction) 48 rocket propulsion system. SEPR had been developing rocket motors based on the BMW-718 system, which had originally been intended to be fitted to the Me 262 fighter in conjunction with the BMW-003 turbojets. Several German scientists aided SEPR in its work. The BMW-718 was evolved into the SEPR-25 rocket, which used a self-igniting nitric acid oxidiser/Tonka fuel combination and which was first tested on the Espadon. After the cancellation of the Espadon fighter programme, two aircraft were used to test the rocket: SO.6020-03 became the SO.6025 with a rocket in an underfuselage fairing, while SO.6020-02 became the SO.6026 with a rocket installed below its jet engine's exhaust nozzle. Both provided much useful data for the Trident programme, the SO.6025 flying six rocket-powered flights and the SO.6026 12.

Experience with the SEPR-25 led to the SEPR-48, which operated autonomously (as opposed to using power derived from a turbojet for its basic functions). The motor had three chambers, which could be lit independently to provide three levels of thrust, and used hypergolic nitric acid and furaline.

Following the abandonment of the Aspin II turbojet, the SO.9000 was then intended to have the Ossau jet as its powerplant, but this, too, was cancelled, leaving the Turboméca Marboré II as the only alternative. This was flown on the SO.6020-01 Espadon, which later tested the SNECMA-designed afterburner, although this proved to be problematical. The SO.9000 would initially fly with the Marboré II without afterburner.

Internally, the circular-section fuselage of the SO.9000 contained, from front to rear, a nose section mounting a long instrumentation boom

Sud-Ouest Trident production list

Designation	Type	Reg'n	Code	First flight	Flight record
SO.9000-01	Trident I	F-ZWRY	'Y'	2 March 1953	94 flights, 24 with rockets
SO.9000-02	Trident I	F-ZWSG	'G'	1 September 1953	crashed on first flight
SO.9050-01	Trident II	F-ZWTT	'T'	19 July 1955	152 flights, 73 with rockets
SO.9050-02	Trident II	F-ZWTY	'Y'	4 December 1955	crashed 7 December on second flight
SO.9050-03	Trident II	F-ZWTZ	'Z'	30 March 1956	202 flights, 27 with rockets
SO.9050-04	Trident IISE	F-ZWUK	'K'	3 May 1957	56 flights, 23 with rockets
SO.9050-05	Trident IISE	F-ZWUL	'L'	22 October 1957	c. 60 flights, c. 43 with rockets
SO.9050-06	Trident IISE	F-ZWUM	'M'	30 January 1958	c. 40 flights, c. 30 with rockets
SO.9050-07	Trident III	–	–	–	virtually complete but unflown

Static tests of the rocket system were a regular feature of the Trident programme; the SEPR-481 of the SO.9000 is shown here. Note the additional pipe added to exhaust turbine gases below the three main rocket chambers.

and containing flight test equipment, a compartment for the nosewheel and then the cockpit. In the event of an emergency, the entire forward fuselage was detached from the rest of the aircraft immediately aft of the pilot's seat, behind which was stowed the escape capsule parachutes. The pilot had two lever quadrants on the left-hand side, one for controlling the turbojets and one behind this for lighting the rocket chambers. Behind the cockpit was accommodation for radios and compasses.

The centre-section of the aircraft was largely given over to the accommodation of fuel, including separate tanks for kerosene, nitric acid, furaline and water-methanol. Space was found for the short main undercarriage units. Immediately aft of the tanks was the turbopump group and turbine which fed fuel to the three rocket chambers in the extreme tail. The three tail surfaces were all-flying, fixed to the fuselage by simple posts. The elevators featured 14° anhedral.

Attached in the mid-upper position were the short wings, which mounted the Marboré II turbojets in tip pods. The wings had simple split flaps inboard and small ailerons outboard. A small leading-edge root fillet was the only blemish on the straight-sided planform. Three perforated airbrakes were arranged around the three tail surfaces.

First flight

After around 15 months of construction, the SO.9000-01 was transported by road from Courbevoie to Melun-Villaroche in January 1953. After a few weeks of ground and taxi tests, the aircraft took to the air in the capable hands of SNCASO test pilot Jacques Guignard on 2 March for an uneventful 15-minute first flight. At the time, the aircraft was still a while from being fitted with its SEPR-481 rocket engine.

The first 11 flights were basic handling/aircraft function test flights, the last one of which tested the ability of the aircraft to turn by using differential tail movements rather than aileron deflection. For two months the Trident was at ONERA's facility at Villaroche for a comprehensive vibration/aeroelasticity test period and subsequent modification/strengthening, after which it resumed flying on 30 June 1953 on a series of envelope expansion missions, punctuated by an appearance and two demonstrations at the Le Bourget air show. On 1 August 1953 the aircraft was grounded for more modifications after 25 flights, all flown by Guignard.

By this time Trident No. 2 was nearing flying status, and Guignard turned his attentions to the second aircraft. It was virtually identical to the first apart from having a slightly thinner wing (6 per cent instead of 7 per cent) and full-span split flaps, the ailerons having been discarded altogether. Guignard took SO.9000-02 for its first taxi run on 26 August, and prepared to take it aloft on the evening of 29 August, a plan frustrated by engine problems. Guignard tried again the next morning, but after a normal 1300-m (4,265-ft) take-off run the aircraft appeared to be losing thrust. At an altitude of only a few meters, Guignard guided the aircraft to miss farm buildings, but instead ran into electricity cables, crashing in a field after a flight officially logged at two minutes. He was badly injured in the crash, but later returned to the Trident programme.

Investigations into the crash revealed that the primary cause was the lack of thrust provided by the Marboré jets; this combined with the new thinner wing and other factors to produce a no-win situation for Guignard, but one which could be avoided in the future with careful planning and reduced take-off weights. Nevertheless, the first aircraft was laid up for over four months before flights began again, on 16 January 1954. Charles Goujon was to undertake the next 49 flights (26 to 74). The renewed phase lasted until 26 April 1954, at which time the aircraft was laid up for fitment of the SEPR-481 rocket motor.

On 4 July 1954 the rocket was ground-tested in a special rig. This employed a series of cable restraints and pipes to exhaust gases from the turbine. With static tests completed, the aircraft undertook runway tests, during which the rocket motor was fired for 11 or 12 seconds. Finally, on 4 September, Charles Goujon took the aircraft aloft for its first rocket-powered flight (No. 44), accompanied by a Dassault Ouragan chase aircraft. The flight only lasted 10 minutes, but during its course one chamber was lit for 83 seconds. Two days later the motor was static-tested with all three chambers working.

Ground rehearsal

Each rocket flight was preceded by static tests which mimicked the intended flight profile. During the second rocket test, on 17 September, chamber No. 1 was lit for 115 seconds, including take-off, while in the next two flights the No. 2 chamber was also lit for six or seven seconds. The next flight almost ended in disaster. Goujon took the Trident off with chamber No. 1 lit, but after about 20 seconds the rocket cut out unexpectedly. At the heavy take-off weight the two Marborés could not keep the Trident aloft, and Goujon had to

The bullet shape of the Trident was marred only by the canopy. Servanty and his team discarded area-ruling as being too complicated, and of marginal benefit above Mach 1.4, although transonic drag was to prove a problem.

SO.9050-01 Trident II

jettison the acid to reduce weight. After a few minutes, he got the aircraft back on the ground – so firmly that the mainwheel tyres blew. Once again, the pathetic thrust of the Marborés had been cruelly exposed.

Engine change

Enough was enough – the Trident was grounded and re-engined with the Dassault MD-30, itself a licence-built version of the Armstrong Siddeley ASV 5 Viper. With its new, more powerful engines, the Trident took to the air again on 17 March 1955 for a series of eight jet-only flights from Istres. On 27 April 1955 (flight No. 57) the rocket tests resumed with a flight from Melun, during which the rocket was relit at 4000 m (13,120 ft). Despite continuing aggravations with the SEPR-481 motor, on 4 June 1955 the aircraft attained Mach 1.2 during a climb on two chambers, and flew supersonically for more than 30 seconds. Later that month the aircraft was displayed again at the Le Bourget air show, Goujon demonstrating a take-off and climb with one chamber lit.

Finally, on 6 July, Goujon got all three chambers lit in an impressive flight which topped out at 14500 m (47,570 ft). On 26 July he achieved Mach 1.4 in the aircraft. Such flights generally used one chamber for about 30 seconds for take-off, followed by a relight at around 9000 m (29,525 ft). The second and third chambers were kicked in soon after each other at around 12000 m (39,370 ft) for the final, three-chamber burst to maximum speed and altitude. The last SNCASO flight (No. 74) occurred on 27 September, and included a barrel roll at Mach 1.2. By this time the first Trident II was ready to continue tests, so SO.9000-01 was transferred to the Centre d'Essais en Vol at Brétigny for rocketless tests into transonic flight. Michel Marias flew a familiarisation sortie on 5 October, followed by D. Ferrigno the next day, a flight which ended in damage to the undercarriage. After repair the Trident was back in the air during November on a series of jet-only flights.

Charles Goujon returned to the aircraft on 12 December to fly a demonstration flight for the CEV during which all three chambers were fired, a speed of Mach 1.53 was attained and a roll was executed at Mach 1.36. Four more rocket flights ensued, all flown by Marias. Various problems forced the cancellation of other flights, and its last certain flight occurred on 7 April 1956. The aircraft may have flown again on 11 July during delivery back to Brétigny for its 94th flight, but it may also have been transported by road. After a few months of ground tests, it was presented to the Musée de l'Air, then at Chalais-Meudon.

Trident II

On 28 January 1953, just as the first SO.9000 Trident experimental aircraft was being completed, the Armée de l'Air issued a major requirement for a lightweight fighter. Three companies received contracts for two prototypes each: SNCASE for the SE.212 Durandal, Dassault for the MD.550 Mystère Delta (Mirage) and SNCASO for the SO.9050 Trident II. At the time this gave massive impetus for the SO.9000 programme: the aircraft had made another step from experimental status

***Left:** A Trident II demonstrates the side-by-side mounting of the two chambers of the SEPR-63 rocket motor.*

***Below:** Here the first Trident II is seen at the Melun static test facility, with chamber No. 1 lit. In addition to cable restraints being attached to the undercarriage, the aircraft was held back by two long cables attached to the fuselage underneath the wings.*

This view of the SO.9050-01 highlights the wider track (for better rough-field performance) and extra height (for missile carriage) of the Trident II's undercarriage. All three units were lowered by a combination of gravity and ram air.

to a prototype for an operational aircraft. After presentation of its design proposal on 30 April 1953, SNCASO received an initial contract for building a static test example of the honeycomb wing intended for the Trident II, and in August 1954 received the final go-ahead and payment for the two prototypes.

In operation the Trident II was intended to be a rapid-reaction interceptor, initially armed with unguided air-to-air rockets. This subsequently changed to a single MATRA radar-guided missile, initially the R.052 and subsequently the R.511. Radar was to be housed in a dielectric nosecone, although a needle shape was fitted to the first aircraft. In effect it was a 'one-shot' fighter, but would be small and cheap enough to be procured in large numbers. Operation from short, semi-prepared strips was required.

At first glance little different from the SO.9000, the SO.9050 Trident II was essentially a new aircraft, although employing the same basic aerodynamic shape. The SO.9050 was approximately 95 per cent of the size of its predecessor, but was considerably lighter thanks to the extensive use of honeycomb structures. The strength of the honeycomb structure allowed the wings to be thinner (6.5 per cent), for lower transonic and supersonic drag. The internal configuration was essentially similar, although the cockpit escape capsule was ditched in favour of a conventional ejection seat (with necessary structural provision made for a return to the capsule if required). A rearward-hinging canopy was fitted, which would blow off by ram air prior to seat ejection. The pilot could command canopy jettison independent of seat ejection. The flaps were changed to the standard deflection type (as opposed to split), while the airbrake arrangement was changed to feature two petals either side of the upper fuselage forward of the tail. A small autopilot and stabilising system were fitted.

Missile carriage

Externally, the main differences were apparent in the undercarriage and rocket propulsion system. The whole undercarriage was made taller to allow the carriage of the missile armament on a centreline hardpoint, while the track was widened by 50 per cent to improve rough-field manoeuvring. The rocket motor system was the SEPR-63, which had two chambers rather than three, with a corresponding drop in thrust. However, the entire system, including chambers, ducting, turbopumps and distributors, was pallet-mounted in the lower fuselage, and could easily be removed as one unit for maintenance. Development of the SEPR-63 had begun in September 1953, and was based closely on the SEPR-481, with the accent on reliability. It was flight-rated for continuous use for up to three minutes.

It had always been intended that the afterburning Marboré II would be the jet powerplant for the Trident II, but the engine continued to be problematical. A programme of 102 flights with wingtip-mounted Marboré IIs (with and without reheat) by the SO.6020-01 Espadon was necessary before the decision was taken, in April 1955, to abandon the Marboré II

The first Trident II flew with a dummy missile from December 1955, initially on jet-only sorties. This weapon was a model of the MATRA R.052 with cruciform tailfins. The intended service weapon was the R.511, which had two lateral tailfins, each with endplate fins.

Two views of the SO.9050-01 highlight the simplicity of the aircraft's design, which would have made it quick and cheap to produce if it had been ordered for service. Like the F-104 Starfighter, the Trident had a very thin laminar-flow straight wing for minimum supersonic drag.

and proceed with a new, more powerful engine, the Gabizo. In the meantime, the first Trident IIs were to be powered by the trusty Viper, also installed in the SO.9000-01.

So equipped, the SO.9050-01 left the factory in May 1955 to begin pre-flight trials at Melun, including static engine runs and taxi tests. On the eighth high-speed taxi test (1 July) the aircraft briefly left the ground, but it was not until 19 July 1955 that Charles Goujon took the aircraft aloft for its first official flight, which lasted 20 minutes. After five flights the SO.9050-01 returned to the hangar for a series of static tests, modifications and fitment of the SEPR-63 rocket motor.

In the interim, SNCASO began a series of tests using five third-scale 'Mini-Trident' models, designated M-200, which were air-dropped from underneath a Sud-Est SE.161 Languedoc (F-BCUT). These flights were usually monitored by a CEV Canberra and Meteor NF.Mk 11, and the model was recovered by a parachute housed in a belly fairing for reuse.

SO.9050-01 returned to the air on 27 October, and was dispatched (via Dijon) to Istres. On its first flight from this base, which was the first flight in the SO.9050 for Jacques Guignard, the aircraft suffered major damage after severe oscillations were encountered after a testing of the airbrakes. A period of repair was followed by further flights, including one where Goujon forgot to raise the flaps from their 20° deflection and took them to 420 km/h (261 mph).

By the beginning of December 1955, SO.9050-02 was ready to join the test fleet. Its first outing was an uneventful 30-minute sortie, but on its second flight on 7 December it ran out of fuel while on approach, crashing about 1 km (0.6 miles) short of the threshold. Jacques Guignard was not badly hurt in the crash, but the aircraft was a write-off. An investigation traced the cause to an inability to transfer fuel, which used gravity, and recommended the installation of electric pumps.

On 15 December 1955 (flight Nos 16/17), Charles Goujon flew two sorties in SO.9050-01 with a dummy MATRA missile under the belly, this being a prelude to the first rocket flights, which began on 21 December. On the second rocket flight one chamber was lit for 2 minutes 11 seconds.

Official evaluation

After modification, '01' was left to continue the flight test programme, which resumed on 24 January. On 16 February (flight No. 25) the SO.9050-01 flew a rocket-powered mission with the dummy missile in place. For the first half of 1956 '01' flew jet-only missions, having returned to Melun. A stay at Brétigny in March allowed CEV pilots Michel Marias and Jean Franchi, and CEAM pilot Jean Auriol, to fly the aircraft. This was the first official evaluation and explored the low-speed regime, including calibration missions with an MS.755 and a flight with the dummy missile in place. Modifications were required, including alterations to the flaps, and they required a series of low-speed test flights and subsequent verification by the CEV pilots. There then followed a tranche of rocket-powered flights which lasted into August.

Meanwhile, aircraft No. 3 had been completed. Back in the original studies for the Trident it had been envisaged that the aircraft could be made pilotless, controlled from the ground by a rated pilot using radio links. This idea, being resurrected again in the late 1990s, offers significant advantages, quite apart from the obvious one of keeping human beings out of danger. The extra weight of the telemetry and equip-

Trident specifications

	SO.9000 Trident I	SO.9050 Trident II	SO.9050 Trident IISE	SO.9050 Trident III
Wing span	6.83 m (22 ft 5 in)	6.22 m (20 ft 5 in)	6.18 m (20 ft 3 in)	6.18 m (20 ft 3 in)
Wing area	16.53 m^2 (178 sq ft)	14.50 m^2 (156 sq ft)	14.50 m^2 (156 sq ft)	14.50 m^2 (156 sq ft)
Wing chord	2.42 m (7 ft 11 in)	2.355 m (7 ft 8.5 in)	2.375 m (7 ft 9.5 in)	2.375 m (7 ft 9.5 in)
Wing aspect ratio	2.83	2.62	2.62	2.62
Wingtip pod length	3.20 m (10 ft 6 in)	3.65 m (11 ft 11.5 in)	3.91 m (12 ft 10 in)	4.12 m (13 ft 6 in)
Fuselage length	12.90 m (42 ft 4 in)	12.77 m (41 ft 11 in)	13.26 m (43 ft 6 in)	13.26 m (43 ft 6 in)
Height	2.84 m (9 ft 4 in)	3.16 m (10 ft 4.5 in)	3.2 m (10 ft 6 in)	3.2 m (10 ft 6 in)
Wheelbase	4.26 m (13 ft 11.5 in)	4.77 m (15 ft 8 in)	4.66 m (15 ft 3.5 in)	4.66 m (15 ft 3.5 in)
Wheel track	1.20 m (3 ft 11 in)	1.80 m (5 ft 11 in)	1.80 m (5 ft 11 in)	1.80 m (5 ft 11 in)
Jet powerplant	2 x Turboméca Marboré II (non-afterburning)	2 x Dassault MD-30 (Armstrong Siddeley Viper ASV.5)	2 x Turboméca Gabizo (non-afterburning)	2 x Turboméca Gabizo (afterburning)
Thrust (each)	3.92 kN (882 lb)	7.26 kN (1,630 lb)	10.79 kN (2,425 lb)	14.71 kN (3,307 lb)
Rocket powerplant	SEPR-481	SEPR-63	SEPR-631	SEPR-631
Rocket thrust (total)	44.15 kN (9,920 lb)	29.43 kN (6,614 lb)	29.43 kN (6,614 lb)	29.43 kN (6,614 lb)
Fuel (kerosene) capacity	835 litres (183.7 Imp gal)	830 litres (182.6 Imp gal)	855 litres (188 Imp gal)	1000 litres (220 Imp gal)
Nitric acid capacity	935 litres (205.7 Imp gal)	805 litres (177 Imp gal)	1000 litres (220 Imp gal)	?
Furaline capacity	550 litres (121 Imp gal)	520 litres (114.4 Imp gal)	520 litres (114.4 Imp gal)	?
Water-methanol capacity	117 litres (25.7 Imp gal)	80 litres (17.6 Imp gal)	90 litres (19.8 Imp gal)	90 litres (19.8 Imp gal)
Empty weight	1465 kg (3,230 lb)	?	1338 kg (2,950 lb)	1356 kg (2,990 lb)
Empty equipped weight	3070 kg (6,768 lb)	2600 kg (5,732 lb)	2815 kg (6,206 lb)	2910 kg (6,415 lb)
Fuel and lubricant weight	2130 kg (4,696 lb)	2305 kg (5,081 lb)	2060 kg (4,541 lb)	2735 kg (6,030 lb)
Maximum take-off weight	5800 kg (12,787 lb)	5150 kg (11,354 lb)	5150 kg (11,354 lb)	5900 kg (13,007 lb)
Wing loading at max. take-off	351 kg/m^2 (72 lb/sq ft)	355 kg/m^2 (73 lb/sq ft)	355 kg/m^2 (73 lb/sq ft)	407 kg/m^2 (83 lb/sq ft)

Above: The dummy R.052-armed SO.9050-01 climbs away with chamber No. 1 ignited. The full two-chamber thrust was only used in the final climb and acceleration to operational altitude.

Right: The Trident II employed a conventional ejection seat (as denoted by the warning triangle). This necessitated a redesign of the canopy, which was designed to blow off backwards under ram air pressure when jettisoned.

ment necessary for radio guidance was far outweighed by the removal of all the equipment (pressurisation, ejection seat, instrumentation, etc.) necessary for piloted operations, while the deletion of the cockpit canopy would have a beneficial effect on drag. The size of the aircraft could be further reduced accordingly, while its performance would increase.

Consequently, SO.9050-03 had been intended to act as a testbed for aspects of a pilotless version, with provision made for guidance and telemetry equipment. However, with the untimely end of the second prototype, Sud-Ouest was obliged to abandon any such plans and divert the third aircraft to the primary flight test programme. It first flew in the hands of Jacques Guignard on 30 March 1956 and began a lengthy series of low-speed jet-only flights which explored aircraft handling in various configurations, including asymmetric thrust. In October it was fitted with an anti-spin parachute, and began inflight relight tests of the turbojets.

US interest

American interest in the Trident II project resulted in a delegation visiting Melun and witnessing a rocket flight by Charles Goujon with the SO.9050-01 carrying a missile. They also saw a live ground ejection by a Major Murray, complete with high-altitude pressure suit attire. Further jet-only flights investigated snaking, allowing new company test pilot Max Fischl to join the team. At this time Sud-Ouest became simply Ouest Aviation for a few months, before being merged with Sud-Est to form Sud Aviation.

Flight tests continued through 1956 and into 1957 with continuing evaluation by CEV pilots interspersed with company flights. On 8 January Charles Goujon took '01' on an envelope expansion flight, which reached 19085 m (62,615 ft) and Mach 1.93. Subsequently, the aircraft was flown by CEAM pilot Jacques Auriol as part of the first Armée de l'Air evaluations. Flights continued until 21 May 1957, when tragedy struck the Trident programme.

On flight No. 152 (the 73rd with rocket power), the SO.9050-01 was lost in spectacular but tragic fashion when the aircraft exploded. Charles Goujon was practising his routine for the forthcoming Paris air show, which entailed using a single chamber take-off and climb-out, followed by a two-chamber climb. The take-off went well and the first chamber shut down. Both chambers were then lit and then extinguished at 166 seconds after take-off. At 195 seconds the aircraft simply blew apart, scattering debris over an area of about 2 km (1.2 miles). 'Charlie' Goujon, the senior pilot on the Trident programme, died instantly.

In the aftermath of the accident, the Trident fleet ('04' had just flown) was grounded pending the inquiry. No cause for the explosion could be ascertained, although suspicion fell largely on chemical decomposition in the hydraulic accumulators. Regular inspections of them, together with other safety precautions such as rigid instructions as to the handling of the rocket fuels to avoid any contamination in the fuselage, were introduced, and flight trials continued.

In February 1957 the SO.9050-03 undertook a few tests of the original telemetry and radio guidance equipment for which it had been intended, among the continuing equipment and handling trials. CEV pilot Jean-Pierre Rozier flew his first flight in a Trident on 21 March 1957, while Roger Carpentier arrived to replace Goujon as a company pilot, taking his first flight on 6 September. On 19 September the aircraft was ferried for its traditional winter test programme at Istres by Carpentier. On its arrival the undercarriage refused to lower, and a wheels-up landing on the grass was the only option, requiring a two-month lay-up for repairs. It was not until 13 May (flight No. 107) that it was eventually flown with rocket power, and it was destined to only fly 27 flights out of its 202 sorties with rocket power. Its final flight was on 30 April 1958, by which time it had also been flown by CEV pilots André Pinier and Jean Coureau.

Trident IISE

By 1955 the Trident programme was showing sufficient promise to justify further development in the form of the Trident IISE (Série Experimentale). These examples became, in effect, pre-production aircraft for the fighter series. Externally, the main difference was the slightly rounded nosecone (designed to house either a Dassault DRA 5A Aladin or Thomson DRA 5B FJ radar), but the major difference was the powerplant. The rocket system was essentially the same (SEPR-631) but the Vipers were replaced by the new Turboméca Gabizo jets, which developed more power. They were not fitted with the intended afterburners, however. The Gabizo had flown 28 sorties installed in the wingtip pods of the venerable SO.6021-01 Espadon. Other modifications included a larger cockpit and a brake parachute mounted above the rocket chambers.

Despite its small, low-drag wings (which featured large but simple unblown flaps), the Trident had a commendably low landing speed (around 185 km/h; 115 mph). This was largely due to the low wing loading once the fuel had been expended.

Even in an operational configuration, the Trident could have been expected to reach 60,000 ft in well under four minutes from brakes-off. Such a performance was deemed necessary at a time when Western Europe's biggest fear was a surprise nuclear attack by high-flying Soviet bombers.

Flight trials of the first Trident IISE, SO.9050-04, by Jacques Guignard began on 3 May 1957, but it was subsequently grounded pending the outcome of the Goujon crash investigation. It returned to the air on 14 August and underwent low-speed trials, including CEV trials by Pierre Faure, Franchi and Rozier. SO.9050-05 first flew, again with Guignard at the controls, on 22 October 1957. It had a Martin-Baker Mk 4 ejection seat in place of the SNCASO E-105B. Guignard flew the sixth aircraft for the first time on 30 January 1958.

In April 1957 Sud Aviation announced a four-company allegiance with SABCA, Fokker and a German manufacturer to jointly market the Trident as a standard NATO interceptor. As a result of this, on 22 November the Trident was flown (jet-only) by a foreign pilot for the first time, when Luftwaffe officer Major Werner flew '05'. This attempt to influence the decisions of European governments came to nothing, but did lay the foundations for the subsequent 'sale of the century' of F-104s.

In early 1958 the three Trident IISE aircraft got swiftly into rocket flights which showed extreme speed/altitude promise thanks to the additional power provided by the Gabizo turbojets. Carpentier took the fifth aircraft to an amazing Mach 1.94 (the highest recorded speed during the whole programme) and 22800 m (74,800 ft). The latter figure easily beat the existing altitude record (then held by a modified Canberra) but could not be ratified.

Further time-to-height record attempts were made in early April, when Guignard took '04' to 15000 m (49,212 ft) in 2 minutes 37 seconds, and 50,000 ft (15240 m) in 2 minutes 49 seconds. Later in the month the same pilot/aircraft combination achieved 18000 m (59,055 ft) in 3 minutes 17 seconds. Further attempts on the 21000-m (68,900-ft) record were thwarted by technical problems. The last of them, on 30 April 1958, was the fourth Trident II's last of 56 flights.

Aiding the X-15 team

During April the Trident programme played host to a NASA delegation from the X-15 programme, which was very interested in the Trident's rocket power and control systems. Pilots Joe Walker and Iven Kincheloe each flew five flights in '05' and '06', including an amazing three rocket flights in one day (22 April) using the fifth Trident II. It was the last official act of this aircraft, for the programme was cancelled a few days later on 2 May 1958. It continued to be flown by the CEV for two months after the cancellation.

On the day of (and despite) the programme termination, Roger Carpentier flew the sixth aircraft on an altitude record flight which captured the world record from the Grumman F11F-1 Tiger. Achieving Mach 1.77 at the time of rocket burn-out, the aircraft continued upwards and topped 24350 m (79,888 ft). The record was short-lived, however, falling soon to the Lockheed F-104. Like the fifth aircraft, the SO.9050-06 continued in use with the CEV for some time. As its swansong, on one of the very last flights of the Trident, on 6 October, Jean-Pierre Rozier took the aircraft to an unofficial altitude record of around 26000 m (85,000 ft). Unfortunately, the altitude radar was not tracking the flight, and it remained an unofficial record.

When the cancellation came, Sud Aviation had four more Tridents under construction in the Courbevoie works with a further six pre-production aircraft planned. SO.9050-07 was almost complete, although all work on these aircraft was stopped. This aircraft was the first of the Trident IIIAs, which had afterburning Gabizo jets fitted, differing externally by having a variable exhaust and an intake centrebody shock cone. The centreline pylon was plumbed for a ferry fuel tank, as well as wired for carriage of the MATRA R.511 missile. Aladin radar was fitted in the nose.

Despite the increased take-off weight, the Trident III could have taken off with one rocket chamber in 475 m (1,560 ft). A standard

The ill-fated second (above) and third (left) Trident IIs differed little from the first. SO.9050-03 was intended to explore the ambitious concept of a pilotless interceptor, which was the ultimate goal of Servanty and the Trident project. However, the loss of the second aircraft meant that 'Z' spent much of its time performing low-speed handling trials, and only flew a handful of auto-guidance/telemetry study flights.

Sud-Ouest SO.9050 Trident IISE cutaway

1 Interchangeable radar nose
2 Nose undercarriage stowage
3 Hydraulic retraction strut
4 Flight control system artificial feel units
5 Rudder pedals
6 Instrument panel
7 Control column
8 Side console panel with jet engine throttle levers
9 Upward-hinging one-piece canopy cover
10 Lightweight ejection seat
11 Oxygen bottle
12 Compressed air bottles
13 Hydraulic reservoir and accumulators
14 Radio and electronics equipment
15 Autostabiliser controller
16 Furaline tank
17 Forward kerosene fuel tanks
18 Ventral missile carriage
19 Main undercarriage stowage
20 Hydraulic retraction jacks
21 Central nitric acid tank

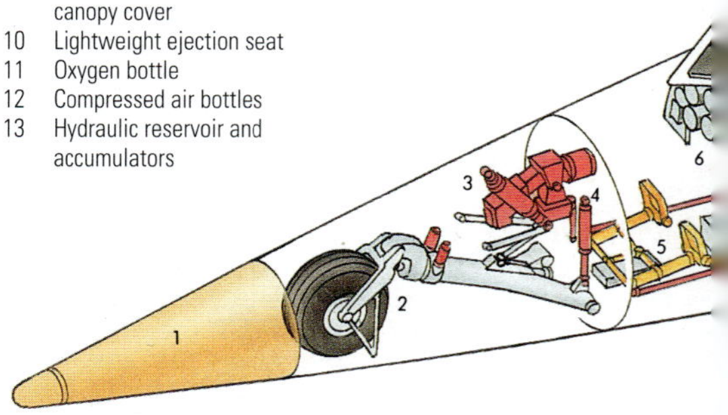

'K' was the first of the Trident IISE aircraft, easily distinguishable by the lengthened and rounded nosecone, intended to house the Aladin radar. The engine nacelles, which contained Gabizos, were also noticeably different to those of the Viper-engined aircraft. A brake chute was carried by the IISE, located above the rocket chambers.

mission would involve a climb to around 18000 m (59,055 ft) at Mach 1.72 in under five minutes, accelerate to Mach 2 for 1.5 minutes for the interception, then decelerate to Mach 1.5 for the return and land. With brake chute deployed it could land in 420 m (1,380 ft). Standard endurance would be 30 minutes, with a radius of action of 160 km (100 miles).

Unbuilt Tridents

Further developments planned included streamlining of the cockpit, lengthening of the fuselage and reduction of the wing thickness to 4 per cent in the Trident IIIB. Trident IIIC and Trident IV studies were also begun, although details are scant. Although the afterburning Gabizo remained the turbojet powerplant of all these projected variants, the SEPR-632 rocket (with Tonka fuel instead of furaline) and SEPR-634 with variable thrust were also under investigation. None of them was to reach hardware stage.

In the period leading up to its cancellation, the Trident programme had been slowly assuming lesser importance and the intended numbers to be procured had fallen. The merger of Ouest with Sud-Est had put paid to the latter's Durandal project as a competitor, but the Mirage remained. By 1956 the Armée de l'Air's plans envisaged the procurement of 19 squadrons of Mirage IIIs and only four (80 aircraft) of Tridents.

Cancellation

As mentioned above, the axe fell on the Trident II programme on 2 May 1958. Nothing could touch the Trident for climb and altitude performance, but it was rigidly limited to one role. On the other hand, Dassault's Mirage was far more versatile, and fitted in well with the Armée de l'Air's gradual move away from the light fighter concept. Various other factors may also have contributed to the Trident's demise: worries concerning the stocking and handling of volatile rocket fuels, long-term corrosion problems, political desires to see Dassault as the prime military contractor, and a squeeze on the defence budget caused by the war in Algeria.

Trident production was briefly reviewed in 1961 but by then the Mirage and its developments were firmly entrenched in the French military machine. Perhaps if development of the aircraft had been achieved more rapidly, the SO.9050 would have stood a high chance of entering service, but it was simply overtaken by events. There is no doubt that it could easily have achieved well over Mach 2, and its altitude and climb performance are more than respectable even in the 1990s. In the event, it was defeated by a more realistic attitude to the provision of air defence, but it was a brilliant example of the technical capabilities of the French aviation industry in the 1950s; for a while, SNCASO and its successors were undoubtedly the most experienced company in the world in terms of rocket-powered flight.

David Donald

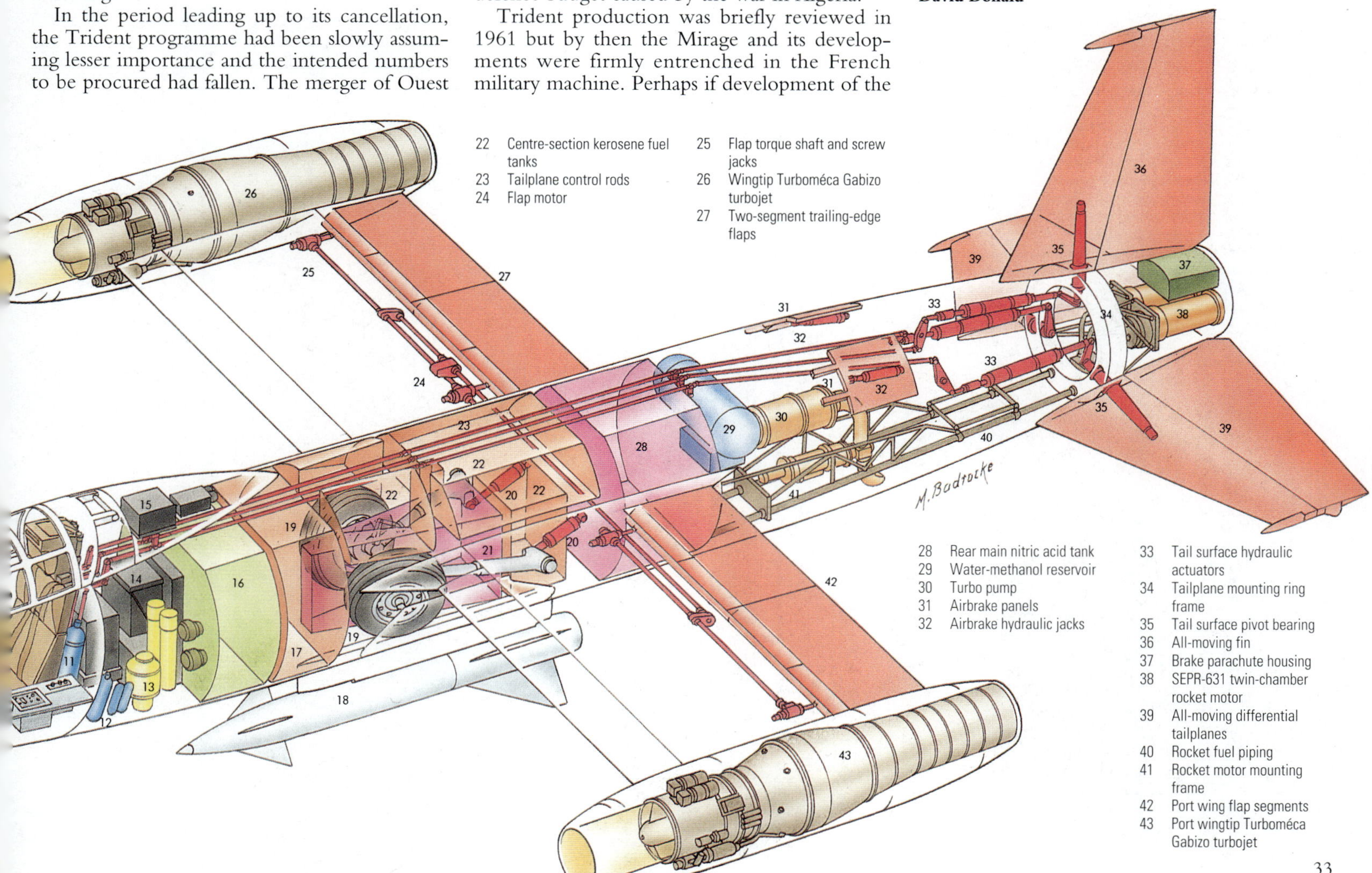

22 Centre-section kerosene fuel tanks
23 Tailplane control rods
24 Flap motor
25 Flap torque shaft and screw jacks
26 Wingtip Turboméca Gabizo turbojet
27 Two-segment trailing-edge flaps
28 Rear main nitric acid tank
29 Water-methanol reservoir
30 Turbo pump
31 Airbrake panels
32 Airbrake hydraulic jacks
33 Tail surface hydraulic actuators
34 Tailplane mounting ring frame
35 Tail surface pivot bearing
36 All-moving fin
37 Brake parachute housing
38 SEPR-631 twin-chamber rocket motor
39 All-moving differential tailplanes
40 Rocket fuel piping
41 Rocket motor mounting frame
42 Port wing flap segments
43 Port wingtip Turboméca Gabizo turbojet

A factory-fresh F-86F-5 flies over the Pacific on a test flight after completion at North American's Inglewood plant. The key aerodynamic feature of the Sabre was its 35° swept wing, which avoided the effects of compressibility encountered by straight-wing designs, in turn allowing the Sabre to enter the transonic speed area with ease (and indeed pass Mach 1 in a dive). Longitudinal problems encountered in this regime with the F-86A were rectified (from the F-86E onwards) by an all-flying tailplane which still incorporated an elevator. This restored the necessary pitch authority at high speeds and became a feature of most subsequent fast-jet designs before the one-piece slab tail was introduced (as fitted to the F-86D). Wing configuration also changed noticeably. This is the original wing with leading-edge slats. Further refinement led to the '6-3 hard wing', which had a fixed, extended leading edge and wing fences. Finally, the 'F-40' or 'slatted 6-3' wing was designed, which restored leading-edge slats to the larger wing, and also extended the wingtips for greater area.

By any criteria, the Sabre was one of the greatest aircraft of all time. Built in huge numbers – including production in Australia, Canada, Italy and Japan – and operated by a large number of air forces, the F-86 also achieved one of the greatest and most emphatic victories in the history of air combat, against a numerically superior and technologically equal enemy. The Sabre's actions in Korea were just one facet of the aircraft's incredible history: it was the backbone of the NATO fighter force in Europe, while radar-equipped versions defended the United States against bomber attack. In a new lease of life it enjoyed a long career in the Air National Guard, and continued in service with Far East and Latin American air arms many years past its planned retirement date. The F-86 broke world speed records, pioneered all-flying tail surfaces, fought the world's first missile engagements and could quite possibly have been the first aircraft to break the sound barrier.

North American F-86 Sabre

The Sabre achieved everlasting glory during the Korean War, when it gained an unprecedented kill-loss ratio over Communist MiG-15s. Here an element of 335th FIS F-86F-10s is seen on its way to the Yalu River in October 1952. The 'element' was the basic combat formation, consisting of leader and wingman. The lead took the shot while the wingman covered him from any other attack. If the wing saw enemy aircraft first, the roles would reverse.

During 1939, the first operational aircraft powered by a gas turbine engine was built. All previous powered aircraft had either inline or radial internal combustion engines, using either gasoline or diesel fuel, turning a propeller. Very simply, the gas turbine used its exhaust gas as power, commonly called thrust. The gas turbine engine pushed the aircraft through the sky, rather than having a propeller pull it.

In Nazi Germany, Ernst Heinkel had installed a gas turbine in his He 178 airframe, which made its first flight on 27 August 1939. Across the Channel in England, British engineer Frank Whittle had one of his new gas turbine designs installed in a Gloster G-40 airframe. These two aircraft ultimately led to an entirely new concept that revolutionised the aviation world – the jet aircraft.

In the United States, very little concern was paid to the new powerplant and its potential. The US War Department was busy simply trying to catch the rest of the world with regard to 'normal' aircraft types. There was a new world war in Europe, and storm clouds in the Pacific. The US was behind all the nations involved in the new world conflict, with regard to high-performance aircraft, and it was not until full development of the Republic P-47 and the Lockheed P-38 that the War Department could expend time and money on things like gas turbines and jet aircraft.

When the P-51 airframe and the Merlin engine were mated in the summer of 1942 to create the P-51 Mustang, considered to be the finest overall fighter aircraft developed during the war, Germany already had a jet fighter aircraft ready for operation that would make obsolete every fighter aircraft type then in service or on the Allied drawing boards, including the Mustang. The Me 262 flew on 18 July 1942, and was ready for operation as early as mid-1943. Only the stupidity of Adolf Hitler, who wanted the aircraft changed into a bomber, kept the German jet from decimating the Allied bomber forces. At 575 mph (925 km/h), the Me 262 was a full 150 mph (240 km/h) faster than the best operational Allied fighter types providing escort to the bomber streams. The RAF did have a jet fighter aircraft – the Gloster Meteor – which made its first combat sortie on 4 August 1944, but it was held back to counter the menace of the V-1 'Buzz Bombs'.

By 1942, a few aircraft manufacturers in America were becoming involved with gas turbine aircraft technology. Using engines borrowed from Whittle, the Bell Aircraft Company built the XP-59 Airacomet, which flew in October 1942. Performance of the XP-59 fell short of expectations, as the aircraft was unable to keep pace even with the latest propeller-driven designs. Lockheed had *Lulubelle,* the XP-80 prototype using a de Havilland Goblin engine, that flew in early 1944. The XP-80 broke the 500-mph (805-km/h) barrier, but was still not competitive with the German jets. Republic was building the XP-84 which offered greater performance, but it was not ready until 1946.

As in the Far East, the Sabre became an everyday sight in Western Europe, where it was operated by most of the local air forces, and by many USAFE units. Among the latter was the 388th Fighter-Bomber Group at Etain-Rouvres AB in France, which flew this F-86F-35. The Block 35 could carry the Mk 12 tactical nuclear bomb, although this example is seen carrying four 200-US gal (757-litre) drop tanks.

On 22 November 1944, North American Aviation initiated a design study, RD 1265, for a jet fighter. Using much P-51 technology, the new jet fighter was straightforward in design. The wing was borrowed directly from the P-51D, having straight leading and trailing edges, and featuring the latest laminar flow shape.

The fuselage was short, circular and very smooth, with an opening in the nose to act as a conduit for air for the General Electric TG-180 gas turbine, a licence-built copy of the de Havilland Goblin gas turbine engine. The NA-134 project was being proposed for the US Navy, which ordered three prototypes, designated XFJ-1, on 1 January 1945.

The US Army Air Force also contacted North American regarding the NA-134 project. On 18 May 1945, North American received a letter contract to build three jet aircraft prototypes, with the designation of XP-86. The requirements called for a day or clear-air fighter type, having a medium range, with a top speed in excess of 600 mph (965 km/h). The 600+ mph requirement caused the most concern for aircraft engineers; not just at North American, either, for aircraft and gas turbine technology simply could not meet such a requirement.

Thin wings and divebrakes

Although based on the Navy NA-134 design, the XP-86 (NA-140) was quite different from its Navy cousin. Using the same laminar flow wing planform, the XP-86 wing was much thinner. Divebrake panels borrowed from the A-36A were to be installed in both upper and lower wings. The powerplant used in both types would be the same, the General Electric TG-180 (military designation J35), an 11-stage, axial-flow compressor which offered 4,000 lb (17.79 kN) of static thrust at sea level.

The fuselage was much more slender, due to the elimination of all the carrier equipment called for in the NA-134 design. North American moved some fuel cells from the fuselage into the wings, and intake duct design studies and wind tunnel tests allowed the engineers to use an elliptical shape which made the fuselage even more slender.

The XP-86 had several features not previously used on fighter aircraft, including a fully pressurised cockpit and hydraulic boost for the elevators and ailerons. Armament was the standard Army Air Force requirement of the era: six Browning M3 0.50-in machine-guns that fired at 1,100 rounds per minute, with 267 rounds for each gun. The XP-86 used the Sperry type A-1B gun/bomb/rocket sight, working with the AN/APG-5 ranging radar.

Each wingtip had a 170-US gal (643-litre) droppable fuel tank. Pylons under the wings could hold up to 2,000 lb (907 kg) of ordnance or additional drop tanks, plus eight rocket launchers to fire the 5-in High Velocity Aircraft Rocket (HVAR). Other Army-specified equipment included self-sealing fuel tanks, armour plate around the cockpit area to protect the pilot, a steerable nosewheel, and the usual Army communications sets – SCR-695A, BC-1206 and AN/ARC-3G.

The XP-86 would be 35.5 ft (10.82 m) in length and 13.2 ft (4.02 m) in height, and have a wingspan of 38.2 ft (11.64 m). Performance was projected to be equal to the other competitors (the P-80 and P-84), but still not meeting the AAF requirement. With a gross weight exceeding 14,000 lb (6350 m), the top speed was estimated to be 582 mph (936 km/h), with a rate of climb of 5,520 ft (1682 m) per minute, a combat range of 1,500 miles (2415 km), and a ferry range of over 2,200 miles (3540 km) with wingtip and underwing drop tanks.

These performance figures were greatly exaggerated, as tests of the swept-wing XP-86 revealed a rate of climb of only 4,000 ft (1220 m) per minute with the J35. The high fuel consumption of the gas turbine would drop the combat range to approximately 500 miles (805 km). Maximum speed of the XP-86 would not have approached the estimated 582 mph, let alone the GOR requirement of 600+ mph. Top speed for the XFJ-1, which was quite similar to the proposed XP-86, did not exceed 550 mph (885 km/h).

On 20 June 1945, the XP-86 mock-up was unveiled at the North American plant in Inglewood, California. Resplendent in a Gloss Pearl Grey paint, the mock-up was built entirely of wood, and consisted of only the fuselage, tail assembly, and port wing. The cockpit and landing gear assemblies were complete. The aft fuselage was pulled from the forward section at the engine break, revealing the TG-180 powerplant. The XP-86 mock-up was quickly approved by Army Air Force officials.

Although construction of the XP-86 with the straight wing proceeded, North American engineers knew that the lack of speed would eventually kill the programme. The XP-86 needed a much more powerful engine, or the engineers had to find some way to reduce the drag encountered at speeds over 500 mph (805 km/h). The answer was, of

Above left: A family portrait shows three classic North American designs. Arguably the best and most successful of the three, the Sabre neatly bridged the gap between the World War II-era fighter (P-51) and the supersonic jet (F-100).

Above: The F-86D introduced a whole new family of Sabres, hastily developed to act as all-weather interceptors. This 31st FIS 'Dog' launches a salvo of rockets during a 1955 Yuma (Vincent AFB) live-fire exercise.

In addition to North American production, lines were opened in Australia, Canada, Italy and Japan. Of these, Canadair's operation was the most prolific, being responsible for supplying most of the non-US NATO aircraft purchasers. The RCAF made much use of the Sabre in fighter and fighter-bomber roles. This immaculate quartet is from Canada's national aerobatic team, the 'Golden Hawks'.

Straight-wing XP-86

North American was swift to join the rush to harness jet power for fighter aircraft, scheming the initial XP-86 design using P-51 aerodynamics as a basis. This would have proved a dead-end street, as the Mustang's thick wing encountered severe compressibility problems (unlike the thin wing of the Spitfire). NAA took the brave, but ultimately vital, step of delaying its design to include the all-important German swept-wing research.

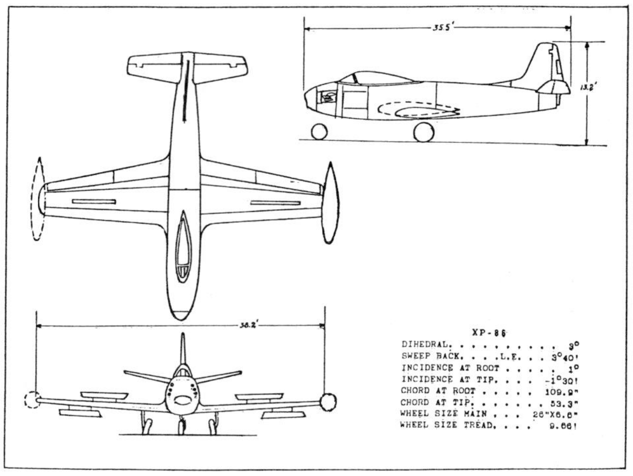

Right: This drawing shows the original straight-wing XP-86 design. It had a P-51D wing planform and tailplane, and A-36A-style speed brakes above and below the wing.

Right: A desk model shows the basic layout of the initial XP-86 design. Elements of the Sabre, notably the canopy and intake layout, are readily visible.

Below: The straight-wing project proceeded as far as a wooden mock-up of the left wing and fuselage, complete with dummy J35 engine. It was unveiled at Inglewood in June 1945.

With the redesign, North American was committing to a concept that had never been successfully proven. All costs already incurred on the straight-winged NA-140 jet fighter would have to be absorbed by the company, although some could be recovered through the US Navy's decision to go ahead with production of the XFJ-1 Fury. In one way, it was quite easy for North American to make such a drastic move because the NA-140 would never be able to meet the Army Air Force General Operational Requirement (GOR), which included a top speed in excess of 600 mph (965 km/h). The thin, straight wing simply would not accommodate a speed that high.

Sweeping the wing had long been known to be one of the answers to the lower drag and compressibility problems associated with high-performance aircraft operating at or near Mach 1. Drag coefficient was significantly lower when the wing was swept; for example, at Mach 0.9, the drag coefficient for a straight wing was approximately 0.05, while for a swept wing it was 0.01. As early as 1944, North American Aviation engineers were working on several swept-wing projects, but the problems associated with wing sweep were as great as the benefits. Sweeping the wing did raise the critical Mach number, thus reducing the drag coefficient and resulting in higher speeds; it also created wingtip stall and low-speed stability problems – which no one had been able to overcome.

On 24 August 1944, Ed Horkey, a North American design engineer, went to Langley Field to study the effects of using a very thin wing on aircraft operating at higher Mach numbers. Horkey was informed by Langley officials that no test data existed for such a thin wing design, let alone a swept wing. In early 1945 Allied forces overran several German aircraft manufacturing and test facilities, including one that was conducting research into the effects of wing sweep. The Messerschmitt Me 262 jet fighter had a mild sweep to the leading edge of its wing, but even this course, sweeping the leading edge of the wing; this would offer a reduction in drag and lead to an increase in speed without an increase in power. The disadvantages were many, especially the loss of stability at high angles of attack, causing severe pitch-up at both low and high speeds. These problems had to be conquered before the XP-86 design could meet its potential.

XP-86 swept-wing development

The decision to radically redesign the XP-86 was both easy and difficult for North American officials to make.

This is the first prototype, seen in the Inglewood workshop prior to its roll-out in August 1947. The intake/nose cap was a fibreglass unit, which initially mounted only the gun camera in the lower lip.

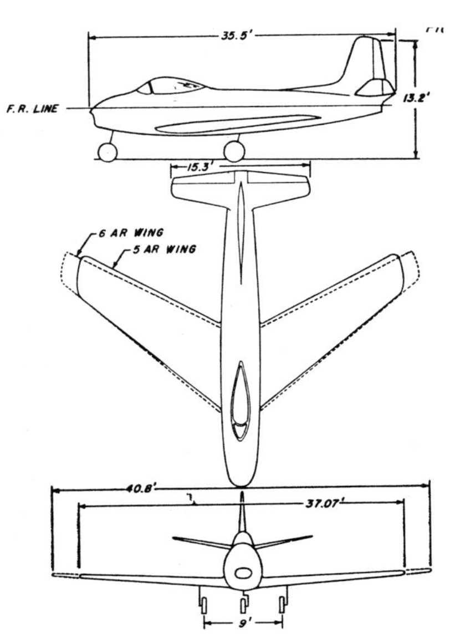

XP-86 prototype

While NAA proceeded with its straight-wing design, studies were being conducted as early as 1944 into the use of swept wings, but there was insufficient tunnel data. In late 1945 such data became available after the capture of German documents and their dissemination by NACA throughout the US aerospace industry. Although NAA received a go-ahead for a swept-wing XP-86 on 1 November 1945, it was not until the next August that work began on constructing the prototype. A year later, the prototype emerged from the factory.

This drawing of a swept-wing XP-86 dates from April 1946, and shows an aircraft with two wings of differing aspect ratios. At this time the aircraft still had straight vertical and horizontal tail surfaces.

Here North American's engineering test pilot George Welch is seen aloft in XP-86 No. 1 during an early test flight in October 1947. It has recently been uncovered that Welch may have exceeded the speed of sound in the XP-86 as early as the first flight on 1 October 1947, two weeks prior to 'Chuck' Yeager's famous flight in the Bell XS-1.

gentle (15°) sweep caused stall problems during landing. Messerschmitt engineers overcame it by the use of a mechanically operated leading-edge movable surface, which operated only during landings. It was also discovered that Messerschmitt had been working on a radically swept (35°) version of the Me 262, called the Pfeilflugel or 'arrow wing'. Luckily, the war ended before German technology could overcome the stability problems of such a drastically swept wing.

George Schairer of the Boeing Company went to Germany after the end of the war, with Theodore von Karman and Robert Jones (an early NACA proponent of swept wings), to investigate German data on swept-wing technology. Schairer was very enthusiastic about the use of wing sweep, proposing that Boeing should incorporate it into the new XB-47 design. He also voiced his opinion that this information be made available to all within the US aeronautical industry, offering to send copies of his information to Bailey Oswald at Douglas, 'Kelly' Johnson at Lockheed, Ralph Bayless at Convair, and Ed Horkey at North American.

Instability solution

It was Larry Green, head of Design Aerodynamics at North American, who finally found an answer to the problems of instability in the swept wing. Green had already been conducting wind tunnel tests on the Curtis XP-55 Ascender at Cal Tech, which indicated that severe non-linear instabilities were present at high angles of attack over a swept wing, causing an extreme pitch-up attitude. Larry Green, Walter Koch (who was newly hired, and spoke fluent German), Dale Meyers and Harrison Storms set up four Recordaks, and, after some coaching from Koch, began translating all the material being funnelled to North American by Wright Field. Within the captured material was considerable data concerning the use of wing leading-edge movable surfaces, commonly called slats, as a possible solution to the instability problems.

The North American Technical Section included Ed Horkey as Chief Aerodynamicist, Harrison Storms, Walt Fellers, Larry Green, Dale Meyers, Bill Wahl, and a host of other specialists. This group finally convinced the powers-that-be that wing sweep would put the XP-86 over the top as far as the speed requirement of the GOR was concerned. On 18 August 1945, 'Dutch' Kindelberger, President of North American Aviation, approved company funding under RD 1369 for the development of a swept wing for the XP-86 proposal to the Army Air Force. Two weeks later a 0.23 scale model of the XP-86, with swept wings, was ready for testing in the wind tunnel. The results were what North American engineers and Army Air Force generals had been looking for. Wind tunnel data clearly indicated that the drag rise and compressibility had been lowered enough to bring the XP-86 into the 600-mph range, even using available gas turbine technology.

In September 1945, the original straight-winged XP-86 fuselage and tail assembly was mated to a 35° swept wing, similar to that found on the advanced Me 262 proposal; it was tested in North American's low-speed wind tunnel, with satisfactory results. On 1 November 1945, General Bill Craigie, head of Research & Development at Wright Field, gave North American the go-ahead for the swept-winged XP-86.

Photographed in December 1947, this is the first XP-86 on the ramp at Muroc, complete with USAF 'buzz' number. The aircraft was fitted with rear-hinged speedbrakes, which were modified to more conventional units later in the month.

Harrison Storms and Ed Horkey convinced the North American engineering staff that the problems could be overcome through the use of a leading-edge slat. Slowly but surely, the North American engineers brought the design to its final shape. The slat design remained a problem and, finally, an entire Me 262 wing was flown in from Wright Field. The Me 262 slat design was of no particular use to the Aerodynamics Group since the German slats were mechanical, being cranked out only during take-offs and landings. Nonetheless, North American's Wing Group found them a treasure-trove of unique ideas. Wing Group disassembled the slats and modified the slat track mechanism to fit the XP-86 wing. The engineers also used the slat lock and control switch from the Me 262. Although not perfect, it was at least a start, and the slat worked. In fact, the first seven aircraft used slat locks and tracks borrowed from captured Me 262 material.

Both 5 and 6 aspect wings were tested in the tunnel, before finally settling on a 5 aspect wing with a 35° sweep. The trailing edge of the wing was extended 4 in (10 cm) at the chord, reducing the angle of the trailing edge, thus

In the late 1940s North American was at the pinnacle of state-of-the-art jet design. In addition to the Sabre (No. 1 shown here), the company had the B-45 Tornado flying (the second XB-45 illustrated).

Above: This was the first aerial photograph of the XP-86 released to the press, and shows graphically the leading-edge slats deployed. They elegantly overcame the problems associated with low-speed stalling inherent in a swept-wing design.

Above right: In December 1947 the first XP-86 was returned to Inglewood for fitment of production-style speedbrakes. At the time it was painted in Pearl Grey, but this was found to suffer from hydraulic fluid corrosion and was removed.

The No. 2 aircraft lines up on the Mines Field runway (on the site of today's Los Angeles International Airport) for its first flight in early 1948.

reducing the trailing-edge separation that was causing some loss of aileron control. Modifying the trailing-edge angle increased the amount of sweep overall to 35.2°.

Originally, the swept wing proposal retained the tail assembly from the straight-winged design. However, by the time the XP-86 mock-up was being built, both the vertical and horizontal tail surfaces were also swept at 35°. Additionally, the horizontal stabiliser was fully trimmable (i.e., both stabiliser and elevator were movable) to achieve a better balance between low-speed control and high-speed flight requirements. Sweeping the tail surfaces caused the overall aircraft length to increase by 2 ft (0.61 m), from 35.5 ft (10.82 m) to 37.54 ft (11.44 m).

The cockpit sat high on the forward fuselage and had a full, blown Plexiglass canopy that offered excellent all-round vision (360°) for the pilot, something not to be matched in any fighter aircraft until the McDonnell/Douglas F-15 Eagle was unveiled some 25 years later. The XP-86 was to have three speed brake doors – a pair of small doors on the rear fuselage sides that opened to the rear, and a larger slab door under the rear fuselage.

The XP-86 was to be armed with six 0.50-in M3 machine-guns mounted in banks of three on either side of the cockpit. Ammunition bays were in the bottom of the fuselage under the gun bay, each 'can' holding a maximum of 300 rounds, although 267 rounds was the normal loading. The gun muzzles were recessed behind individual frangible 'doors' that opened in 1/20th of a second when the trigger was pulled. All radio and radar antennas were to be enclosed in fibreglass fairings within the design of the aircraft. The engine that would power the prototype was the Chevrolet-built, General Electric TG-180 (J35-C-3) rated at 4,000 lb (17.79 kN) static thrust. However, production aircraft were slated to be powered by the GE TG-190 (J47) engine offering 5,000 lb (22.24 kN) static thrust.

Wing construction

The design of the wing was not the only innovation in the XP-86 design. The wing was of a totally new construction and manufacturing process. The conventional rib and stringer wing construction was replaced by a double skin structure with 'hat sections' between the layers that provided room for the installation of self-sealing wing fuel tanks. The wing skins were tapered throughout their length and width, being 0.250 in (6.35 mm) thick at the wingroot, tapering down to 0.064 in (1.625 mm) at the joint with the outer wing skin, and 0.032 in (0.813 mm) at the wingtip. So complex were these tapered skins that they required special milling machines, which took 45 minutes to complete a single skin. The fuselage was unique in that it was divided into two sections, joined near the wing trailing edge. Splitting the fuselage at this juncture provided easy accessibility to the engine and accessories.

On 28 February 1946, the mock-up of the swept-winged XP-86 received Army Air Force approval. In August 1946, basic engineering drawings were made available to the manufacturing division of North American, and metal was finally cut for the new aircraft. So excited was the Army Air Force over the prospect of the new swept-winged XP-86, and its projected much higher performance over contemporary fighter designs, that a contract was awarded to North American on 20 December 1946, to build 33 production P-86As. No YP-86 service test aircraft were built. On 8 August 1947, the wait was over: that morning, the doors of North American's Inglewood factory opened to reveal the first swept-winged production aircraft in the world – XP-86 No. 1, serial 45-59597, nicknamed the 'Silver Charger'. Six days later, the 689 Board completed its inspection of the first prototype.

XP-86 No. 2

The second XP-86 was completed with production-style airbrakes (as shown right). The aircraft did not have armament fitted, but did feature the necessary wiring and had a Mk 18 gunsight installed. All three prototype aircraft were powered by the Chevrolet-built J35-C-3 engine (licence-built de Havilland Goblin) but were later re-engined with the J47.

F-86A

The first Sabre contract was placed as early as November 1946, for 33 P-86As (a number finally raised to 554). The aircraft were very similar to the third prototype apart from the J47-GE-1 engine. The first production aircraft flew on 20 May 1948, and the first examples were handed over to the USAF on 28 May.

Left:* *In the early 1950s, the USAF began testing Dayglo paint. This 56th FIG F-86A was one of many test aircraft. Red, yellow and blue paints were also trialled.

This is one of the cold weather test P-86A-1s, seen carrying a pair of 200-US gal (757-litre) drop tanks. The latter were very useful for extending range, but bit heavily into the advertised top speed of 670 mph (1078 km/h).

Above:* *This P-86A-1 was another of the cold-weather test aircraft sent to Ladd Field, Alaska, hence the red wingtips and tail. It is seen here at Inglewood in the late summer of 1948. In common with all other Dash 1 aircraft, 47-608 had the gun port retractable doors and rounded windscreen.

During the next month, North American engineers conducted taxi and brake tests at Mines Field, which adjoined the North American factory at Inglewood (Mines Field is now Los Angeles International Airport). On 11 September 1947, the XP-86 was disassembled and trucked to the North Base area of Muroc Dry Lake Army Air Base, now known as Edwards AFB. The XP-86 was then reassembled and all systems were retested and adjusted in anticipation of the first flight. On the morning of 1 October 1947, George 'Wheaties' Welch, chief test pilot for North American, taxied the XP-86 to the edge of the runway at Muroc, released the brakes and pushed the throttle forward. Three thousand feet (915 m) down the runway at Muroc, the XP-86 lifted smoothly off the dry lake bed runway for the first time.

First flight report

Everything about the first flight went smoothly, and 30 minutes later Welch made a final circuit over the base, pulled the lever to lower the landing gear, and began his approach for a landing. Ed Horkey recalled, "Ed Virgin, Head of Engineering Flight Test, Jim Sullivan, and I were clustered around the ground radio listening to George's excited chatter about the first flight. The first flight went very smoothly, with each item on the First Flight Card being checked off satisfactorily. George could tell from the speeds he was obtaining, versus the power settings on the J35, that he was riding something that was pretty fast. After about a 30-minute flight, it became time to land and George lowered the flaps and landing gear.

"The main gear lock lights were in the green, but the nosewheel light did not show the gear was down and locked. We had him make a pass, and we could clearly see the nose gear was down about 45°. George tried everything he, and we, could think of. Nothing worked. Decision time was rapidly coming upon us. Ed Virgin and I were immediately unanimous in letting George make the decision on whether to jump or bring the aircraft in. The company would not influence a decision to save the aircraft if it meant jeopardising George's life.

"George radioed that he would stay with the aircraft and try to bring her home. But he was going to try the landing on the dry lake bed and not on one of the runways. He made a smooth, very nose-high approach. Touching down on the lake bed, George let the aircraft just coast along with no brake application. As the aircraft slowed and the nose started irretrievably over, the nose gear swung forward and locked into place. The only thing heard on the radio was George quietly exclaiming over and over, 'Lucky. Lucky.'

"We found out later that someone in landing gear design or hydraulics was not impressed with the nose gear load data that had been furnished them by the wind tunnel and aerodynamics crew. They installed a cylinder/piston size on the nose gear retraction system that was too small but easy to obtain – not the one called for in the specs. Normally, nosewheels rotated down to the rear, so that air loads

Record-breaking F-86As

The new fighter was a natural for a USAF attempt on various speed records. On 15 September 1948, Major Robert L. Johnson took the record at Muroc with a speed of 670.981 mph (1079.8 km/h). On Armed Forces Day (20 May) 1950, Captain Richard Creighton set a record flying from San Francisco to Los Angeles in another F-86A.

Below left:* *Captain Creighton's F-86A-5 is seen in the colours of the 71st FS, to which both aircraft and pilot were assigned. Creighton later scored five kills in Korea to add to his two P-51 kills from World War II.

Below:* *Robert Johnson chats with NAA engineers at Muroc prior to his record flight. The aircraft, F-86A-1 47-611, was a stock production aircraft complete with full armament.

Sabre into service

Deliveries to front-line units were delayed by a production halt caused by problems with the J47 engine, but got under way on 15 February 1949, when the 94th 'Hat-in-the-Ring' Fighter Squadron received its first two aircraft. By June the entire 1st Fighter Group was equipped with F-86As, and was swiftly followed by the 4th, 33rd and 81st. In November 1950, the first 4th FIG Sabres were dispatched to Korea.

***Above:** This line-up of F-86As shows the first aircraft delivered to the 1st Fighter Group at March AFB, California, in February 1949. The aircraft were F-86A-5s, with retractable gun blast doors, and were flown in with 240-US gal (908-litre) drop tanks.*

***Far right:** The Sabre was initially assigned to units with strategic air defence roles. These units were redesignated as fighter interceptor squadrons and wings in January 1950, and came under the aegis of the newly-created Air Defense Command. Here an F-86A sits in the alert barn at March AFB, resplendent in the famous unit insignia of the 94th FIS. This squadron, and the rest of the 1st FIG, was responsible for the air defence of the Los Angeles region, which contained many important military facilities (including Edwards AFB) and much of the nation's aviation manufacturing capacity.*

would make sure the gear came down even if the hydraulics failed. However, the XP-86 nose intake duct layout precluded this approach, and the nose gear rotated down toward the front, against the air stream. The immediate fix on the XP-86 was to use two of the original cylinder/pistons, then replace them later with the larger, correct one."

Other than the nose gear problem, Welch had only one complaint about that first flight: the J35 did not produce enough power. With only 4,000 lb (17.79 kN) of static thrust, the XP-86 had a rate of climb of only 4,000 ft (1219 m) per minute. However, since the J35 was not the engine slated to power the production aircraft – they would have J47s, with 5,000 lb (22.24 kN) thrust available – no one got too excited. Especially in light of what happened next while, still using J35 power.

First through the sound barrier?

On 14 October 1947, Chuck Yeager took the rocket-powered Bell XS-1 beyond the magic number of Mach 1.0 – the first piloted vehicle to do so. But George Welch may have beaten that date in history during some of the routine tests with the XP-86. Welch began complaining to the engineers about some unusual fluctuations in his airspeed and altitude indicators. During flight in the transonic range close to Mach 1.0, shock waves will effect both the airspeed and altimeter readings.

Ed Horkey mused, "Had George gone Mach 1 before 14 October 1947? This is an intriguing question. Recently discovered data in the North American archives seem to indicate that possibility. Following the first flight and corrections to the nose gear assembly, the rest of North American's Phase One Flight Tests up to Flight 32 showed a great capability of the aircraft to fly, analyse the data, make any required changes, and to fly again quickly. George had been telling me that he was getting oscillation of the airspeed and altimeter readings, indicating Mach 1.0 on the pitot head. At that time, North American had no way of calibrating airspeed indicators into the transonic range.

"NACA had set up a flight test operation at Muroc, later known as Dryden Center. They put a tracking theodolite (like a surveyor's transit) together with a large radar receiver which measured speeds very accurately at any altitude above Muroc. It was the same system that had tracked Yeager in the XS-1. We heard about it and talked Walt Williams, NACA Director, into tracking George in the XP-86. They asked Welch to dive the XP-86 in a certain pattern, after which they would give us his speed and Mach number. Lo and behold, George hit a reading of Mach 1.02 and 1.03. The date was 19 October 1947 – five days after Yeager's flight in the XS-1. The tests were flown again on 21 October with the same results. But George had been performing some of those very same flight patterns during tests before 14 October 1947.

"Just like the people involved in the XS-1 programme, everyone involved in the XP-86 flight test programme was immediately sworn to secrecy. In fact, Stuart Symington, the first Secretary of the new independent United States Air Force, called 'Dutch' Kindelberger and told him not to let out anything concerning the XP-86 going over Mach 0.935. It would remain a secret for many years."

Even if George Welch did not exceed Mach 1.0 during

***Right:** In the foreground is the F-86A which took the world speed record. Behind it are newly completed F-86As, still wearing chrome yellow anti-corrosion paint. Much of the assembly process was accomplished in the open air of southern California, and the aircraft kept their paint until immediately before delivery to the Air Force.*

***Far right:** A problem which dogged the Sabre was lack of range. This F-86A (49-1172) was modified by Boeing with a refuelling receptacle for tests. Although these were successful, the equipment was not adopted. The Sabre had to extend wheels and flaps to keep station with the Boeing KB-29 tanker.*

Left: An important early task of the Sabre was the air defence of the nuclear bomb programme at Alamogordo and Los Alamos. The 81st FG at Kirtland AFB, New Mexico was given this job. In late 1951 the 81st moved to England, although the 93rd FIS (illustrated) stayed behind.

those early Phase I tests (tests flown by North American company pilots), the Air Force was impressed. On 16 October 1947, Fixed Price Contract W33-038-ac-16013 was granted to North American Aviation, authorising production of 33 P-86A aircraft. This contract was supplemented that same day to include production of 190 P-86B aircraft, a strengthened P-86A for rough-field operations. Advancements in tyre and brake systems nullified the need for the P-86B, and the contract was amended on 16 December 1947, changing the production order to an additional 188 P-86As and two P-86Cs.

This dramatic shot captures an F-86A-5 firing a full salvo of 5-in (12.7-cm) HVAR rockets from wing stubs over the Nellis ranges in 1952. A full load of HVARs could not be carried with any other ordnance or drop tanks.

Air Force testing

Phase II Flight tests (tests flown by Air Force pilots) began in early December 1947. Major Ken Chilstrom was the Phase 2 Air Force pilot. "In late November 1947, North American Aviation called Colonel Al Boyd, Chief of Air Force Flight Test Division, and recommended delaying the start of the Phase II flight tests because of heavy rains at Muroc, resulting in the flooding of the dry lake bed. Colonel Boyd suggested I visit Muroc and inspect the conditions to determine if I could operate from the runway at North Base. After a few days at North Base evaluating the lake bed, the runway, and the XP-86, I called Colonel Boyd and recommended we proceed with Phase II tests using North Base.

"Colonel Boyd notified North American that the Air Force would begin flying the Phase II tests of the XP-86 immediately. North American expressed concern because of the extremely short runway conditions at North Base. However, the Air Force prevailed and I made my first takeoff on 2 December 1947. This flight was a get-acquainted flight and, since there were no squawks, I asked that the XP-86 be refuelled for a second flight that day. This allowed for performance checks and speed points at intermediate altitudes.

"I was very impressed with the XP-86's speed improvement over the Republic XP-84 Thunderjet, with the same engine but having a straight wing. The maximum speed for the XP-84 was 615 mph [990 km/h], while the XP-86's maximum speed was in excess of 650 mph [1046 km/h]. Our remaining Phase II flights were accomplished in 11 flights totalling 10 hours and 17 minutes – all in six days. The XP-86's performance envelope was investigated up to Mach 0.9, and altitudes near 45,000 ft [13715 m]. My conclusion of the Phase II tests, and supported by our data, was that the Air Force now had the very best jet fighter developed to this date, anywhere in the world."

In early 1948, XP-86 prototypes No. 2 (45-59598) and No. 3 (45-59599) became available for testing. They were different from the No. 1 aircraft, as well as different from each other in several areas. Both Nos 1 and 2 had different fuel gauges, a stall warning system built into the control stick, a bypass for emergency operation of the hydraulic boost system, and hydraulically actuated leading-edge slat locks. The No. 1 aircraft was the only one to have an onboard fire extinguisher. The No. 3 prototype was the only XP-86 with fully automatic leading-edge slats that opened at 135 mph (217 km/h), and the only prototype to have full armament, including a Mk 18 gyroscopic gunsight with manual ranging. Both Nos 2 and 3 were equipped with SCR-695-B Identification Friend or Foe beacons, and the AN/ARN-6 radio compass set.

Finally, the No. 1 aircraft was the only one with the reverse, or rear-opening, side fuselage dive brakes, in addition to having a large ventral brake under the fuselage. A new aft section had been constructed for use on the No. 3 prototype, with production-style speed brakes installed.

Below left: This F-86A belonged to the aerobatic team formed from personnel and aircraft at the Wright-Patterson AFB test centre, and is seen at the 1951 National Air Races held at the Ohio base. The aircraft was painted with Dayglo scallops and black trim on the fuselage, wings and tail.

Below: One of the units at Nellis AFB, Nevada, was the 3596th Fighter Squadron, nicknamed 'The Cadillac Flight'. These aircraft were the machines which always appeared in Air Force publicity photos taken at the base. The badge on the nose was that of Air Training Command, with the word 'Nellis' painted above.

The 23rd Fighter Interceptor Group was the last F-86A unit within Air Defense Command, having been established at Presque Isle, Maine, on 12 January 1951. One of the constituent squadrons was the 75th FIS. The 23rd FIG inherited the traditions of the AVG 'Flying Tigers', although no trace of this can be found in the markings of the time.

These brakes had hinges at the front, and opened out and down into the airstream. Air Force had approved the new brake design, but the new aft section would not be finished until late in the year. The ventral brake was eliminated, and the new aft section was installed on the No. 1 prototype in late January following test flight No. 77. The other two prototypes were completed with production-style speed brakes.

Many significant events took place in the early P-86 development programme during the spring of 1948. In March, the first P-86A production aircraft, 47-605, came off the assembly line at Inglewood. The 689 Board passed it on 15 March. In May the rest of the world was informed that George Welch had exceeded Mach 1.0 in the XP-86, the first aircraft to do so ('aircraft' being defined as a vehicle that takes off from the ground, flies, then returns and lands – all under its own power). The date was set as 26 April 1948. This flight did take place, but George Welch was not the pilot.

Ed Horkey recalled the day. "A visiting British pilot came over and was checked out in the XP-86. He was told about the phenomenon he might encounter (i.e., breaking the sonic barrier), and the secrecy restrictions. Unfortunately, he had an open radio channel and all the nearby towers got an earful of his going through Mach 1.0. I understand that he was severely disciplined. However, the facts soon became common knowledge throughout the aviation industry. I suppose the media never brought it to the public's attention, which would tarnish the otherwise exotic story they already had (Yeager and the XS-1). The 14 June 1948 issue of *Aviation Week* announced to the world that the XP-86 had gone supersonic."

It has been said that the 26 April flight took place after the XP-86 had been re-engined with the General Electric TG-190 (J47) engine rated at 5,000 lb (22.24 kN) static thrust – but that did not take place until later in the XP-86 test programme.

On 20 May, the first flight of a production P-86A took place. The Air Force accepted its first two P-86As on 28 May. The very next day, Air Force officials placed a verbal order for an additional 333 P-86As, bringing the total production of the P-86A/F-86A to 554 aircraft.

On 18 September 1947, the United States Congress made the Air Force a branch of service distinct from its original parent, the US Army. In June 1948, the new US Air Force redesignated all Pursuit aircraft as Fighter aircraft, changing the prefix from P to F. Thus, all XP and P-86A aircraft became XF and F-86A. The three prototypes continued to serve in various test and evaluation missions well into the 1950s, being designated, at least unofficially, as YP-86s. The YP-86 designation was seen stencilled on the data information of the No. 1 aircraft in a film dated 1951. The No. 1 aircraft crashed and was destroyed in September 1952, while Nos 2 and 3 were retired from service in April 1953.

F-86A

Production of the P-86 began with the P-86A. North American had received an order on 20 November 1946 from the Army Air Force to build 33 P-86As, although the prototype was still under construction. Although no service test or YP-86s were ever built, the initial batch of P-86A-1s served as such. The Army estimated that the initial block of P-86As would cost approximately $438,999 per aircraft, including spares, manuals, and additional equipment. This proved to be overly exaggerated, for the 'fly-away cost' of a P-86A turned out to be $178,408.

The P-86A was the production version of the third prototype XP-86 – with one exception, the engine. The P-86A had full military equipment, including six M3 0.50-in machine-guns with a rate of fire of 1,100 rounds per minute (rpm). Each gun was fed by an ammunition canister in the lower fuselage holding up to 300 rounds per gun (rpg). The ammunition bay door also served as the first 'step' for entry to the cockpit. Initially, the P-86As were delivered with a Sperry Mk 18 GBR sight, having manual ranging.

The cockpit itself remained essentially the same as the XP-86, although certain military equipment such as radios and IFF equipment was added. Additionally, the P-86A was equipped with the type T-4E-1 ejection seat assembly, with a manually jettisoned canopy. The P-86A had two underwing hardpoints for weapons carriage: two small pylons could be installed to carry either a pair of 206.5-US gal (782-litre) drop tanks, or a pair of 1,000-lb (454-kg) bombs. Four zero-length stub rocket launchers could be

Below: This F-86A was assigned to the 116th FIS, Washington ANG in 1954. This was one of the units which had been activated in 1951 during the Korean crisis and dispatched as part of the 81st FIG to England, flying F-86As. It returned to the US in November 1952, and acquired Sabres of its own in 1954.

Right: One might at first glance be excused for thinking that this is one of the F-86s captured by Communist forces during the Korean War, or that it is an early aggressor aircraft. However, it is an F-86A of the Fighter School at Nellis, crudely painted to resemble a MiG-15 for the movie Sabre Jet. All of the flying sequences in the film, which starred Robert Stack, were flown by Nellis instructors.

Left: The first YF-93 cruises over California on an instrumented test flight. The F-93 was much bigger than the Sabre, principally to accommodate the afterburning J48 (Rolls-Royce Tay) engine and more fuel for the penetration mission. The area-ruling and extra thrust made the F-93 considerably better performing than the standard Sabre.

F-86C/F-93

Although beginning life as the YF-86C, the YF-93 'penetration interceptor' had little more than its wing in common with the Sabre. Embodying the latest advancements in aerodynamics, including an area-ruled fuselage, the F-93 would have escorted bombers to distant targets and fought opposing interceptors with a battery of 20-mm cannon. The design lost out to McDonnell's F-88, later to become the F-101 Voodoo.

Above: The YF-95A and YF-86C sit on the Muroc dry lake in early 1950. By the end of that year, the aircraft would be redesignated as YF-86D and YF-93, respectively.

Left: The No. 1 prototype YF-93A is seen at Edwards prior to its first flight. The small radome covered a ranging radar as used on the F-86A.

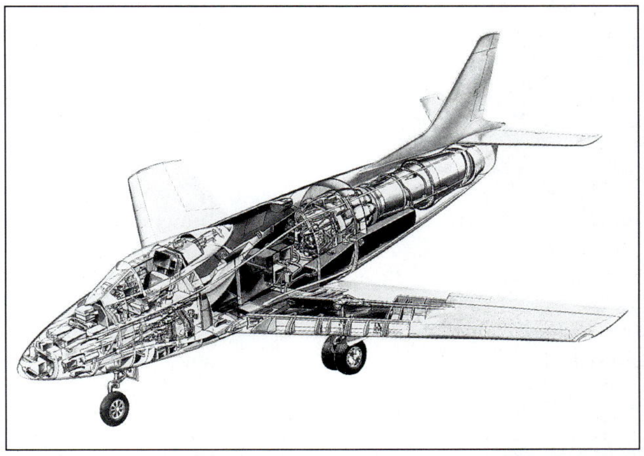

Left: A cutaway view of the YF-93A. The aircraft was to have been armed with six 20-mm cannon and would have had a range of more than 2,000 miles (3240 km).

Below: After the cancellation of orders for 188 production F-93s, the two aircraft were bought by NACA and used for a variety of research tasks. Conventional intakes were fitted and they proved to be more efficient than the original recessed design.

installed under each wing to fire the 5-in HVAR rocket, which could be carried in pairs on each launcher.

The major difference between the prototype aircraft and the production aircraft was the installation of the General Electric TG-190 turbojet engine, military designation J47-GE-1. The J47-1 was rated at 4,850 lb (21.57 kN) thrust at sea level. It would seem that the J35's rating was somewhat exaggerated, based on a comparison of performance figures. With both the XP-86 and the P-86A having the same gross weight – 13,395 lb (6076 kg) – the top speed at sea level for the J35-powered XP-86 was 600 mph (965 km/h), but jumped to 679 mph (1093 km/h) with the J47-powered P-86A. Service ceiling rose from 41,200 to 46,000 ft (12560 to 14020 m). The rate of climb almost doubled, being 4,100 ft (1250 m) per minute in the XP-86 and 7800 ft (2,377 m) per minute in the P-86A.

The initial block of 33 production aircraft, serials 47-605/-637, were designated P-86A-1. The first P-86A came off the assembly line at Inglewood in January 1948 (minus J47 engine), being inspected and approved by the 689 Board on 15 March. George Welch made the first flight on 20 May 1948, with the Air Force taking delivery of the first two examples eight days later. They, however, were bailed back to North American for test use.

Rough-field variant

The second production variant would have been the P-86B had not the Army Air Force requirements been changed before the type got off the drawing board. One of the AAF requirements within the first contract specifications was for the P-86 to be capable of rough-field operations. This called for a beefier landing gear assembly, and larger wheels and tires. North American would have bulged the fuselage an additional 7 in (18 cm) in the landing gear bay area to house the bigger wheels and tires. However, advancements in both high-pressure tyres and brake assemblies led to the AAF cancelling this portion of the GOR. North American had already contracted with the Air Force on 16 October 1947 to build 190 P-86Bs when the rough-field requirement was dropped. On 1 December 1947, North American submitted a proposal to change the contract, replacing the P-86B with an additional 188 P-86As and two P-86C 'Penetration Fighter' prototypes. The Air Force approved the contract change on 16 December 1947, with the additional aircraft being designated P-86A-5 (serials 48-129/-316).

Several significant changes took place throughout the production of the F-86A-5. Beginning with the first aircraft, the rounded windscreen assembly was replaced

Above: A pair of Ashtray Sabres at K-13. Each of the seven Ashtray conversions were unique and virtually hand-built at the Tachikawa maintenance facility in Japan. These RF-86As had a K-9 camera mounted horizontally in the ammo bay area.

RF-86A

Although Sabres were very precious fighter assets in Korea, the type was also coveted by the reconnaissance units. A handful of F-86As were subsequently modified by and for the 67th TRW, beginning with two Honeybucket aircraft with a single K-25 camera and followed by the Ashtray aircraft with two K-9s. The aircraft wore 4th FIG markings and often operated within a four-ship of standard fighters.

Above: 'Every Man a Tiger' was the motto of the 15th TRS based at Kimpo with RF-86A Honeybucket Sabres. These aircraft were several converted FY 1948 F-86As, all veterans of the 4th FIG. This aircraft was shot down by AA fire on 27 June 1952, killing the commander of the 15th, Major Jack Williams. Note the 'dicing' camera in the intake top lip in place of the radar ranging unit.

with a V-shaped one having armoured glass. The sliding portion of the canopy was jettisoned by an explosive charge tied into the ejection seat sequence. The gun compartments and ammunition bays were heated. Stainless steel oil tanks and lines were installed. A new canopy defrosting system and inflatable canopy seal were incorporated from the 160th aircraft, 48-289. At the same time, the leading-edge slats were completely redesigned, with new slat tracks and elimination of the slat locks.

On 28 May 1948, two weeks after the first two P-86A-1s had been delivered to the Air Force, North American received authorisation to build an additional 333 A-5s (serials 49-1007/-1339). These aircraft incorporated all the changes put into effect during the previous production runs. Additionally, the combat capabilities were greatly enhanced by the installation of the Sperry type A-1B GBR sight which used the AN/APG-5C ranging radar. When it worked, it was quite an improvement over the old Mk 18 GBR sight with manual ranging. The new production A-5s also incorporated completely revised wiring in the cockpit to both simplify production and reduce maintenance hours in the field. The brand-new 120-US gal (454-litre) 'combat drop tanks', developed specifically for the F-86, were also introduced during this production run. All these assembly-line changes were retrofitted to previously built F-86As.

Although the XP-86 had 'unofficially' broken the sound barrier in May 1948 (and even more unofficially in October 1947), no official speeds had been recorded or announced for the newest Air Force jet. In September 1948, the Air Force decided to try for the world speed record, then held by US Marine Corps Major Marion Carl in the Douglas D-558-1 Skystreak at 650.796 mph (1047.326 km/h).

The record try would come at the Cleveland National Air Race held over the Labor Day weekend at the Cleveland Municipal Airport. Air Force Major Richard L. Johnson brought the cold weather test aircraft, F-86A-1 No. 47-608, to Cleveland from Wright Air Development Center near Dayton, Ohio. On Sunday, 5 September 1948, Major Johnson flew the F-86A through the 3-km (1.86-mile) speed course that General Electric had laid out over Cleveland Airport. Major Johnson made six passes, averaging 669.480 mph (1077.394 km/h). Unfortunately, the cameras only worked on three of the passes, and the Federation Aéronautique Internationale (FAI) would not certify the record.

A few days later the Air Force made the decision to try again, this time over Muroc Dry Lake. Once again Major Richard L. Johnson was the pilot. The aircraft this time was the armament test aircraft being flown out of Muroc, No. 47-611. On 15 September 1948, Major Johnson took the F-86A through the high desert air over Muroc the required six times. This time the FAI cameras operated perfectly, and at the end of the day Major Johnson and the F-86A

F-86A Target tugs

These F-86As were assigned as target tugs with the Utah (above) and Montana (left) ANGs and are seen at Nellis AFB in 1955 during a gunnery meet. Aircraft used as tugs for live-fire exercises were painted in brilliant colours to make them highly visible to pilots coming in to fire on the target sleeve (known as the 'rag'). There was no specified scheme, although naturally orange and yellow were used.

F-86E

First flying on 23 September 1950, the F-86E introduced many new and important features, including a more powerful engine. F-86Es were dispatched to Korea from June 1951 to replace the tired As of the 4th FIG and to help establish the 51st FIG as the second Sabre wing in the warzone. NAA production for the USAF was augmented by Canadair.

Right: The thing that made the F-86E different was the all-flying tail. This unit had hydraulic power controls, whereas the elevator on the A was mechanically actuated. The new system required 'artificial feel'.

Top: The first F-86E, 50-579, was used for tests of the 'fighter-bomber wing' which had hardpoints for carriage of bombs or an extra pair of drop tanks. The new hardpoints were outboard of the original pair, and are seen here with 500-lb (227-kg) bombs fitted.

were the new world record holders for top speed. The F-86A had averaged 670.781 mph (1089.488 km/h), besting the previous record by more than 20 mph (32 km/h).

In the autumn of 1948, problems with the J47-GE-1 production, and within the engine itself, brought F-86A production to a halt. By late December, General Electric had rectified the production problems, and upgraded the engine for the F-86A to the J47-GE-7, which offered 5,340 lb (23.75 kN) thrust. F-86A production was resumed and deliveries to the first combat squadrons started.

The Sabre reaches the squadrons

On 15 February 1949, the 94th Fighter Squadron at March AFB, California took delivery of its first two F-86As. The 94th FS was one of the squadrons within the 1st Fighter Group, whose mission was the air defence of southern California. Most of the primary military aircraft manufacturers were in and around Los Angeles – Douglas, Lockheed and, of course, the North American plant. One of the first things the 1st FG crews did was to hold a contest in March 1949 to come up with an 'official' name for their new aircraft. The F-86 had unofficially been referred to as the 'Silver Charger'. Of the 78 entries, the chosen name was Sabre, which the media consistently referred to as 'Sabrejet'.

By June 1949, the 1st FG was fully operational with three squadrons of F-86A-5s, 83 aircraft. Next to be equipped was the 4th FG defending the nation's capitol, the 81st FG based at Kirtland Field near the atomic bomb plant at Alamogordo, New Mexico, and the 33rd FG at Otis AFB, Massachusetts, to defend the northeastern approaches into the US. In January 1950, all units whose primary mission was air defence were redesignated as Fighter Interceptor Groups (FIGs) or Wings (FIWs) within Air Defense Command.

Above: The first Air Force unit operational with the F-86E was the 33rd FIG at Otis AFB, Massachusetts. The 33rd had been equipped with F-86As, but most of its aircraft had gone to Korea with the 4th FIG in November 1950. In mid-1951 many of the 33rd's brand-new F-86Es were also diverted to the warzone.

Before the F-86A was phased out of USAF service into the National Guard, two more groups were equipped with it – the 56th FIW at Selfridge AFB, Michigan in 1950 and the 23rd FIW at Presque Isle AFB, Maine in January 1951.

The F-86A continued to be upgraded as problems were encountered or newer equipment became available. The last 24 F-86A-5s (Nos 49-1316/-1339) had the type A-1B GBR sight and AN/APG-5C ranging radar replaced by the type A-1CM GBR sight, using the AN/APG-30 ranging radar. The APG-30 radar was a better unit, with a range from 150 to 3,000 yd (137 to 2743 m), that locked on to a target at 1,800 yd (1646 m). Some F-86As had the A-1CM GBR sight unit combined with the older AN/APG-5C radar. These aircraft were redesignated F-86A-6. Aircraft having the A-1CM GBR sight and AN/APG-30 radar were redesignated F-86A-7.

This Sabre of the 42nd FIS based at Chicago's O'Hare Airport in 1955 was one of the last five F-86Es built. The 42nd had been one of the squadrons under the control of the 56th FIG which was disbanded in February 1952, and its assets taken over by the 501st Air Defense Group.

Right: Some of the most colourful Sabres ever were the F-86Es of the 56th FIW involved in trials of the then-new Dayglo paints in 1952.

Above: The 1952 paint trials resulted in the adoption of Dayglo orange as the most effective recognition colour for air defence fighters and some other types. Aircraft assigned to northern climes were trimmed in a colour named Arctic Red, as was this 144th FIS F-86E seen in the late 1950s at Anchorage.

The F-86E-10 used by Major Fred Ascani on his record-breaking flight taxis out at Detroit. This aircraft was later sent to Korea and assigned to the 51st FIG at Suwon, wearing the name This'll Kill Ya.

Some of the aircraft were re-engined with the J47-GE-13 engine rated at 5,450 lb (24.24 kN) thrust, which did not change their designation. All F-86As came off the assembly line with the pitot head located within the air intake duct. False readings could occur due to the increased air flow within the intake duct, so North American moved the pitot head to the tip of a short boom extending from the leading edge of the right wingtip. All F-86As were retrofitted with the wingtip pitot boom as they went through one of the many IRAN (Inspect and Repair As Necessary) facilities.

YF-93A/F-86C penetration fighter

Toward the end of World War II, the US Army Air Force, and indeed all the Allied Air Forces, were pulling all the range they could from both existing and any future design proposals. These aircraft proposals were designated 'long-range penetration fighters'. As the name implies, their mission was penetration of any enemy defences as escort for bomber aircraft, against targets far beyond the ranges of standard fighter aircraft. The first jet fighters, with their inherent lack of range (the F-86A had a range of less than 600 miles/965 km), could never be considered for the 'penetration fighter' mission. An entirely new design was needed to meet AAF requirements for a penetration fighter.

Three aircraft manufacturers came up with penetration fighter proposals – McDonnell had the XF-88, Lockheed entered the XF-90, and North American offered the F-86C. The F-86C would use much existing F-86A technology, such as the main wing and tail assemblies, to keep the cost down. The wing had leading-edge slats for low-speed control. The primary flight controls were mechanically operated (i.e., cables) with a hydraulic boost as found on the F-86A. The complete stabiliser was adjustable, similar to the F-86E. There was no nose intake duct as on the F-86A; the intakes were the new NACA flush-mounted designs, which were actually recessed, one to each side. This design was chosen as it was felt that it would reduce drag enough to compensate for the slight loss of intake performance. The nose would come to a blunt point, which covered the AN/APG-30 ranging radar.

The fuselage was a totally different design from any other F-86, the first to have the so-called 'Coke bottle shape', i.e., the fuselage was pinched in just aft of the cockpit. Designed by North American engineer Larry Green, who referred to it as the 'Gibson Girl Shape', the fuselage design reduced drag at high Mach speeds that built up along the fuselage. The fuselage was much larger in diameter and 8 ft (2.4 m) longer than the F-86A.

There were two reasons for the increased size: 1) The F-86C would have an internal fuel capacity of 1,561 US gal (5909 litres), which was needed to meet the 'penetration fighter' range requirement; 2) The F-86C was going to be powered by the Pratt & Whitney copy of the Rolls-Royce Tay engine, which was larger in diameter and longer than the J47. This new engine, designated J48-P-1, had a centrifugal-flow compressor with a double-sided impeller, and was equipped with an afterburner. The J48 was rated at 6,250 lb (27.79 kN) of static thrust, with 8,000 lb (35.58 kN) of thrust in afterburner. The J48 had a variable exhaust outlet, with two clam-shell doors to increase or decrease the outlet opening size. Armament for the F-86C was six M24 20-mm cannons, with a rate of fire of 800 rounds per minute. There were 225 rounds per gun available.

Everything about the F-86C was bigger and heavier than on the F-86A. It was 44.1 ft (13.44 m) in length (36.6 ft/11.16 m on the F-86A), with a wingspan of 38.9 ft (11.86 m) (37.1 ft/11.3 m on the F-86A). The combat weight was 26,516 lb (12028 kg), compared to 16,357 lb (7420 kg) for the F-86A. The landing gear was much beefier in design to support the added weight, and had dual wheels for the main landing gear.

Record-breaker

In addition to the better-known F-86A and D absolute speed records, the F-86E was used for an assault on the closed-circuit speed record in 1951. A team from the Air Force Flight Test Center at Edwards AFB used four aircraft in the attempt at Detroit on 17 August 1951. The record was taken by Major Fred J. Ascani in aircraft '2' (F-86E-10 51-2721) at a speed of 635.31 mph (1,023 km/h), at the same time breaking the 100-km speed record for jets.

Right: The aircraft used for the record attempt were painted with Dayglo noses and large recognition numbers.

A Utah Air National Guard F-86E cruises over terrain uncharacteristic of its home state. Utah's 191st FIS converted to refurbished F-86Es, many of them Korean War veterans, from 1956. After only two years in the day-fighter role, the 191st gave up its Es and re-equipped with F-86Ls.

Even with the additional weight, the added thrust of the J48 with an afterburner took the F-86C's performance to a higher level than the much lighter F-86A. The top speed rose to 708 mph (1140 km/h) at sea level. Rate of climb was 11,960 ft (3645 m) per minute in afterburner. Service ceiling was 46,800 ft (14265 m). The range without external fuel tanks was an astonishing 1,967 miles (3165 km), compared to the F-86A, with its 200-US gal (757-litre) underwing ferry tanks, at 1,052 miles (1693 km). The wing could be fitted with underwing pylons for carriage of additional fuel tanks or up to 2,000 lb (907 kg) of ordnance.

The new design was so radically different from the F-86A that the Air Force redesignated the new aircraft as YF-93A in 1948. The initial order in 1948 was for 120 F-93As, but in January 1949 the Air Force suddenly cancelled the entire penetration fighter programme, and funding was limited to the two YF-93A prototypes (49-317 and 49-318) that were already under construction. The reason was the projected performance of the new all-jet B-47, which was so fast that it would not need a fighter escort. All funds for the penetration fighter programme were subsequently channelled into the XB-47 and XB-52 programmes.

The first flight of the YF-93A (49-317) was made by George Welch on 24 January 1950. Both YF-93As were flown extensively as test and evaluation aircraft for North American, the Air Force and NACA. One of the tests was research into intake design, and the first prototype was fitted with a standard set of intakes that protruded from the fuselage into the air stream. The results indicated that the standard intakes were a better design for high-speed operations. Test results were used in the designs of most of the 'Century Series' of fighter aircraft from F-101 through F-106. Both aircraft were eventually bailed to NACA, being based at the NACA Ames Laboratory facility at Moffett Field until the late 1950s, when they were scrapped.

Reconnaissance Sabres

One of the primary missions of any air force since World War I has been that of aerial surveillance of the enemy. Troop deployments, road and rail traffic, air defences, bomb damage assessment – all have been covered under the blanket of air reconnaissance. During the Korean War, air reconnaissance was performed by a number of different aircraft types and squadrons. The LT-6 Mosquitoes flew forward air control; RF-51D Mustangs reconnoitred the road and rail net of North Korea. In high-threat areas near the Yalu River and the MiGs, reconnaissance was performed by RF-80 Shooting Star and RB-45C Tornado jets. The MiGs made life miserable for the RF-80s and RB-45s, in spite of having F-86 Sabre escorts; neither type was fast enough to do the job in 'MiG Alley'. A reconnaissance version of the F-86 was needed, but no such project was in the works by either North American or the Air Force.

Except for the very long-range, high-altitude missions, all tactical reconnaissance during the Korean War was the mission of the 67th Tactical Reconnaissance Wing at Kimpo AB. Around the middle of 1951, several pilots in the 67th made a request for clearances to build a reconnaissance version of the F-86 – if possible. Majors Bruce Fish and Ruffin Gray, along with Captain Joe Daley, began a daily campaign with FEAMCOM about the project. They were told it could not be done – there was simply no room in an F-86 for the long-range cameras needed for the mission.

Far left: This F-86E was extensively modified during the Korean War period with a gloved wing (extended fixed leading edge), and a modified canopy with an extended windshield.

This F-86E-1 was one of two aircraft used to test an inflight-refuelling system which employed refuelling probes mounted to each wing drop tank. The tests were successful, but by the time the concept had been validated the Sabre was becoming obsolete, overtaken by the F-100.

F-86Es on test

Below: An Aerojet rocket was installed on this F-86E as part of 1956 investigations into the high-Mach flight regime.

Above: All of the F-86Fs that were dispatched to Europe flew the route from Newfoundland, to Greenland, to Iceland, and finally to the UK. Thus all aircraft carried Arctic Red markings for visual sightings in case they were forced down in snowy terrain. This aircraft is seen bound for the 21st FBW at Chambley AB, France.

Right: Major C. L. Hewitt checks the paperwork for the first F-86F (51-2850) delivered to the Air Force, with J. S. Smithson of NAA. The early Fs were built at Inglewood, but the demands on the factory were such that a second line was opened at Columbus, Ohio. The first Columbus-built variant was the F-20, the initial example of which first took to the air in May 1952.

The three officers persisted, and were constantly seen crossing the runway at Kimpo to inspect the F-86As of the 4th FIG for possible camera installations. Colonel Harry Thyng, commander of the 4th FIW, finally got tired of seeing the three reconnaissance pilots in his maintenance facilities, and offered them a 'class 26d' F-86A forward fuselage to work with. The three men took the F-86A nose to the maintenance hangers of the 67th TRW to examine it and try to fit a camera set-up into it somewhere. The people at FEAMCOM seemed to be correct: a camera simply would not fit. At least not mounted normally.

The maintenance crews of the 67th found that by removing the lower pair of 0.50-in guns and ammunition canisters, there was enough room for a small focal length camera. They installed a K-25 bomb scoring camera from an RB-26C, and mounted it horizontally in the right side of the fuselage. A series of mirrors was then installed to allow the camera to shoot vertically through a small opening cut into the lower fuselage. Externally, except for the very small opening under the right side of the nose, the reconnaissance Sabre looked identical to the fighter aircraft.

Following an inspection by Colonel Edwin 'Chick' Chickering, commander of the 67th TRW, who enthusiastically approved the modified mock-up, a pair of tired F-86As was pulled from the 4th FIG inventory and made ready for the conversion. Known as Project Honeybucket, the two F-86As (48-187 and 48-217) were ferried to Tachikawa AB, Japan, where all major F-86 maintenance was performed. FEAMCOM personnel modified both aircraft identically to the mock-up created by the 67th TRW crews. A single K-25 was installed in the lower right fuselage, shooting into the mirror installation devised by the Kimpo pilots. All three 0.50-in guns in the left fuselage, and the remaining single 0.50-in the right fuselage, remained operational. However, the guns were rarely charged prior to a mission because the vibration could knock the delicate mirror set-up out of adjustment.

Honeybucket mission

Captain Joe Daley brought the first Honeybucket (48-187) back to Kimpo in October 1951. Outwardly it looked exactly like the standard F-86As of the 4th FIG, black and white ID bands and all, and was parked on the 4th FIG ramp until mission time. Missions were usually flown with the Honeybucket as flight lead of a four-ship flight of 4th FIG F-86s.

Even with the limited capabilities of the single camera installation, FEAMCOM and the 5th AF recognised the potential of the Honeybucket Sabres. In late 1951, FEAMCOM authorised conversion of six more F-86As under Project Ashtray. Although the camera installation was similar, the Ashtray aircraft were much different from the

F-86F

The F model introduced the uprated J47-GE-27 engine, which provided a major increase in combat performance that was felt immediately after the variant reached Korea in September 1952. The first F flew on 19 March 1952 and initially differed only in powerplant from its predecessor. Later, numerous sub-variants were produced, including the F-25/30 fighter-bomber and F-35 nuclear bomber. The '6-3 hard wing' was introduced part-way through the production run and retrofitted to many earlier aircraft.

The 50th Fighter-Bomber Wing at Hahn AB, West Germany was a stalwart of USAFE throughout the Cold War. Among its assigned squadrons was the 81st FBS, one of whose F-86F-30s (with a '6-3' wing) is seen here in 1954. This variant introduced the dual-store wing which could mount ordnance on its inboard pylon. The Far East Air Force black-and-yellow identification bands were worn by Sabre units in Europe, providing quick ID in air combat.

Above: Seen at Eielson AFB, Alaska, this pair of F-86F-30s was assigned to the 720th FBS. Although designated as a SAC fighter-bomber unit, the 720th flew air defence missions.

Above: Following the end of the Korean War, three Sabre groups (4th, 8th and 18th FBGs) remained in Korea. In November 1954 the 18th moved out to Okinawa, and its place in Korea was taken by the 58th FBG. Lady Ann was an F-86F assigned to the group's 69th FBS, photographed at a snowy Osan (K-55) in the winter of 1956.

Left: Air defence of southern West Germany was the task of the 36th Fighter Day Group at Bitburg AB. This F-86F-25 served with the unit's 53rd FDS.

prototype Honeybucket machines. All the Ashtray aircraft had both gun bays emptied, and had a pair of K-9 cameras installed in place of the K-25. Being much larger than the K-25, the K-9 installation required bulging of the lower fuselage just forward of the wing leading edge. Both Honeybucket aircraft were brought up to Ashtray standard.

All Ashtray aircraft differed from each other. Some aircraft retained the two upper guns and their ammunition supply; most had them completely removed and replaced with ballast. Some had a K-14 'dicing' camera installed in the upper forward part of the nose in place of the APG-30 ranging radar. Some had open apertures for the cameras, while others had sliding doors that opened only when the camera was used. All Ashtray aircraft were painted in the markings of the 4th FIG, including the change from black and white ID bands to black and yellow ID bands in early 1952. The Ashtray aircraft were officially designated RF-86A, and all were assigned to the 15th TRS at Kimpo.

Being an 'in-the-field' modification, there were bound to be problems with all the Honeybucket/Ashtray aircraft. Photos were often fuzzy or blurred due to two major faults with the installation: 1) The camera installation, which required a multi-mirror set-up, was very vulnerable to vibration. 2) The K-9 camera itself, and the K-25 that followed, were both used in propeller-driven aircraft that had relatively low speeds. The RF-86As were much faster and the camera was just not suitable for the high-Mach runs made by the RF-86As. Lieutenant Bill Cress, 15th TRS pilot, came up with a modified mirror installation that solved most of the vibration problem. The slow-speed cameras themselves continued to be a problem until replaced by the higher-speed K-14.

Seven '48 model F-86As, all taken from 4th FIG inventories as new F-86Es arrived, had been modified to RF-86A standard by the end of the war (serials 48-183, -187, -195, -196, -217, -246 and -257). One aircraft, 48-217, flown by Major Jack Williams, commander of the 15th TRS, was shot down by North Korean anti-aircraft fire on 27 June 1952. Major Williams was killed in action.

F-86E

The next production variant was the F-86E (NA-170). The prototype YF-86D actually flew before the E model in December 1949, but the first production F-86D did not come off the assembly line until June 1951. Externally, at first glance, the F-86E differed little from the F-86A. It was a subtle external feature that made the F-86E a vastly different aircraft, with much greater combat effectiveness over the F-86A: the 'all-flying tail'.

Sabre pilots had been complaining that the flight controls were 'strange' in the transonic speed ranges. They seemed to reverse, i.e., if the pilot wanted to pull up and his speed was near Mach 1, the aircraft continued to go down. Several accidents were the result of this 'control reversal'. In actuality, the controls did not reverse, they simply did not

The ramp at Nellis is full of F-86Fs for the 1955 Worldwide Gunnery Meet. On the left are aircraft from the Itazuke-based 8th FBW, while on the right are the striped-tail Sabres of the 366th FBW from Alexandria AFB, Louisiana. A pilot from the 366th was the event's top scorer. He was Major Manuel 'Pete' Fernandez, third-highest scoring US ace in Korea.

Above: This 461st FDS, 86th FDW F-86F was one of several tested with various camouflage schemes in the mid-1950s, none of which was adopted. The wing was based at Landstuhl.

Right: This F-86F was the personal mount of General Spicer, commander of Air Training Command.

Above: Many Sabres ended their days as range targets and airfield decoys. Before such aircraft became available, this quite convincing mock-up was exhibited next to an F-86F-30 at Wiesbaden.

Right: 55-3816 was the first of the F-86F-40s to have a revised wing with extended tips. The return to leading-edge slats also involved the removal of the wing fences as fitted to the '6-3 hard wing'.

Below: No. 2 Sqn, SAAF, was assigned to the 18th FBG and completed over 2,000 fighter-bomber missions in F-86Fs in the final year of the Korean War.

respond effectively. In the transonic speed ranges, when the pilot pulled the control stick back to pull up, the air loads over the elevators were so great that the hydraulically boosted controls were inadequate to move the elevators. Thus the aircraft continued to go in the original direction.

The answer was to increase the amount of hydraulic boost actuating the elevator system. F-86A elevator controls were actuated by cables, with a hydraulic boost. On the F-86E, the cable system was eliminated, being replaced with a fully hydraulic system having greatly increased boost for the controls. It was tested on an F-86A in mid-1949.

The pilot had regained control of the aircraft, but it was still sluggish in the transonic speed range. North American's engineers had a dilemma. The horizontal stabiliser/elevator was aerodynamically correct in size for the aircraft, but the size of the elevator had to increase to regain manoeuvrability near Mach 1. The engineers decided to change the entire stabiliser/elevator operation.

The F-86A had a stabiliser that was movable by an electric motor which could change the angle of incidence to trim out excessive air loads. The North American engineers decided to gear the stabiliser and elevator together, which, for all intents and purposes, created a larger elevator surface. As the pilot called for more elevator, the stabiliser would move in conjunction with the elevator, creating a greater angle of attack; thus, better control was achieved at all speeds.

It was called the 'all-flying tail', and, together with the new, completely hydraulic flight controls (only the rudder remained cable controlled), the system became 'irreversible'. The fully hydraulic controls had their drawbacks, too. The pilot lost his 'feel' for the aircraft handling. Air loads were no longer transmitted back to the control stick. The North American engineers came up with a bobweight and bungee system that created an artificial 'feel' on the stick. Externally, the fuselage was bulged immediately in front of the stabiliser to cover the gearing mechanism that operated the stabiliser.

Internally, there were several significant changes. The type A-1CM gunsight, working with the AN/APG-30 radar rangefinder as had been installed in the last 24 F-86A-5s, would be standard on the F-86E. Engine thrust was increased with installation of the J47-GE-13 engine rated at 5,450 lb (24.24 kN) static thrust. George Welch made the first flight in F-86E 50-579 on 23 September 1950.

Es into service

The initial production run was for 60 F-86E-1s (serial 50-579/-638), with the first aircraft being delivered in February 1951 to the 33rd FIG. Both the 33rd and 1st FIGs began receiving F-86E-1s in the early spring of 1951 to replace some of the old '48 models that had been acquired when the 4th FIG had been sent to Korea, gathering new aircraft along the way to debarcation. By June 1951, it was obvious that the 4th FIG in Korea had two problems: 1) The F-86As that had been in combat almost every day since December 1950 were becoming tired and needed to be replaced. 2) There were more MiGs across the Yalu River every day, far more than even the veteran 4th FIG pilots would eventually be able to handle.

In late June 1951, the Air Force decided to re-equip the 4th FIG with F-86Es, and to make the 51st FIG, then flying Lockheed F-80C Shooting Stars, the second combat F-86 group, again equipped with F-86Es. The first E models sent to Korea were aircraft taken from active air defence units in the United States. Aircraft from both the 1st and 33rd FIGs were flown to San Diego, loaded aboard a Navy escort carrier, and shipped to Korea. The first aircraft arrived in July 1951, and were flown directly to the 4th FIG at Kimpo. The 51st FIG began to transition to the F-86E in September 1951, flying its first combat sorties on 2 December 1951.

The bulk of the F-86Es that were committed to Korea arrived aboard USS *Cape Esperance* and *Sitkoh Bay* in early November 1951. They were brand-new F-86E-5s straight off the assembly line. The F-86E-5 (serial 50-639/-689) was identical to the E-1 except for some minor changes in cockpit switching and a couple of minor internal system upgrades. Both the E-1 and E-5 shared the same wing, V-shaped windscreen, and weapons capabilities with the F-86A. Performance levels – i.e., speed, rate of climb, range, etc. – were identical to the F-86A.

The next variant produced was the F-86E-6, which was not built by North American Aviation. As MiG activity increased with each day the war in Korea continued, the

Taiwan Straits

The Chinese Nationalist Air Force (CNAF) began to receive Sabres in 1955 when the first of 320 aircraft were supplied from USAF stocks. Many of them were Korean War veterans, including many aces' aircraft. In 1958, these aircraft saw combat again when Taiwan and the People's Republic of China clashed over the Taiwan Straits, air battles that saw the first use of guided AAMs in combat. Around 30 MiG-17s were claimed for two CNAF air-to-air losses. It is now believed that many of the victorious Sabre pilots were in fact US Navy flyers.

***Above:** These Sabres are from the CNAF's 28th Fighter Squadron, 1st Fighter Wing and are seen in September 1956. The aircraft were brightly coloured, including a version of the Korean War-style identification bands.*

***Below:** Pilots of No. 28 Squadron scramble for their F-86Fs.*

***Left:** The CNAF gunnery team at the 1960 Flying Brothers SEATO Gunnery Meet. This aircraft (51-13185) wears a pair of MiG-kill stars dating from the conflict of two years before.*

USAF wanted to add a third squadron to the 51st FIG at Suwon. North American was already at peak aircraft production and the new plant in Columbus, Ohio would not be ready for some months. The USAF did not want to again strip aircraft from the inventories of its air defence squadrons for duty in Korea, so it contacted Canadair Ltd, which had been licensed to build F-86E aircraft beginning in 1951, as Sabre Mk 2s. Sixty aircraft were purchased under contract AF-9386. The first aircraft purchased was Sabre Mk 2 No. 19244, and was built on 2 February 1952. Delivered to the USAF between April and July 1952, the new aircraft were designated F-86E-6 (serials 52-2833/-2892). With few exceptions, the entire production of Canadair E-6s was sent to squadrons in Korea, serving with both the 4th and 51st FIGs.

The total of 111 F-86E-1s and E-5s, plus the 60 E-6s, would have been the last of the E series except for a problem with production of the new engine at General Electric. The next aircraft off the assembly line should have been the F-86F (NA-172), having the new J47-GE-27 engine rated at 6,090 lb (27.05 kN) static thrust. General Electric could not meet the production deadline for the -27 engine, so North American, with Air Force approval, built the first 132 aircraft with the J47-GE-13 engine, as installed in previous E models. These aircraft were designated F-86E-10 (serials 51-2718/-2849).

The fuselage of the E-10 had provision to accept the -27 engine when it became available. Some aircraft, especially those in Korea, were re-engined with the -27 engine during one of the trips through the IRAN facilities. One other significant change was the replacement of the V-shaped windscreen with a new, flat, armoured glass unit, which provided better forward protection and vision than the V-shaped unit. Minor changes were made to the instrument panel and various switches, all corresponding with the possible installation of the -27 engine. The first E-10s came off the assembly line in September 1951, with many going straight to the combat squadrons operating in Korea.

The final E variant was, again, the result of production problems with the -27 engine. The F-86F-15 was supposed to have the -27 engine, type A-4 gunsight, and repositioned control systems to eliminate a problem with total loss of hydraulics if a single vital spot were disabled during

This is an F-86F-30 of No. 11 Fighter Squadron. This unit used the F model from 1956-58 before upgrading to the F-86D, which remained in service until 1970.

Guard Fs

The first ANG use of the F-86F was by one squadron (123rd FIS, Oregon ANG) which was called to federal active duty on 1 March 1951 as part of the Korean War call-up, albeit equipped with F-51Ds at the time. It remained at Portland, however, where it converted to the F-86F in early 1952. By the end of the year it was back under state control, flying Mustangs again. It later regained F-86Fs, one of a small number of ANG units to operate this variant, most of which were exported after front-line USAF service.

This F-86F was assigned to the 123rd FIS, Oregon ANG in 1955. The badge was that of a diving red eagle.

Test Fs

Right: F-86Fs were employed on a wide variety of test programmes. This F-86F-30 had a Rocketdyne AR2-3 engine installed under the fuselage which added another 6,000 lb (26.70 kN) thrust. Unlike other rocket engines, the AR2-3 used JP-4 fuel, and could be air-started several times, although duration was only 2.8 minutes. So equipped, the JF-86F made 31 flights in 1960, attaining Mach 1.22 in level flight and 71,600 ft (21825 m).

This F-86F-30 (52-5143) was modified to evaluate the use of the F-86F as a bomber-destroyer, equipped with three of the retractable 2.75-in (7-cm) rocket trays similar to those used on the F-86D. In addition to the ventral tray, a 53-round tray was mounted either side of the forward fuselage. This awesome firepower was not adopted, as firing the side trays blinded the pilot.

combat. The first seven F-15s came off the assembly line in April 1952. The remainder of the 100 F-15s were completed with J47-GE-13 engines, being designated F-86E-15 (serials 51-12977/-13069). These aircraft were delivered between April and December 1952, serving with Air Training Command and Air National Guard squadrons. Many of the E-15s were subsequently retrofitted with both the -27 engine and the '6-3' solid leading-edge wing. No F-86E-15s went to Korea.

F-86F

The J47-GE-27 engine finally became available in quantity during early 1952 and production of the F-86F began almost immediately. The first F-86F-1 (51-2850) made its maiden flight on 19 March 1952. Other than the engine change, the F-1 was identical to the E-10, with the same weapons capabilities, wings and flight control systems, including the new flat, armoured windscreen. Installation of the -27 engine made the F-86F a vastly improved aircraft over the other variants. With 6,090 lb (27.09 kN) static thrust, and the same weight as the E-10, the F-86F's top speed rose to 688 mph (1107 km/h) at sea level, and well over 600 mph (965 km/h) at 35,000 ft (10668 m). This was an increase of more than 10 mph (16 km/h) over the -13 powered F-86E. Service ceiling was pushed another 2,000 ft (609 m) to 52,000 ft (15850 m), bringing the pilots in Korea closer, but still not equal, to the MiGs.

One great advantage of the -27 engine was the increase in rate of climb, which jumped over 2,500 ft (762 m) per minute to 9,850 ft per minute. No longer could the MiG drivers 'zoom and sun' with impunity through the F-86 formations. The Sabre pilots in 'MiG Alley' could now close on the MiG at any altitude, even during a climb. The -27 engine also offered slightly better fuel economy, and the combat radius was increased to 430 miles (692 km) with a pair of 120-US gal (454-litre) combat drop tanks.

North American built a total of 78 F-86F-1s (serials 51-2850/-2927), the first of which was delivered to the 84th FIS at Hamilton AFB in June 1952. The F-1 was operational in Korea with the 4th FIG by September of that year. The F-5 introduced a wing modification that strengthened the drop tank attachment point, enabling the carriage of new 200-US gal (757-litre) combat drop tank. This increased the combat radius to 463 miles (745 km). Every mile increase in the combat radius meant another few precious seconds in 'MiG Alley', seconds that could mean the difference between a kill or being killed. North

Pilotless Sabres

The last Sabres in US service have seen out their days with the Army and Navy on various drone and test programmes. Many missions, such as ECM pod testing against live weapons (below), can only be carried out on NOLO (NO Live Operator) flights. Below is an Army QF-86E at White Sands, while right is an NWC Sabre.

Above: This former Boeing chase CL-13 Mk 5 flew with Flight Systems Inc.

Right: A QF-86 meets its end at the hands of an AIM-9.

Below: USN QF-86Hs of the PMTC.

American built 16 F-86F-5s (serials 51-2928/-2943).

The F-86F-10 introduced the new AC type A-4 GBR gunsight, replacing the type A-1CM used on all previous models. The type A-1CM was a good unit, but it suffered from being a little too complicated and fragile for use in the rather spartan combat arena of Korea. Sperry and the USAF even constructed a special maintenance trailer under Project Sightline, which offered the latest and best maintenance equipment available to service the A-1CM. It alleviated the problem somewhat, but the A-1CM remained a source of contention for the pilots when it did not work during a combat engagement. The type A-4 GBR sight, using the same AN/APG-30 radar rangefinder, was a much simpler and more reliable unit to operate, and especially to maintain. All other equipment on the F-86F-10 remained the same as on previous models. North American built 34 F-86F-10s (serials 51-12936/-12969).

Damage limitation

Next off the assembly line was the F-15, which introduced the repositioned control systems. Combat in Korea had shown that there were several vital areas in the F-86 that one good hit could severely damage, often completely wiping out the entire system. One such area was the parking brake. The hydraulic lines for all the systems ran through the parking brake, and one hit in this area could drain the entire hydraulic system of fluid, leaving the pilot with no flight controls. All these vital areas were identified, and either repositioned, encased in armour plate, or given a back-up system in case of failure.

Problems with production of the -27 engine brought F-15 production to a halt after only seven aircraft were built (serials 51-12970/-12976). Six of the seven are known to have been operational in Korea with the 4th FIG.

Production of the Sabre in all variants (the D was also now in production) severely strained the production facilities at North American's Inglewood plant. In 1950, North American sought, and was granted, a lease of the old Curtiss Aircraft plant in Columbus, Ohio from the US Navy. Many thousands of SB2C Helldivers had been built at the plant during World War II, but it had sat empty for the preceding five years. As soon as the plant was refurbished and brought to standards acceptable to the USAF for building the Sabre, a contract was issued to build F-86Fs.

The first Columbus-built variant was the F-86F-20, virtually a copy of the Inglewood-built F-15, with the provisions to carry the 200-US gal drop tanks, the repositioned control systems, and the -27 engine. Some minor cockpit changes related to switching and the installation of the AN/ARC-33 radio equipment. North American/Columbus built 100 F-86F-20s (serials 51-13070/-13169), the first flight of one being in May 1952. The Air Force added a suffix to the official designation to identify the factory: all Inglewood-built aircraft carried the suffix NA, while Columbus-built aircraft had NH, e.g., F-86F-15-NA or F-86F-20-NH. None of the F-20s served in Korea.

Next off the North American assembly lines was a Sabre to meet an Air Force requirement for a fighter-bomber variant. All F-86s had two underwing hardpoints and up to four launch fittings per wing to fire the 5-in HVAR rocket. The carriage of any type of ordnance on the underwing pylons meant that no underwing fuel tanks could be carried, thereby considerably shortening range. Another pair of hardpoints was needed.

The F-25 and F-30 introduced the dual-store wing, which featured an additional pair of hardpoints at about 50 per cent of the wingspan. They were in addition to the standard pair just outboard of the main landing gear. All four hardpoints could handle either the 120- or 200-US gal (454- or 757-litre) drop tanks. However, only the inner pair was capable of carrying ordnance, up to 1,000 lb (454 kg) on each pylon. Thus, an F-86F with the dual-store wing could have a pair of 1,000-lb bombs plus two 200-US gal drop tanks on a typical mission. The first of 859 F-86F-30-NAs (serials 52-4305/-5163) came off the assembly line in October 1952. Deliveries of the first of 600 F-86F-25-

Above: NAA supplied conversion kits for export Sabres to turn them into RF-86Fs. The RoKAF's 10th Fighter Wing had a squadron of these aircraft, which had been built as F-25/30s, modified to F-40 standard and then given the RF conversion.

Above left: Many surplus F-86Fs went to foreign users. Here, newly refurbished aircraft await delivery to Venezuela's Grupo Aéreo de Caza 12 at McClellan AFB.

The eight factory-built RF-86Fs supplied to the 15th TRS were quite different from the Haymaker aircraft, featuring a side bulge to house the film magazine in the gun bay. The vertically-mounted cameras were less prone to shake. They arrived in Korea before the end of 1953, this example being seen at Kimpo in early 1954 with NAA 'tech rep' Ozzie Neidermann.

RF-86F

Experience with the Honeybucket/Ashtray RF-86As led to the conversion of three F-86F-30s to reconnaissance configuration under the codename Haymaker. These aircraft employed K-14 cameras. Initial field modifications were followed by eight NAA-designed and -built RF-86Fs, which had K-22 main cameras mounted in a bulged fairing on the fuselage sides. They arrived in Korea too late see action.

Left: This is one of the three Haymaker RF-86Fs, identified by the fairing on the lower fuselage side and lack of fuselage bulge. The horizontally-mounted cameras had to use a mirror to bend the image through 90°. Like the RF-86As, they wore 4th FIG markings to make them less conspicuous. They were operated by the 15th Tactical Reconnaissance Squadron at Kimpo (K-14) from June 1953.

Japanese F-86Fs

The Japanese Air Self-Defence Force re-equipped with Sabres as its first post-war fighter from 1955, with the delivery of 180 F-86Fs from the US. A shortage of pilots led to a proportion of these aircraft being returned unused. At the same time, Mitsubishi was instigating production of Sabres at Nagoya, under licence to North American, eventually completing 300 aircraft. They were all F-86F-40s with the slatted '6-3' wing and the J47-GE-27. They remained in service as trainers until the 1980s.

***Right:** Sabres of 1 Hikotai fly over Mount Fujiyama. The nearest aircraft is an F-86F-30, that leading the formation an F-25, and on the right is a Mitsubishi-built F-40, the others being US-made.*

***Right:** All of the 300 Sabres assembled by Mitsubishi were to the advanced F-86F-40 standard. This example carries a dart target for aerial gunnery.*

***Far right:** 64-6241 was one of 18 Mitsubishi F-86F-40s converted to RF-86F configuration in 1961-62. All these aircraft served with 501 Hikotai until their replacement by RF-4Es in 1979.*

The 'Blue Impulse' team flew the F-86F for 21 years from 1960. The aircraft initially retained natural metal with a black/yellow checkerboard on the fin, before adopting a blue/white scheme over natural metal. In 1963 the familiar base white with blue trim scheme appeared.

***Far right:** Seen in May 1982, this Fuerza Aérea Argentina F-86F undertakes a rocket attack during a training exercise. The Argentines retained a handful of Sabres for weapons training purposes, and when the Falklands/ Malvinas conflict erupted, thoughts turned to reactivating them for front-line use against British forces. They were initially considered for relocation to the islands themselves prior to the British Task Force arriving, and later for emergency deployment after the British landings at Ajax Bay, San Carlos Water.*

NHs (serials 51-13170/-13510 & 52-5272/-5530) began in January 1953.

Fighter-bomber F-30s were rushed to Korea in January 1953 to begin the conversion to F-86s of two existing 5th Air Force fighter-bomber groups, the 18th and 8th FBGs. Conversion of these two groups accomplished two Air Force goals: upgrading the last F-51D- and F-80C-equipped groups still operational in Korea, and doubling Sabre strength in the theatre to counter the ever-increasing MiG forces north of the Yalu. The Communists had over 1,000 MiG-15s available at the bases between the Yalu River and Mukden, Manchuria, which were opposed in January 1953 by less than 150 F-86s.

The increase in control offered by the full power flight controls developed with the F-86E prompted North American engineers to explore how best to use the new-found control at high Mach numbers. One of the things discovered in the wind tunnel tests was that elimination of the leading-edge slats, making a smoother edge for the wing to cut the air flow, lowered the drag coefficient. By making that edge even sharper, drag was lowered even more – especially at or near Mach 1.

On the other end of the scale was a loss of low-speed control, which had originally been alleviated through the use of leading-edge slats. The loss of control was more evident at low speeds, especially in take-off and landing. The stall speed rose from 128 to 144 mph (205 to 232 km/h). Landing approach speeds rose similarly, making the new Sabre a very hot landing aircraft when compared with slat-winged variants. Some of the penalties were alleviated by increasing the size of the wing. North American extended the wing leading edge 6 in (15 cm) at the wingroot and 3 in (7.6 cm) at the wingtip, creating the so-called '6-3' wing. The increase also increased the angle to 35.7°. A 5-in (12.7-cm) high wing fence was installed at 70 per cent of the wingspan to correct air flow problems over the ailerons caused by the new leading edge.

The end results were worth it, as top speed increased to 695 mph (1118 km/h) at sea level, and manoeuvrability was greatly increased at combat altitudes. The '6-3' wing added about 1.5*g* to the manoeuvrability at 35,000 ft (10668 m). Since the '6-3' extension occurred in front of the main wing spar, North American's engineers made use of the available space to install a leading-edge fuel tank, which increased internal fuel capacity from 435 to 505 US gal (1647 to 1911 litres).

The '6-3' solid leading-edge wing was installed in three batches. The entire wing leading edge was held in place by a piano-type hinge, so North American devised a kit to convert existing slatted wing aircraft to the new solid leading edge. Fifty of these kits were rushed to Korea where they were installed on aircraft flown by aggressive pilots, i.e., pilots who flew the aircraft right on the edge and were not afraid to challenge the MiGs any time and any place. Large numbers of these kits were eventually sent to Korea and installed on all the combat F-86Fs (and some Es) in the theatre.

Left: RoKAF F-86Fs taxi for a mission at Suwon. Apart from the national markings, this 1956 scene looks little different from the days of the war.

The '6-3' wing was incorporated into the production run of both the F-25 and F-30 at different points, starting with the 171st F-86F-25-NH (51-13341), and the 200th F-86F-30-NA (52-4305). All subsequent F-86Fs were built with the '6-3' wing installed at the factory. Interestingly, although most historians credit the F-86F-25 with being the leading MiG-killer in Korea, no F-25s were sent to Korea. During the war, the media considered everything with a '6-3' solid leading edge to be a F-25, when in fact many of the combat aircraft with the kit installation were early Fs, from F-1 through F-15, plus large numbers of F-30s.

South Korea began operating the Sabre in 1955 and received 122 ex-USAF F-86Fs, most of which were upgraded with the F-40 wing and Aero 3B Sidewinder launch rails. Here examples of the original natural metal and later camouflage schemes are seen during the March 1969 Focus Retina exercise at Taegu AB.

Nuclear and reconnaissance Fs

The last F model off the North American assembly line was the F-35, which had a nuclear capability, being able to carry a 1,200 lb (544-kg) Mk 12 atomic bomb with a yield of up to 20 kT under the port wing on the inner pylon. All other pylons would carry drop tanks. The F-35 pilot had to use a toss-bomb technique requiring use of an M-1 Low Altitude Bombing System (LABS) computer to aid in finding the correct launch point to 'toss' the bomb. The F-35 was otherwise similar to other F-86Fs.

North American built 264 F-86F-35-NAs in two batches (serials 52-5164/-5271 and 53-1072/-1228), with the first aircraft being nuclear operational in January 1954. The F-35s were almost exclusively assigned to squadrons operating from NATO bases in Europe very close to the Iron Curtain.

Towards the end of 1952, the 15th TRS sought authorisation to re-equip with newer aircraft. The F-86F was already in service with both the 4th and 51st FIGs, and new aircraft were arriving each day. North American Aviation was working on a factory-built RF-86, but it was still many months away. Again, FEAMCOM authorised a conversion of several F-86F aircraft to RF-86F under Project Haymaker. Several brand-new F-86F-30 aircraft went to the Tsuiki REMCO facility in Japan after a short combat stint with one of the groups in Korea.

At Tsuiki, the aircraft had all armament, radars and the gunsight removed. A camera suite identical to that of the Ashtray RF-86A was then installed, but using K-14 cameras in place of the slower speed K-9s. Again, the K-14s had to be mounted horizontally, shooting through a mirror complex with an aperture in the bottom of the fuselage. The K-14 'dicing' camera was now mounted between the two vertical cameras, with an aperture on the fuselage bottom. As with the RF-86A, the fuselage was bulged to cover the camera suite installation. The Tsuiki REMCO facility built three Haymaker RF-86F-30s, serials 52-4330, -4357, and -4529.

The Haymaker RF-86F-30s began equipping the 15th TRS at Kimpo in 1953, flying side by side with the Ashtrays that remained in service. Once again, the RF-86Fs were marked identical to aircraft of the 4th FIG, including painting on fake gun ports. The mission profiles were identical to the RF-86A. It would take off as lead in a flight of four 4th FIG F-86s. Near the target area, often north of the Yalu River, the RF-86F broke down and away from the rest of the flight. The RF-86F pilot would then make a high-Mach run over the target while the rest of the flight orbited nearby.

The results of both the Ashtray and Haymaker programmes were successful in spite of the shortcomings of a 'field-modified' installation. No Haymaker aircraft were lost. In June 1953, the first North American RF-86F production aircraft began arriving in Korea. The factory-built aircraft were a vast improvement over the Haymaker aircraft. Using all the available information that was coming in daily from the pilots of the 67th TRW in Korea, North American engineers fixed all the problems before the aircraft ever flew. The camera suite was the latest high-speed unit, using a pair of K-22s and a K-17 'dicing' camera.

The factory camera suite, however, was not mounted horizontally, and used no mirrors to obtain vertical photos. The K-22s were mounted vertically which, with their longer focal length, took the main body of the camera and the film magazines outside the fuselage contours of the F-86. North American solved this by simply creating a large

Pakistani Sabres meet their nemesis, standing next to a Folland (HAL) Gnat. This very nimble fighter scored heavily over the F-86 in both Indo-Pakistan wars, earning itself the nickname 'Sabre-Slayer', although the traffic was far from one way. This Gnat was captured in the 1971 war when its pilot, Squadron Leader Brij Pal Singh Sikand, was forced to land at a Pakistani base.

Indo-Pakistan Wars

The Sabre formed the backbone of the Pakistani Air Force during both the 1965 and 1971 wars with India, proving itself as a worthy opponent against often more capable fighters. The initial F-86F batch was bolstered for the second conflict by Sabre Mk 6s, and some aircraft were modified to carry Sidewinders.

Above: Sqn Ldr Mohammed Alam was commander of No. 11 Sqn, PAF. Flying an F-86F, he claimed nine kills (and two damaged) in the 1965 war.

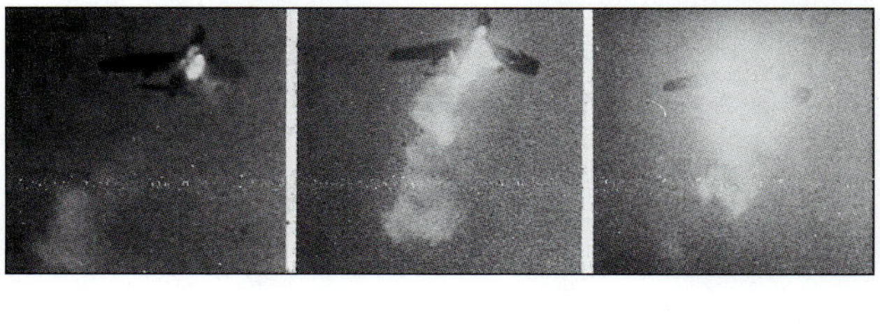

Left: Gun camera film shows one of the two No. 14 Sqn Sabres that were shot down on 22 November 1971 by No. 22 Sqn, IAF Gnats. This combat, in which a third F-86 was damaged, was a prelude to the 1971 war.

Transonic Trainer

On 14 December 1953 NAA flew its TF-86F prototype (52-5016, above), which had been developed in response to a USAF requirement for a high-performance trainer. This aircraft was lost after a few flights, but was replaced by a second aircraft (53-1228, left), which differed in being fitted with the '6-3' wing. Although no orders were forthcoming, the second TF-86F had a long and productive career as a trainer and test/chase platform.

The second TF-86F in flight graphically demonstrates the '6-3 hard wing' with which it was fitted, and the 63-in (1.60-m) forward fuselage extension necessary to accommodate the second cockpit.

bulge on the gun bay door, which covered the film magazine. Ballast, needed to realign the aircraft's centre of gravity, was added to the forward fuselage, totalling almost 750 lb (340 kg).

The cockpit of the factory-built RF-86F had an elongated canopy to counter a buffet caused by the bulged fuselage. All camera windows had sliding doors. Factory aircraft had the new '6-3 hard wing' with leading-edge fences. North American built eight RF-86Fs for the US Air Force (serials 52-4377, -4379, -4492, -4800, -4808, -4822, -4823, and -4864). None of the factory-built RF-86Fs were completed in time to join the combat during the war in Korea. However, all the RF-86Fs were involved in clandestine and standard reconnaissance missions after the war ended.

In spite of the success in combat of the RF-86A and F programmes, the Air Force chose a reconnaissance version of the Republic F-84F as its next-generation tactical reconnaissance aircraft – the RF-84F Thunderflash. However, interest in the RF-86F by Japan, South Korea and Nationalist China kept the type in front-line service into the 1980s. North American Aviation provided conversion kits to Mitsubishi Heavy Industries, which was in the process of assembling F-86F-40 aircraft. Mitsubishi converted at least 18 aircraft to RF-86F-40 standard. The 501st Hikotai finally turned in its RF-86Fs in favour of RF-4E Phantoms on 1 October 1979. South Korea had one squadron of 10 RF-86Fs still flying missions in the late 1980s. These aircraft included F-86F-25 and -30 airframes, brought to F-40 standard, then to RF configuration. The Taiwanese Air Force on Formosa had seven RF-86Fs, all modified similarly to the South Korean RF-86Fs.

F-86F-40

During the early 1950s, with war raging in the skies over Korea, many nations were interested in obtaining F-86 aircraft to defend their borders against the Soviet threat. Most simply bought surplus F-86s that became available as the US Air Force transitioned into the supersonic era with the F-100 Super Sabre. NATO members equipped their air forces with Canadair-built Sabres. Nations of the Pacific Rim were also very interested in the Sabre, especially Japan in the wake of the attempted Communist take-over of South Korea. Japan was interested not only in re-equipping its air force, but also in licence-building the Sabre in an effort to bolster its war-ravaged economy.

In late 1953, the Allied Nations – minus the USSR, of course – decided to let Japan begin to re-equip its military forces. At the top of the list was the Japanese Air Self-Defence Force, or JASDF, for whose squadrons the US would supply F-86Fs. Part of the agreement was that the majority of the Sabres intended for the JASDF would be built in Japan. Mitsubishi Heavy Industries, builder of the famed Zero fighter, signed a joint production agreement

Below right: The No. 2 TF-86F carried out armament trials, including the carriage of two 1,000-lb (454-kg) bombs under the wing pylons. Unlike the No. 1 aircraft, '228 had gun armament (two 0.50-in/12.7-mm machine-guns) fitted from the start.

Right: The second TF-86F is seen at Edwards, wearing the badge of the AFFTC on the fin and the ARDC on the fuselage. To cure directional stability problems the aircraft was built with an enlarged dorsal fin, and was subsequently further modified with a shallow ventral fin.

Gunval

Combat in Korea quickly revealed the inadequacy of the Sabre's six-gun armament. A handful of aircraft were modified with four 20-mm cannon and tested under combat conditions.

A ramp full of secret aircraft: this is the 335th FIS Gunval line at K-14 in early 1953. Note the revised blast plate configuration of the F-86F-2s, which were armed with four T-160 20-mm cannon. The middle aircraft, 51-2867, was flown by Colonel George Jones, 30th ace of the war. He shot down two MiG-15s with Gunval aircraft, although overall the combat evaluation was inconclusive.

with North American on 13 July 1954, allowing Mitsubishi to licence-build a version of the F-86F: the F-86F-40. The F-40 was a combination of all the best qualities that had been developed through the F-86 family, plus one new innovation. The fuselage, weapons system and flight controls were standard F-86F. The engine chosen was the J47-GE-27 engine rated at 5,910 lb (26.28 kN) of thrust. The wing would be the '6-3' wing, but with leading-edge slats, and would incorporate the multiple stores capability developed for the fighter-bomber Sabre. Wingspan was increased 12 in (30 cm) at each tip.

Installation of the extended wingtips gave the F-40 an outstanding turning ability over all the other variants, including the famed MiG-killer Fs with the '6-3 hard wing'. The leading-edge slats reduced the stall speed from 144 mph (232 km/h) on the '6-3 hard wing' Fs to 124 mph (200 km/h) in the F-40. The slat actuators and wingtip extensions added about 250 lb (113 kg) to the overall weight, but performance was almost identical to that of a standard F-86F. The first F-86F-40 (No. 55-3816) was completed in October 1955 at the North American Inglewood plant.

Although Mitsubishi was in the process of gearing up to build the new Sabre, it would be many months before the first aircraft would be completed. Cold War tensions dictated that the USAF ordered North American to reopen the F-86F assembly line that had closed down in June 1954 following the last F-86F-35 off the assembly line. The USAF ordered 215 F-86F-40s on 27 June 1955, with a further order of 65 on 27 March 1956. The first of these North American-built F-40s were shipped to Japan by sea in 1956.

Mitsubishi was not going to build the Sabre 'from scratch'. It would obtain parts kits supplied by North American that included fuselage, wing, and tail assemblies, J47 engine, landing gear, and cockpit assemblies. Arriving by ship, the kits would then be reassembled by Mitsubishi at its plant in Nagoya. The first 70 kits were sent to Japan on 19 August 1955, and the first Mitsubishi F-40 (55-5048) made its initial flight on 9 August 1956.

North American supplied two additional kit contracts for 230 aircraft, making a total of 300 Mitsubishi-assembled F-86F-40s. The last Mitsubishi F-40 came off the assembly line on 25 February 1961. Late in that final contract, an additional kit was supplied to Mitsubishi, containing Aero 3B pylons and installation equipment to use the Philco-Ford GAR-8 (AIM-9B) Sidewinder air-to-air missile.

The much improved overall performance of the F-40 led to a USAF decision to retrofit large numbers of its remaining F-86F inventory with the extended wingtips and leading-edge slats. Again, North American supplied kits to the USAF squadrons containing the new wing leading edge, slat assemblies, wingtip extensions and new ailerons. (The original aileron was part of the wingtip, while the F-40 aileron was separate.)

Many Sabre-equipped nations also converted their aircraft to F-40 standard through the use of the kits. Only the Canadair and Australian Avon Sabres were not equipped with the F-40 wing kits, although both types could accept the installation. Two countries were equipped with Mitsubishi F-86F-40 Sabres – Pakistan and, of course, Japan – but F-40 conversion kits were supplied to others, including South Korea, Nationalist China, the Philippines, Portugal, Spain and Saudi Arabia.

TF-86F Transonic Trainer

The TF-86F was an answer to an Air Force request for a very high performance trainer aircraft to replace the Lockheed T-33A. North American proposed a lengthened F-86F in early 1953 to meet the requirements. A new F-86F-30, one of the early aircraft without the '6-3' wing, was pulled from the Inglewood assembly line and taken to the modification facility. Construction began on 9 September 1953.

Left: An NAA employee 'paints' the F-95A designation on the nose of the prototype YF-95. Noteworthy features, modified on the production machines, were the V-shaped windscreen and rearward-sliding canopy. Note also the pitot tube inside the intake.

Below: This is the second prototype, seen flying from Edwards in 1951. By this time the designation had changed from YF-95 to YF-86D.

Neither prototype was fitted with armament or radar, being intended solely for aerodynamic and systems testing. This is No. 1, with spin parachute fitted.

After initial tests were completed, the No. 1 YF-86D was used to test aspects of the Sabre 45 (F-100 Super Sabre). It was fitted with a 45° wing, new jetpipe and low-set stabiliser.

YF-95/YF-86D

Delays to the Northrop F-89 Scorpion and its F-102 follow-on caused something of a panic in the USAF, which urgently needed a radar-equipped interceptor. Lockheed (with the F-94) and North American responded with derivatives of existing designs to bridge the gap, although both F-94 and the F-86D Sabre gave excellent service for many years. Little of the F-86A design remained in the F-86D, and it was initially assigned the new designation of F-95 to reflect this fact.

This 'Dog' was an F-86D-35 assigned to the 16th FIS at Naha, Okinawa in August 1954. When F-86Ds were committed to the Far East, the Air Force discovered that most of the runways that they would use were too short for safe operation. Accordingly, the F-86D-45 with brake parachute was developed to overcome the problem.

The fuselage was lengthened 63 in (160 cm) to make room for the student cockpit in front of the instructor's cockpit. Due to the modification to the fuselage, the aircraft's centre of gravity had shifted to the rear. North American engineers countered this by moving the wing assembly forward 8 in (20 cm). The entire cockpit area was covered by a single bubble canopy that opened clam-shell style, as on the F-86D and the T-33A. The wing, tail assemblies and engine remained standard F-86F. The wing retained the leading-edge slats for low-speed stability.

Power for the TF-86F was the J47-GE-27 engine rated at 5,910 lb (26.28 kN) of static thrust. No armament, radar or gunsight was installed. The first flight of the TF-86F Transonic Trainer (52-5016) came on 14 December 1953, with North American test pilot Ray Morris at the controls. Performance was on a level with the single-seat variants, as the TF-86F weighed only 100 lb (45 kg) more than a standard F model. It had a top speed of 692 mph (1114 km/h), with both rate of climb and service ceiling matching the F-86F. Range was an additional 300 miles (483 km) due to additional internal fuel tanks.

Sadly, after only nine flights, the TF-86F crashed on 17 March 1954, taking the life of North American test pilot Joe Lynch. Just days later, despite the crash of the prototype, the Air Force authorised construction of a second TF-86F. It differed from the first prototype in having the '6-3' wing with extended wingtips developed under the F-86F-40 programme. The No. 2 TF-86F would be armed with a pair of M3 0.50-in machine-guns, with 100 rounds per gun, and underwing pylons for carriage of drop tanks or ordnance. A small ventral fin was added to the aft fuselage to counter what was thought to have caused the crash of the first prototype.

The second TF-86F (53-1228) made its first flight on 5 August 1954, and was delivered to the Fighter School at Nellis AFB on 31 January 1955. One week after delivery of the TF-86F, the Air Force suddenly cancelled quantity orders for the Sabre Transonic Trainer. The USAF had already authorised a trainer version of the 'next-generation fighter' – the TF-100 Super Sabre. However, the second TF-86F saw extensive service, first as a trainer for F-86 crews at Nellis, both US and foreign pilots, and later at the Air Force Flight Test Center at Edwards AFB, as a chase aircraft for many of the programmes under development at Edwards. It served in that role well into the 1960s.

Above: J. Slade Nash flew this F-86D-20 to capture the first 'Dog' speed record with a figure of 968.505 mph (1124.104 km/h).

Record-breaking 'Dogs'

The F-86D twice broke the world speed record, flying low-altitude runs over the Salton Sea in California. Captain Slade Nash set the first record on 18 November 1952 in an F-86D-20. On 16 July 1953 Lieutenant Colonel William Barnes used an F-86D-35 to capture the record.

Left: A USAF cameraman operates the central tracking unit as an F-86D streaks at 125 ft (40 m) above the Salton Sea record track.

Below: This F-86D-30 was involved in the 1953 record effort, although it was a D-35 which took the record at 715.697 mph (1151.77 km/h).

Project Gunval

Throughout the Korean War, it was painfully obvious that the standard Sabre armament of six 0.50-in machine-guns was inadequate against the MiG-15. Although the MiG was lighter than the Sabre, it had armour plate in all the right places. Fifth AF pilots complained that, on many occasions, they expended all their ammunition (1,800 rounds), only to watch the MiG flee back across the Yalu River to probably fly and fight again. Experiments with explosive 0.50-in ammunition were tried in 1951, but the results were disappointing.

The obvious answer was the 20-mm cannon. Several types were available, including the M24, the Navy Oerlikon, and the new T-160 20-mm cannon. The T-160 was a gas-operated, belt-fed, electrically-fired weapon that fired 1,500 rounds per minute. Based on a Mauser design for the Luftwaffe, the T-160 was developed jointly by the Springfield Arsenal and North American. A division of Ford Motor Company would manufacture the new cannon. North American engineers redesigned the entire forward fuselage of a standard F-86E to accept installation of four of the new T-160 cannon; both gun bays had to be completely changed. The guns had to be spaced further apart vertically, with a totally new muzzle blast panel. The ammunition canisters were in the standard position, low on the fuselage, but each canister held only 100 rounds or about six seconds' fire.

Left: An F-86D-15 lets fly with a full volley of 'Mighty Mouse' rockets. Easily visible are the four tail fins which were clustered together when the rocket was in its launcher, and which sprung open as the projectile left the confines of the tube. Universally called 'Mighty Mouse', the official term for the weapon was FFAR (Folding-Fin Aircraft Rocket).

Rocket ship

Until a few aircraft were modified to carry Sidewinders, the F-86Ds were universally armed with the 2.75-in (7-cm) 'Mighty Mouse' rocket, 24 of which could be carried in a retractable ventral tray. The pilot could select single, group or full salvo firing, although when faced with a Soviet bomber target only a full salvo was a realistic option.

Right: A rear view shows a 'Mighty Mouse' test at the Air Proving Ground at Eglin, the rockets having flash heads to allow camera tracking. The rockets were fired sequentially over a half-second period, and naturally dispersed to ensure a wide area coverage to maximise the chances of a hit. Rocket firing was normally performed automatically, taking cues from the E-4 system, although there was manual back-up.

During the design stage of the installation, it was thought that gun gas in minor amounts would have little effect on the performance of the jet engine. Gun gas is highly explosive, so it would have to be removed from the gun bays to eliminate any chance of explosion. North American engineers designed small 'doors', cut into the interior of the intake duct, to extract the gun gas. All four guns fired simultaneously.

North American pulled a test nose from the assembly line and made the installation in early 1952. The test nose was ground-tested at the North American firing range between the two main buildings at the Inglewood factory. Ten thousand rounds were fired through each weapon. Structural integrity of the nose and the gun mounts suffered cracks and broken rivets and bolts due to the much heavier pounding of the large-bore cannon. North American had to redesign the gun mounts and strengthen the nose around the guns.

When the Air Force and North American were satisfied with the ground test results, the manufacturer received approval to build several test aircraft. Other than the installation of the T-160 cannon, the test aircraft would all be built to F-86F specifications, with the AC type A-4 GBR sight, AN/APG-30 ranging radar, J47-GE-27 engine, and the '6-3 hard wing'. North American built a total of 10 aircraft. Four F-86E-10s were pulled from the assembly line (51-2803, -2819, -2826 and -2836), and six F-86F-1s followed (51-2855, -2861, -2867, -2868, -2884, and -2900). All 10 aircraft were redesignated F-86F-2.

The first aircraft was 51-2803. George Welch flew all the initial flight tests in -2803, firing the weapons over the Pacific firing range near Catalina Island. All test flights were between 10,000 and 25,000 ft (3048 and 7620 m), with no problems being encountered. North American began deliveries of the remaining F-86F-2s to the Air Force Armament Test Center at Eglin AFB. Testing would be conducted under the auspices of Project Gunval, the commander of which was Lieutenant Colonel Clayton Peterson.

In December 1952 eight of the Gunval aircraft were

An F-86D of 'C Flight' of the 37th FIS makes a run on the target sleeve during the March 1955 deployment to Yuma for live-fire practice. The rocket tray has yet to extend from its position just forward of the wing joint. The 37th was based at Ethan Allen AFB, Vermont, as part of Northeast Air Command. Since the unit regularly flew across the border into Canada on intercept missions and cross-training exercises, the high-visibility Arctic Red markings were applied.

Above: This F-86D-60 is from the 498th FIS, photographed on its way to the annual Yuma rocket-firing competition. The 498th 'Geiger Tigers' (from Geiger AFB, Washington) were among the most 'colourful' squadrons in the Air Force, and NAA made a colour movie about their time at Yuma. The D-60 was the last production block, and featured a brake parachute as standard.

Above right: The 327th FIW at McChord AFB, Washington established the 'Sabre Knights' aerobatic team using the F-86D, the aircraft being drawn from the 325th FIS.

shipped to Japan aboard the escort carrier USS *Windham Bay*, arriving at Kisarazu later that month. The aircraft were made combat ready by the 6408th Maintenance Support Squadron at Tsuiki. On 1 January 1953, Lieutenant Colonel Peterson took seven of the Gunval aircraft to Kimpo for extensive combat testing with the 4th FIG. The Gunval project was assigned to the 335th FIS, commanded by the legendary 'Grey Fox', Lieutenant Colonel Vermont Garrison. One Gunval aircraft remained at Tsuiki for further testing. Combat missions began in the first week in January. Almost immediately, problems were encountered that resulted from the T-160 installation.

George Welch had flown all the test firings at altitudes between 10,000 and 25,000 ft – with no problems. Combat in Korea took place at altitudes exceeding 40,000 ft (12192 m), usually above 45,000 ft (13716 m). On one of the first missions that MiGs were encountered, Major John Moorehead engaged one of the MiGs at 46,000 ft (14020 m). When Major Moorehead fired a long burst from the cannon, the engine immediately shuddered and suffered a flameout. Luckily, Major Moorehead got a restart at around 20,000 ft (6096 m) and landed safely back at Kimpo.

About a week later, Captain Murray Winslow was not as lucky. Captain Winslow engaged a MiG at about 45,000 ft, and opened fire with all four cannons. Again, the F-86F-2 shuddered and the engine stalled. Captain Winslow could not restart the engine and had to eject over the ocean below. Gunval Sabre 51-2861 crashed into the Yellow Sea.

Something was drastically wrong. The Gunval project was grounded immediately, pending further tests. It transpired that large amounts of gun gas were being ingested into the intake, much larger amounts than the engineers had expected. With the higher altitude and lesser amounts of oxygen for the engine to run on normally, the gun gas was causing a compressor stall, commonly known as a flameout.

The first thing the Gunval team did was to weld shut the doors that bled gun gas directly into the engine intake duct. Next, a selector switch was installed in the cockpit allowing the pilot to choose either two or four guns firing. One-in (2.5-cm) holes were drilled in the aft portion of the gun bay doors to alleviate gun gas build-up. These changes seemed to cure most of the compressor stall problems.

However, Captain Lonnie Moore, flying Gunval Sabre No. 51-2803, suffered first a compressor stall and then a turbine failure. He, too, was forced to eject over the Yellow Sea. Test photos indicated that large amounts of gun gas were forming ahead of the guns, and being ingested directly into the nose intake. North American Aviation engineer Paul Peterson (no relation to the Gunval commander) came up with the answer. He realised that something was needed to break up the gun gas as it exited the muzzles, before it had a chance to enter the intake. He designed a small horseshoe-shaped clip to be installed in the recessed muzzle trough of each weapon. The clip broke up the gun gas, deflecting it away from the aircraft. Peterson's deflector clips cured the compressor stall problems of the Gunval Sabres. North American made kits that were sent to Korea for installation on the combat test aircraft. Subsequently, the clips were incorporated into the M39 cannon installation in the production of F-86H-5s.

Gunval statistics

The Gunval combat tests in Korea lasted a total of 16 weeks, beginning in mid-January 1953. Gunval pilots flew a total of 282 combat missions. Although the project was a 335th FIS assignment, Gunval pilots were drawn from throughout the 4th FIG. MiGs were engaged 41 times, with the following results: six MiGs destroyed, three probables, and 13 damaged. Two Gunval Sabres were hit by MiG cannon fire. Major Ray Evans took a 37-mm hit in the intake and Lieutenant Colonel Don Rodewald was hit twice in the wing by 23-mm cannon fire. Both aircraft returned safely to K-14. Project Gunval was completed on 1 May 1953, and the aircraft were returned to the US, eventually being assigned to the Colorado Air National Guard 'Minutemen' aerobatic team.

Two additional F-86Fs (51-2916 and -2926) were completed with installation of Oerlikon 206RK 20-mm cannon taking the place of the T-160s. These aircraft were redesignated F-86F-3, and were delivered to the Armament Test Center at Eglin in April 1954. The Oerlikon installation was not very successful. The guns were much heavier than the T-160s, resulting in a shift in the aircraft's centre of gravity; the barrel life was too short; and the stoppage rate was unsatisfactory. The F-86F-3s were assigned to Air Proving Ground Command for further tests in 1954-55, being redesignated JF-86F in 1957, and eventually scrapped.

Although the Gunval combat tests in Korea were inconclusive due to the limited ammunition supply, the weapons

Beginning in 1954, F-86Ds were deployed to bases in the European/ Mediterranean theatre to provide air defence for bases operating SAC bombers. This aircraft is from the 324th FIS, dispatched to Sidi Slimane in Morocco in July 1958. In that year two squadrons of 'Dogs' in Spain were directly assigned to SAC.

Right: The flight line at Vincent AFB, Arizona groans under the weight of interceptors gathered for the 1956 Yuma Rocket Meet. Here (from left) are an 84th FIS F-89H, and F-86Ds of the 498th and 497th FIS.

This F-86D-60 was from the 512th FIS, based at RAF Bentwaters in England. Europe-based Sabres deployed to Wheelus Field in Libya for their live-firing exercises. F-86Ds in Europe routinely carried 120-US gal (454-litre) drop tanks due to the length of time missions usually took, which often involved weather diversions.

themselves were extraordinary. They were later mass-produced by Ford under the designation of M39. The M39 20-mm cannon were the main armament of the early 'Century Series' aircraft, both the F-100 Super Sabre and F-101 Voodoo having four M39 cannons.

F-86D 'Sabre Dog' interceptor

The F-86D programme was the result of the slippage of another programme – the Northrop XF-89 Scorpion. The Scorpion was supposed to be the USAF all-weather interceptor of the future, at least through 1954, which is when the supersonic '1954 Interceptor', the Convair F-102, was slated for rollout. However, problems with the XF-89 prototype, including a bad tail buffet that could end a flight disastrously, led to the Air Force investigating other aircraft for the all-weather interceptor programme. This included a modified Lockheed TF-80C – the F-94 Starfire – and a modified Sabre.

North American had a programme underway for a possible all-weather version of the F-86 as early as March 1949, when the first F-86As were entering service with combat units. There was one major difference between the North American proposal and all the other interceptor designs – the North American design would be a single-seat aircraft. Almost all previous all-weather or night-fighter designs had been multi-place. Aircraft such as the Northrop P-61 Black Widow, the Mosquito night-fighter, even the German Bf 110G – all were multi-place aircraft. They had a pilot to fly the aircraft, and at least one other person to run the radar system. The US Navy/Marine F6F-5N and F4U-2 were notable single-seat exceptions. All these aircraft had the very simplest of radar units added to the existing cockpit layout.

The North American design would be developed, from the beginning, around the most sophisticated radar equipment available, and then combined with the most sophisticated airframe of the era – the F-86A. North American planned to pull off this engineering miracle by employing some of the earliest computers used in aviation. The computer would handle many of the chores normally performed by the pilot during an intercept, such as flight

Photographed high over the Slovenian Alps, this is one of the 130 F-86Ds received by the Jugoslovenske Ratno Vazduhoplovstvo for interception duties. They were replaced by MiG-21s and Oraos.

'Dog' Sabres Overseas

Left: The Philippines operated 20 F-86D-35s between 1958 and 1969. Some had Sidewinder capability.

Below: The JASDF received 122 ex-USAF F-86Ds from 1958. The three red stripes and golden dolphin tail markings identified the 3rd Fighter (AW) Wing.

Above: South Korea was another recipient of ex-USAF F-86Ds. This is a D-50 of the 10th Fighter Wing, fitted with Aero 3B launch rails and AIM-9B Sidewinders.

Right: Denmark's three squadrons of 38 F-86Ds were also Sidewinder-capable. This colourful example served with 726 Eskadrille.

F-86K

Although outwardly similar to the F-86D, the K differed considerably in many areas. It was cannon-, rather than rocket-, armed, necessitating a small fuselage stretch, and the fire control system was downgraded for export. Originally intended solely for production (using NAA-supplied parts) at Fiat's Caselle plant, the K was also built by the parent company.

Above: Fiat built F-86Ks for Italy, France, West Germany, Norway and the Netherlands. In AMI service it was nicknamed the 'Kappone', and served with five Aerobrigati (1ª – illustrated, 4ª, 5ª, 36ª and 51ª). Despite the 'MM' on the fin, the AMI used USAF serials.

Top right: 52-3630 was was the first YF-86K prototype, itself a conversion from an F-86D-40. It first flew on 15 July 1954.

control and engine performance. This left the pilot free to locate and track the target as previous all-weather aircraft radar operators had done.

The new F-86 interceptor would be powered by a new engine from General Electric, with an afterburner unit that had been developed jointly by GE and North American. The new J47-GE-17 engine, having 6,650 lb (29.58 kN) of thrust in afterburner, had an electronic fuel control to feed the exact amount of fuel needed by the engine for optimum performance for the mission. It would take almost two years to develop the electronic fuel control, and many more years to perfect it. When it worked, the instantaneous response of the engine made all the work worthwhile.

Hughes Aircraft Company was to develop the fire control system, not only for the F-86 interceptor, but also for the Lockheed and Northrop designs. The Hughes E-3 Fire Control System (FCS), with a 50-kW AN/APG-36 radar unit, was developed in July 1949. The APG-36 had an 18-in (46-cm) antenna dish, and a range of about 10 miles (16 km). However, the E-3 system was never intended to be the production unit the Air Force wanted, as the range was too short. The E-4 Fire Control System, with 250 kW of power, would provide the targeting information for the production interceptors.

The E-4 system used the AN/APG-37 radar, which had a range of up to 30 miles (48 km). The E-4 system had an AN/APA-84 computer integrated with the APG-37 radar, which determined the best possible lead collision course to the target. Approximately 29 seconds before firing time, the pilot chose the number of rockets he would fire – six, 12, or a complete salvo of 24. The APA-84 computer would automatically fire the selected amount of rockets as soon as the target was within range. It took slightly over three seconds to extend the rocket tray, fire all the rockets, and retract the tray. If the E-4 system became inoperable, the Sabre interceptor would have a manual lead computing sight as a back-up.

Extensive changes in the fuselage were necessitated by the new engine and radar installations. The 18-in (46-cm) radar antenna dish would be covered by a 30-in (76-cm) radome, which necessitated a complete redesign of the entire forward fuselage in which the engine air intake was moved under the radome and given a more horizontal opening. The J47-GE-17 engine with afterburner was longer and had a greater diameter than the standard J47. This called for a completely new rear fuselage that was much greater in diameter than the F-86A, and was 4 ft (1.22 m) longer between the engine break and the tail pipe opening.

Although the first prototype aircraft would have the F-86A sliding canopy with V-shape windscreen, production aircraft would have a clam-shell opening canopy and flat, armoured windscreen. The vertical tail and rudder assembly were essentially the same as found on the F-86A, but the horizontal stabiliser and elevator were a completely different unit than that found on the day fighters. It was a single-piece unit similar to that developed for the F-86C (YF-93), using the same flight control system that had been developed for the F-86E, i.e., the 'all-flying tail'.

Rocket armament

Finally, the armament used on the F-86 interceptor would be completely different from all other interceptor aircraft. Instead of machine-guns or cannon, it would fire small air-to-air rockets, the 2.75-in Folding Fin Aircraft Rocket (FFAR), commonly called the 'Mighty Mouse' rocket. The 2.75-in FFAR, developed jointly by the Navy and North American, was based on the German R4 rocket that B-17 crews had encountered over Europe. It had a 7.53-lb (3.4-kg) warhead, a range of 4,500 yd (4115 m), and a speed in excess of 2,500 ft (762 m) per second. The stabilising fins were foldable, being clustered around the aft end of the rocket and snapping into position after clearing the launcher.

North American developed the internal launcher for the new interceptor after making the decision in 1950 to change to the all-rocket armament. The launcher, referred to as 'the tray', held 24 FFARs internally. At the firing point, the tray extended from the underside of the fuselage in half a second. The rockets could then be fired singly, in groups, or salvoed. The rockets were fired automatically by the E-3 or E-4 FCS, but the pilot could override the FCS and fire the rockets manually.

Since the new aircraft was almost an entirely new design (only the main wing and landing gear remained from the F-86A), the Air Force opted to give it an entirely new designation: F-95A. The first F-95A (No. 50-577) was completed in November 1949, and trucked to Muroc on

Above: The Luftwaffe purchased 88 F-86Ks to equip a single all-weather fighter unit. JG 74 'Mölders' ('JD') formed at Ahlhorn in 1961. The Geschwader had started life (without aircraft) in 1960 as JG 75 at Neuburg, and some aircraft were painted with the 'JE' code.

Right: The KLu received 63 F-86Ks to equip Nos 700, 701 and 702 Squadrons. Six were Fiat-built and the remainder were from NAA production. The F-86 was known locally as the 'Kaasjager' (cheese-fighter).

NATO Defenders

The F-86K was specifically developed in answer to a European requirement for a radar-equipped interceptor, and all 341 aircraft (120 NAA, 221 Fiat) were supplied to NATO air arms. The type entered service from mid-1955, initially with the AMI, which retired its last example in July 1973.

***Above:** Norway took 64 F-86Ks for service from 1955 with 337 (illustrated) and 339 Skvadrons. Norway used wartime RAF-style two-letter squadron codes.*

***Below:** Two escadrons of F-86Ks served with EC 13 at Colmar, augmenting Meteor NF.Mk 11s in the all-weather role from 1956. They served until 1962.*

***Left:** Like many Sabres, the Dutch F-86Ks were fitted with Sidewinder launch rails.*

28 November 1949. Following reassembly and ground testing, the F-95A, with George Welch at the controls, made its first flight on 22 December, minus the fire control system and armament.

The US Congress would not appropriate money for any new aircraft designs, no matter how advanced. They would, however, purchase a development of an existing design. With this in mind, the Air Force redesignated the F-95A to YF-86D on 24 July 1950. The second of two F-95As (No. 50-578) was completed in late 1949. Both F-95A prototypes were completed using various systems taken from other Sabre programmes, with the wing, landing gear and canopy coming from the F-86A.

Fire-control installation

The first Hughes E-3 FCS was installed in the second F-95A during May 1950, and flight tested in September 1950. This aircraft was subsequently bailed to Hughes for extensive development tests of both the E-3 and E-4 FCS over the next two years. The retractable rocket launcher was installed in the first prototype YF-86D in late 1950, and test fired for the first time in February 1951. Both F-95As (YF-86Ds) were powered by the J47-GE-17 engine rated at 5,000 lb (22.24 kN) static thrust, with 6,650 lb (29.58 kN) of thrust available in afterburner.

The first production aircraft was the F-86D-1, which started to come off the Inglewood assembly line in March 1951. The Air Force was so excited about its new 'one-man interceptor' that it ordered 979 F-86Ds before the first aircraft came off the assembly line. This, of course, was in response to the Soviet detonation of an atomic bomb in 1949. The D-1 had most of the features called for in the production order specification – clam-shell opening canopy, slab stabiliser, and production version of the J47-GE-17 engine, which had 5,425 lb (24.13 kN) static thrust, with 7,500 lb (33.36 kN) available in afterburner.

The rear fuselage of the D-1 was redesigned to have a much smaller exhaust opening than the prototypes, and small vortex generators were added to both the stabiliser

***Below:** 'Kappones' of the 51ª Aerobrigata wear the unit's black cat and three green mice badge above the 6º Gruppo Caccia Ogni Tempo badge.*

Venezuela took 74 F-86Ks, most of which came from Luftwaffe stocks. They served with three squadrons until 1969. At least five were subsequently passed to Honduras.

Follow-On

Under Project Follow-On, 981 F-86Ds were modified with the necessary datalink equipment for SAGE operation. In addition, these F-86Ls were rewinged with the F-40 wing ('slatted 6-3' with extended wingtips) and re-engined with J47-GE-33s.

***Right:** This pristine F-86L flew with the 456th FIS at Castle AFB, California in 1958. The rebuilt Ls were given new block numbers one number greater than their original. Thus an F-86D-45 became an F-86L-46, etc.*

***Above:** Seen on the Nellis alert ramp in March 1958 are F-86Ls from the 94th FIS.*

***Right:** This F-86L was from the 3555th FLMSq. It is shown with the rear fuselage removed to provide quick and easy access to the J47-GE-33 engine. The F-86D, K and L had rudimentary afterburners.*

This F-86L was also assigned to the 3555th Flightline Maintenance Squadron at Perrin AFB, Texas. The unit was responsible for training mechanics and crew chiefs, and its aircraft were kept in full operational condition. Dayglo bands began to appear in late 1958. Note the extended ventral rocket tray.

and the rear fuselage to break up potential drag in these areas. All the D-1s were equipped with the E-3 FCS.

Interestingly, the aircraft serial number ranges of the D-1 through the D-15 were all numbered previous to that of either prototype.

The first flight of the F-86D-1 (No. 50-455) took place of 8 June 1951. The performance specifications for the D-1 were certainly impressive, despite the vastly different aerodynamics of the D fuselage. Weighing 19,975 lb (9060 kg) for a typical interceptor mission – i.e., two 120-US gal (454-kg) drop tanks and a full load of 2.75-in FFARs – the F-86D-1 had a top speed of 692 mph (1114 km/h) at sea level. An F-86F, with the '6-3' solid leading-edge wing, had a top speed of 695 mph (1118 km/h) – but weighed over 3,000 lb (1360 kg) less than an F-86D. Rate of climb on the D-1 was 17,750 ft (5410 m) per minute in afterburner. Service ceiling was 55,400 ft (16885 m). Combat radius was only 277 miles (446 km) when the aircraft was employed as a point defence interceptor, requiring full afterburner take-offs and mission profiles without drop tanks.

North American produced 37 F-86D-1s (Nos 50-455/-491). Problems with production of the E-3 Fire Control System, and recurring problems with the electronic fuel control, kept deliveries of the F-86D many months behind schedule. The first D-1 was delivered in March 1951, but the last was not delivered until October 1952. Problems with the electronic fuel controls meant that GE engine production was almost 18 months behind schedule well into 1952.

Next off the Inglewood assembly line was the F-86D-5, the first to be equipped with the much more sophisticated Hughes E-4 FCS. Developed and tested on the second prototype YF-86D (50-578) for more than two years, the E-4 was five times as powerful as the E-3 system. The E-4 would eventually be used in all three major Air Defense Command interceptor types of the era – the F-86D, F-89D and F-94C – but not before major changes were made, not only to the E-4 system, but also to the production facilities at Hughes, which suffered from some major quality control problems. The first production D-5 (50-492) was delivered to the USAF on 13 July 1952 – and promptly bailed back to Hughes for extended testing of the E-4 FCS. North American built 26 F-86D-5s (Nos 50-492/-517).

Rudder power and rapid turn-rounds

The F-86D-10, of which 36 were built (Nos 50-518/-553), introduced a full power rudder without a rudder trim tab. Previous types had all been cable-operated with a trim tab. The F-86D-15 introduced a single point refuelling receptacle for faster mission turn-round times. North American built 54 D-15s (Nos 50-554/-576 and 50-704/-734). Other changes on the D-15 included installation of the AN/ARC-27 command radio.

The next several variants had minor internal changes. North American built 188 F-86D-20s (Nos 51-2944/-3131), which had a fuel filter de-icing system. The D-20s were delivered between May and September 1953. Eighty-eight D-25s (Nos 51-5857/-5944) followed, with droppable 120-US gal (454-litre) underwing fuel tanks. The D-30 reintroduced a rudder trim tab, removing the power-operated rudder assembly. North American built 200 D-30s (Nos 51-5945/-6144).

The F-86D-35 replaced the RC-103 Zero Reader installed in previous variants, with the AN/ARN-14 Omni-Directional Ranging Set. All 350 D-35s (Nos 51-8274/-8505) were completed by December 1953. However, recurring problems in December 1952 with the electronic components (the E-4 FCS, electronic fuel control, and the new ARN-14 Ranging Set) kept well over 300 airframes from being completed until late December 1953.

An F-86D captured the world speed record that had been held by an F-86A since 1948. On 18 November 1952, Captain Slade Nash took the second D-20 (No. 51-2945) over the FAI instrumented course set up over the Salton Sea in California, averaging 698.505 mph (1124.104 km/h). Seven months later, on 16 July 1953, Lieutenant

F-86Ls in the Guard

Large numbers of F-86Ls served with ANG units, beginning in 1957, with the peak years being 1958-60. In 1960 26 squadrons were flying the L, but by the end of 1961 the number was down to six. The last survivors were the aircraft of the 196th FIS/CA ANG, which were finally replaced in May 1965.

***Above:** The 194th FIS flew the L model from Fresno, California. As nearly half of the L conversions were performed at NAA's Fresno plant, the California Guard was naturally an early recipient. The 194th kept its aircraft until 1964.*

***Left:** This F-86L flew with the 108th FIS, Illinois ANG. The Guard units took most of the Ls, as the active-duty Air Force was already transitioning to the F-102A Delta Dagger.*

***Far left:** This shark-mouthed F-86L was assigned to the 146th FIS, Pennsylvania ANG.*

Colonel William Barnes put the first D-35 (No. 51-8274) through the same 3-km (1.86-mile) course, averaging 715.697 mph (1151.77 km/h). Both record-holding aircraft were production F-86Ds, with full armament and electronics. The course was flown at an average of 125 ft (38 m) above the ground.

The difference in record speeds by similar aircraft was due to a higher ambient temperature, installation of a new fuel amplifier, and addition of a new ceramic liner around the exhaust nozzle. Both modifications were incorporated into the final 97 D-35 production aircraft. F-86Ds also held the world speed records over a 100-km (62-mile) course of 690.185 mph (1110.71 km/h) and 707.876 mph (1139.185 km/h) over a 15-km (9.3-mile) course, both set on 2 September 1953.

D-40 details

The F-86D-40 introduced several new features. It had the latest J47-GE-17B engine, rated at 5,425 lb (24.13 kN) static thrust, with 7,500 lb (33.36 kN) thrust available in afterburner. The D-40 instrument panel added a glide path indicator and an exhaust temperature gauge. North American built 300 D-40s (Nos 52-3598/-3897). Problems with the electronic fuel control became so acute in December 1953 that the Air Force grounded the entire F-86D fleet following the destruction of 13 aircraft by engine fires and explosions.

The F-86D-45 introduced a drag chute installation in a small fairing just under the rudder. North American had traded rocket armament information in exchange for drag chute technology being developed by Lockheed. Installation of the 16-ft (4.88-m), ring slot drag chute was necessary as the USAF had begun operations with the F-86D in the Far East to counter Cold War tensions rising in the area. The USAF sent 52 F-86Ds to bases in Japan late in 1953. Runways in Japan and on Okinawa and Formosa were much shorter than those normally used by the F-86Ds of Air Defense Command, necessitating the drag chute installation. North American built 300 D-45s (Nos 52-3898/-4197), with the final 62 having the J47-GE-33 engine. The -33 engine had 5,550 lb (24.68 kN) of static thrust, with 7,650 lb (34.02 kN) available in afterburner.

The final three variants had minor instrument and electronics updates. North American built 301 F-86D-50s (53-4198/-4304 and 52-9983/-10176), 225 F-86D-55s (53-557/-781), and 399 F-86D-60s in three batches (53-782/-1071, 53-3675/-3710, and 53-4018/-4090). All were externally similar to the D-45, with the drag chute in the tail. The flyaway cost of a standard F-86D was $343,839. At the same time, the USAF ordered Project Pull-Out, which essentially brought 1,128 older model F-86Ds of various blocks to F-86D-45 standard. Project Pull-Out was completed between 15 July 1954 and September 1955. In September the final production F-86D (53-4090) was built and delivered to Air Defense Command. Counting the two F-95As (YF-86Ds), the Air Force accepted a total of 2,506 F-86D aircraft.

At that time, Air Defense Command had 20 F-86D wings, totalling 1,405 aircraft, a full two-thirds of all units in ADC. All F-86D squadrons were under Air Defense Command, US Air Forces/Europe, or Far East Air Force

Thailand became the only foreign operator of the F-86L when it acquired ex-USAF aircraft for the defence of the nation's capital, Bangkok. Based at Don Muang Airport, the Ls provided top cover for USAF wartime operations at Thai bases, a role also undertaken by RAAF CA-27 Sabres.

Sabre Colours

United States

The prototype Sabre was finished in Pearl Grey, but this was removed in favour of natural metal. In the 1960s anti-corrosion grey became the standard scheme, while at the end of the 1960s the few surviving F-86Hs received T.O. 1-1-4 tactical camouflage.

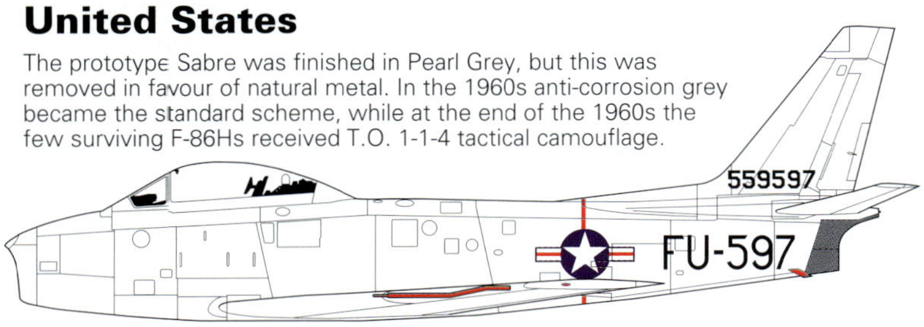

In Korea the fuselage and wingtip identification sashes were standard. The four Sabre wings introduced different tail markings: this aircraft wears the triple-flash markings of the 8th FBW. The 4th had a yellow fin sash, the 51st had black checkers and the 18th FBW had a large tricolour fin-flash.

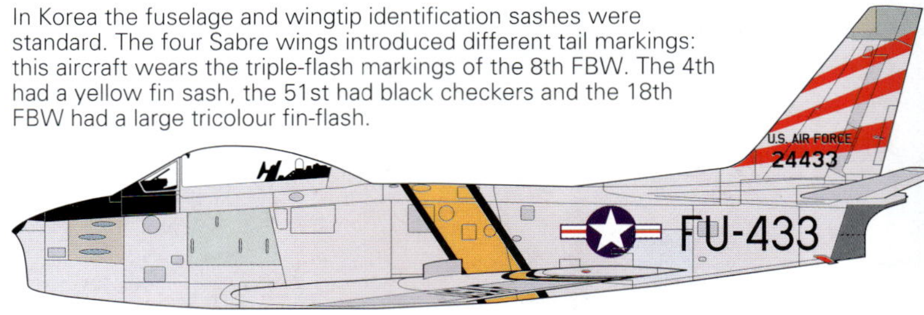

Argentina

The FAA's F-86Fs initially served in standard natural metal finish, but were subsequently painted in a three-tone dark green/mid-brown/grey camouflage scheme. The serial was prefixed 'C' (for *caza* – fighter).

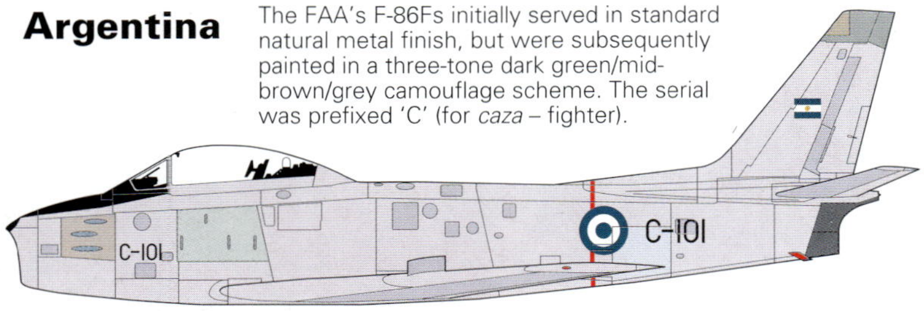

Denmark

Danish F-86Ds served in natural metal. The original RAF-style two-letter squadron codes gave way to a single type designator ('F') and the 'last three' of the USAF serial.

Australia

The Avon Sabre, with its slightly altered nose contours, first appeared in natural metal but spent most of its life in anti-corrosion silver. RAAF unit markings (No. 76 Sqn shown here) were usually bright.

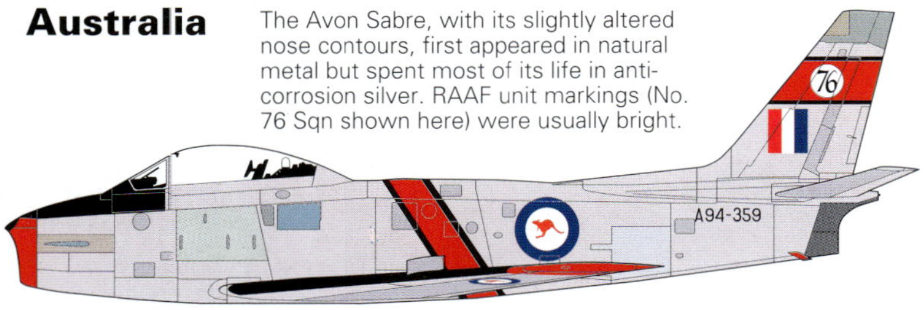

This Sidewinder-armed CA-27 Sabre Mk 32 was assigned to No. 79 Sqn, RAAF, and is seen on alert at Ubon RTAFB, Thailand in the summer of 1968. RAAF Sabres provided top cover for Thai bases from 1962.

Ethiopia

The initial batch of EAF Sabres flew in natural metal, but later deliveries may have served in anti-corrosion grey, especially as they flew into the 1970s.

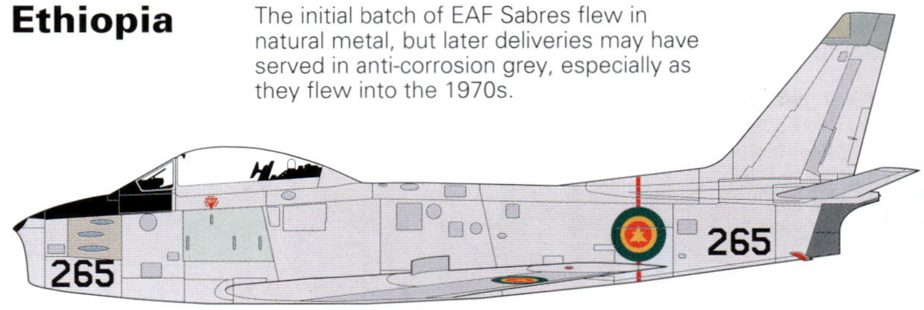

France

The French Ks flew in natural metal with simple national insignia applied. The serial was the original USAF number, applied in stencil-style lettering.

Canada

Canada's Sabres were initially completed without a base paint scheme, although from 1955 most acquired a two-tone grey/green camouflage scheme as most front-line aircraft served with the Air Division in Europe.

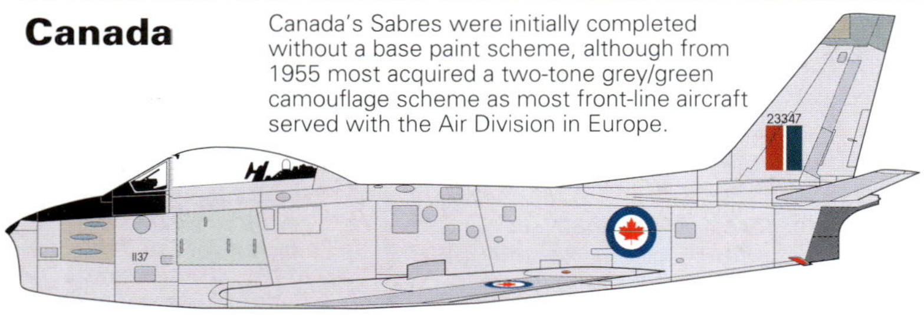

This CL-13B Sabre Mk 6 served with No. 430 'Silver Falcons' Squadron and is seen during an open house at Chaumont AB, France in 1957. The two-tone camouflage was considered more effective in Europe.

Greece

Greece had both Sabre Mk 2s (ex-RCAF) and F-86Ds (ex-USAF), both variants serving in natural metal. Some aircraft had unit insignia applied.

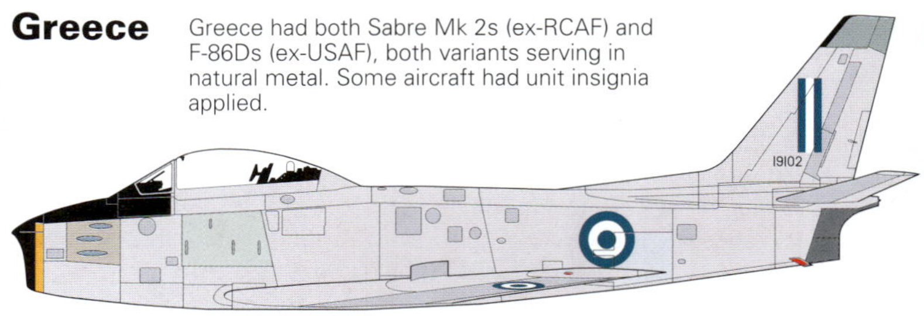

Honduras

The first FAH Sabres were from Yugoslavia, and arrived in standard RAF camouflage. Subsequently, various green/brown camouflage schemes were applied.

Colombia

Colombia's Sabre Mk 6s were acquired from Canadair, and arrived in standard RCAF two-tone grey/green camouflage. Different schemes were applied later, including a three-tone scheme of two greens and a grey.

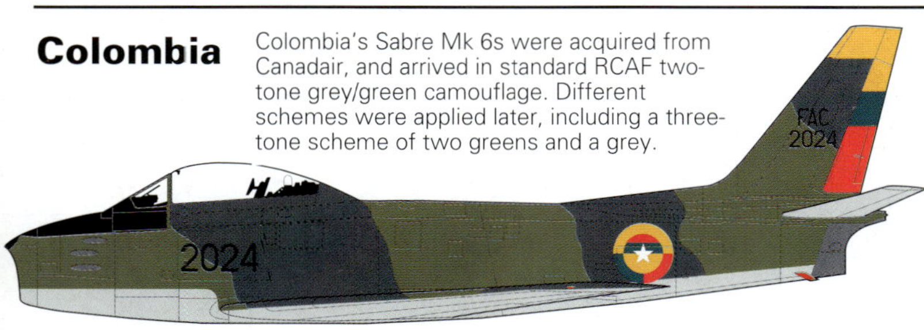

Indonesia

The TNI-AU's CA-27 Sabres were all ex-RAAF, and were delivered with the anti-corrosion silver paint they had worn previously. They retained RAAF serials (A94-xxx).

:rew training

'he all-weather Sabre interceptor was originally intended to be a two-man aircraft, for which design began in May 1948. The backseater would have been esponsible for radar-controlled interception and navigation, but the performance limitations inherent in a two-seater, plus the problems of the resulting reduction ı fuel tank space, led to its eventual abandonment. The availability of an improved, automated AI radar, which considerably reduced the operator's workload, was nother important factor in this decision.

In practice, the USAF took delivery of an F-86D fleet that was far from standardised in terms of its avionics capabilities, not to mention flight characteristics. The JSAF was forced to admit that the 'Sabre Dog' pilot required more training than the crew for any other Air Force type, including the six-engined B-47 Stratojet! -86D crew training was carried out by the all-weather school at Perrin AFB, Texas, using an Erco simulator to duplicate the D-model's cockpit controls, including he radar's attack modes.

Fuel capacity

To provide sufficient range on a combat mission, F-86Ds invariably carried two 120-US gal (454-litre) external fuel tanks. From F-86D-25-NA batch aircraft, air-droppable 'combat' tanks of the same capacity could be carried. Experience in Korea resulted in the F-86F-5s being able to carry a 200-US gal (757-litre) combat drop tank. A 'dual store' provision was built into the F-86F-30, which added another pair of wing pylons and allowed the carriage of four tanks. With the '6-3' wing, extra fuel could be carried in a wing leading-edge fuel tank.

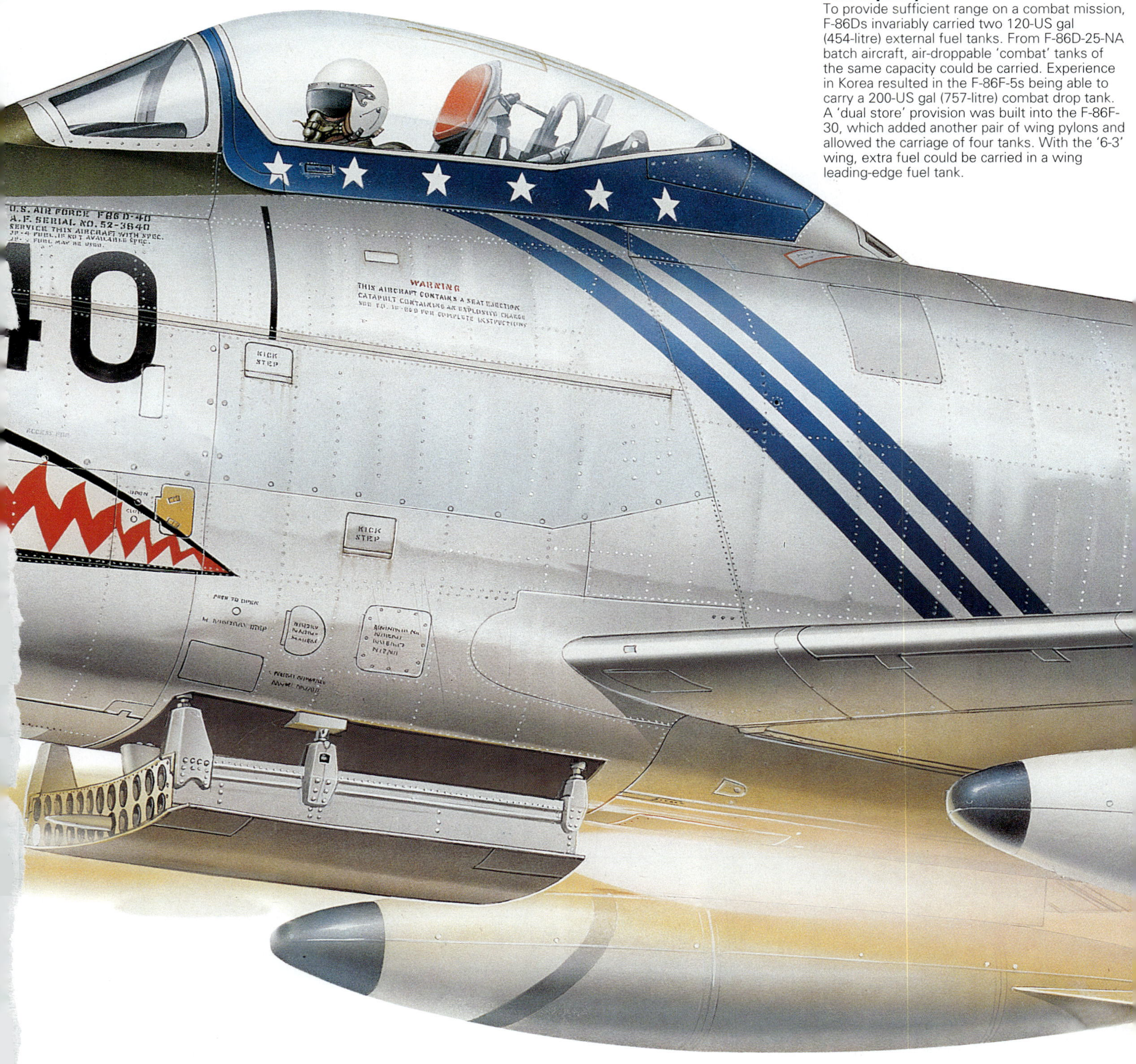

lighty Mouse' rocket armament

'etractable rocket pack contained the F-86D's air-to-air armament – 24 2.75-in (7-cm) folding-fin aircraft rockets FARs). Known as 'Mighty Mouse' rockets, they were originally developed for use by the US Navy and were sed on the German R4 rocket produced for the Messerschmitt Me 262. With an all-up 18-lb (8.2-kg) weight ıd 7.55-lb (3.4-kg) warhead, the 'Mighty Mouse' had a velocity of 2,500 ft (762 m) per second, plus the speed the aircraft, and a range of 13,500 ft (4114 m). During flight training, rockets were fired at a target towed ,000 ft (1829 m) behind a B-45. Known by pilots as the 'rag', it consisted of a 6 x 30-ft (1.83 x 9.14-m) plastic ıesh panel with spinning metal discs to reflect radar energy.

Iran

The IIAF operated F-86Fs, which served in natural metal and later anti-corrosion paint. The 90 Sabre Mk 6s passed on to Pakistan wore Luftwaffe schemes with hastily-applied Iranian insignia.

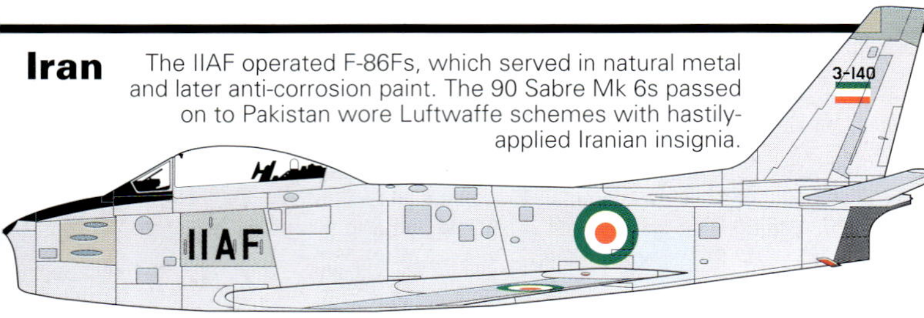

Italy

Italy's Sabre Mk 4s were initially supplied in RAF-style camouflage, although many were later stripped back to bare metal. The F-86Ks served in natural metal, as displayed by this 51ª Aerobrigata example.

Japan

The Sabre enjoyed a lengthy career in JASDF service. For the first years all served in natural metal, but in the later years they were painted in silver. Unit markings were typically flamboyant.

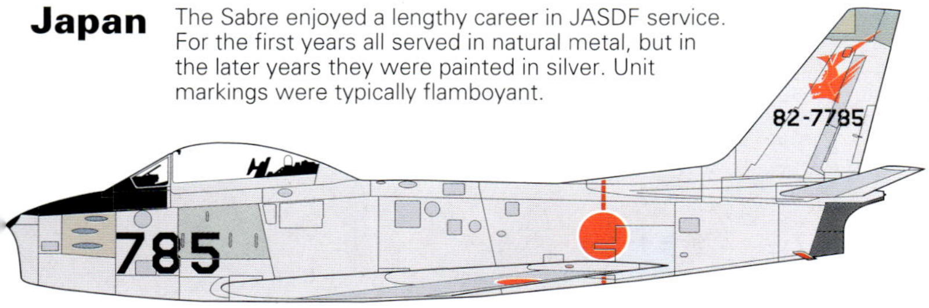

Malaysia

Although delivered in standard RAAF anti-corrosion silver, the Malaysian CA-27 Avon Sabres acquired a single-tone dark green upper surface camouflage.

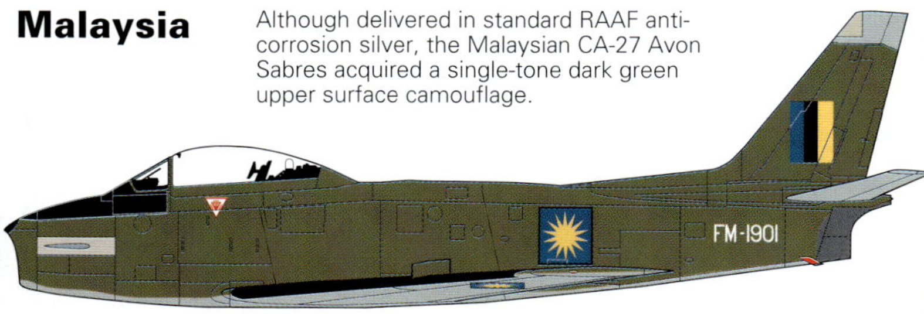

Netherlands

The KLu's F-86Ks served in natural metal. Like most such aircraft, a black or dark green anti-glare panel was applied forward of the windscreen. The serials consisted of the 'last three' of the USAF serial prefixed by 'Q'.

Norway

Natural metal was the base scheme for Norway's Sabres, with colourful unit markings applied. The tricolour fin-flash and 'FN' codes on this aircraft indicated 331 Skvadron.

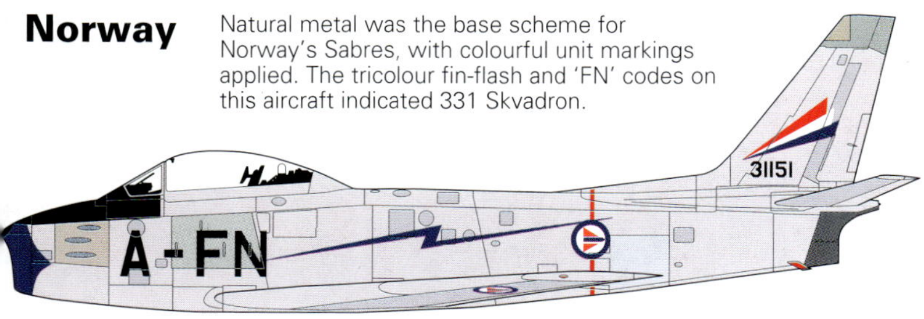

Pakistan

Initially serving in natural metal, the PAF's Sabres acquired this more warlike single-tone dark green scheme. The Sabre Mk 6s acquired via Iran initially retained their Luftwaffe colour scheme.

Peru

In common with most other Sabre recipients of the 1950s/early 1960s, Peru operated its F-86Fs in natural metal. The most notable feature was the giant fin-flash.

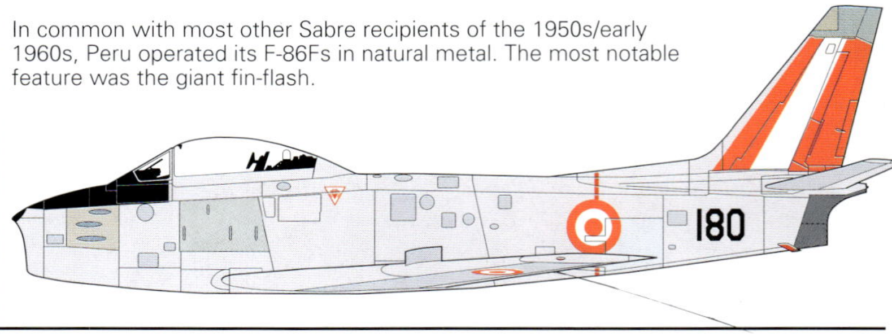

Philippines

The PhilAF's F-86F Sabres retained natural metal base finish, to which were added colourful unit, identification and national markings. This aircraft carries the markings of the 7th TFS.

Portugal

Portuguese Sabres initially flew in natural metal, with the large side-numbers being the last three digits of the FAP serial. For the latter portion of their career they wore ADC-style light grey.

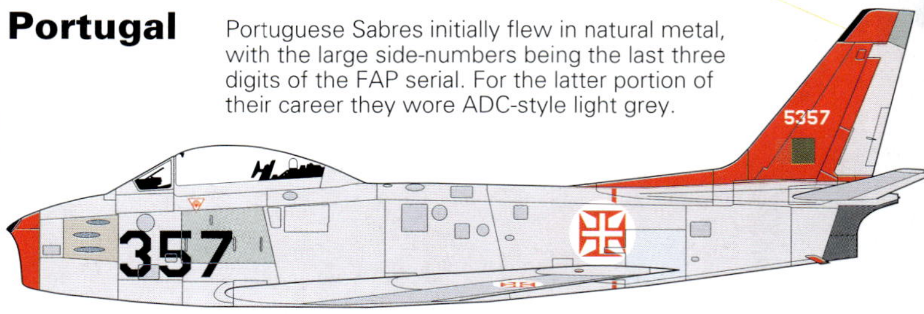

Saudi Arabia

Saudi Arabia's F-86Fs were initially delivered in natural metal, and wore USAF-style buzzcodes with fin and tail stripes. The latter disappeared when anti-corrosion grey was introduced in the mid-1960s.

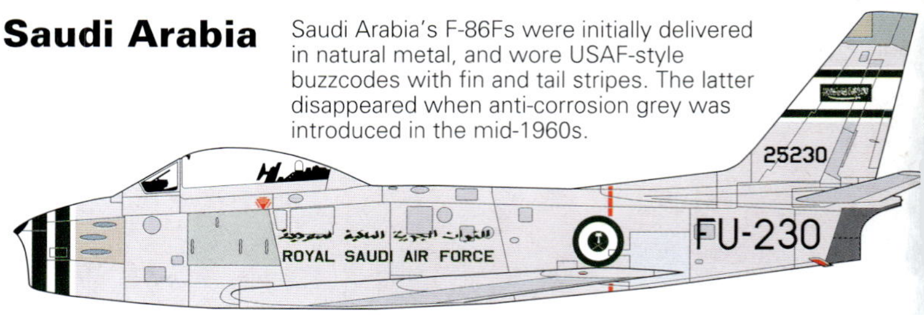

This line-up of No. 7 Squadron F-86Fs shows aircraft in the anti-corrosion grey paint. Note that they carry the late-style 206.5-US gal (782-litre) drop tanks without fins.

South Africa

In Korea SAAF F-86Fs wore the 18th FBW fin-flash and USAF yellow ID sashes. The Sabre Mk 6s (illustrated) originally served in natural metal, with the original national insignia of a springbok in an RAF-style roundel.

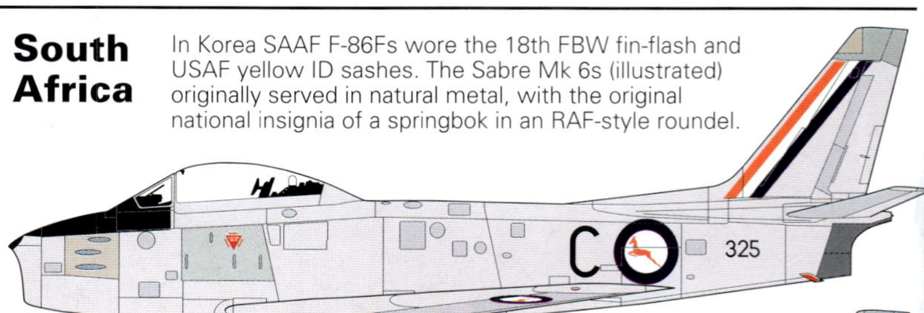

The 1961 declaration of a full republic brought with it a change in national insignia, although the springbok was retained. A green/brown camouflage was applied to SAAF Sabres late in their career.

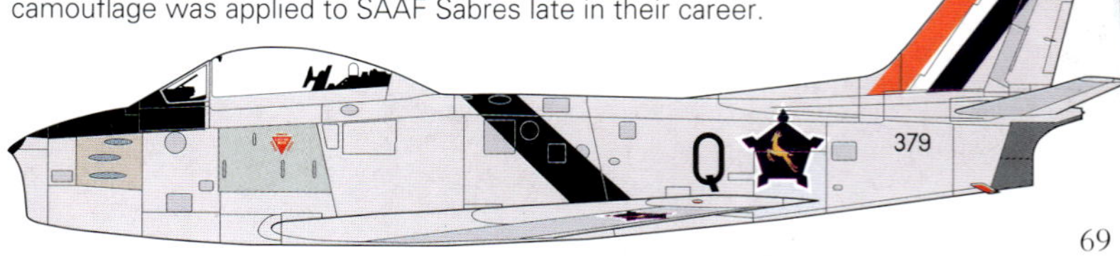

Radar and fire control system

Among the changes introduced with the 'Dogship' all-weather interceptor, the most significant were the AN/APG-36 radar set (AN/APG-37 on later production aircraft) housed in a 30-in (76.2-cm) plastic nose radome, and the E-4 fire control system to which it was connected. Development of this system was dogged by delay and quality control problems but was eventually successful in producing a reliable system to equip not only the F-86D, but also the Northrop F-89D and Lockheed F-94C.

The E-4 system featured three elements – radar target location, electronically computed aiming and rocket armament – which together addressed the problems of successfully locating and downing an enemy bomber at night. During the early search phase of an intercept mission the APG-36's 18-in (45.7-cm) radar scanner swept through 68.5° left and right of centre in a 3.5-second cycle; it could also scan through 33.5° up and 13.5° down. Its detection range was about 30 miles (48 km), and when it detected a possible target the radar displayed it as a dot on the pilot's radar scope. Once the radar was locked-on to the target, the onboard AN/APA-84 computer calculated a lead collision course. The pilot was required to follow this by keeping the steering dot on the radar scope within a 1-in (2.54-cm) reference circle, steering more precisely when the auto tracking system indicated there were fewer than 20 seconds left. After selecting six, 12 or all 24 rockets, the pilot depressed the fire switch, the time of firing being determined by the APA-84 computer. When the firing circuit was triggered, the rocket pack extended in half a second and was able to fire 24 rockets in 0.2 seconds, sending the 'Mighty Mice' toward a target, by then 1,500 ft (457 m) away, in a 'fan' pattern in order to ensure that the target was destroyed.

An 'X' on the pilot's scope indicated that the rockets had fired, and the rocket pack retracted automatically in 3.3 seconds. When the target was fewer than 780 ft (237 m) away, an '8' appeared on the radar scope as a collision warning. If the E-4 system became unserviceable, or was affected by ground clutter, an optical lead computing sight could be used, but only in good visual conditions.

USAF 'Sabre Dog' units

F-86Ds entered service in 1951 with the 97th Squadron, followed in 1952 by the 45th, 51st, 84th, 357th and 432nd Squadrons; then, in 1953, by the 2nd, 4th, 5th, 11th, 13th, 14th, 18th, 31st, 37th, 40th, 41st, 42nd, 49th, 56th, 68th, 85th, 86th, 95th, 323rd, 325th, 326th, 330th, 331st, 431st, 445th, 465th and 496th Squadrons; from 1954, the 47th, 54th, 83rd, 444th, 460th, 519th, 520th and 539th Squadrons; from 1955, the 322nd, 324th, 327th, 329th, 332nd, 337th, 354th, 456th, 518th and 538th Squadrons; and, from 1956, the 87th Squadron.

By mid-1954, 1,026 of Air Defense Command's 1,405 interceptors were 'Dogships'. Most were based in the continental US, although the type saw limited service in Korea (briefly, after the war, in 1953), Japan, the United Kingdom, the Netherlands and Spain. Once passed to Air National Guard units in the late 1950s, D models continued to see service outside CONUS, in Hawaii and Puerto Rico, into the 1960s.

498th Fighter Interceptor Squadron

Constituted as the 303rd Bombardment Squadron (Light) on 13 January 1942 and activated on 10 February, this unit was redesignated the 303rd Bombardment Squadron (Dive) on 27 July. Based in the southern US during this period, the unit served in the operational and replacement training role until disbanded on 1 April 1944. Reconstituted as the 498th Fighter-Interceptor Squadron on 20 June 1955, it was activated on 18 August, equipped with F-86Ds inherited from the 520th FIS. These the unit flew until 1956, when they were replaced by F-102s.

North American F-86D-40-NA Sabre
498th Fighter Interceptor Squadron 'Geiger Tigers'
84th Fighter Group
Geiger AFB, Washington, 1956

South Korea

RoKAF F-86Ds and Fs originally wore standard USAF colours (natural metal, ID sashes) with colourful local embellishments. The aircraft which survived into the 1970s were painted in a green/brown camouflage.

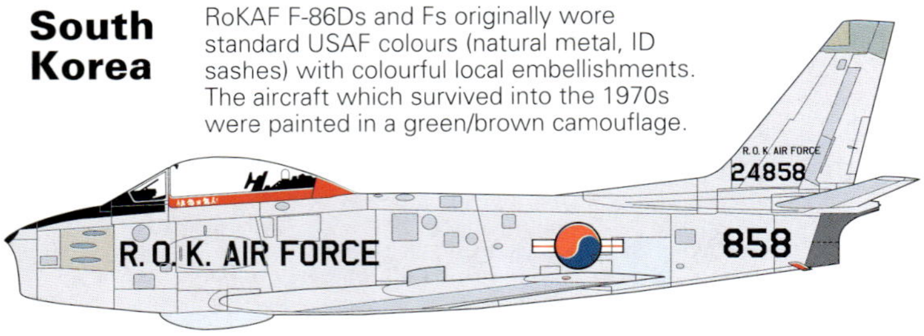

Spain

Natural metal was again the order of the day for Spain's F-86Fs, although anti-corrosion silver was later applied. The national markings included a black cross on the fin.

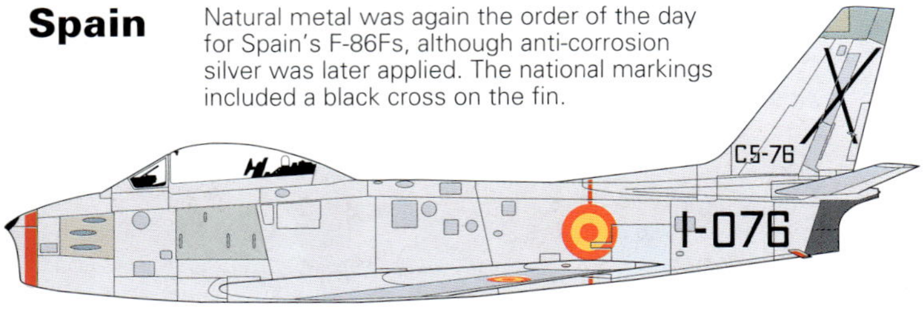

In Spanish service the Sabre was known as the C.5, hence the EdA serial on the fin. The red line through the roundel denoted the position of the rear fuselage break.

Taiwan

RoCAF F-86s were ex-USAF and many retained the Korea identification band. This was later embellished. The blue-white rudder stripes were standard.

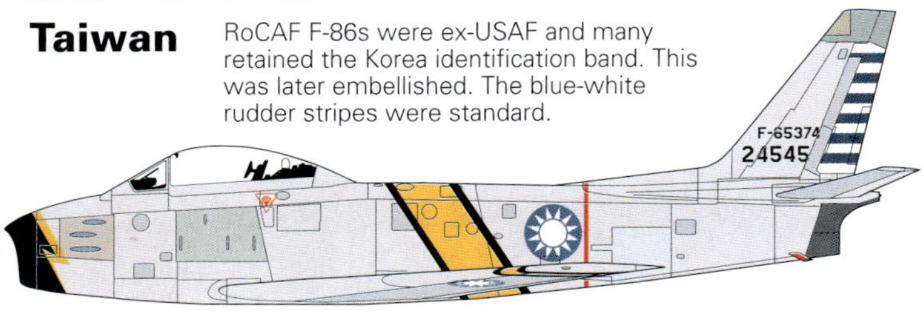

Taiwanese Sabres were among the most colourful as units modified the fuselage/wingtip sashes and nose markings, and applied unit insignia. Natural metal gave way to anti-corrosion silver, as seen here.

Thailand

In common with most Sabre recipients, the RTAF left its F-86Fs in natural metal when they were received. A noteworthy feature was the application of two different serials.

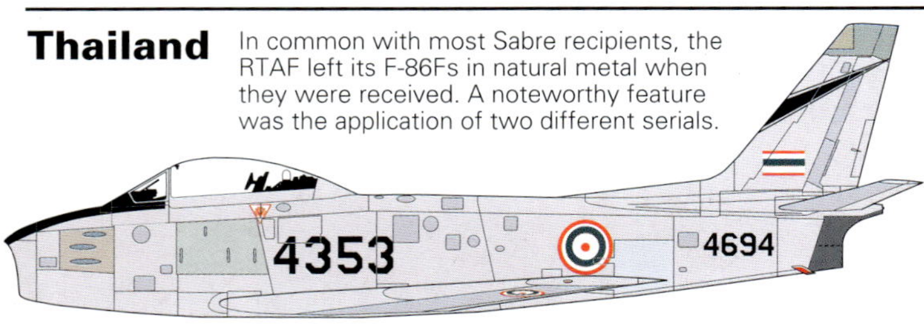

RTAF F-86Fs served until 1966, and provided air defence for Thai bases used by USAF aircraft. These aircraft have their original USAF serials on the fin.

Turkey

The majority of Turkish Sabres flew in standard natural metal, with old-style square national insignia. A few survived long enough to wear a three-tone camouflage and carry the later roundel.

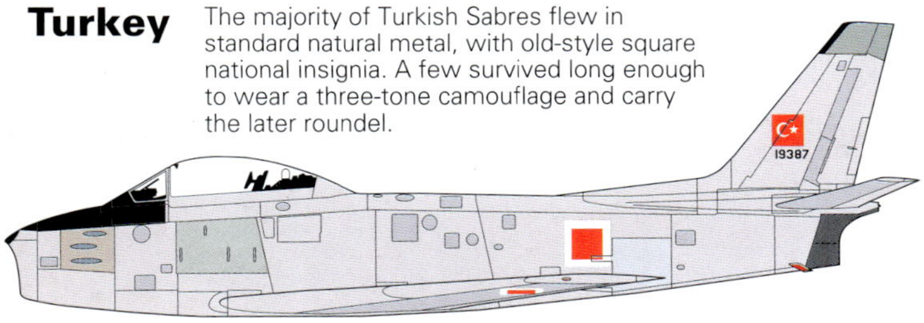

United Kingdom

Although delivered in natural metal, RAF Sabres served in a similar grey/green camouflage as that applied to RCAF aircraft.

Traditional squadron markings were applied to RAF Sabres, as displayed by this No. 92 Sqn aircraft landing at its base at Linton-on-Ouse.

Venezuela

Venezuela's F-86Fs flew in natural metal, while the F-86Ks wore anti-corrosion grey. The fin-flash left no doubt as to the operating nation.

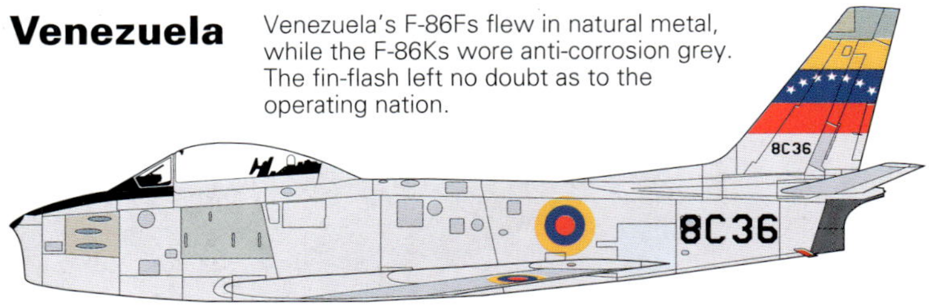

West Germany

German Sabres were delivered in natural metal, but soon acquired a camouflage scheme consisting of two dark green tones. Shown is a WS-10 Sabre Mk 5.

This Sabre Mk 6 wears special markings for 1./JG 72. German Sabres wore two-letter, three-digit codes, the first letter (J) denoting the role (Jäger) and the second the Geschwader.

Yugoslavia

JRV Sabres served in both natural metal and grey/green camouflage. Most of the F-86Ds ended their days in camouflage, while the Sabre Mk 4s were mostly delivered in standard RAF camouflage, although many were later stripped.

F-86 Sabre details

Above: Jettisonable fuel tanks were vital to the Sabre's combat success. A variety were developed for the F-86, the most common being the 120-US gal (454-litre) combat tank seen here. They were quickly expended in combat and new tanks had to be manufactured in Japan to a local design, offering 200-US gal (757-litre) capacity.

Right: A pair of hydraulically-operated airbrakes was positioned on the lower rear fuselage of all Sabres. The F-86D unit was less complex.

Above: The rear fuselage of the Sabre could be removed for full access to the engine (in this case a J47). The combustion chambers of this axial-flow turbojet can clearly be seen here.

Right: On the F-86D, the radar was the AN/APG-37, with a range of 30 miles (49 km). The open bay seen here behind the radar on a 496th FIS 'Dog' housed the inverters for the E-4 Fire Control System.

Above: The APG-30 gun-ranging radar was shoehorned into a remarkably tight space by North American. The radar had a maximum range of about 9,000 ft (2740 m), and made a lethal combination with the A-4 gunsight. This is an F-86F, seen at K-13 in late 1952.

F-86E cutaway

1 Radome
2 Radar antenna
3 Engine air intake
4 Gun camera
5 Nosewheel leg doors
6 Nose undercarriage leg strut
7 Nosewheel
8 Torque scissor links
9 Steering control valve
10 Nose undercarriage pivot fixing
11 Sight amplifier
12 Radio and electronics equipment bay
13 Electronics bay access panel
14 Battery
15 Gun muzzle blast troughs
16 Oxygen bottles
17 Nosewheel bay doors
18 Oxygen servicing point
19 Canopy switches
20 Machine-gun barrel mountings
21 Hydraulic system test connections
22 Radio transmitter
23 Cockpit armoured bulkhead
24 Windscreen panels
25 A-1CM radar gunsight
26 Instrument panel shroud
27 Instrument panel
28 Control column
29 Kick-in boarding step
30 Used cartridge case collector box
31 Ammunition boxes (267 rounds per gun)
32 Ammunition feed chutes
33 0.5-in (12.7 mm) Colt Browning machine-guns
34 Engine throttle
35 Starboard side console panel
36 North American ejection seat
37 Rear view mirror
38 Sliding cockpit canopy cover
39 Ejection seat headrest
40 ADF sense aerials
41 Pilot's back armour
42 Ejection seat guide rails
43 Canopy handle
44 Cockpit pressure valves
45 Armoured side panels
46 Tailplane trim actuator
47 Fuselage/front spar main frame
48 Forward fuselage fuel tank (total internal fuel capacity 434.4 US gal/ 1644 litres)
49 Fuselage lower longeron
50 Intake trunking
51 Rear radio and electronics bay
52 Canopy emergency release handle
53 ADF loop aerial
54 Cockpit pressure relief valve
55 Starboard wing fuel tank
56 Leading-edge slat guide rails
57 Starboard automatic leading-edge slat, open
58 Cable drive to aileron actuator
59 Pitot tube
60 Starboard navigation light
61 Wingtip fairing
62 Starboard aileron
63 Aileron hydraulic control unit
64 Aileron balance
65 Starboard slotted flap, down position
66 Flap guide rail
67 Upward identification light
68 Air conditioning plant
69 Intake fairing starter/generator
70 Fuselage/rear spar main frame
71 Hydraulic system reservoirs
72 Longeron/main frame joint
73 Fuel filter de-icing fluid tank
74 Cooling air outlet
75 Engine equipment access panel
76 Heat exchanger exhaust duct
77 Engine suspension links
78 Fuselage skin plating
79 Engine withdrawal rail
80 Starboard side oil tank
81 General Electric J47-GE-27 turbojet
82 Bleed air system primary heat exchanger
83 Ground power connections
84 Fuel filler cap
85 Fuselage break point sloping frame (engine removal)
86 Upper longeron joint
87 Engine bay air cooling duct
88 Cooling air outlet
89 Engine firewall bulkhead
90 Engine flame cans
91 Rear fuselage framing
92 Fuel jettison pipe
93 Fuselage top longeron
94 Fin/tailplane root fillet fairing
95 Control cable duct
96 Fin spar attachment joint
97 Tailplane/rudder control cables
98 All-moving tailplane hydraulic jack
99 Tailfin construction
100 Flush HF aerial panel

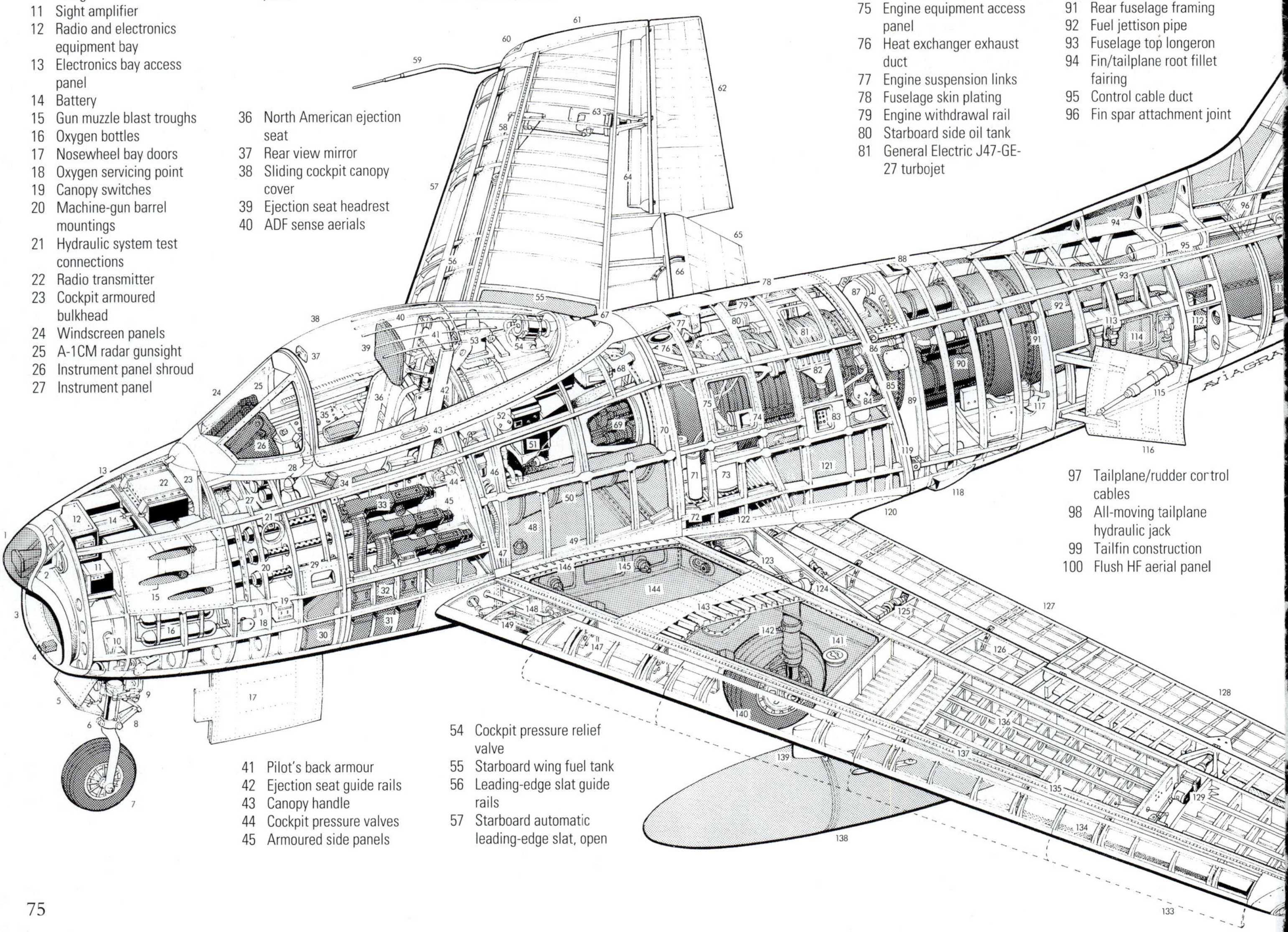

'Sabre Dog' variants and the F-86K

Originally known as the F-95A in an attempt to justify the larger unit cost of the new model (which had only 25 per cent parts commonality with the fighter-bomber variants), the F-86D was subject to numerous improvements throughout its production life. Successive production 'blocks', each identified by a separate North American design number, introduced new features, mainly concerning their powerplants and avionics, as follows:

D-5	Hughes E-4 fire control system (replacing E-3 in D-1 aircraft)
D-10	power rudder (trim tabs deleted)
D-15	single-point ground refuelling; AN/ARC-27 command radio
D-20	fuel filter de-icing system
D-25	120-US gal (454-litre) wing drop tanks for combat missions
D-30	automatic approach control; manual rudder and trim tabs reinstated
D-35	AN/ARN-14 Omni-Directional Ranging Set
D-40	J47-GE-17B producing 7,500 lb (73.55 kN) thrust in afterburner; glide path indicator; exhaust temperature gauge
D-45	drag chute; from aircraft 52-4136, 7,650 lb (75.02 kN) J47-GE-33
D-50 } D-55 } D-60 }	generally similar, with internal electronics modifications

During the 1950s, technological advances allowed considerably improved communications between ground radar warning systems and airborne interceptors, which had been using World War II era detection and control techniques. In 1953 MIT developed the SAGE (Semi-Automatic Ground Environment) datalink system. This allowed threat information gathered by surveillance radars to be quickly processed by computer and transmitted to a receiver in the interceptor. Here it was presented to the pilot in a usable form as the heading, speed, altitude, bearing and range of a potential target, and fed into the E-4 fire control system which automatically positioned the aircraft for a lead-collision attack. The need for voice communication was eliminated.

Under Project Follow-On, low-time F-86D airframes, beginning with the older examples, were withdrawn and fitted with SAGE and other related equipment, namely the AN/ARR-39 datalink receiver, AN/ARC-34 command radio (replacing the older AN/ARC-27) and an AN/APX-25 Identification Friend or Foe (IFF) transponder (replacing AN/APX-6). An AN/ARN-31 glide slope receiver was also installed. Externally, the SAGE aircraft were identifiable by a small blade aerial protruding from the lower left fuselage ahead of the wing. All were also brought up to F-86D-45 airframe standard, which included the installation of the J47-GE-33 engine. An adaptation of the '6-3' wing was fitted (with leading-edge slats retained). These changes warranted a new designation, the 981 F-86Ds so-treated becoming F-86Ls.

To meet the requirements of a number of NATO countries, the F-86K was developed for supply under MDAP. Originally a cannon-armed two-seat version was proposed, but in the event the K model was a reworked F-86D in which the (then-secret) E-4 fire control system was replaced by a simpler MG-4 radar set. Four nose-mounted Pontiac M24-1 20-mm cannon were substituted for the rocket armament.

Engine installations

Sabres were powered by a variety of engine types during their development. Chevrolet-built 4,000-lb (17.8-kN) J35 axial-flow turbojets were installed in the prototype XP-86s, but were replaced in production aircraft by the more powerful J47 derivative, which was the same size as the former but had an extra compressor stage and produced 5,200 lb (23.1 kN) of thrust. An afterburner was added to the variant fitted to the F-86D all-weather aircraft, while the F-86H was powered by the General Electric J73, an enlarged and uprated version of the J47. To adequately feed the new engine, a larger air intake was required, so use of this engine necessitated a major fuselage redesign in which it was effectively split lengthways and a 6-in (15.2-cm) plug inserted. Canadian and Australian production led to two other engine variations.The use of the Avro Canada Orenda turbojet (first used in the CF-100 all-weather interceptor) was contemplated from the beginning of the Canadair Sabre programme. Slightly larger in diameter than the J47, the Orenda required larger frame apertures over the engine bay and other minor structural changes. Commonwealth Aircraft Corporation (CAC) chose the new axial-flow Rolls-Royce Avon, originally built to power the English Electric Canberra, for its aircraft. Like the F-86H, the CAC Sabre had a modified fuselage; a 3-in (7.6-cm) deep splice in the engine air intake increased intake area. The Avon was shorter, wider and 400 lb (181.4 kg) lighter than the J47, and was therefore mounted further aft to maintain the aircraft's centre of gravity.

Wing development

Starting life as the NA-140, North American's USAAF jet fighter design was derived from the US Navy's NA-134 jet project. Both were straight-winged aircraft, although the NA-140 was a longer, slimmer machine with much greater fuel capacity and thus more weight. On 30 August 1944 the USAAF ordered two prototypes and a static test example of the latter as the XP-86. (The Navy followed on 1 January 1945 with an order for an XFJ-1 prototype.) By mid-1945, captured data from German swept-wing research was becoming available, which suggested that compressibility drag increases could be postponed with mild wing sweep back, allowing higher speeds. In light of this new data, North American sought permission from the Navy and Army Air Force to redesign the NA-134 and NA-140; the Navy declined to take advantage of this new data (though straight-winged FJ-1 production was to total just 30 aircraft), but the USAAF proved more willing to accept the risks apparent in the reworked fighter. The XP-86 design was to be modified and 20 production P-86s ordered.

The XP-86/P-86A's new wings featured 35° of sweep and full-span, automatic leading-edge slats. The latter addressed the problem of poor low-speed handling characteristics caused by wingtip stall. In the F-86E, the 'all-flying' tail (denoted by the fairing below the tailfin housing its controls), became the primary control surface, the elevators merely increasing its effect. Combined with hydraulic ailerons, this improved aircraft control throughout the transonic speed range.

To make best use of the improved control offered by the new tail at high speeds, NA engineers eliminated the leading-edge slats from the next variant, the F-86F. To compensate for the loss of low-speed control resulting from this change, the aircraft's leading edge was extended 6 in (15.2 cm) at the wingroot and 3 in (7.6 cm) at the tip. Known as the '6-3' wing, this had a sweep angle of 35.7° and incorporated a 5-in (12.7-cm) high wing fence at 70 per cent of the wing span to correct aileron air flow problems created by the new leading edge. Although the Sabre was now a 'hot landing' aircraft, it had a top speed of 695 mph (1118 km/h) at sea level and much improved manoeuvrability. The '6-3' wing was introduced on the 171st production F-86F-25-NH and the 200th F-86F-30-NA, and was retrofitted to earlier production F models and a few F-86Es.

With the F-86F-40 came a further improvement in low-speed handling, as this batch of aircraft (built for delivery to Asian operators under the MDAP) featured a 12-in (30-cm) wingtip extension and reintroduced the leading-edge slats. The correspondingly increased wing area improved handling and eliminated roll-and-yaw tendencies at low speeds, and reduced both the stalling speed and take-off run of the aircraft. These benefits persuaded the USAF to retrofit F-86F-25 and -30 aircraft to -40 standard.

On Canadair-built aircraft, the '6-3' wing was fitted to the Orenda-powered CL-13A Sabre Mk 5; leading-edge slats were reintroduced on late-production Canadair CL-13B Sabre Mk 6s. The first batch of 21 Commonwealth-built Sabre Mk 30s had 'slatted' wings, although these aircraft were later modified to Mk 31 standard with a 'non-slatted', '6-3' wing. All subsequent production (90 Mk 31s and 32s) was to this latter standard.

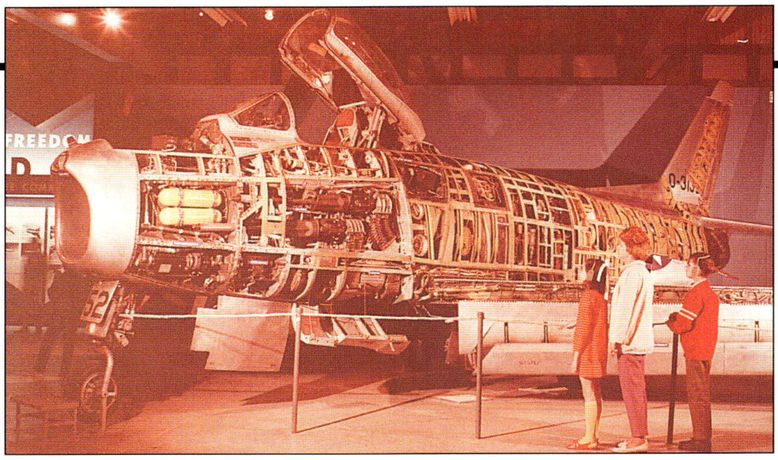

Above: This F-86H, 53-1352, had its skin removed for display at the US Air Force Museum. The 20-mm M39 cannon mounted on the cockpit sides can be seen clearly.

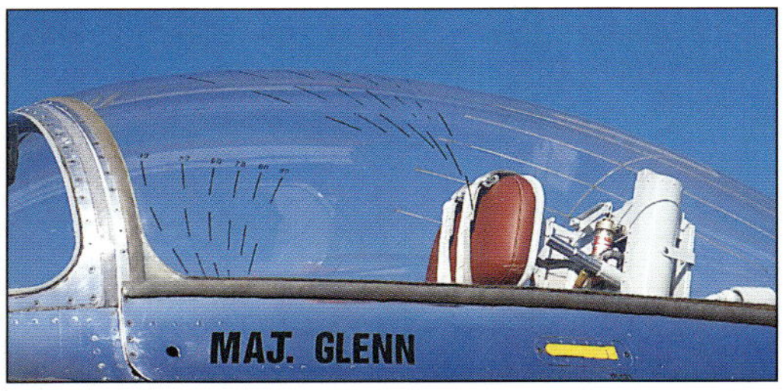

Above: F-86 fighter-bomber pilots could line up the horizon with these canopy markings to achieve the correct dive angle in an attack.

Above: The slatted wing on many Sabres, such as this JASDF F-86F-40, was retracted by air pressure and extended in the low-speed flight regime.

Right: The cockpit of an SAAF F-86F shows some variation in the placement of instruments compared to the A's cockpit. Dominating the centre of the panel is the gyro compass indicator, which has displaced the turn-and-bank indicator and VSI to the bottom of the main panel. There was no radar scope as such, radar information being presented on the A-1CM or A-4 gunsight.

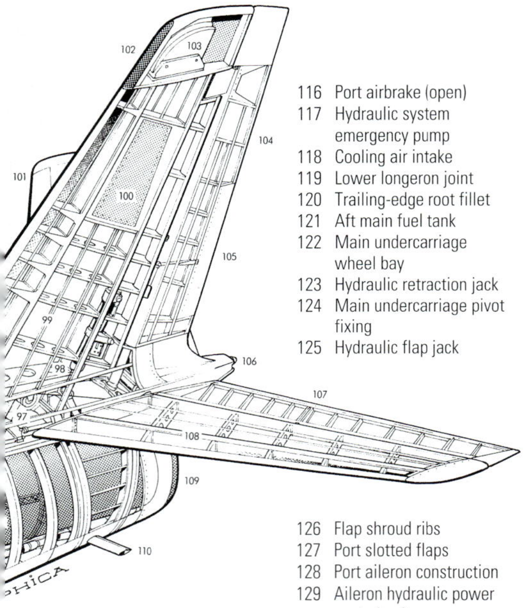

101 Starboard tailplane
102 Fintip dielectric aerial fairing
103 ADF aerial
104 Rudder construction
105 Rudder trim tab
106 Tail navigation light
107 Port elevator/tailplane flap
108 All-moving tailplane construction
109 Engine exhaust nozzle
110 Fuel jettison
111 Heat shrouded jet pipe
112 Power control compensator
113 Emergency hydraulic valves
114 Airbrake housing
115 Airbrake hydraulic jack
116 Port airbrake (open)
117 Hydraulic system emergency pump
118 Cooling air intake
119 Lower longeron joint
120 Trailing-edge root fillet
121 Aft main fuel tank
122 Main undercarriage wheel bay
123 Hydraulic retraction jack
124 Main undercarriage pivot fixing
125 Hydraulic flap jack
126 Flap shroud ribs
127 Port slotted flaps
128 Port aileron construction
129 Aileron hydraulic power control unit
130 Gyro compass remote transmitter
131 Wingtip fairing
132 Port navigation light
133 Port automatic leading-edge slat, open position
134 Leading-edge slat rib construction
135 Front spar
136 Wing rib and stringer construction
137 Wing skin/leading-edge piano hinge attachment joint
138 120-US gal (454-litre) drop tank
139 Drop tank pylon
140 Port main wheel
141 Fuel filter cap
142 Main undercarriage leg strut
143 Fuel tank bay corrugated double skin
144 Port wing fuel tank
145 Tank interconnectors
146 Skin panel attachment joint strap
147 Slat guide rails
148 Fuel feeders
149 Aileron cable drive

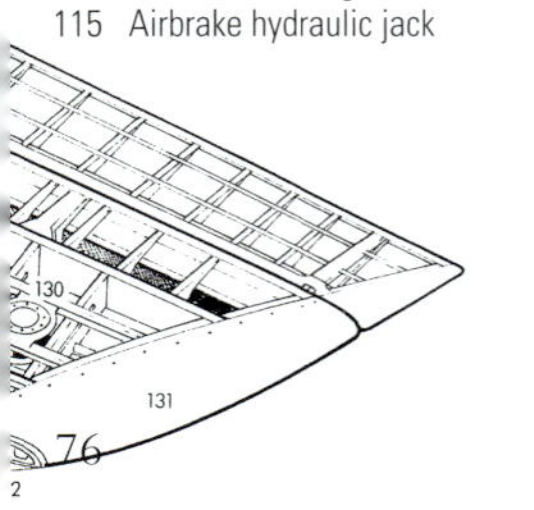

Left: This is the cockpit of an F-86F-1 of the 39th FIS, on alert at K-13 in 1953. The F had the A-4 gunsight interfaced with the APG-30 ranging radar.

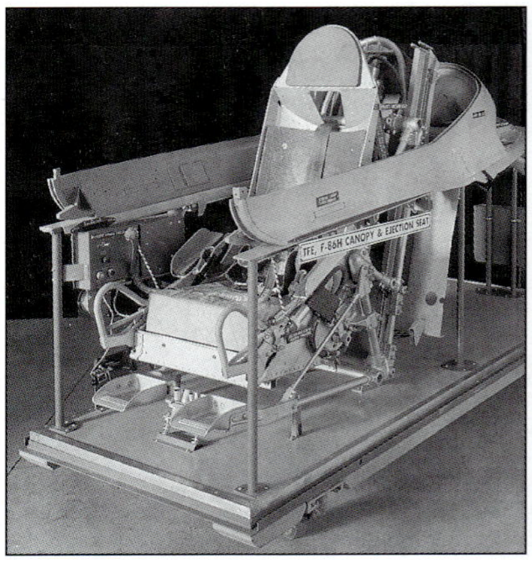

This is the NAA T-4E-1 ejection seat of the F-86A (left). The F-86H seat (above) was made by Air Products Inc. Upgraded D and K models, and CL-13s, had Martin-Baker seats.

F-86 Sabre Weapons

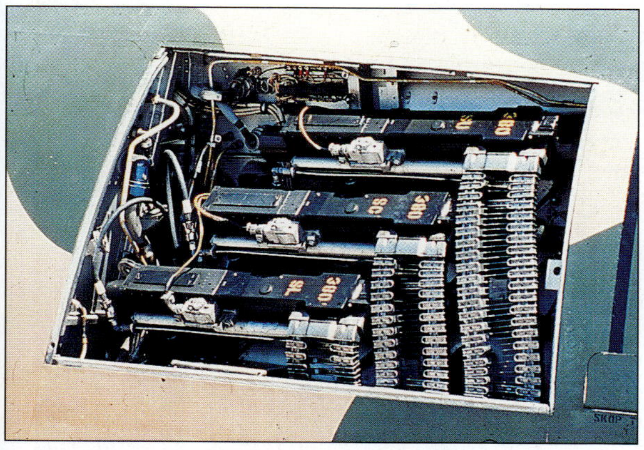

***Above:** Primary armament of the majority of **Sabres** was the same as that of the **P-51 Mustang** – six 0.50-in **Browning** machine-guns. The guns were mounted at an angle for best use of space and were fed from cans in a lower bay. Total ammunition capacity was 1,800 rounds, which, with an average rate of fire of 20 rounds per second, gave about 80 seconds of firing.*

***Left:** This shot of night firing with a **Canadair Sabre** shows the concentration of firepower available with six machine-guns. Attempts to increase the fire on the target by adding cannon were never wholly successful on **US** day-fighter **F-86s**.*

***Above:** Technicians clean 'Mighty Mouse' rocket trays at Yokota, Japan. The 'Mighty Mouse' with its 24 rockets was a potentially devastating weapon – when all the elements of its fire-control system worked properly. This view shows the rear of a tray with the electrically-operated firing pins over the end of each tube.*

***Above and left:** The **F-86** was one of the first fighters to be armed with air-to-air missiles. The **AIM-9 Sidewinder** (orginally the **GAR-8**) was first used on the **F-86F**, but appeared on other versions, including the **K** as seen at left (note two 20-mm cannon ports). The **AIM-4 (GAR-4) Falcon** (above) was not adopted as a standard fit.*

***Right:** This **F-86A** (the World Absolute Speed Record aircraft) was used in hoist tests to prove that **HVARs** could be fired safely from the **Sabre**.*

***Left:** Although the **F-86A-F** series was used almost exclusively as fighters by the **USAF**, bombs and rockets were used in action in **Korea**. Back in the **States**, this **F-86A** of the **Fighter School** at **Nellis AFB**, where **Sabre** advanced training was undertaken, is seen with a pair of 100-lb practice bombs in place of the usual drop tanks.*

*This shot of an **F-86A** shows the guns and ammunition, **M43, M44** and **M47** (white phosphorus) bombs, **HVARs** (High Velocity Aircraft Rockets), rocket pods, fuel tanks (240-**US** gal ferry tank at left, 120-**US** gal combat tank underwing) and chemical weapons tanks (behind the **HVARs**).*

*The **F-86F** was the first model with an extra hardpoint, allowing fitment of another pair of pylons and carriage of weapons in addition to underwing tanks. This **R-3** cluster bomb aboard an **F-86F-25** was fitted for trial purposes in April 1953.*

Sabre 'Hog'

At first glance similar to earlier day-fighter Sabres, the F-86H was a very different beast indeed. The large J73 engine required a major redesign of the fuselage, which was deeper and longer, and the aircraft incorporated many other improvements. It was built with three wing standards: original, 'hard 6-3' and F-40 'slatted 6-3', and during the production run armament changed from machine-guns to cannon. From the start the H was nuclear-capable, with LABS toss-bombing equipment.

Above:* *This was the third F-86H-1, seen at the AFFTC with instrumentation boom fitted. The aircraft is carrying 5-in (12.7-cm) rockets on underwing stubs.

Above:* *This family portrait at Edwards in 1953 shows the first F-86H in the foreground, together with the first F-86D-1 and first F-86F-5. The extra size of the H, particularly the depth of the fuselage, is immediately apparent.

Above right:* *NAA test pilot Joe Lynch made the first flight (seen here) of the YF-86H (52-1975) on 9 May 1953. Although the J73 engine offered nearly double the thrust of the first J47s, the H was only 10 mph (16 km/h) faster. This was indicative of the fact that the Sabre had reached the limit of its development potential.

control, with the exception of two squadrons that were transferred to Strategic Air Command in 1959. The 431st and 437th FISs, both based in North Africa, were sent to the B-47 bases at Torrejón and Zaragoza, Spain, where they stood alert against attacks on the SAC bases. By June 1961, all F-86D aircraft had been removed from both Air Force and Air National Guard inventories. Only the squadrons equipped with the F-86L remained on active duty.

A few nations acquired some of the F-86Ds that had been phased out of service with USAF. Denmark purchased 38 aircraft, South Korea 40 and the Philippines 20, and an unknown number of F-86Ds were sent to the Nationalist Chinese Air Force on Taiwan. The largest purchaser of the D model was Japan, which obtained 122 F-86Ds.

F-86K

The F-86K was the North American Aviation answer to a requirement by the Western allies for an all-weather interceptor to counter the Soviet bomber threat. In particular, NATO countries were anxious to have such an aircraft due to their close proximity to the Soviet border, and the often terrible weather conditions that prevailed over the continent. On 22 January 1953, Air Material Command laid down the requirements for the Mutual Defense Assistance Program interceptor. The new aircraft had to have an all-weather capability, had to be armed with 20-mm cannon, and had to have a two-man crew. North American countered with a modified version of their successful F-86D 'one-man interceptor'. The new aircraft would be designated as the F-86K.

Neither the Air Force or North American wanted the F-86K to use the Hughes E-4 Fire Control System. It was still brand-new and very secret – and it was full of problems that the Air Force did not need in the F-86K. North American designed a simplified fire control system, the MG-4. The MG-4 used the same AN/APG-37 radar as found in the D, and the AN/APA-84 computer to put the K model on a collision course to the target. A modified AC type A-4 gunsight assembly was installed in the K.

Armament was four M24-A-1 20-mm cannons, with a rate of fire of 800 rounds per minute. To make room for the 20-mm cannon installation and ammunition supply, the fuselage of the F-86K was lengthened 8 in (20 cm) just forward of the wing leading edge. The gun bays and muzzle ports were then cut into the forward fuselage. Large vent holes were cut into the gun bay doors to relieve the gun gas build-up that been experienced with the Gunval F-86Fs in Korea.

Production model F-86Ks would have the J47-GE-33 engine, which had 7,650 lb (34.02 kN) of thrust available in afterburner. They would have the same electronic fuel control as found on the F-86D. All other major assemblies of the F-86K were the same as those found on the F-86D – wing, leading-edge slats, landing gear, tail assembly with drag chute, and the flight control systems. Two F-86D-40s (52-3630 and 52-3804) were pulled from the assembly line and modified to K specifications, and designated YF-86K. North American test pilot Ray Morris took the first

This F-86H-1 was employed as a chase aircraft by Lockheed during the F-104G International Starfighter programme. It is carrying 206.5-US gal (782-litre) drop tanks on the outboard wing pylons, and what appears to be a high-speed camera installation on the port inboard pylon. The aircraft is one of the first 15 production aircraft, which were built with the original slatted wing, but is seen here after retrofit with the extended F-40 wing.

Command stripes
The four red stripes denoted the aircraft of the 101st's commanding officer. His deputy's aircraft usually wore two stripes in the same position.

Fuselage
To incorporate the new engine, the basic Sabre fuselage was deepened by six inches (15.2 cm) by adding a fuselage splice along its length. The tailpipe area was also extended 14 in (35.6 cm) to cover the increased length of the J73.

North American F-86H-10 Sabre 101st Tactical Fighter Squadron Massachusetts ANG Logan Field, Boston 1964

Cannon
Due to Air Force delays in ordering the T-160 cannon, the F-86H-1 was delivered with the six 0.50-in calibre M3 machine-guns of the standard day-fighter Sabres. Beginning with the -5, two pairs of 20-mm M39A2 cannon with 150 rounds per gun were installed. This weapon had a higher rate of fire than the M3 machine-gun – 1,500 rounds per minute compared to 1,100 – and proved more suitable for ground attack purposes. Each cannon weighed about 110 pounds (50 kg) more than a machine-gun, however, leading to a significant increase in armament system weight despite there being two fewer guns in total.

Engine
The 'Hog Sabre' was powered by the General Electric J73-GE-3/3A which was a development of the afterburning J47-GE-17 used in the F-86D, K and L. The H's engine produced 9,200 lb (40.94 kN) take-off thrust compared to 7,500 lb (33.38 kN) for that of the D. This new powerplant had a larger intake area but with the same diameter and length as the J47. This was achieved by relocating some accessories below the engine in turn resulting in the need for a larger external intake and increased fuselage diameter.

Mark 12
Primary weapon of the few F-86Hs to serve in regular USAF squadrons was the Mk 12 *Brok* nuclear bomb. This weapon, weighing 1,200 lbs (544 kg) with an explosive yield of 10-20 kilotons, could also be carried by the F-86F-35. This sleek bomb had folding fins to ensure ground clearance – the lack of which prevented use of the larger and more efficient Mk 7. Only 250 Mk 12s were produced. Normal carriage was a single weapon under the port wing balanced by a pair of drop tanks on the starboard wing.

The two fighter squadrons of the Massachusetts ANG have long played on the heritage of the people from which their personnel are drawn. The 101st from the western part of the state style themselves the 'Irish Guard', while the 131st FS from the east are the 'Polish Guard' and decorate their aircraft with a suitable red and white trim. Both units operated F-86Hs from 1958 to 1964.

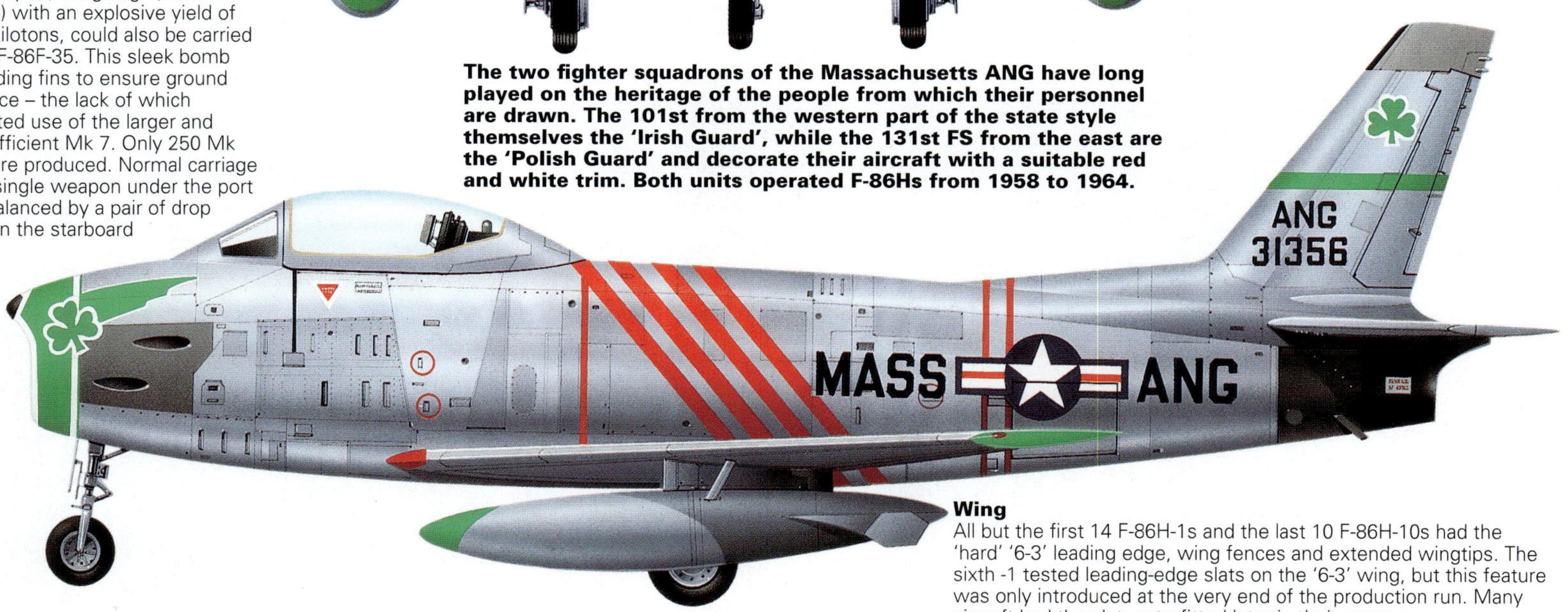

Wing
All but the first 14 F-86H-1s and the last 10 F-86H-10s had the 'hard' '6-3' leading edge, wing fences and extended wingtips. The sixth -1 tested leading-edge slats on the '6-3' wing, but this feature was only introduced at the very end of the production run. Many aircraft had the slats retrofitted later in their careers.

Right: F-86Hs of the 430th FBS line the ramp at Thule AB, Greenland during one of the Highflight deployments that sent units to the European theatre to support NATO. The 430th was normally part of the 474th FBW at Cannon AFB, New Mexico, and was on its way to Wheelus AFB in Libya. Note the four-cannon armament.

This colourful F-86H-10 was the mount of 50th FBW (Hahn AB, West Germany) commander Colonel Fred Ascani (of speed record fame). The fin stripes were in the colours of the wing's constituent squadrons.

Below right: During the 1961 Berlin Crisis several ANG units were called to active duty and dispatched to Europe. This 131st FBS F-86H from the Massachusetts ANG is seen at Phalsbourg in France.

Below: Among the Berlin Crisis activations was the 138th TFS and its F-86Hs. This aircraft is seen en route to Phalsbourg AB from where it would undertake air defence missions, even though the primary role of the 138th was nuclear.

YF-86K (52-3630) on its maiden flight on 15 July 1954.

The F-86Ks would be built in two separate batches, and by two different companies – North American's Inglewood plant and Fiat of Italy. North American provided 50 sets of parts to Fiat in May 1953, which Fiat assembled at its factory in Turin. NATO officials wanted more F-86Ks than Fiat could assemble at the time, so North American put the F-86K into limited production at the Inglewood factory, building 120 F-86Ks before production was halted. The first North American-built production F-86K (54-1231) made its first flight on 8 March 1955; the first of the Fiat-assembled F-86Ks (53-8273) made its on 23 May 1955. Colonel Arthur DeBolt, North American Aviation's representative in Italy, was at the controls for the latter.

The North American-built Ks (54-1231/-1350) were divided between Norway, whose air force received 60 aircraft, and the Netherlands Air Force, which had 59 in its inventory. Eventually, Fiat received 221 sets of parts to build the F-86K, the last 45 of which had the '6-3' extended wing, with leading-edge slats as found on the F-86L. Many of the Netherlands Ks were also retrofitted with the long-span F-86L wing. Many of the F-86Ks could fire the GAR-8 missile, known to the world as the AIM-9 Sidewinder. Sidewinder-equipped Ks had Aero 3B launch rails installed under the wing just inboard of the landing gear. Fiat-built F-86Ks equipped squadrons in Italy (65 aircraft), France (60 aircraft), and West Germany (88 aircraft).

The first Ks to enter service were the Fiat-built examples, with the 1ª Aerobrigata in mid-1955. By 1964, the F-86K was being phased out of service with NATO and replaced by the Lockheed F-104S Starfighter. However, as soon as one country phased out the K from service, another nation would purchase them for its own use. Dutch F-86Ks were overhauled after being phased out, and began service with the Turkish Air Force (60 aircraft) in 1964. The last French F-86Ks were phased out in August 1962. West Germany gave up its Ks in January 1966. Some of the French and Dutch Ks were transferred to Italy in 1962/63. The last Dutch Ks were phased out in June 1964, with Norway following in 1966/67. Many were sold to Venezuela (74 ex-German), which then sold them to Honduras (five), which flew them well into the 1970s.

F-86L – Project Follow-On

The F-86L was the solution to a problem that had plagued all-weather operations throughout the early 1950s, whether the interceptor was an F-86D, F-94 or F-89: slow or incomplete communications between the GCI radar operator and the interceptor pilot, often resulting in either a missed intercept or one that came too late to stop the impending bomber attack. The Lincoln Laboratory at the Massachusetts Institute of Technology had developed a computerised datalink system that would bridge the communications lag. It was called SAGE, an acronym for Semi-Automatic Ground Environment. The SAGE system telecommunicated all available GCI radar information to the interceptor at the exact instant the GCI operator saw it. Thus, the pilot got the heading, speed, altitude and range to target information at the same moment as the GCI operator, without any voice communication at all. The SAGE system used the AN/ARR-39 datalink, which automatically recomputed the lead-collision course to the target despite changes in the target speed or manoeuvres.

The SAGE system was installed under Project Follow-On. Specific low-time airframes taken from blocks D-10 through D-60 were sent through the Follow-On programme at the North American plants in Fresno and Inglewood, starting in May 1956. Along with the

'Hogs' in the Guard

Large numbers of F-86Hs were turned over to the ANG from 1957, and served with a total of 14 squadrons on fighter-bomber duties. It was a popular and long-lived aircraft, the final example being retired from the 138th TFS, New York ANG, in January 1971.

AN/ARR-39 datalink, all Follow-On aircraft replaced the ARC-27 command radio with the ARC-34 radio, and the APX-6 IFF system with the APX-25. A new AN/ARN-31 glide slope receiver was also added. SAGE system aircraft had a small blade antenna protruding from the lower left fuselage, just ahead of the wing.

All Follow-On aircraft were brought to F-86D-45 specifications before starting on the electronics upgrades, including addition of the drag chute in the tail. Other external changes included two protruding cooling scoops on the rear fuselage, replacing the older NACA-design recessed cooling ducts. The '6-3' wing with extended wingtips as developed for the F-86F-40 was adapted to the F-86D wing. This wing was 12 in (30 cm) longer at each tip, had the '6-3' wing chord addition, and was equipped with leading-edge slats.

The aircraft were also equipped with the latest engine, the J47-GE-33. The maximum take-off weight for an F-86L was 20,275 lb (9196 kg) with a pair of 120-US gal (454-litre) underwing tanks and equipped for the area defence mission profile; this was slightly over 300 lb (136 kg) heavier than a similarly equipped F-86D. Although slightly heavier, the performance figures for the D and L were almost identical. The modified aircraft were redesignated F-86L.

The first flight took place on 27 December 1955. That aircraft had just the SAGE equipment installed, and the first true conversion incorporating all the Follow-On changes did not take place until May 1956. All F-86L block designations were changed to reflect their original F-86D block numbers. Thus, an F-86D-10 became an L-11, a D-40 became an L-41, and so on through block L-46. Blocks 50, 55, and 60 just changed the type from D to L, e.g., F-86D-50 became L-50.

The first F-86Ls were delivered to the 317th FIS at McChord AFB in late November 1956. Eighteen months later, the US Air Force had received 576 F-86Ls. By the time the last L was being delivered, the type was already being phased out in favour of the '1954 Interceptor' – the Convair F-102A and F-106A interceptors. Of the total of 981 F-86Ls, North American's Inglewood plant converted 575 aircraft from D to L, and the Fresno plant converted another 452. The remaining 52 aircraft were converted at the Sacramento Air Material Area at McClellan AFB.

The 108th FIS, Illinois Air National Guard began conversion to F-86Ls in October 1957. Eventually, 24 ANG squadrons were equipped with F-86Ls. The variant completely phased out of Air Force service into the ANG by 1960, where they served until the summer of 1965, when the 196th FIS, California ANG phased out its F-86Ls in favour of F-102As. Only one nation other than the United States had F-86Ls in its inventory: Thailand purchased 10 F-86Ls, for service with No. 12 Squadron at Don Muang Airport into 1966.

F-86H: the 'Hog' Sabre

The F-86H (NA-187) was supposed to be the ultimate Sabre design. Every problem would be addressed in the H – bigger engine, heavier firepower, nuclear capabilities, longer range. All that anyone envisioned the Sabre could do, the F-86H would be able to do. And do it better than any other fighter type in the USAF.

The H would be powered by the brand-new J73-GE-3 engine rated at almost 9,250 lb (41.14 kN) static thrust. The J73 was much larger in every way than the previous J47, and required a lot more air than the J47. This meant a

***Above:** This red-painted F-86H-10 was flown from Nellis on target-towing duties – note the towing equipment under the wing pylon.*

Target tugs

Sabres regularly performed the target-tug duty, being assigned to gunnery training units or individual squadrons. Many Hs were used in this way. Surplus F-86Hs were also converted to drones for weapons tests.

***Left:** This F-86H-10 was assigned to the 104th TFS, Maryland ANG and is seen in June 1963 while carrying a TDU aerial dart target. By this date Sabres had mostly acquired silver anti-corrosion paint.*

This brightly marked F-86H-5 was the mount of the legendary Colonel George Lavin, Jr, commander of the 413th Fighter Day Group at George AFB, California, in 1955.

***Left:** During the 1968 Pueblo Crisis two Guard F-86H squadrons (104th and 138th TFS) were called to federal active duty. This pair is from the 138th TFS, New York ANG, which deployed to Cannon AFB, New Mexico, during the crisis to operate a forward air controller school. By this time the surviving H models had acquired T.O.1-1-4 tactical camouflage.*

Canadair Sabres

Canadair contributed over 1,800 Sabres, virtually all built for NATO air arms, notably the RAF, RCAF and Luftwaffe. Initial production was of an F-86E equivalent, but the majority were built as Sabre Mks 5 or 6 with the Orenda engine. This made the Canadair Sabre a better-performing aircraft than its USAF counterpart, and it ruled the roost in Europe as far as fighters were concerned.

***Above:** Canadair supplied 60 Sabre Mk 2s (as F-86E-6s) to the USAF to cater for shortages caused by the war in Korea. This example was assigned to the Air Force Academy.*

***Top right:** RCAF 19101 was the first Canadair-built Sabre, the one-off Sabre Mk 1. It was supplied to Cartierville in kit form, and was in fact an F-86A-5 built, but not assembled, on the NAA Inglewood line. The aircraft first flew from Dorval on 8 August 1950.*

***Right:** Sabre Mk 2s of No. 441 'Silver Fox' Squadron fly from North Luffenham in Leicestershire. Both of these aircraft were written off in non-fatal accidents: 19149 (front) at Zweibrücken in 1954 and 19152 in 1953 near Wells, England. It would appear that the fuselage roundel decal on '149 was applied without cuts for the airbrake, causing its early demise.*

bigger fuselage was needed. North American engineers split the fuselage longitudinally, splicing an additional 6 in (15 cm) into the depth of the fuselage from front to rear. Additionally, the fuselage was lengthened by over 2 ft (60 cm), and widened a few inches. The air intake duct was increased a similar amount. Other fuselage changes included installation of the clam-shell opening canopy that had been introduced on the F-86D. The cockpit was more spacious than any previous variant, and had a new ejection seat, again developed for use in the D model. The deeper fuselage allowed internal fuel tank capacity to be increased from 435 to 570 US gal (1647 to 2158 litres).

The vertical tail assembly was 3 in (7.6 cm) taller and wider through the chord, but had a smaller rudder. The horizontal control surfaces were changed from the 'all-flying tail' design with a split stabiliser and elevator, to a single-piece slab that was one-third larger than the earlier units, but still all-movable. The first 15 aircraft off the assembly line were completed with the old-style slatted wing, without the '6-3' extension. The '6-3 hard wing' was added later.

Armament was the same as all previous F-86s – six M3 0.50-in machine-guns, with the type A-4 GBR gunsight using the AN/APG-30 radar rangefinder. The new high-speed 20-mm T-160 cannon was the weapon slated for installation in the F-86H, but development had slowed and the weapons were not ready when the first aircraft started coming off the assembly line. Since the H was developed as a fighter-bomber with a nuclear strike capability, an M-1 LABS toss-bombing computer was installed.

The prototype F-86H (52-1975) came off the Inglewood assembly line in late April 1953, making its first flight on 9 May. The performance was what had been expected with the larger engine. Top speed rose to 707 mph (1138 km/h) at sea level, and over 617 mph (993 km/h) at 35,000 ft (10668 m). Service ceiling went up to 51,500 ft (15697 m). The rate of climb jumped to an astounding 12,160 ft (3706 m) per minute. Even though the H weighed almost 10,000 lb (4536 kg) more than the F model, the combat radius was about the same – 532 miles (856 km) – due to the increase in internal fuel supply.

All but the first two prototypes would be built at the North American plant in Columbus, Ohio, the first leaving the plant in September 1953. The initial production run was for 113 F-86H-1-NHs (52-1977/-2089). Problems with both the airframe and engine developments (the J73 could not meet the 150-hour qualification tests) held up deliveries to the first operational wing, the 312th FBW at Clovis AFB, New Mexico, until the autumn of 1954.

Next off the Columbus line would be the H-5, with the J73-GE-3A engine. The H-5 was the first type armed with the new T-160 20-mm high-speed cannon, standardised as the M39. The M39 had been combat tested with the 4th FIG in Korea under Project Gunval and had a rate of fire of

A Sabre Mk 2 of No. 410 Squadron is seen at its Dorval base in 1951. The 'Cougars' were the RCAF's first jet squadron (1948 – Vampires), and its first Sabre squadron, equipping with the new fighter three years later. The unit moved to North Luffenham in November of 1951 where this aircraft (19122) was written off in a landing accident in February 1953.

over 1,500 rounds per minute. Ammunition supply was limited, however, to a total of only 600 rounds – about six seconds' worth. North American built 60 F-86H-5s (52-2090/-2124 and 52-5729/-5753).

The H-10 was nearly identical to the H-5, having only some minor internal electrical system changes and installation of the J73-GE-3E engine. Three hundred F-86H-10s were built (53-1229/-1528) before production of all types of F-86 was halted on 16 March 1956

Although the first 14 H-1s were completed with the standard F-86F dual-store wing with leading-edge slats, the rest of the H-1 production, all of the H-5s, and the first 290 H-10s were built with the '6-3' solid leading-edge wing. The final 10 aircraft were completed using the so-called 'F-40' wing, which had the '6-3' chord increase, a 12-in (30-cm) extension on each tip, and the leading-edge slats reinstalled for low-speed control. Extending the wing increased the angle of wing sweep to 39°. Eventually, all remaining Hs in both Air Force and Air National Guard inventories were retrofitted with the extended 'F-40' wing.

Although the H was supposed to be the ultimate Sabre, and lived up to that promise after all the bugs were worked out, the airframe design was at its limit and was unable to meet the requirements for the new fighter generation. Those aircraft would be supersonic in level flight, something the H could never achieve. By the time the Hs were fully operational with five wings in 1956, they had already been made obsolete by the Sabre 45, commonly known as the F-100 Super Sabre.

The Air Force had phased the H models out of service into the Air National Guard by mid-1958, where they soldiered on for over 12 more years. The last H was not phased out of service with 'The Boys From Syracuse', the 138th TFS, New York ANG, until 8 January 1971. That was short-lived, as the Navy brought them out of retirement to act as MiG-17 simulators with 'Top Gun'. Many an F-14 jock was very surprised to find an old F-86H stuck to his tail in the early 1970s. The F-86H truly was 'The Last Of The Sport Models'.

Canadair Sabres

When Canada wanted to re-equip the Royal Canadian Air Force with a modern jet aircraft, it opted for North American's F-86. The RCAF was already equipped with F-51D/K Mustangs and AT-6 Harvard trainers, both North American products, and the company was building the best day fighter aircraft in the Western world – the F-86A Sabre. However, it would be a fight to bring another US-built aircraft into the RCAF. The Canadian press, as well as many members of the government, wanted a British aircraft for the RCAF. The only types available were the de Havilland Vampire and the Gloster Meteor, neither of which could approach the performance of the Sabre.

In August 1949, the Canadian and US governments came to an agreement that allowed Canadair Ltd to licence-build a version of the Sabre. Canadair already had a connection with North American, having built T-6 Harvard trainers during World War II. North American would supply all the engineering drawings, some 46,000 in all, and all the sub-assemblies necessary to begin production.

The first Canadair-built Sabre was the Mk I, actually an F-86A-5. North American shipped the aircraft in sub-assemblies (wings, tail assemblies, fuselage, engine, etc.) to the Canadair plant at Cartierville, Quebec in late 1949. North American and Canadair engineers worked together to get the production and assembly jigs built, and the assembly lines started. In July 1950, the first aircraft was finished. The Canadair CL-13 Sabre Mk I (serial 19101) was rolled out in early July 1950. Since the runway at Cartierville was too short to allow jet aircraft operations, the Mk I was towed to nearby RCAF Dorval for initial flight tests. Following the usual taxi and braking tests, the Mk I was ready for its first flight. On 8 August 1950, test pilot Al Lilly took it into the air for the first time.

Canadair built just the single Mk I, since the contract with North American was to build a version of the F-86E.

Above: 49-1069 was the F-86A converted to take the Orenda 3 engine. The USAF designated the aircraft F-86J. It flew during 1950.

Orenda power

The first two production Canadair Sabre versions (Mks 2 and 4) retained the J47, but a shortage of these engines and the promise of the Avro Orenda powerplant resulted in a Sabre being tested with the Canadian engine as early as 1950. Fitting the slightly larger Orenda required a redesign of the fuselage structure and engine bearers.

19200 was built as a Sabre Mk 2, and first flew as such on 14 June 1952 with the original J47. After 12 GE-powered flights it was re-engined with the Orenda 3 to become the sole Sabre Mk 3. It flew again on 25 September 1952, remaining an evaluation vehicle for the remainder of its career, although it was used by Jacqueline Cochran for a world speed record over a 15-km course in June 1953.

Sabres for Britain

Sabres were acquired in haste to provide the RAF with swept-wing fighter capability pending delivery of the indigenous Hawker Hunter. Canadair built the aircraft, and the US paid for them through MDAP funds. A total of 428 Sabre Mk 4s arrived between October 1952 and December 1953 during a major ferry operation code-named Becher's Brook (an infamous fence on the Aintree Grand National racecourse). Two squadrons were assigned to home defence and 10 squadrons were established in West Germany. Their service life was brief.

Above: XB982 was used by Bristol as a testbed for its Orpheus 801 engine (which in production form powered the Fiat G91). It is seen here on its first Orpheus-powered flight in the hands of Godfrey Auty on 3 July 1958 at Filton.

The RAF's Sabres were delivered in natural metal but soon acquired standard camouflage. The springbok badge identifies No. 26 Squadron, which flew Sabre F.Mk 4s from Oldenburg between November 1953 and June 1955. By mid-1956 all of the RAF's dozen squadrons of Sabre F.Mk 4s had transitioned to the Hunter F.Mk 4, allowing the Sabres to be reallocated to other NATO countries.

Sabre Mk 5

Designated CL-13A by Canadair, the Sabre Mk 5 combined the Orenda engine with the F-86F's '6-3' wing. All were initially earmarked for the RCAF, although 75 were transferred to the Luftwaffe.

Above: The Mk 5 was the definitive Canadair Sabre, although there were many variations during production. These 1954-built aircraft have all the modifications made to the type except for the slatted wing, which returned on the last 415 Canadair Sabres manufactured.

Above right: Sabre Mk 5 23362 spent all of its 10-year flying career with the Sabre OTU at Chatham and was photographed there in July 1957.

Right: This Mk 5, 23275, was modified with aft fuselage blisters by Canadair to test Richard Whitcomb's area rule. The performance gain was marginal and the study was terminated.

They were designated CL-13 Sabre Mk 2. The Mk 2 was identical to the North American-built F-86E-1 with the 'all-flying tail', V-shaped windscreen, and an American GE J47-GE-13 engine rated at 5,200 lb (23.13 kN) of thrust. The first flight of a Mk 2 (19102) came on 31 January 1951, only four months after the first flight of the North American F-86E-1.

Canadair built a total of 350 Sabre Mk 2s (19102/-199 and 19201/-452) between January 1951 and August 1952. Included in that total were 60 aircraft purchased by the US Air Force to replenish combat losses in the Korean War, as mentioned previously. Designated F-86E-6 by the USAF (52-2833/-2892), the first aircraft was delivered to the US Air Force on 2 February 1952, after going through the Fresno North American plant to have American equipment installed. Most of the 60 Canadair F-86E-6s were delivered to squadrons in Korea, replacing the war-weary F-86As and any combat losses.

RCAF Sabre operations began with No. 410 Squadron at Dorval, which received its first Mk 2 on 10 April 1951. Both 441 and 413 Squadrons equipped in the summer of 1951. The Sabre-equipped No. 1 Fighter Wing was rushed to Europe almost before the transition into the Sabre was completed, bolstering NATO squadrons that were facing a growing MiG threat with various inferior aircraft types.

A lack of J47s and development of the Avro Orenda turbojet engine led to the next variant, the Sabre Mk 3. However, the actual first Sabre to have an Orenda engine was a North American Aviation project. In August 1949, North American pulled F-86A-5 No. 49-1069 from the assembly line, and modified the fuselage formers and engine mounts to accept the larger Orenda engine. Designated F-86J by the USAF, the Orenda-powered F-86 first flew in 1950. With 6,000 lb (26.68 kN) of thrust, it had a much greater overall performance than any J47-powered Sabre. Performance was so much better that Canadair started its own Orenda Sabre project, which resulted in the sole Mk 3. Canadair pulled a Mk 2 (19200) from the assembly line and performed virtually the same fuselage modifications as made by North American to the F-86J. An Orenda 3 engine was then installed in place of the J47.

Mk 3 first flight

First flown on 29 September 1952, the Mk 3 was destined to be only a test and evaluation aircraft to develop the final production version of the Orenda Sabre. However, it was notable as the aircraft in which Jacqueline Cochran set many international speed records, including a world speed record over a 15-km (9.3-mile) course, when she was clocked at 675.471 mph (1087.04 km/h) on 3 June 1953.

The production version of the Orenda was not ready before the next Canadair Sabre variant was produced. The CL-13 Sabre Mk 4 would again use the American J47-GE-13 engine, and was virtually identical to the E-10 with the flat windscreen. First flown on 28 August 1952, most of the Mk 4 production run of 438 aircraft (19453/-890) was taken by the Royal Air Force, 428 Mk 4s being delivered between December 1952 and December 1953. The first RAF Sabre Mk 4 unit was No. 67 Fighter Squadron, which began operations on 8 May 1953. In 1956, following their replacement in the RAF by Hawker Hunters, the Mk 4s

The Sabres of the Air Division, such as this 441 Squadron aircraft based at Marville, soon acquired camouflage befitting the tactical environment. This is a Sabre Mk 6 with the slatted '6-3' wing, seen in February 1957.

Sabre Mk 6

Canadair's final production variant was the CL-13B Sabre Mk 6, which featured the uprated Orenda 14 and introduced the slatted wing part way through production. The majority went to the RCAF for service in Europe. Flown with typical Canadian skill and aggression, the Sabre Mk 6s were unbeatable for some time in the late 1950s in NATO air combat exercises, especially the no-rules, unofficial contests that were a part of the European fighter pilot's everyday life.

Canadair CL-13 Sabre Mk 2 No. 434 Squadron, No. 3 Wing, RCAF Zweibrücken 1954

Armament
All Canadair Sabres were completed with the same six-gun armament as USAF F-86s. The Sabre Mk 2 had two underwing pylons for bombs or fuel.

Export Sabre Mk 2s
The first three Sabres for the RAF were Mk 2s (designated F.Mk 1) loaned in preparation for the delivery of the main batch of F.Mk 4s. After phasing out of RCAF service the surviving Mk 2s went to Greece (106) and Turkey (107).

The Sabre Mk 2 was the Canadian-built equivalent of the F-86E. After assembly of an F-86A as the sole Mk 1, production switched to the Mk 2, of which 350 were built, all with J47-GE-13 engines. The more powerful Orenda engine was not fitted until the Mk 5 model. Improvements to the Mk 2 kept pace with North American developments, although the US block number system was not applied to Canadian aircraft.

19232
Sabre Mk 2 19232 was the 131st Sabre built by Canadair at Cartierville, Quebec. The aircraft was taken on strength by the RCAF on 23 November 1951. After a fairly brief career during which it served with Nos 413 and 434 Squadrons and the OTU, the aircraft was transferred to Turkey in June-July 1954, one of 107 Mk 2s supplied to this country from RCAF stocks. Its subsequent use and fate is unknown.

No. 434 'Bluenose' Squadron
The sixth RCAF unit to receive the Sabre, after Nos 410, 439, 413, and 421 Squadrons and 1(F) OTU, No. 434 Squadron formed with Mk 2s on 1 July 1952 at Uplands. In February 1953, No. 3 (F) Wing was formed at Zweibrücken, West Germany and the aircraft of No. 434 Squadron flew to join it as part of Operation Leap Frog III on 7 March. Together with Nos 413 and 427 Squadrons, the 'Bluenoses' served in the air defence role at Zweibrücken, occasionally deploying to French Morocco for gunnery training.

Wing
The Sabre Mk 2 was fitted with the wing of the F-86E, complete with leading-edge slats. The '6-3 hard wing' was incorporated into Canadair Sabre production beginning with the 701st example. Both the '6-3' wing extension and slats were incorporated into all Sabres built in Canada, from the 1,401st on (an Orenda-powered Mk 6). This restored the low-speed handling characteristics and made these late-model aircraft the best-handling of all Sabres.

Markings
This aircraft wears the 'schooner' of No. 434 Squadron on a blue fuselage chevron, this marking having previously been carried in a disc on the tail. The well-weathered national insignia is of a more complicated and realistic type than that later adopted by the RCAF. The Canadian red ensign flag of the period began to replace the RAF fin flash on RCAF aircraft from the end of 1953. Sabres of the Air Division were the first aircraft on which they were noted.

Rearming the Luftwaffe

Having established a fighter-bomber and reconnaissance arm (with Republic F/RF-84Fs), the Luftwaffe ordered 225 Sabre Mk 6s (the last Sabres to be built at Montreal) to equip three day-fighter wings. This delivery was preceded by 75 Sabre Mk 5s which were used to kick-start the extensive training effort. The operational Mk 6s entered service in mid-1959, and served with eight Staffeln. JG 71 converted to the F-104G Starfighter in 1964, while in 1964/66 the other two wings became light attack units flying the Fiat G91R. Luftwaffe Sabre Mk 6s were modified to become Sidewinder-capable.

***Left:** Waffenschule 10 was established at Oldenburg in 1958 as the Sabre training unit. This aircraft was the first Sabre Mk 6 to be delivered to the unit.*

***Below:** JG 72 was the second Sabre unit to form, initially flying from Leck although later moving to Oldenburg. The third unit, JG 73, was based at Pferdsfeld.*

***Above:** The 75 Sabre Mk 5s for the Luftwaffe came from surplus RCAF stocks, and were fitted out by Scottish Aviation at Prestwick before delivery. All served with WS-10 on type training duties.*

***Above centre:** The stylised tulip design and Richthofen 'R' identifies the Sabres of JG 71, the first operational Luftwaffe unit. The Geschwader was commanded by Major Erich Hartmann, the highest-scoring fighter pilot of all time, and the tulip was his personal marking during the war. He accepted the first of the unit's Sabre Mk 6s on 6 June 1959.*

***Right:** Turkey operated Sabre Mk 2s from July 1954. They were augmented by a few NAA-built F-86Fs.*

***Below:** Under MDAP, the AMI received 179 ex-RAF Sabre Mk 4s after rework by British companies and reassignment of RCAF serials. This aircraft wears the black lancer badge of 2ª Aerobrigata Intercettori Diurni.*

were transferred to other European air forces, notably Italy, which received 180 aircraft, and Yugoslavia with 121.

The Canadair CL-13A Sabre Mk 5 was the first production variant to use the Orenda powerplant. On 21 July 1953, Canadair rolled out the first Mk 5 (23001), powered by the Orenda 10 engine rated at 6,500 lb (28.91 kN) of thrust. The overall performance of the Mk 5 was significantly greater than any J47-powered Sabre, either North American or Canadair. Top speed rose to over 696 mph (1120 km/h) at sea level, and service ceiling went over 50,000 ft (15240 m). Time to climb was literally cut in half due to the 9,700 ft (2956 m) per minute rate of climb available with the Orenda engine. The increased power also cut into the range, reducing it more than 20 per cent over a similar F-86F.

The Mk 5 used the '6-3 hard wing' developed for the F-86F-25/-30. As with US Air Force Sabres, this '6-3' wing leading edge could be, and was, retrofitted to large numbers of Mk 4 aircraft, and even some Mk 2s. The first flight of a Mk 5 took place on 30 July 1953. Canadair built a total of 370 Sabre Mk 5s, dividing the production run between the RCAF and the West German Bundesluftwaffe, which received 75 aircraft.

Following closely on the heels of the Mk 5 was the

CL-13B Sabre Mk 6. Initially, the Mk 6 differed from the Mk 5 only in having the two-stage Orenda 14 engine, which offered 7,275 lb (32.35 kN) of thrust. However, during the production run, the wing was changed from the '6-3 hard wing' with fences to a '6-3' wing with leading-edge slats. Reinstallation of the slats recovered the lost low-speed stability and lowered the stall speed. The slats were retrofitted to many of the Mk 5 aircraft already in service.

The first flight of the Mk 6 (23371) came on 19 October 1954. The performance of the Mk 6 was truly outstanding considering the age of the original airframe design, and was totally the result of the power increase from using the Orenda 14 engine. The Mk 6 had a top speed of 710 mph (1142 km/h), and a rate of climb exceeding 11,800 ft (3597 m) per minute. At 55,000 ft (16764 m), the service ceiling was over 7,000 ft (2134 m) greater than any F-86F, and on a par with both the MiG-15bis and the MiG-17.

The initial batch of 292 Mk 6s was built and delivered to the RCAF, followed by six Mk 6s for the Colombian Air Force, 34 for South Africa, 90 more for the RCAF, and a final batch of 225 for West Germany. South Africa had operated a squadron of Sabres during the Korean War, but these aircraft were 'loaned' to No. 2 Squadron, SAAF by the US 5th Air Force. They were returned following the end of the war in 1953, when No. 2 Squadron rotated home.

On 9 October 1958, the last Canadair Sabre Mk 6 came off the assembly line. Canadair had built a total of 1,815 CL-13 Sabres between August 1950 and October 1958.

Commonwealth Aircraft Corporation Sabre

Late in 1950, when 5th Air Force Sabres were showing the world they could beat the best the Soviets could field in Korea, the Australian government made the decision to upgrade the Royal Australian Air Force. None of the forthcoming European designs could stay with the Russian MiG-15, so Australia turned to the US to put its air force on a par with the best in the West. The country opted for the North American F-86.

To say that the Commonwealth Aircraft Corporation (CAC) Sabre was just another licence-built Sabre would be a vast understatement. Although it looks very similar to its North American cousin, almost the entire fuselage structure was different. The wing, vertical tail, and horizontal stabiliser assemblies were virtually identical, however.

Two of the main things the RAAF wanted to change in the basic F-86 design were exactly the same two changes sought by the USAF pilots fighting in Korea – additional

thrust and heavier armament. Both changes would necessarily cause a major redesign of the fuselage. The RAAF chose the Rolls-Royce RA-7 Avon engine, which had 7,500 lb (33.36 kN) of static thrust. The RA-7 Avon engine was approximately the same size as the J47, but weighed almost 400 lb (181 kg) less. This caused the centre of gravity of the aircraft to move, which CAC engineers corrected by moving the engine further aft than the J47 – it was then discovered that the engine mounts would be out of the forward fuselage structure. With this in mind, CAC redesigned the forward fuselage structure, lengthening it at the aft break point. This moved the fuselage break point to the rear, from station 236.25 to 262.75, and the engine mounts were again within the confines of the forward fuselage.

Fuselage splice

The Avon engine needed a larger volume of air than the J47. CAC engineers split the forward fuselage from a point just under the cockpit, and spliced in a 3.73-in (9.5-cm) triangular piece. The intake itself was enlarged 4 in (10 cm) to meet the new fuselage contours. The intake duct was enlarged a corresponding amount, giving 25 per cent more air to the Avon engine than was available to the J47. The much greater thrust of the Avon required a larger exhaust nozzle, which also increased the depth of the rear fuselage slightly. None of these changes increased the overall length of the CAC Sabre.

Armament was a pair of 30-mm ADEN cannon, a development of the Mauser MG213, which had a rate of fire exceeding 1,200 rounds per minute and a 2,600 ft (792 m) per second muzzle velocity. The ADEN cannon were mounted in the original 0.50-in machine-gun bays, but staggered, and the starboard weapon was mounted inverted and 7.9 in (20 cm) forward of the port weapon. The ammunition bays were in the original F-86 position, and had a capacity of 162 rounds, which were electrically fed to the gun breeches. The fuselage, from the gun bays forward, had to be strengthened considerably to withstand the heavier pounding of the high-velocity cannon.

Other changes to the fuselage included a repositioning and redesign of the two fuselage fuel tanks, and the addition of accessories such as hydraulic pumps and generators, which were not mounted on the Avon engine but were integral with the J47. A Plessey propyl nitrate liquid fuel starting system replaced the electric starter of the J47. When the redesign of the fuselage was complete, only the cockpit area, windscreen and canopy remained from the original North American design. The wing used on the prototype aircraft was a standard F-86E/F wing with leading-edge slats, and the flight control system was that developed for the F-86E. The stabiliser/elevator assembly was the North American 'all-flying tail'.

With its crisp and precise handling, the Sabre was an admirable formation aerobatics tool, especially the Orenda-powered Canadair aircraft that had greater thrust. Probably the best known of the Sabre teams was Canada's own 'Golden Hawks', which flew 317 displays between 1959 and 1963 using the Sabre Mk 5. Other Canadian Sabre teams were the 'Prairie Pacific Team' (Cold Lake), the 'Sky Lancers' (No. 2 Fighter Wing, Grostenquin) and the 'Fireballs' (No. 3 Fighter Wing, Soellingen). The last two represented RCAF Europe in the 1954/55 display seasons.

The JRV operated an aerobatic team using CL-13 Sabre Mk 4s which were locally designated F-86E(M). The team's machines were painted in a special blue and yellow scheme.

Sabre aerobatic display teams

CL-13 Mk 4 PANs flew with the Italian 'Frecce Tricolori' team (above left). Other Italian Sabre teams were the 'Lancieri Nero' (below right – 2ª Aerobrigata) and the 'Cavallino Rampante' (above right – 4ª Aerobrigata). Note the underwing smoke generators.

Spain's Ala de Caza 1 established an F-86F team called the 'Ascuas' (Arrowheads). The name was in memory of an Ala 1 pilot, killed in a crash, whose callsign was 'Ascua'.

Above: The 'Sabre Knights' of the 325th FIS (George AFB) were one of the premier US teams. They initially flew the F-86E (illustrated) before transitioning to the F-86D.

Right: Greece's Sabre Mk 5 team (1958-64) was called 'Hellenic Flame'.

Below: Turkey had a Canadair Sabre 2 team, known as the 'White Swans'.

Aussie Sabres

Following the poor performance of the RAAF's Meteors in Korea, Australia eagerly sought the F-86. Moves to obtain F-86Es were replaced by licence-production of the Sabre by the Commonwealth Aircraft Corporation. Some 112 Avon-powered CAC Sabres were built, in four versions.

The prototype CA-26 Avon Sabre, A94-101, was equipped with a slatted wing and a UK-built Avon. It is preserved today at RAAF Pt Cook.

A94-922 was the first production Sabre Mk 31, and it was used to test the de Havilland Firestreak missile at the Woomera range. The missile pack was housed in a ventral fairing.

The CA-27 looked outwardly similar to US or Canadian Sabres but was very different internally. The revised forward fuselage and intake profile was distinctive to the trained eye, but a far more obvious feature was the single 30-mm ADEN cannon in each side of the nose. This is a Sabre Mk 32 with the improved Avon Mk 26 and strengthened wing.

The prototype was designated the CAC CA-26 Sabre. The first aircraft carried the serial A94-101. The initial CA-26 was completed in early July 1953, with ground testing commencing on 20 July. In late July, the CA-26 prototype was disassembled and trucked from the CAC factory at Fishermans Bend in Melbourne to Avalon RAAF Base, where it was reassembled and readied for the first flight. On 3 August 1953, Flight Lieutenant W. Scott took the CA-26 into the air for the first time.

The RAAF placed an initial order for 70 CAC Sabres, the first production types being designated CA-27. The initial 22 CA-27s were further designated as the Mk 30 (serials A94-901/-922). The Mk 30 was identical to the prototype and was powered by imported Avon RA.7 engines. First flight of a production Mk 30 came on 13 July 1954, and the aircraft was delivered to the RAAF on 18 August.

Next off the assembly line were 20 Mk 31s (A94-923/-942), which used the CAC licence-built Avon Mk 20 engine. These aircraft were also the first to be equipped with the '6-3 hard wing' as used on USAF F-86Fs. All previous CA-27 Sabres had the '6-3' wing retrofitted at this time. The 70-US gal (265-litre) leading-edge fuel tanks installed in USAF F-86Fs were tested in A94-938, before being incorporated into the CAC production run and retrofitted to all previous Mk 31 aircraft.

The last 28 aircraft of the original RAAF order were completed as Mk 32s (A94-943/-970), having an improved Avon Mk 26 engine with an anti-surge feature. The Mk 26 engine had an electronically controlled fuel pump tied in to the fire control system, which automatically lowered the amount of fuel whenever the guns were fired. This reduced the possibility of a compressor stall, something well known to the North American engineers who had worked so hard on the Gunval project.

The Mk 32 aircraft had the strengthened '6-3' wing with additional hardpoints for carriage of up to four drop tanks, or a pair of 2,000-lb (907-kg) bombs and two drop tanks, as found on USAF fighter-bomber F-86Fs. An additional 20 Mk 32 aircraft (A94-971/-990), identical to previous Mk 32s, were ordered by the RAAF in July 1957. A final production order was placed in 1959 by the RAAF, for 21 more Mk 32s (A94-351/-371), again being identical to previous Mk 32 aircraft. The last CAC Sabre, A94-371, was delivered to the RAAF on 19 December 1961.

Right: AIM-9-equipped CAC Mk 32 Sabres with the 'dual store' wing rest at Butterworth, Malaysia. This wing modification was retrofitted to earlier aircraft and allowed the carriage of external fuel tanks as well as AAMs.

Below: Mk 32s of the No. 75 Squadron aerobatic team, the 'Black Diamonds', line up at Richmond, NSW in September 1963. Note the external smoke pipe.

Missile fighter

One final modification to the CAC Sabre was the provision to carry the Philco-Ford AIM-9B Sidewinder heat-seeking missile. Combat tested by the National Chinese on their F-86Fs in 1958, the Mach 2.5 AIM-9B was the weapon of choice for most of the air forces of the world, both West and East, for the air-to-air mission. The RAAF had proposed a Sidewinder installation for its Sabres as early as 1956, mounted on a pair of Aero 3B pylons just inboard of the main landing gear.

The first Sidewinder-equipped CAC Sabre, A94-946, was tested in 1959, with the first Sidewinder 'kill', a target drone, coming in November 1959. Operations with No. 78 Fighter Wing at RAAF Butterworth in West Malaya commenced in February 1960. All existing Mk 31 and Mk 32 aircraft were retrofitted with the Sidewinder capability. The addition of the Sidewinder kept the CAC Sabres as a viable air defence weapon into the last half of the 1960s. Top cover for several of the USAF installations in Thailand was flown by RAAF CAC Mk 32 Sabres during the Vietnam War.

CAC built a total of 112 Avon Sabres between 3 August 1953 and December 1961, which equipped six RAAF squadrons: No. 2 OTU, and Nos 3, 75, 76, 77, and 79 Squadrons. The last Avon Sabre was retired from the RAAF on 31 July 1971. That was not the last flight of an operational Avon Sabre, for the first of 18 Mk 32 Sabres were delivered to the Royal Malaysian Air Force in October 1969. In February 1973, the first of 18 Mk 32s were delivered to the Indonesian Air Force, all surplus RAAF aircraft. When the Malaysian Air Force phased the Mk 32 out of service, five of its aircraft were supplied to Indonesia in July 1976. The CAC Sabre, originally just an interim aircraft for the RAAF, thus had a service life in excess of 25 years. **Larry Davis**

Right: CAC Sabres of No. 75 Squadron are seen during Exercise Sea Cobra at Korat, Thailand with French Vautours, RAF Hunters, RAAF Canberras, an RAF Valetta, Thai T-6s and a USAF C-130.

Commonwealth Aircraft Corporation CA-27 Sabre Mk 32 No. 76 Squadron RAAF Williamtown 1963

Smoke system
For use by the squadron display teams, a pipe for adding smoke oil to the jet efflux was routed partly externally along the fuselage, there being little room for it within the crammed rear section of the Avon Sabre.

ingine and fuselage
AAF Sabre Mk 32s were tted with the Avon 26 axial-ow turbojet rated at 7,500 (33.38 kN) thrust at take-ff. A propyl nitrate liquid uel combustion starter eplaced the electric starter f other Sabres.
As with the F-86H, the icorporation of a new ngine (as well as cannon rmament) meant a edesign of the fuselage. he same method as used n the H was used, hereby a fuselage 'splice' vas added. This was 3.73 in .47 cm) deep and ran from ist aft of the intake lip to ne rear end of the clear anopy. Additionally, the uselage break was moved ft and there were odifications to the tailpipe accommodate the horter, wider Avon.Overall here was only 40 per cent uselage commonality etween CAC Sabres and ne F-86F.

National insignia
From 1956 Australian Sabres wore the new kangaroo insignia on the fuselage, with the earlier RAF-style roundel above and below the wings.

In 1960, No. 76 was the fourth RAAF squadron to receive the Sabre, after Nos 75, 3 and 77. The squadron was reformed as part of No. 81 Wing at Williamtown to replace Nos 3 and 77 Squadrons when they were sent to Malaya. No. 76's Sabres were replaced by Mirage IIIs in 1966. During this relatively short period of existence, the squadron formed two aerobatic teams, the 'Black Panthers' (1962) and the 'Red Diamonds' (from 1963). This aircraft is in the markings of the latter team.

nnon
e CAC Sabres had two 30-mm ADEN nnon, each with a capacity of 180 rounds d a rate of fire of 1,200-1,400 rounds per nute. The gun bay and doors were npletely redesigned and the structure from nose to the windscreen arch much engthened. The gun aperture on the totype and many Sabre 30s was shorter d without the aft brace fitted to later craft.

A94-947
Sabre Mk 31 A94-947 was delivered to the RAAF in October 1956. Its career ended when it crashed into the sea off Williamtown in December 1963, one of 19 CAC Sabres that were destroyed in crashes in RAAF service.

Sidewinder
AIM-9B Sidewinder AAMs were fitted to Mk 31 and 32 Sabres from 1960. Two could be carried, although there was a proposal for a four-missile configuration. The DH Firestreak was trialled but rejected for a number of reasons, including the amount of airframe and fire-control system modification needed to make full use of the missile's capabilities.

F-86 Sabre Operators

Four units (4th, 8th, 18th and 51st) eventually flew the Sabre in Korea, all wearing the yellow fuselage identification sash. Karen's Kart, a 25th FIS F-86E-10, was flown by Lt Col Albert Kelly, commander of the 51st FIG. The black checkerboard was adopted by the 51st in mid-1952 to distinguish the unit's aircraft from those of the 4th.

United States of America

F-86A Sabres entered service with the USAF in February 1949, beginning with the 1st Fighter Groups at March AFB, followed by the 4th and 33rd groups. The 4th Fighter Group was dispatched to the Korean War in 1950. F-86Es were initially assigned to these three units, plus the 51st FIG, which became the second Sabre unit in Korea.

The F-86F was also rushed to Korea, to equip the 8th and 18th FBGs, as well as the two fighter units. Other Fs entered service with CONUS-based fighter-bomber units, and also became the mainstay of USAFE, where some units had a tactical nuclear role.

Several ADC squadrons flew day-fighter Sabres, but the primary version in service was the radar-equipped F-86D and F-86L modification, which was compatible with the SAGE system.

F-86Hs were assigned to a few active-duty fighter-bomber wings, including one in Europe, but mostly to the Air National Guard, which flew the last operational USAF Sabre sortie in 1970.

United States Air Force

The following is a list of active-duty Sabre units with details of variants flown.

F-86A wings
1st FIW, 4th FIW, 23rd FIW, 33rd FIW, 56th FIW, 81st FIW

F-86E wings
1st FIW, 4th FIW, 33rd FIW, 51st FIW, 56th FIW

F-86F wings – TAC or US-based
322nd FBW, 366th FBW, 401st FBW, 450th FBW, 474th FBW, 479th FBW

F-86F wings – USAFE
21st FBW, 36th FDW, 48th FBW, 50th FBW, 86th FBW, 388th FBW, 406th FBW, 81st FBW (78th TFS only)

F-86F wings – FEAF
4th FIW, 8th FBW, 18th FBW, 35th FIW, 49th FBW, 51st FIW, 58th FBW, 67th TRW (15th TRS with RF-86A and RF-86F)

F-86H wings
50th FBW, 83rd FBW, 312th FBW, 413th FBW, 474th FBW

Independent squadrons – SAC
720th FBS (F-86F), 497th FIS (F-86D)

Independent squadrons – USAFE
45th FDS (F-86F), 357th FIS (F-86D and F), 431st FIS (F-86D), 461st FBS (F-86F), 525th FIS (F-86D), 526th FIS (F-86D)

F-86D squadrons – FEAF
4th FIS, 16th FIS, 25th FIS, 26th FIS, 39th FIS, 40th FIS, 41st FIS, 68th FIS, 339th FIS

Air Defense Command squadrons
2nd FIS (F-86A and D), 5th FIS (F-86D), 11th FIS (F-86D and L), 13th FIS (F-86D and L), 14th FIS (F-86D and L), 15th FIS (F-86A, D and L), 18th FIS (F-86A and F), 31st FIS (F-86D), 37th FIS (F-86D), 42nd FIS (F-86D and L), 45th FIS (F-86F, then to USAFE), 47th FIS (F-86F, D and L), 49th FIS (F-86F, D and L), 54th FIS (F-86D), 56th FIS (F-86F, D and L), 60th FIS (F-86A, E and D), 62nd FIS (F-86A, D and L), 63rd FIS (F-86A, F, D and L), 71st FIS (F-86A, D and L), 74th FIS (F-86A and E), 75th FIS (F-86A, E and D), 82d FIS (F-86D), 83rd FIS (F-86D), 84th FIS (F-86F), 85th FIS (F-86D and L), 86th FIS (F-86D), 87th FIS (F-86D), 93rd FIS (F-86A, E, D and L), 94th FIS (F-86A,E, D and L), 95th FIS (F-86D and L), 97th FIS (F-86A, E and D), 318th FIS (F-86D), 322d FIS (F-86D and L), 323rd FIS (F-86D), 324th FIS (F-86D and L, then to USAFE), 325th FIS (F-86E and D), 326th FIS (F-86D), 327th FIS (F-86D), 329th FIS (F-86D and L), 330th FIS (F-86A, F, D and L), 331st FIS (F-86D and L), 332nd FIS (F-86D and L), 337th FIS (F-86D and L), 354th FIS (F-86D and L), 413th FIS (F-86D), 432nd FIS (F-86F and D), 440th FIS (F-86D then to USAFE), 44th FIS (F-86D and L), 445th FIS (F-86D), 456th FIS (F-86D and L), 460th FIS (F-86D), 465th FIS (F-86D), 469th FIS (F-86A and D), 496th FIS (F-86D then to USAFE), 497th FIS (F-86D then to SAC), 498th FIS (F-86D), 518th FIS (F-86D), 519th FIS (F-86D), 520th FIS (F-86D), 538th FIS (F-86D and L), 539th FIS (F-86F, D and L)

In addition to these units there were many second-line users, trials units and training organisations, notably the Fighter School at Nellis AFB, Nevada.

Sabre advanced training was carried out at Las Vegas AFB (now Nellis AFB). The Fighter School taught air-to-air and air-to-ground gunnery. This F-86A has wing racks fitted.

***Below:** Sweet Mudder was the personal mount of the commander of the 329th FIS at George AFB, 1958. The 329th was assigned to the Los Angeles Air Defense Sector, covering southern California's aircraft plants.*

Not a camouflaged USAF F-86 variant, but an ex-RAF Canadair Sabre Mk 4 seen en route to the Yugoslavian air force, via Dübendorf, Switzerland, where the aircraft was reputedly test flown. During delivery these machines were known as F-86E(M)s and displayed their RCAF serial numbers and a spurious USAF 'buzz number', in this case FU-494 (from RCAF 19494).

One of two authorised USAF Sabre display teams, the 'Skyblazers' flew F-86Fs with the 48th FBW from Chaumont AB, France. This F-86F-35 is seen at Orly during the 1955 Paris Air Salon.

United States Navy

US naval use of the Sabre began in 1970/71 when the Navy bought the first of around 200 ex-ANG H-models (reputedly for $2 each!). A number were assigned to VX-4 'Evaluators' at NAS Point Mugu (and later at China Lake) for use as aggressor aircraft simulating MiG-17s, but plans to introduce the type into the 'Top Gun' programme were foiled by parts support problems and the H model's unreliable ejection seat. Other USN Sabre operation has been largely confined to the service's drone programme. Flying from the Naval Air Warfare Center Weapons Divisions at China Lake and Point Mugu, the Sabre has been one of the Navy's main pilotless drone types used in the testing of air-to-air missiles. The balance of the F-86Hs were used initially and retained provision for a pilot. However, by the early 1990s drone operations were carried out using at least 50 QF-86Fs converted from ex-RoKAF and ex-JASDF aircraft. They carried their former US DoD serial numbers.

United States Army

Flight Systems Incorporated undertook the conversion of Canadair-built Sabres for the Army's drone programme testing ground-based air defence systems. Designated QF-86Es, these aircraft were operated over the White Sands missile range from nearby Holloman AFB, New Mexico. They were often fitted with external jamming pods.

Seen at Mojave in October 1984, Sabre Mk 5 23331, stripped of its paint but still showing evidence of its previous RCAF ownership, awaits delivery to the US Army and a likely violent end as a target on the Army's White Sands, NM range.

Many ex-Air National Guard F-86Hs ended their lives in the US Navy's drone programme as QF-86Hs. This example is seen at China Lake in April 1974. The China Lake Sabre unit was nicknamed the 'Polish Air Force'.

Air National Guard

National Guard use of the Sabre began during the Korean War, when three Guard units (116th, 126th, 148th) were equipped with F-86As and the 123rd FS with F-86Fs for active duty in the US and Europe. Mainstream ANG use of the air superiority variants (F-86A/E/F) began in the November 1953 when the 186th FIS, Montana ANG was equipped, and ended in 1960. Thirty-one squadrons were equipped, as follows:

104th MD (1955-1957), 107th MI (1955-1956), 113th IN (1956-1958), 115th CA (1955-1960), 116th WA (1951-1952 and 1954-1955), 119th NJ (1955-1958), 120th CO (1958-1960), 121st DC (1954-1957), 123rd OR (1952 and 1953-1955), 126th WI (1951-1952 and 1953-1954), 141st NJ (1955-1958), 142nd DE (1954-1958), 144th AK (1955-1957), 152nd AZ (1956-1957), 156th NC (1954-1959), 163rd IN (1955-1958), 165th KY (1956-1958), 170th IL (1953-1955), 171st MI (1955-1956), 172nd MI (1954-1955), 176th WI (1953-1954), 186th MT (1953-1956), 190th ID (1953-1955), 191st UT (1955-1958), 192nd NV (1955-1958), 194th CA (1954-1958), 195th CA (1955-1960),196th CA (1954-1958), 197th AZ (1953-1957), 198th PR (1954 1958) and 199th HI (1954-1958)

The ground-attack F-86H was a longer-lived version in ANG service. From 1957, 14 squadrons were equipped with the type, the last relinquishing their H models as late as 1970. The following ANG squadrons flew the F-86H:

101st MA (1958-1964), 104th MD (1957-1970), 118th CT (1957-1959), 119th NJ (1962-1964), 121st DC (1957-1960), 131st MA (1958-1964), 136th NY (1957-1960), 137th NY (1958-1961), 138th NY (1957-1970), 139th NY (1957-1970), 141st NJ (1962-1964), 142nd DE (1958-1962), 167th WV (1957-1961) and 198th PR (1960-1967)

Radar-equipped interceptor Sabres (the F-86D and F-86L) equipped 26 fighter interceptor units between August 1956 and May 1965. Florida's 159th FIS was the first unit to receive D models; California's 196th FIS was the last ANG unit with F-86Ls. The full list of 'Sabre Dog' Guard units is as follows:

141th TX (1957-1960), 120th CO (1960-1961), 122nd LA (1957-1960), 124th IA (1958-1962), 125th OK (1957-1960), 127th KS (1958-1961), 128th GA (1960-1961), 133rd NH (1958-1960), 146th PA (1957-1960), 147th PA (1958-1961), 151st TN (1957-1960), 156th NC (1959-1960), 157th SC (1958-1960), 159th FL (1956-1960), 173rd NE (1957-1964), 181st TX (1957-1964), 182nd TX (1957-1960), 185th OK (1958-1961), 187th WY (1958-1961), 190th ID (1959-1964), 191st UT (1958-1961), 192nd NV (1958-1961), 194th CA (1958-1964), 196th CA (1958-1965), 197th AZ (1957-1960), 198th PR (1958-1960) and 199th HI (1958-1961)

In the autumn of 1958, the 101st TFS, the so-called 'Irish Guard', received F-86Hs, flown by the unit until March 1964. This aircraft, an F-86H-10 serialled 53-1515, was the CO's aircraft.

Right: An Idaho ANG (190th FIS) F-86A formates with an RCAF Vampire F.Mk 3 of No. 442 (City of Vancouver) Squadron, some time in the early 1950s. The 190th FS operated the A model for just over a year.

Left: Two units assigned to the Texas ANG flew the F-86L – the 181st FIS from June 1959 and the 182nd FIS from early 1958. Here 53-0766 is seen with its 'Mighty Mouse' pack lowered.

National Air and Space Administration

NASA and its predecessor, NACA, operated various Sabres over the years. Those which were assigned NASA/NACA numbers were F-86A (136) and JF-86Ds (204 and 205) at Langley, Virginia, while Ames (at Moffett Field) operated F-86As (116 and 135), YF-86D (149), F-86D (216), F-86E (157 – variable stability tests between 1955 and 1959), F-86F (228) and YF-93s (139 and 151). Additional Sabres were temporarily assigned but remained on USAF charge. The latter category included two F-86Fs used by Dryden (at Edwards AFB) for pitch-up research in 1954.

F-86F NASA 228 was assigned to the Ames Laboratory at Moffett Field to investigate phenomena in the transonic and supersonic speed ranges. Armament was removed and the '6-3' wing fitted during these tests in the early 1960s.

Many a publicity photograph of the first flight of a new Boeing airliner also featured Canadair Sabre Mk 5/6 N8686F. Boeing flew the aircraft as a chase machine between 1974 and 1991, when it was donated to the Museum of Flight, Seattle.

Civil operators

Tracor Flight Systems Incorporated (previously Flight Systems Inc.) has been associated with Sabres for some years. Flight Systems was engaged in the conversion of Canadair Sabres to QF-86E drone standard for the US Army from 1975. Other aircraft entered service with the company's trials fleet, performing such roles as target-towing. In 1997, TFSI operated five Sabres in its trials fleet. They were two ex-RCAF Mk 5s (one acquired in 1976, the other in 1981), an ex-RCAF Mk 6 (1983) and two former Luftwaffe Mk 6s (1979), one of which has also served with the SAAF.

The Boeing Company was a long-time user of civilian Sabres, obtaining an ex-RCAF Mk 5 in late 1962. Registered N8686F, it notably flew chase on the first flights of both the B.737 and the B.747. Sold to Flight Systems in 1974, it was replaced by another ex-RCAF Mk 5 upgraded to Mk 6 standard with an Orenda 14. Also registered N8686F, this machine served until 1991. Lockheed Aircraft Corporation is also known to have operated a Sabre chase aircraft.

The Sabre has also become popular among the warbird fraternity, with about 50 airworthy aircraft in the US and more under restoration. The fliers include single examples of the A, D, E, H and L, and 11 Fs. The remainder are CL-13s. Outside of the US there are two flying Sabres: an F-86A in the UK and a CA-27 Mk 32 in Australia.

N860AG (52-4666) is one of the few F-86Fs restored to flight. This aircraft served with Venezuela and Bolivia before recovery by Dixie Air Parts of San Antonio. Many ex-USAF aircraft had their spars broken on retirement.

Above: Tracor Flight Systems still flies five Sabre Mk 5s (illustrated) and 6s from Mojave.

Below: Four Sabres were gathered for the USAF's 50th anniversary air show at Nellis AFB in 1997.

Argentina

Fuerza Aérea Argentina

Twenty-eight F-86F-30s were delivered to the FAA in 1960 (under Operation Sabre) after an attempt to buy Canadair aircraft came to nought. They were modified to F-40 standard and were operated by three squadrons with nine aircraft each. From their El Plumerillo base, FAA Sabres saw action assisting in foiling an attempted *coup* in April 1962. Retirement was planned for the late 1970s, when the last 12 or so were offered to Venezuela and Uruguay; both deals fell through. The unsold aircraft were then returned to service, initially with Escuadrón de Caza-Bombardero I of Grupo I de Caza-Bombardero. At the time of the Falklands War trials were conducted to ascertain whether the Sabres could be operated from Port Stanley, but this proved impractical. Sixteen aircraft were lost in operational accidents. In June 1986, a fatigue-related fatal accident led to the grounding of the last FAA aircraft, on 3 July.

***Above:** FAA Sabres were serialled C-101 to C-128 and were initially unpainted.*

***Right:** Aircraft were camouflaged prior to the aborted sale to Venezuela. Surviving FAA F-86s re-entered service in 1982.*

Australia

Royal Australian Air Force

Having failed to secure NAA-built Sabres for use in Korea, the RAAF looked to CAC, which proposed an Avon-engined F-86F to be known as the CA-26 Sabre. Only one CA-26 was built; production aircraft were designated CA-27. The RAAF received its first Sabre on 18 August 1954 (in all, 111 production Sabres were built). It was delivered to the Sabre Trials Flight of No. 2 OTU (the flight was renamed No. 2 OCU in 1958) at Williamtown and was followed by Nos 3 (from March 1956), 75 (April 1955), 76 (1960), 77 (November 1956) and 79 Squadrons (May 1962). From 1958, three of these units served in Malaya, while No. 79 flew the type from Ubon AB, Thailand during the Vietnam War. The last RAAF Sabres were retired by No. 5 OCU on 31 July 1971. A number were sold to the air forces of Indonesia and Malaysia, one of the latter's aircraft (A94-983) later returning to Australia where it is now a member of the RAAF Historic Flight.

***Left:** No. 76 Sqn's 'Red Diamonds' display team was equipped with Sabre Mk 32s from 1962.*

***Above:** No. 78 Wg Sabres were based at Butterworth, Malaysia as part of Australia's SEATO commitment.*

Bangladesh

Bangladesh Defence Forces/Bangladesh Biman Bihani

After the 24-Day War of December 1971, the BDF/BBB salvaged five Sabre Mk 6s abandoned by the retreating Pakistan Air Force. With help from defecting PAF personnel, they were made airworthy and flown from Tezgaon. After MiGs were delivered in 1973, a lack of spare parts led to the Sabres' withdrawal later in the year.

Presumably taken in 1973, this view shows four of Bangladesh's five Sabres with new MiG-21s.

***Above and below:** Ten serial numbers (650-659) were allocated to the FAB's Sabres, though some sources suggest that nine or 11 aircraft were delivered.*

Belgium

Force Aérienne Belge

Five F-86Fs are known to have been allocated to the FAB in June 1955. Though no trace of these aircraft has been found in Belgian records, it is assumed that they were evaluated by the FAB. Certainly they were never operational; Hawker Hunters and Republic F-84F Thunderstreaks were delivered, instead.

Bolivia

Fuerza Aérea Boliviana

One of the last F-86 operators, the FAB took delivery of the first of about 10 ex-FAV F-86Fs in 1973. They equipped Brigada Aérea 21, Grupo Aéreo de Caza 32 at Santa Cruz. Overhauled in Argentina by FMA, about four survived in 1993.The last examples are believed to have been retired in the early 1990s, making the FAB the last air force to fly F-86s operationally.

Burma

Tamdaw Lay

In 1975, the Tamdaw Lay received 12 ex-Pakistani Sabre Mk 4s. Funding problems led to their withdrawal in the early 1980s.

RCAF Sabres were stationed in Europe from late 1951. Camouflage was applied to these aircraft in 1955. Mk 6 23403 was delivered to No. 413 Squadron in March 1955, and later served with No. 430, with whom it was written off in the following February.

Canada

Royal Canadian Air Force

Canadair built 1,815 CL-13 Sabres, the RCAF's No. 410 Sqn receiving its first examples in April 1951. Eventually four wings were equipped with Sabres; in all, 23 units (including the OTU and the 'Golden Hawks' aerobatic team) operated the type at one time or other. The various marks became operational on the following dates: Mk 2s in May 1951 (350 aircraft in all); Mk 4s in November 1952 (71); Mk 5s in February 1954 (370); Mk 6s in April 1955 (390). The Sabre Transition Unit retired its last aircraft in November 1968, the type being officially phased out on 9 December.

The RCAF's Sabres initially flew in natural metal; this aircraft served with No. 416 Squadron.

Ethiopia

Ye Ityopya Ayer Hayl

A dozen F-86Fs equipped the Imperial Ethiopian Air Force's (IEAF) first interceptor squadron at Debre Zebit from July 1960. Others are believed to have been delivered later, possibly from Iran, bringing total strength to 25 aircraft. Detail regarding retirement dates is sketchy; some sources say the last Ethiopian F-86s had been retired by 1976; others suggest that as many as 12 fought in the 1978/79 war with Somalia. Whether these aircraft served after these dates is unknown; F-86s were noted at Debre Zebit in 1986.

Ethiopia's enigmatic F-86Fs appear to have served in natural metal.

Colombia

Fuerza Aérea Colombiana

Six Canadair Sabre Mk 6s (some sources say Mk 4s; FAC personnel refer to the aircraft as F-86Es) were sold to the FAC in June 1956, with whom they equipped 1º Escuadrón de Caza-Bombardero, replacing F-47D Thunderbolts. In 1963, two ex-EdA F-86Fs arrived as attrition replacements, and the type was finally retired in 1966.

Chile

Fuerza Aérea de Chile

Twenty-five F-86Fs were scheduled to enter FAC service in 1966; they were never delivered.

Sabre 2025 was the fifth of six Canadair Sabres for the FAC.

France

Armée de l'Air

Sixty Fiat-built F-86Ks were delivered to the French between September 1956 and June 1957. Some, if not all, were fitted with Sidewinder launch rails. The first unit to receive the type was ECTT 1/13 'Artois' (initially at Lahr, Germany), followed by ECTT 2/13 'Alpes', both units being based as Colmar. When the former re-equipped with Mirages in 1962, a third Sabre unit was formed, ECTT 3/13 'Auvergne'. Twenty-two aircraft were returned to Italy in July 1962, the final Sabres being retired the following month after further Mirage III deliveries. Most of the remainder were destroyed under the terms of the MAP agreement.

EC 2/13 'Alpes' F-86Ks originally carried '13-Hx' codes, before changing to the '13-Px' series. Part of the aircraft's USAF serial appears on the tailfin.

Denmark

Kongelige Dankse Flyvevabnet

Fifty-nine mainly ex-USAFE F-86Ds were received by the Royal Danish Air Force (RDAF), the first 38 arriving from 26 June 1958, the rest following in 1960. Another three were bought in 1962 as spares sources. Eskadrilles 723, 726 and 728 flew the 'Sabre Dog' until 31 March 1966, surviving airframes then serving as decoys.

Initially, F-86Ds were not available for export under the MAP, given to the sensitive nature of their advanced fire control system. Denmark's F-86Ds were the first examples exported. Martin-Baker ejection seats were fitted.

F-86 Sabre Operators

Greece

Elliniki Polmiki Aeroporia

Ex-RAF Canadair Mk 4s were operated by the EPA from July 1954. The first of about 106 machines equipped No. 341 Squadron; Nos 342 and 343 Squadrons were similarly equipped in 1955. On 12 May 1961, the first of 35 F-86Ds arrived to re-equip No. 343 Squadron, surviving Canadair aircraft going to No. 337 Squadron between 1958 and 1962. In 1966 the Sabre fleet was stored. The D models were operated until 1966/67; a few remained as decoys in 1993.

The exact number of CL-13 Sabres, like this one, delivered to the Royal Hellenic Air Force is unclear.

Below: Greece also acquired ex-USAF F-86Ds, which served with 337 Mira.

Honduras

Fuerza Aérea Hondurena

Honduran Sabres came from various sources. In 1976, eight ex-Yugoslav (originally RAF) Sabre Mk 4s (F-86E(M)s) were supplied, in crates, from Florida. They equipped Escuadrón Sabre and were joined the following year by four ex-USAF F-86Fs. Four (some sources say five) possibly ex-FAV F-86Ks had already been delivered in 1969, though only two were ever considered airworthy. They possibly saw action shortly after the 'Soccer War' of that year, but the K models proved an expensive liability; all were retired in 1980. The other Sabres were still in use in 1986, but were replaced by Super Mystères.

Above: FAH 1101 was the second of the four F-86Ks to arrive from Venezuela in 1969. Their FAH careers appear to have been short and expensive.

FAH 3001 (below right), seen at Key West, Florida finished in an unorthodox colour scheme in July 1976, and 3002 (above), are both Canadair CL-13s.

This TNI-AU CA-27 still carries its RAAF serial number (A94-990) on its tailfin. Note the twin 30-mm ADEN cannon armament.

Indonesia

Tentara Nasional Indonesia-Angkatan Udara

In April 1972, 18 ex-RAAF Commonwealth Aircraft Corporation Sabre Mk 32s were given to the Tentara Nasional Indonesia-Angkatan Udara (TNI-AU). The first arrived in February 1973. Five more ex-Malaysian air force aircraft arrived in 1976, as attrition replacements. All Sabres were initially operated by No. 14 Squadron (renamed SAT SERGAP F-86 Squadron in 1974). The survivors were withdrawn and replaced by A-4s in the 1980s.

Iran

Imperial Iranian Air Force

A number of F-86Fs were flown until the early-1970s. Exact numbers and dates are unknown, though the 'Golden Crown' display team was among the units equipped. Iran is also known to have facilitated the sale of 90 ex-Luftwaffe Sabre Mk 6s to Pakistan (then under a United Nations arms sales embargo) in 1966. These were 'sold' to Iran and delivered, but then left for Pakistan for 'overhaul'. They were never returned.

Seen at Vahoati Air Base in April 1964, this is one of the F-86Fs delivered to the IIAF.

Iraq

Royal Iraqi Air Force

In 1958, five aircraft of a large order of F-86Fs were delivered, but the overthrow of King Faisal II in July saw the US veto further arms sales. Little is known of their service in Iraq; they are believed to have been passed on to Pakistan.

Israel

Heyl Ha'Avir

Israel ordered 24 Sabre Mk 6s in 1955. At least eight were allotted serial numbers; one was painted in Israeli markings. However, the Canadian government halted the deal as a reaction to the Suez Crisis the following year.

Sabre Mk 6 6036 was among the first of 24 aircraft intended for Israel. After the sale was vetoed, it served with No. 434 Squadron, RCAF. The Heyl Ha'Avir purchased Dassault Mystère IVs instead.

Italy

Aeronautica Militare Italiana

The first of 63 Fiat-built F-86Ks for the AMI was delivered in November 1955, equipping 6º, 17º and 23º Gruppi of 1º Stormo, the last being delivered in 1957. (In all 121 Sabres were built by Fiat.) The first of 179 ex-RAF Canadair Sabre Mk 4s were delivered in 1956. Designated F-86E(M), they equipped 20 squadrons within 8º, 9º, 10º, 12º, 13º, 14º Gruppi until 1963. Five AMI Mk 4s served with a UN force in the Congo in 1962, flown by Philippine air force pilots. The F-86Ks were augmented by aircraft from Holland (eight NAA-built F-86Ks) and France (22 Fiat-built F-86Ks) returned in the early 1960s; 12º, 21º and 22º Gruppi of 51ª Aerobrigata were also equipped with this variant. The last AMI Sabre flight (by a 23º Gruppo aircraft) was on 27 July 1973.

Above: Still carrying its USAF serial number, this K model served with 51ª Aerobrigata. The aircraft were allocated AMI 'MM' serial numbers, but they were little used. All examples were eventually modified to carry AIM-9s.

Below: This Sabre Mk 4 (19852) wears the codes of 4ª Aerobrigata and was XB696 in RAF service. The camouflage was as applied by Canadair when new. In Greek service these aircraft were sometimes referred to as F-86E(M)s and also equipped the 'Hellenic Flame' display team between 1958 and 1964.

F-86Fs (including Mitsubishi-built examples like this one) were the mainstay of Japan's fighter force into the 1960s.

Japan

Japanese Air Self-Defence Force

Third largest user of the Sabre, the JASDF flew 480 F-86Fs and 122 F-86Ds. The 135 ex-USAF F models were received between December 1955 and early 1957; most were Korean War veterans and were brought up to F-86F-40 standard, though the last 45 were never flown and were returned to the US, partly due to a JASDF pilot shortage. Mitsubishi went on to build 300 F-86F-40s from 1956 to 1961 and converted 18 additional NAA-built aircraft to RF-86F reconnaissance standard. Hikotais 1 to 10 and the 'Blue Impulse' display team were equipped with F models. Thirty aircraft were 'mothballed' in 1967 and in the late 1970s reinstated, after a major rebuild which included the substitution of a fuselage from a retired aircraft. The F-86Ds were delivered from January 1958, going to Hikotais 101, 102, 103 and 105, serving until October 1968. Retired from front-line units in 1980, the last F-86F was retired in March 1982; many were later returned to the US under the terms of MAP.

Below: Tell-tale fuselage 'bulges' identify this as one of 18 Mitsubishi-modified RF-86Fs which served with the 501st Hikotai.

Below: The 105th Hikotai was one of four all-weather interceptor units established to operate 122 F-86Ds until October 1968.

Malaysia's 10 ex-RAAF CA-27s represented AUS$10 million in aid.

Malaysia

Tentara Udara Diraja Malaysia

CAC found its first foreign recipient for the CA-27 Sabre in the TUDM, which was given 10 Sabre Mk 32s by the Australian government in October 1969. Six more aircraft followed in 1971, along with two non-flying examples for ground instruction. No. 11 Squadron flew the type until 1975/76, when Northrop F-5As were delivered. The Sabres then went to a newly formed No. 12 Sqn which operated them until later in 1976, after which several were sold to Indonesia.

Dutch F-86Ks never carried KLu serials; the 'last three' of their USAF serials were used with a 'Q' prefix. These are No. 700 Sqn aircraft.

Netherlands

Koninklijke Luchtmacht

Delivered by ship between October 1955 and April 1957, the 57 NAA-built F-86Ks were supplemented by six Fiat K models in 1957. Three squadrons were equipped: Nos 700, 701 and 702. In 1960, all were given long-span wings and Sidewinder capability. All were phased out in June 1964, eight aircraft having gone to Italy in 1963.

Norway

Royal Norwegian Air Force

The first Norwegian Sabres were 59 F-86Ks delivered in September 1955 (60 were ordered; one crashed in the US and was not replaced until 1960). A hangar fire in March 1956 claimed four aircraft. They were replaced by four Fiat-built aircraft three months later. The F-86Ks were issued to Nos 337 and 339 Skvadrons and, later, to Nos 332 and 334, replacing F models. The last were retired in July 1967, most being scrapped. From March 1957, the RNoAF replaced its F-84Gs with 90 ex-USAF F-86F-35s (relieved of their nuclear capability). Six attrition replacements, comprising six Fiat-overhauled aircraft and 19 from the US, followed in mid-1960 and January 1961, respectively. All were brought up to F-86F-40 standard and equipped Nos 331, 332, 334, 336 and 338 Skvadrons until March 1966. By then many were grounded by wing fatigue problems. As MAP aircraft some F models were passed on to Saudi Arabia and Portugal.

Below: Norway's K models were committed to the defence of NATO's northern tier until 1966/67. This No. 332 Skvadron aircraft carries AIM-9B Sidewinder rails.

Bottom: No. 336 Skv was among those units to fly the F-86F.

Pakistan

Pakistan Fiza'ya

In 1954, Pakistan began receiving the first of 120 F-86F-40s under the MDAP; the last arrived in 1958 and were the last Sabres built. They served with Nos 5, 11, 14, 15, 16, 17, 18, 19 and 20 Squadrons at different times. Many saw action (and scored aerial victories) in the war with India in September 1965. In 1966, 90 ex-Luftwaffe Canadair Sabre Mk 6s were acquired via Iran (the PAF referred to these aircraft as F-86Es), the combined fleet seeing further action in the 1971 war. The last aircraft were withdrawn in 1980 after a number of fatigue-related accidents.

Above: For the first few years of their service with the Pakistani air force, the F-86Fs remained unpainted.

Above: F-86F-40 55-3854 was built in 1956 and was among the final batch of Sabres built, purely for export.

Below: Sabre Mk 6 1764 was photographed at Masroor in March 1981, shortly after retirement.

Peru

Fuerza Aérea Peruana

The FAP received its first jet aircraft, 15 ex-USAF F-86Fs, from July 1955. Between five and 11 others are believed to have been delivered later. They equipped Escuadrón de Caza 12 (later Grupo de Caza 12) and at least one other unit. Wing spar cracks caused the FAP major problems, and surviving aircraft were replaced in 1979/80 by Sukhoi Su-22s.

Three of the initial batch of 15 F-86Fs are seen in California prior to delivery to the FAP in 1955.

Pilots 'scramble' to their F-86Ds, 20 of which were supplied to equip an all-weather interceptor unit to work with the US Pacific Air Force in defence of Southeast Asia.

Philippines

Philippine Air Force

Between 36 and 40 mainly ex-Taiwanese F-86Fs were acquired from 1957. The 6th, 7th and 9th Tactical Fighter Squadrons were equipped with the type; a fourth all-weather unit was equipped with 20 F-86Ds, a year later. The latter saw just 12 years' service, but the F models were upgraded to F-86F-40 standard and were in use (by the 9th TFS) until at least 1979; some sources suggest that the last three were not withdrawn until 1984.

The Hukbong Himpapawid ng Pilipinas (HHP), as the 'Phil. Air Force' is known locally, flew a mixture of F-86F-25s, -30s and -35s built at North American plants at Inglewood, CA and Columbus, OH.

Portugal

Força Aerea Portuguesa

Fifty F-86Fs were delivered to the FAP in 1958, with 15 ex-Luftwaffe Canadair Sabre Mk 6s following later. Esquadra 51 (and briefly, Esq. 52) operated the type, deploying eight to Portuguese Guinea between 1961 and 1964. All were brought up to F-40 standard, including Sidewinder capability. The last six FAP Sabres were withdrawn in July 1980.

Portuguese F-86Fs, like this example, flew 577 ground-attack and close-support missions over Guinea between 1961 and 1964. Though all the aircraft that took part in these missions were hit by ground fire at one stage or another, none was lost. The last such sortie was flown on 24 October 1964, when FAP T-6 Texans took over the air-to-ground mission.

Rhodesia

Rhodesian Air Force

Rhodesia negotiated the purchase of 28 ex-Venezuelan K models in 1975, but the deal collapsed before any of these aircraft were delivered.

Saudi Arabia

Royal Saudi Air Force

Sixteen ex-USAF F-86Fs were supplied in 1958. Three others (from Norway?) may have been supplied later, though for spares use only. Little use is believed to have been made of the aircraft; some served with No. 7 Squadron, but all were phased out between 1966 and the early 1970s.

Above: F-86F 52-5230 is seen in full RSAF markings, though still carrying its USAF 'buzz' number, in this rare colour air-to-air view.

Below: No. 7 Squadron flew the RSAF's small fleet of F-86Fs from Dhahran during the type's limited service.

South Africa

South African Air Force

Twice operators of the Sabre, the SAAF first employed F-86F-30s during the Korean War, when No. 2 'Cheetah' Squadron (attached to the 18th FBW, USAF) flew 22 examples from January 1953 until the end of the war. Six were written off, the rest going to Taiwan via MAP. In April 1954, 34 Canadair Sabre Mk 6s were bought for service with Nos 1 and 2 Squadrons. Front-line examples were retired in October 1979, and the last examples flew with No. 85 Advanced Flying School in April 1980. Ten were sold to Flight Systems of the US.

Above: One of the USAF F-86Fs loaned to the SAAF in 1953 is seen here in SAAF markings.

Right: Towards the end of their service, the SAAF's Sabre Mk 6s obtained in the mid-1950s were finished in this camouflage scheme.

South Korea

Republic of Korea Air Force

Ex-USAF F-86Fs were supplied to the RoKAF from 1955; about 85 were delivered in all, equipping units of the RoKAF's 10th Wing. Another 27 followed in 1958, around 10 of which were RF-86F aircraft. Other MAP aircraft are also known to have been supplied, including at least one ex-EdA F-86F. Two day fighter wings of three squadrons each were equipped, along with an all-weather unit which flew 40 F-86Ds from November 1960. Remaining D-models had been retired by 1978/79, but at least three F-86Fs survived until 1987.

***Above:** Little RoKAF Sabre unit detail has been released. Towards the end of the type's career, in the late 1980s, plans existed to convert a number into cruise missiles.*

***Below:** Its afterburner alight, this RoKAF J47-GE-33-engined F-86D-50 'Sabre Dog' is about to hurtle skyward. The D models were retired in the late 1970s.*

Spain

Ejército del Aire

The EdA took delivery of 270 F-86Fs from 1955 to equip three wings, each with three squadrons of 25 aircraft. All remaining aircraft were brought up to F-86F-40 standard by CASA. The last examples were withdrawn on 31 December 1974, and a few remain as range targets.

F-86Fs were known as C.5s to the EdA. This C.5, at the Museo del Aire at Cuarto Vientos, wears the colours of the EdA's 'Ascuas' display team.

Taiwan

Chinese Nationalist Air Force

Among the 320 F-86Fs handed over to the CNAF from November 1954 were a number of famous ex-USAF Korean War veterans. Some of these aircraft were to see further action against Chinese MiG-17s during the 1958 Formosa Crisis, in which 29 MiGs were claimed shot down. All these aircraft had the '6-3 hard wing' but were converted to F-86F-40 standard. One hundred were still in service in 1977, this total possibly including approximately 15 F-86Ds delivered later. Two reserve units may have flown Sabres into the 1980s. Seven RF-86Fs were also delivered in the 1950s.

CNAF F-86Fs are seen getting airborne from Clark AFB in the Philippines in 1961. Taiwan's Sabres were among the few examples to see combat twice in their careers in the service of different countries.

Thailand

Royal Thai Air Force

From 1961, 40 F-86Fs were supplied to equip three squadrons, including Nos 13 and 43 Squadrons. The RTAF also took delivery of the only exported F-86Ls, 15 (some sources say 20) being supplied in 1964 for No. 12 Sqn. The F models were retired in 1966, the F-86Ls in 1976.

***Right:** This RTAF F-86L, among the only examples of this variant exported, served with No. 12 Squadron from 1964. They were replaced by F-5s in the mid-1970s.*

***Left:** No. 43 Squadron markings are carried by this F-86F. Others served with No. 13 Squadron. Survivors are believed to have been in use as airfield decoys in the early 1990s.*

Turkey

Turk Hava Kuvvetleri

Four Sabre variants have equipped THK units. In July 1954 the first of 102 Canadair Sabre Mk 2s was delivered. They were later augmented by 12 ex-USAF F-86Fs as attrition replacements. Units so-equipped were Nos 141, 142 and 143 Squadrons, the last Mk 2s/F models being retired in 1966. Up to 50 D models and 40 K models, drawn from ex-Netherlands stocks, followed in the early 1960s. The last Turkish Sabres were retired in 1969.

Tunisia

Armée de l'Air Tunisien

Tunisia's air force acquired jet combat aircraft only nine years after it was established – 15 ex-USAF F-86F Sabres (some sources say 12) in 1969, for use as fighter-bombers. All were replaced in 1978, though rumours suggested that 12 more were delivered from the US in 1983.

Despite direct support from Canadair, the THK suffered major spares shortages from the late 1950s. This Sabre Mk 2 (F-86E(M)) is seen soon after delivery in the mid-1950s.

This F-86D-35 appears to carry the tail badge of the 44th Tactical Fighter Squadron and has an AIM-9 Sidewinder launch rail fitted.

United Kingdom

Royal Air Force

In October 1952 the RAF took delivery of its first swept-wing fighters, three Canadair Mk 2s loaned for pilot conversion prior to the delivery of the first of 428 Sabre Mk 4s from December (438 were to have entered RAF service, but 71 were loaned to the RCAF, 10 of which were written-off in accidents). In all, 13 squadrons were equipped with the Sabre, the first of which, No. 67 Squadron, was operational from May 1953. Other units were Nos 3, 4, 20, 26, 71, 93, 112, 130 and 234 Squadrons based in Germany, Nos 66 and 92 in the UK and No. 229 OCU, as well as various training and test establishments. By May 1956, all had been withdrawn. Many went to Italy and Yugoslavia; one (XB982) went to Bristol Siddeley as an Orpheus engine testbed.

***Left:** Sabre F.Mk 4 XB813/M is seen while on strength with No. 229 Operational Conversion Unit.*

***Lower left:** These No. 112 Squadron Sabre Mk 4s wear the unit's famous wartime shark-mouth marking. The lead aircraft, XB978/N, later served with the air forces of Italy, Yugoslavia and Honduras.*

Uruguay

Fuerza Aérea Uruguaya

Twelve ex-Argentinian F-86Fs were to be delivered to the Fuerza Aérea Uruguaya in late 1976, but the US State Department vetoed the sale.

Venezuela

Fuerza Aérea Venezolana

Thirty ex-USAF F-86Fs were delivered between October 1955 and December 1960, in three batches, for Escuadrón de Caza 36 and, possibly, EdC 37 and 38. Fifty-one Fiat-built ex-Luftwaffe F-86Ks were delivered by sea in 1966. Some went to EdC 34 and 35, but about 19 remained in storage and never flew. (Four were sold to Honduras in 1969.) All had long-span wings and Sidewinder capability. (Some sources suggest that the number delivered was 70; others suggest 74, the balance being made up of NAA-built K models.) The F-86Fs were retired 1971, nine going to Bolivia; the F-86Ks were withdrawn in the early 1970s.

***Right:** The FAV's F-86Ks proved a maintenance headache; in service they wore this light grey overall.*

***Below right:** Four F-86Fs, like this one, joined an attempted coup on 1 January 1958 in which they strafed the presidential palace at Miraflores.*

***Above:** JG 74 briefly operated Sabre Mk 6s during 1960/61 before taking over JG 75's F-86Ks. Initially natural metal, all were camouflaged after 1961.*

***Left:** Now retired to the Deutsches Museum, KE-105 first flew in January 1958. The 'KE' code indicated use by Messerschmitt as a trials and chase plane.*

West Germany

Luftwaffe

The first of 75 ex-RCAF Sabre Mk 5s were operational from 18 December 1957. From 1959, 226 Mk 6s entered service. One of the principal operators of the type, the Luftwaffe took delivery of 88 Fiat-built F-86Ks, beginning in January 1957. Three wings of CL-13s and two squadrons of F-86Ks were eventually equipped, though a number of the latter remained stored until 1960; some never flew in West German service. In 1962, all were equipped with Martin-Baker ejection seats and were made Sidewinder capable. The K models were retired in 1966; 51 (including some stored examples) were sold to the FAV. The Sabre Mk 5s were retired in March 1962,.and most were scrapped. In December 1966, the Sabre Mk 6s followed suit. Ninety Mk 5s and 6s were then sold to Pakistan, via Iran, and another 50 were sold to Portugal. Between December 1966 and April 1974, Condor Flugdienst flew Mk 6s as target tugs.

Yugoslavia

Jugoslavensko Ratno Vazduhplovstvo

Another user of ex-Royal Air Force Sabre Mk 4s, the JRV took delivery of 121 aircraft from 1956. After overhaul in the UK these aircraft were known as F-86E(M)s. In 1961, about 130 ex-USAF D models were supplied, and served until around 1980. The ex-RAF aircraft were replaced in the mid-1970s.

A camouflaged F-86D (above) is seen banking on the approach to its base. The first JRV F-86E(M)s (right) were delivered in RAF camouflage; later, they were finished in natural metal.

FACs

Forward Air Control in Southeast Asia

Above: An OV-10A of the 19th TASS at Bien Hoa lets loose smoke rockets at a VC target near Lai Khe in South Vietnam in late 1969. The Bronco could carry four rocket pods or cannon pods in addition to machine-guns built into its sponsons.

Above left: The FAC's job was mostly a lonely one. For the O-1 pilot, it meant circling the battlefield for hours in an unarmoured, underpowered light plane, talking to two or three allied units at once and calling down the application of force on an enemy that was often in very close proximity to friendly troops.

The role of Forward Air Controller in the Vietnam War grew from the relatively primitive techniques of World War II and Korea to become a sophisticated, highly co-ordinated operation using purpose-built aircraft. The FAC's life had less glamour and more danger than that faced by the actual combat pilots he controlled.

Manoeuvring a Cessna O-1 Bird Dog at treetop level under hostile fire was not a job that drew a vast number of volunteers in the US Air Force, or any other military service. Being a FAC (forward air controller) meant living under primitive conditions, facing almost as much risk as an infantryman while on the ground, and confronting more risk than a fighter pilot while in the air. As the US became more deeply embroiled in its Vietnam adventure, the fighting intensified. FACs added the Cessna O-2 Skymaster and North American OV-10 Bronco to their arsenal, expanded the fighting to Laos and North Vietnam, and established a tradition of courage and duty.

FACs went to the middle of pitched engagements between opposing ground forces. They provided surveillance over assigned areas and, when no fight was going on, became adept at spotting anything unusual. Once an area of known enemy activity had been identified by visual or radio reports, the FAC called upon attack weapons, typically artillery, helicopter gunships, or fighter ground-attack aircraft. The FAC marked enemy positions using smoke rockets and gave corrections by radio to pinpoint attacks. Once the attack had been completed, the FAC observed the effect, often at low level with bullets flying, and radioed the results back.

The allied nations fighting in Vietnam approached the FAC mission differently – the US Air Force, Army, Marine Corps and Navy as well as Australia, New Zealand and South Vietnam itself all had FACs – but all had to learn as they went along, often at considerable price. The USAF provided the bulk of forward air controllers throughout the war. Most FACs also pulled duty as air liaison officers (ALOs) on the ground, operating with infantry troops at forward locations.

FAC genesis

In 1961, a study of the Vietnamese Air Force (VNAF) revealed that there was no system for directing or controlling air strikes. As a result, a system was established for control of tactical air in 'small war operations' – the size Americans

What the FAC's job was all about: F-100Ds streak past an L-19. The 'fast movers' did what the man in the Bird Dog said, but with a difference in cruising speed of nearly 500 mph (810 km/h), everyone had to have their wits about them to avoid collisions.

expected the Vietnam War to remain – along lines developed by the Air Ground Operations School at Keesler AFB, Mississippi. On 30 December 1961, Thirteenth Air Force at Clark Field, Philippines, which was then in charge of US involvement in Vietnam, drew up a plan that created an air operations centre and called for the assignment of forward air controllers. The air operations centre became operational at Tan Son Nhut airfield, outside Saigon, on 14 January 1962, manned by USAF and VNAF personnel. For a time, a small number of USAF personnel flew Cessna L-19 Bird Dogs borrowed from the VNAF. The L-19 was redesignated O-1 on 1 October 1962.

Forward air control in Vietnam began in earnest with the USAF decision to send American men and aircraft to support Saigon's embattled government during the 1961-63 Kennedy administration. A handful of pilots trained as FACs were sent to Vietnam on 2 February 1962 in a deployment that was initially known as Jungle Jim, and later as Farm Gate. These men helped spot targets in North American T-28 fighter-bombers that were among the first USAF aircraft to reach Southeast Asia. O-1 Bird Dogs followed. It appears that about a dozen Bird Dogs were acquired on an informal basis by the USAF prior to 1963, when it received 22 ex-Army ships designated O-1F.

The US Army began flying FAC missions and training the Vietnamese to do the same. However, a strong sentiment developed 'in country' to turn this mission over to the US Air Force which had done the job in the 1950-53 Korean conflict.

It was probably Captain Douglas K. Evans, the first American FAC, who devised the rocket launcher for smoke rockets on the Bird Dog. Various methods of marking a target were debated, and different ones were used at times, including grenades that emitted coloured smoke and magnesium parachute flares, but the 2.75-in rocket projectile with a 3.5-in white phosphorus warhead became standard.

With the Vietnam build-up, hundreds of Korean War-era O-1 Bird Dogs were recalled from the Reserves and National Guard units, flown to Wichita for modernisation, and then taken by cargo plane to Vietnam. Here, forward air control (FAC) tactics were refined.

Though FAC duty was initially the job of US Army and Vietnamese Air Force (VNAF) Bird Dogs, the US Air Force took over the mission. On 17 June 1963, the first USAF FAC squadron was activated at Bien Hoa air base under Lieutenant Colonel John J. Wilfong. The 19th TASS initially had just four Cessna O-1A Bird Dogs, although strength rose to 22 aircraft by September, when a FAC training centre was set up at Nha Trang. At this juncture, the myth was being maintained that Americans in Vietnam were functioning as 'advisers', and the rules of engagement required Vietnamese markings and a Vietnamese crew member on any aircraft that performed actual FAC duties in a combat situation. More than one American flew with a Vietnamese whom he grabbed at random ("the houseboy in our barracks, anybody," one American said) or who was asleep – although it was difficult to remain asleep after the target-spotting action began.

Soldier spotters

US Army forward air controllers, also flying Bird Dogs, remember that their rules were different. At no time did soldiers find themselves required to have a 'token' Vietnamese observer onboard, nor were they cautioned to be defensive unless fired upon. The Army was still getting accustomed to the helicopter at the start of the 1960s – it had been slow to do so – and made less than fully effective use of its formidable fleet of light, fixed-wing aircraft, some of which were in temporary storage. To meet demands of the growing commitment to Vietnam, O-1s were pulled from storage, spruced up, and shipped to Saigon.

American soldiers were busily introducing the Bird Dog to their ARVN (Army of Vietnam, i.e., South Vietnam) allies and were using the aircraft in its traditional role as an artillery spotter and observation ship. More than

By 1964, when this picture was taken, US FAC pilots were an established part of the scene. Burt Lassman was a FAC for Special Forces flying an O-1, nominally belonging to the VNAF. His personal weapon is a vintage M3 'grease gun'.

Three L-19s of the 3rd GAO (Group, Artillery Observation) at Da Nang cruise off the coast of South Vietnam in the 1961-62 period. This unit was later designated the 114th Observation Squadron.

50 Army O-1 Bird Dogs were in South Vietnam in 1963 when the service had only 6,000 personnel there.

The US Army had employed the O-1D (TL-19D) Bird Dog as a fixed-wing trainer. By 1964, it was discontinuing this type of flight instruction and was returning O-1Ds to Cessna for modification and onward shipment to Vietnam.

The Army Bird Dogs were modified with two underwing bomb racks under each wing, giving the aircraft the capability (just as on Air Force O-1F models) to carry up to eight smoke rockets. In May 1963, the 73rd Aviation Company under Major John S. Kark took these aircraft to Vietnam. They were shipped by sea and reassembled by Air Vietnam civilian workers at Tan Son Nhut airfield near Saigon. The 73rd flew over 30,000 combat hours during its first year in Vietnam and attained a 'mission capable' rate of 93 per cent. Army pilots served as FACs, among other duties, until the USAF took over the FAC mission in Vietnam in the late 1960s – at which time the USAF acquired the O-1D airframes, too.

The US Army also operated E model Bird Dogs, some of which eventually reached the USAF. These aircraft were updated at the factory with armoured pilot seats that were retrofitted to other Bird Dogs in the field. Thereafter, the Army retained a number of in-country O-1s, primarily for the artillery observation (AO) role, directing artillery fire from fire support bases and providing liaison support for scattered Special Forces outposts.

In a bizarre incident on 19 March 1964, two Cambodian T-28s shot down a USAF O-1F and killed its pilot, USAF Captain Uwe-Thorsten Scobel – perhaps the only aerial victory for a T-28 and the only air-to-air loss of a Bird Dog.

Tough job

The mission of the FACs was to find targets and mark them with smoke rockets for attention by fighters or ground fire. The work was risky, especially in those early years when the lightweight Bird Dog was the only mount provided. It was generally agreed that the degree of risk was directly proportional to the aggressive spirit of the FAC pilot involved.

Originally, all Air Force FACs were fighter-qualified pilots. Later in the war, there were two categories, informally dubbed A-FACs and B-FACs, the latter employed as SCARs (strike control and reconnaissance). "A lot of very junior people controlled more ordnance than a lot of generals did," remembers Lieutenant Colonel Bob Kirkwood of the FAC's duties. "Permission to expend ordnance in-country had to come from a FAC. The bad guys knew that if a FAC didn't see them, they wouldn't get bombs down on their heads. If they didn't think we saw them, they wouldn't shoot at us. But when they did, all hell broke loose." Kirkwood also remembered that – in contrast to his experience flying fast jets – "the hardest part of the job was FAC procedures – reading the map, talking the right lingo on the radio with the Army, and stuff like that."

'Mac the FAC'

Major William McAllister, soon known as 'Mac the FAC', was bolder than most when he

Above: About 20 L-19s had been supplied to the VNAF in 1954 and used by 3 GAOs. Note the twin rocket tubes on this 1961-62 view.

Below: By May 1966, when this picture was taken at Phan Thiet, the L-19 had become the O-1 and nearly 90 more had been delivered to the VNAF.

Above: The 19th TASS was the first 'official' USAF FAC squadron, and for a time applied this rather outrageous visage to its O-1Es. Note the camera-wielding observer in his cramped rear-seat position.

Below: A pilot of the 19th TASS, Captain Ken Hugley, discusses the location of suspected VC positions with an ARVN officer, possibly his observer, March 1966. The 19th's main base was Bien Hoa near Saigon.

began flying in 1964, assigned to the 22nd ARVN Division. McAllister earned a reputation for spotting Viet Cong efforts at concealment – about 60 per cent of a FAC's time was spent reconnoitring to find the enemy, including the tactic of using foliage to disguise infantrymen as 'walking trees'.

On 25 March 1965, McAllister covered a detachment of Vietnamese Marines pinned down in a narrow valley surrounded by 3,000-ft (914-m) mountains some 50 miles (80 km) north of Qui Nhon. In marginal weather with a ceiling lowering from 1,200 ft (365 m), 'Mac the FAC' endured heavy fire from small-arms and automatic weapons to direct a series of attacks by A-1E Skyraiders against Viet Cong troops, enabling the ARVN Marines to gain their objective. McAllister remained in the area, a target for enemy gunners, while a helicopter from Qui Nhon evacuated two US Marine advisors who had been wounded. Low on fuel and with engine problems McAllister finally limped home. He was later awarded the Air Force Cross for the mission.

Above: A pair of 19th TASS O-1Es, both wearing the 'dog mouth' insignia, get airborne from Phu Cat in February 1966. The 19th were then attached to the Army's 1st Cavalry Division.

That night, after dark, the ARVN Marines again called for help. Grabbing the first in-commission Bird Dog he could find, McAllister headed back to the scene, flying under a low overcast that extended up to 8,500 ft (2590 m). After finding the valley, which was barely wide enough for tight 360° turns, he called for flares. The assigned C-123 Provider flare ship could not enter the valley under a 500-ft (152-m) ceiling. McAllister told the C-123's pilot to climb above the overcast and drop from 10,000 ft (3048 m) using a radar fix from Pleiku. When

Cessna O-1 Bird Dog

The high-wing, fixed-gear Bird Dog eventually became the symbol of all forward air control operations in Vietnam, but when FAC pilot Stokes Tomlin first saw the aircraft, he thought it was "decidedly a down-scale experience from flying an F-100." Tomlin later warmed to the O-1, which was already a seasoned veteran but was new to the US Air Force. "I got to like being able to fling that little Spam can around."

The Cessna L-19 Bird Dog was already being blooded in Vietnam when its designation was changed to O-1 on 1 October 1962. It was a nimble, lightweight, all-metal craft with pilot and observer in tandem, although FACs rarely carried a 'guy in back'. The L-19 was powered by a 213-hp (159-kW) Continental O-470-11 flat-six piston engine. With a wing span of 36 ft (10.97 m), a maximum take-off weight of 2,400 lb (1089 kg) and a maximum speed around 130 mph (209 km/h). The Bird Dog looked functional and handled in a forgiving manner.

Although artillery spotting had been its intended duty when developed for the US Army during the 1950-53 Korean War, the Bird Dog needed some modifications – the addition of four shackles – to accommodate 2.75-in 'Willie Pete' (white phosphorus) smoke rockets. In the end, it was left with a flight duration that could rarely be stretched to three hours, and not quite enough power to accelerate out of dangerous situations. FACs piloting the O-1 Bird Dog quickly learned to weave abruptly to evade Viet Cong gunfire.

The FAC treated the Bird Dog as his domain and fitted it out as he chose. Tomlin installed an aiming sight consisting of a plastic stick on the engine cowl. Captain Michael P. Curphey installed an M60 machine-gun in the backseat so that he could operate it with a lanyard from the front. It was not uncommon to carry an M16 rifle wedged into the narrow space between the pilot's right hand and the side of the aircraft, ready to use if nothing else worked. The pilot typically wore flight suit, helmet (a ballistic helmet after 1967), a sidearm dangling from a canvas web belt, and a package of survival gear – rations, mirror, knife, canteen. The O-1 lacked armour around the cockpit, engine and fuel tanks, so a 'flak jacket' usually enshrouded the pilot's torso and sometimes an extra one resided beneath his buttocks.

While pinpointing a target for 'fast movers', the FAC relied on devices that ranged from a grease pencil mark on the windshield to an abrupt barrel roll to keep his adversary in sight and at a measurable distance. The smoke rockets were fired after activating an arming switch on the cockpit left side. The rockets detonated on impact.

One of the FAC's biggest challenges was to handle communications. He used FM radio (AN/ARC-44) for contact with ground troops, his VHF set (AN/ARC-73) to talk to the C-130 airborne command post ('Hillsborough') and his UHF unit (AN/ARC-45 or -47) to talk with the tactical warplanes being directed into action.

The first O-1s went to the ARVN (South Vietnamese army) and to USAF flyers in Vietnam, although the 19th TASS had only 21 on charge at the end of 1964. When the US began its build-up in 1965, the USAF took over virtually all FAC duties and eventually operated five TASS squadrons with 30 aircraft each at 49 airfields and FOLs (forward operating locations). O-1A, E, F, and G models were nearly identical.

O-1s were in the war until its end. During the evacuation of Saigon in 1975, one even landed on the carrier USS *Midway* (CVA-41).

***Above:** An O-1D of the 73rd Aviation Company waits at Ban Me Thuot in the II Corps area, March 1964. Note the blacked-out fuselage national insignia and the orange strips on the wings, which aided recognition from above.*

***Below:** This USMC O-1B (OE-1) Bird Dog is seen being refuelled on the dirt strip at Cam Duc in South Vietnam. Many of the Marines' O-1s were USMC Korean War veterans, while others were handed down from the Army or USAF.*

A number of O-1s in Vietnam wore experimental colour schemes such as this 'tiger-striped' O-1F of the 117th Aviation Company, US Army, seen at Nha Trang in September 1963. Some such aircraft were used on missions into Cambodia and Laos.

the first flares fell off-target, he steered the flare ship into position for accurate release, using dead reckoning. The intense light of the flares placed McAllister in double jeopardy: he was in danger of being blinded by the same brilliant light that outlined him as a tempting target for the Viet Cong. Still, McAllister remained over the enemy, directing additional flare ships to the scene and at times firing an M1 Garand rifle at the Viet Cong troops below. The enemy attack stalled and McAllister limped home again from a marathon, three-hour sortie. Sadly, he was killed soon afterward, in an accident on what would have been his final mission before going home.

Home for the 19th TASS was Nha Trang in the central eastern part of South Vietnam. The oldest air base in the Republic, having been built by the French in 1949, Nha Trang was used primarily by the VNAF for flight training until the huge US build-up of the mid-1960s. By 1970 it was dominated by the US presence with FAC aircraft very much in evidence. This was also home of the Tactical Air Support Group (TASG), nominal HQ of USAF FAC units.

By 1965, the American role in the war was no longer limited to Vietnam. Now, US airmen in Laos were waging a private war managed by the US ambassador in Vientiane, G. McMurtrey Godley. That year, two-man teams were sent to Udorn, Thailand for FAC missions in northern Laos. Soon, they were replaced by the Ravens, who are discussed in more detail later.

Organisation

With the build-up of US forces in Vietnam in 1965, it became more and more difficult to answer the question soldiers have asked for centuries: "Who's in charge here?" There was now an out-country operation in Laos and eventually there was another at Nakhon Phanom, Thailand (the 23rd TASS). Meanwhile, for ease of communication, the US command divided South Vietnam into four regions: I, II, III and IV Corps, each with its own Direct Air Support Center (DASC) manned by USAF and Vietnamese personnel. The DASC's job, in part, was to receive requests for tactical air support (i.e., for FAC assistance) and forward them to the MAC-V (Military Assistance Command, Vietnam) operations centre in Saigon. In the South Vietnamese capital, priorities were determined, requests were accommodated, targets were 'fragged', and tactical air power was directed to the scene, where a FAC was usually already onboard.

In-country, FACs spent much of their time not with fellow airmen, but with the soldiers they supported. The four FAC squadrons in-country – namely, the 19th TASS at Bien Hoa (III Corps), the 20th TASS or COVEY FACs at

Below: Army O-1D (formerly TL-19D) 57-2779 is seen at An Heip, a dirt strip in the IV Corps area in 1963. The former trainer TL-19s were converted for the FAC role by the removal of the dual controls and the addition of rockets.

Above: This rather enigmatic O-1F was photographed on 13 March 1966 over South Vietnam. The inverted national insignia is a removable placard suggesting a change of identity could be made to suit the circumstances.

Right: This shark-mouthed O-1E is getting the preflight walkaround before a mission in December 1966. The aircraft belonged to the Army's 183rd Aviation Company.

Da Nang (I Corps), the 21st TASS at Pleiku (II Corps), and the 22nd TASS at Binh Thuy (IV Corps), all reporting to the 504th Tactical Air Support Group (TASG) at Bien Hoa – had detachments spread all over the map. A FAC was more likely to bunk with his army counterpart than to have a conversation with his squadron commander. To further confuse the situation, the 20th TASS flew some missions into North Vietnam, where command and control arrangements were different.

From 1965 on, FACs had a role in every major campaign. In October 1965, the US First Air Cavalry Division began a series of skirmishes, marking the first time a main-force American unit had come up against North Vietnamese regular troops. The first and second battles of Ia Drang followed. This was widely regarded as a milestone, indeed a turn of the tide, because the Viet Cong and North Vietnamese never again won a major campaign on the battlefield – even though, as it was to turn out, persistence would win them the war. USAF and US Army FACs were busy at Ia Drang, and the air cavalry concept drew support from tactical air power directed by heroic Bird Dog pilots.

'FAC-U'

Throughout the early part of the US commitment, there was a 'FAC School', also called 'FAC-U' (FAC University). To supplement Stateside training of FACs, a Theater Indoctrination School (Detachment 1, 504th TASG) was established at Binh Thuy in the Mekong Delta region in August 1966. The school was moved to Phan Rang in February 1968. The only one of its kind in Vietnam, the school trained USAF and allied pilots in techniques of identifying targets and directing air strikes. Pilots newly assigned to the theatre were taught advanced techniques to supplement whatever training and experience they already had. Further training with their assigned unit was also normal before being 'cut loose' to fly in combat independently. A separate course taught combat-qualified FACs how to transition to new aircraft when the O-2 and OV-10 came along. Yet another course trained pilot instructors.

One FAC remembers, "the Air Force was fairly structured in its checkout programme at Phan Rang, but MACSOG was more lenient. [The Military Assistance Command's 'Studies and Observations Group' was running special operations into North Vietnam and Laos.] I flew the U-17 in training and found it had better range than the O-1. [The U-17 was a Cessna 180 variant used by the VNAF for liaison work and visual reconnaissance.] This airplane was good for more than the O-1's 2.5 hours but its visibility was not so good and it carried no rockets." When training at the 'schoolhouse', he continued, "the front prop on the O-2 sat 10 in [25 cm] lower than the rear prop, so when taxiing you shut down front engine and got the prop horizontal."

Little lessons like that were not taught Stateside, apparently, so the school was invaluable. A newly assigned pilot began at Phan Rang with a two-week in-country checkout. After training at Phan Rang, he went to the division to which he was assigned for training before flying operationally. When a wind-down of forces began, the school was closed in November 1969, after which time all in-country training was accomplished at the pilot's assigned squadron.

Between 1965 and 1968, the US struggled to combat North Vietnamese infiltration and Viet Cong insurgency by continuously increasing its military presence on the ground in South Vietnam. Total US strength increased from 23,000 at the end of 1964 to 536,000 at the end of 1968. The American role in the war was

O-1 weapons

Although the FAC's job was not to attack the enemy directly, a certain amount of offensive/defensive capacity was often provided in the field. Normal weapons fit was one or two pairs of 2.75-in white phosphorus (WP) or smoke rockets (shown right) for target marking, although HE warheads could also be carried. To give the observer some defensive capability when things got hairy, an M60 machine-gun was sometimes fitted in the left rear window as seen on these USAF (below) and US Army (below right) O-1s.

Above: 'Hit my smoke!' – an O-1 gets down low in the thick of the action. Getting this close was actually dangerous and inefficient as there was little time to identify and accurately locate tagets. The poor climb performance of the O-1 kept the pilot in range of enemy small-arms fire for too long.

Right: Due to heavy losses, later in the war FACs were ordered to keep above 1,500 ft (457 m), out of rifle range. This O-1E is not far above this as the pilot rolls in to smoke-mark a target in November 1966.

'micro-managed' by the White House, and was strongly influenced by the war's growing unpopularity at home, the collapse of Lyndon Johnson's hopes for re-election, and the arrival of the Nixon administration. The result was that the rules of engagement changed frequently – the 'out-country war' over North Vietnam was on again, off again, until a bombing halt in 1968 – while ground fighting remained intense. There was never a let-up in the FAC mission at any point during this tumult, and in the minds of many the FAC emerged as a kind of 'lone wolf' warrior, always on the scene, always pressing the fight, no matter what the top brass were saying or doing.

Not Vietnam, but Florida. While the FACs plied their trade in Southeast Asia, the 4410th Combat Crew Training Squadron trained their replacements over the Everglades. The 'invasion stripes' were actually red and white .

TacAir system

Beginning in 1965, the US and its South Vietnamese ally built up a tactical air control system to employ FACs and fighter-bombers effectively in support of ground combat operations. The system handled the flow of aircraft from take-off to the target area, and return to base. Known as the Tactical Air Control System (TACS), it assured positive radar control in all areas where significant combat operations were indicated. Without this system it would have been impossible to deploy forces from one numbered region to another.

For example, a fighter-bomber scheduled for a pre-planned mission in the sector known as I Corps could be diverted with a minimum of disruption to II Corps. On arrival in the assigned area, the strike aircraft would be instructed to fly a FAC. The forward air controller might be a USAF flyer in a Bird Dog or a VNAF O-1 or U-17 from an observation squadron.

The TACC (Tactical Air Control Center), located at Tan Son Nhut, became the major hub of the system that eventually developed. It was in close proximity to the Saigon headquarters of both the VNAF and the USAF, and commanders of both used its facilities. It was from the TACC that air operations were planned, co-ordinated, executed and monitored. Subordinate to the TACC were outlying DASCs (Direct Air Support Centers) assigned to each of the Corps headquarters, with a direct line of communication to the TACC.

DASCs were responsible for the deployment of aircraft located with their sector, usually in support of ground operations. They reacted quickly to any change in the enemy threat, diverting aircraft from a preplanned target to an immediate threat. Operating under each DASC were numerous TACPs (Tactical Air Control

Below and left: These two Bird Dogs are of the 19th TASS. The aircraft at right is a former TL-19D (or TO-1D) seen at its Bien Hoa base in January 1966. The O-1E below was seen a few months later 'in the field' at Gi Lang in I Corps. The tail badge reads: 'THE PADDY RAT FAC-KERS'.

***Above:** In addition to target marking for 'troops in contact' and working the 'Trail', FACs patrolled fortified outposts such as this one, looking for signs of possible impending Viet Cong attacks.*

***Below:** O-1E* **The Rebel** *was one of many individually-marked O-1s, and reputedly well-known to the Viet Cong. Snoopy the dog was adopted as an unofficial insignia by many FAC units and aircrew.*

Parties) manned by one or more VNAF/USAF personnel and positioned with forces such as corps, field divisions, battalions and other units, including the airborne FACs. A communications network linked all three levels of command and control, giving the TACC overall control of the air situation at all times. Additional control and information was provided by a radar network which covered all of South Vietnam and beyond, monitoring all strike aircraft. This gave real-time information to FACs with unprecedented effectiveness.

Marines

The US Marine Corps, which always seeks to provide organic air support to its ground combat troops, was the only service to operate the O-1C (originally, OE-2) Bird Dog II. This was not a variant of the O-1 but a newer and heavier aircraft employing the wing and tail structure of the Cessna 180, with a strengthened fuselage and increased fuel capacity. In the 1950s, the Bird Dog II had become the first liaison aircraft designed and manufactured with a built-in provision for target marking rockets. It was also the first aircraft in its class designed from the outset with flak curtains and armoured seats for crew protection.

With both Bird Dog and Bird Dog II liaison craft, two Marine squadrons – VMO-2 and VMO-6 – operated mainly in the Da Nang area. The Marines eventually replaced their Cessnas with the North American OV-10 Bronco, a process which began in 1968.

In strict Marine terminology a FAC was a ground-based controller, the Bird Dog/Bronco crews actually flying the FAC(A) mission (A = airborne). FAC(A)s also flew helicopters, as did their brethren in the Army. The Marines also introduced a third form of fighter control, known as TAC(A) (tactical air control – airborne). This was performed from 1966 by rocket-armed Grumman TF-9J Panthers and later by Douglas TA-4F Skyhawks. The 'fast-FAC' concept was also field-tested by the USAF using F-100Fs, but it was only the USMC that fully embraced the idea.

Palace Gate

In December 1966, under a programme dubbed Palace Gate, the US Air Force recruited pilots with World War II and Korea experience who were near retirement, and assigned them to refresher flight training. Some later went to C-123 Providers and other aircraft types, but most became forward air controllers. Typically, these 'retread' pilots were given brush-up flying in whatever was available – many who came from Strategic Command logged time in the twin-engined U-3 'Blue Canoe', the military version of the Cessna 310 – and were then sent to Hurlburt Field, Florida to be introduced to the Cessna O-1 Bird Dog. After survival school, they arrived in Vietnam and spent a brief introductory period at the group headquarters for all FACs in Vietnam. In 1966, this was at Can Tho. Subsequently, they went to one of the tactical air support squadrons (TASS) scattered around the country. As pilot Bob Kirkwood remembered, "The TASS provided airplanes, bullets, paperwork and harassment but had no operational control. The group controlled all of us in-country."

As the war continued in Vietnam, another war, fought in secret in Laos, went all but unnoticed. The US was involved there from 1962 on, and the FAC mission in Laos began with a handful of USAF enlisted men, called 'Butterflies', who flew in the Helio Couriers and Pilatus Porters operated by Air America. This short-lived effort was replaced on 5 May 1966 when a highly classified programme, variously dubbed Steve Canyon and Project 404, selected about 120 USAF officers and support personnel to operate O-1 Bird Dogs in Laos. This group became better known under their callsign, RAVEN. The 'Raven FACs' were military men posing as civilians, assigned to help the pro-West forces of Laos's General Vang Pao. They flew forward air control missions in a war that was never acknowledged in public.

The men flew extraordinary missions, sometimes flying a dozen sorties in a day. Here is the tale of one of them.

Wilbanks

With darkness closing in on 24 February 1967, O-1 pilot Captain Hilliard A. Wilbanks of the 21st TASS uncovered a planned Viet

***Above:** The 'Ravens' operated a clandestine war in Laos. Despite official denials, many Americans were flying Laotian-marked O-1s and other types against VC, NVA and Pathet Lao forces.*

***Left:** An unmarked Laotian Air Force O-1 taxies out with a Lao observer in the back. Often this was done to maintain the fiction that any Americans killed or captured were just 'advising' the local forces.*

***Below:** Despite the introduction of more modern types such as the O-2, the O-1 soldiered on. Both these aircraft belonged to the 19th TASS at Cam Ranh Bay in 1971.*

***Left:* An O-2A patrols the Delta region of South Vietnam during 1969 with a pair of LAU-3 rocket pods underwing. In this case the observer appears to be wearing the 'hard hat'.**

***Below:* Although looking like a Vietnam action scene, this is actually an early-model O-2 under test with civillian markings in the US. O-2s were mostly new-built, but some were reworked Model 337s pulled from dealerships.**

Cessna O-2 Skymaster

Early in the Bird Dog's Vietnam experience – while the North American OV-10 Bronco was being developed separately – the USAF sought a FAC aircraft with better endurance than the Bird Dog, and with better suitability to carry a forward air navigator (FAN) as a second crewman. This aircraft became the O-2, an 'off-the-shelf' purchase of the well-established civilian Skymaster.

The twin-boom, twin-engined, high-wing, tricycle-gear Cessna O-2 Skymaster was based on the push-pull concept, with engines driving one tractor and one pusher propeller. Powerplant was two 210-hp (157-kW) Continental IO-360-GB flat-six piston engines. With tricycle landing gear, wing span of 38 ft 2 in (11.63 m), maximum speed around 206 mph (332 km/h) and a maximum take-off weight of 4,630 lb (2100 kg), the O-2 offered greater speed, range and endurance than its Bird Dog predecessor, but was not without its own drawbacks – the most obvious being that the pilot did not sit on the centreline, and had to make 'clearing' turns to gain vision to starboard.

Efforts were made to optimise the O-2 for FAC duty by adding extra windows, ordnance stations, and extra fuel not found in its civilian equivalent. Endurance increased to six hours and in at least one instance reached seven, although FAC pilot Major Robert C. Mikesh spoke of feeling "glued to the seat" after that time. Like its predecessor, the O-2 had a complete radio kit. It carried two LAU-59/A rocket launchers each packing seven 2.75-in rockets. It was capable of carrying two SUU-11/A external 7.62-mm gun pods.

Cessna built or rebuilt about 700 O-2s, most O-2As for FAC duty and a few as O-2Bs for propaganda work (dropping leaflets). A small number of O-2As at Nakhon Phanom, Thailand were painted black for night operations against North Vietnamese infiltration routes. O-2s equipped all five TASS squadrons and a handful reached the Vietnamese air force.

Cong ambush on the ARVN 23rd Ranger Battalion and its American advisors at Di Linh, 100 miles (160 km) northeast of Saigon. It was nearly dark as Wilbanks pinpointed VC soldiers and warned US Army Captain R. J. Wooten. A firefight began and the Bird Dog orbited overhead as Wilbanks fired a white phosphorus rocket into the VC troops. The marker smoke began to rise just as two helicopter gunships arrived and opened fire. A third helicopter was hit and Wilbanks ordered all three out, knowing that two flights of fighters were on the way.

But a bayonet and knife charge by the VC began before the fighters could arrive. Wilbanks attacked the Viet Cong with another smoke rocket. This apparently distracted them and they began shooting at the Bird Dog instead of pressing the assault on Wooten and the Rangers. Again, Wilbanks banked and attacked with a smoke rocket. The Bird Dog has become a fighter-bomber in its own right. Yet another pass followed, and again intense ground fire swirled around the aircraft. Wilbanks fired another rocket, his last. He knew he had no more. So did the Rangers and the VC. It was time to pull off the target and wait for the fighters – but that would might give the VC time to regroup and overrun the Rangers.

Instead of leaving, Wilbanks pointed his O-1 at the enemy, took his hands off the controls, and began shooting out the window with an automatic rifle. As the Bird Dog careened over the treetops, he grabbed the controls to recover the aircraft and evade fire. Now, the Viet Cong were off-balance and confused. Wilbanks loaded another clip and attacked again. "Each pass, he was so close we could hear his plane being hit," Wooten said later. A second FAC approaching the scene tried to contact Wilbanks but there was no reply. Wilbanks unleashed his third rifle-firing pass, and it became the last.

Another Ranger advisor, Captain Gary F. Vote, said, "He was no more than 100 feet [30 m] off the ground and almost over his objective, firing his rifle. Then he began the erratic moves, first up, then down, then banking west

Above:* Tiger Pause *was the name of this O-2A tied down and well-protected in its revetment. The door cut-outs that restored some of the pilot's starboard-side visibilty can be clearly seen here.

***Left:* The other O-2 version used in Southeast Asia was the O-2B. These aircraft were civillian C.337s adapted for the 'psywar' mission by the addition of a speaker and tape player in the starboard baggage door and a chute for dropping leaflets in the floor. Thirty-one were purchased, and like this 9th SOS aircraft, many were given highly unusual colour schemes.**

Left: Aircraft names and nose-art, not all of it particularly tasteful, flourished in the highly individualistic world of the FACs.

Below: Baby Jane II was an O-2A of the 21st TASS and was pictured at Phu Cat on 22 November 1970.

The 'Butterfly' FACs were predecessors of the Ravens in the secret war in Laos. 'Butterfly 44' was Charlie Jones (right) seen with his Laotian-civil-registered Turbo-Porter at Nakang, 1966.

right over my position. I thought he was wounded and looking for a friendly spot to land. I jumped up and waved my arms. But as he banked again, I could see that he was unconscious. His aircraft crashed almost 100 m [328 ft] away." The fallen Bird Dog came to rest in a no man's land between the opposing forces.

Wilbanks was alive when Vote pulled him from the wreckage. Meanwhile, the two helicopter gunships that now doubled as rescue aircraft returned. They fired their remaining ammunition into the Viet Cong and swooped over the fallen Bird Dog to pick up its pilot. Four times, they tried to set down in no man's land. Four times, Viet Cong guns drove them off.

Another FAC arrived and directed two F-4 Phantoms to rake the Viet Cong with 20-mm gunfire. After repeated efforts, a helicopter finally picked up Captain Hilliard Wilbanks. His award of the Medal of Honor, the first to a FAC (and the first of two in Vietnam), had to be posthumous. He died in the helicopter en route to a treatment centre.

Skymaster

The Cessna O-2, with its odd pusher-tractor engines and twin-boomed configuration, began operations on 1 January 1967 with the 20th TASS at Da Nang. This derivative of the civilian Skymaster took some getting used to: the pilot sat off the centreline and had to make clearing turns to the right to have visibility to both sides. The O-2 was faster and could reach farther and carry more, but it never seemed to win over pilots as the O-1 had done.

According to FAC Captain Bob Kirkwood, the O-2 was "at best a stopgap. It was never a good FAC plane. Visibility was not as good as the O-1 or OV-10. It had decent range but was not as manoeuvrable and had a sluggish rate of climb. There were problems with the prop controls on the front propeller. The prop would overstress if power was applied in a dive and would run away. Also, the cooling of the rear engine not good."

In late 1967, O-2s also began to reach the 23rd TASS at Nakhon Phanom. Some aircraft of the latter group were painted black for night operations over North Vietnamese supply routes.

OV-10 Bronco

In the following year, the North American OV-10 began to enter service with both USAF and USMC FAC units. This purpose-designed aircraft at last gave the FAC a real chance to shoot back, as it was armed with four machine-guns and could carry heavy rocket loads. Although the performance and range were better than the figures for the O-1 and O-2, one disadvantage was the louder noise it made, which rendered it less 'stealthy' than the Bird Dog.

Blessed with outstanding visibility from both seats, the OV-10 rapidly established itself as the pricnipal FAC aircraft of the later part of the war. The 15 OV-10As fitted with the Pave Nail laser designation system also played a part in pioneering the employment of laser-guided weapons

The 504th TASG was deactivated on 15 March 1972 as the US continued a drawdown of forces in Southeast Asia. Now serving under the wing commands in their local regions, the three remaining TASS squadrons (20th, 21st and 23rd) fought through the massive battles at Quang Tri and An Loc in 1972 and the continuing interdiction efforts against the Ho Chi Minh Trail.

BAT 21

In the spring of 1972, North Vietnam launched a massive invasion of the South in its final attempt to wrest victory on the battlefield. FACs were involved in furious fighting. Especially difficult was the running gun battle that began when an EB-66 crew member, Lieutenant Colonel Iceal 'Gene' Hambleton, was shot down along the DMZ and was seeking to evade capture. FACs from Da Nang (20th TASS) and Nakhon Phanom (23rd TASS) were among the dozens of aircraft covering Hambleton as he fought to survive while the spring offensive exploded around him. Hambleton's story was later covered in the book and movie entitled *Bat 21* (his radio callsign was BAT 21-B).

US Army helicopters tried to rescue Lieutenant Colonel Hambleton, but the North Vietnamese guns drove them off and downed one – a UH-1 'Huey', callsign BLUEGHOST 39. Three of its crewmembers were killed and one was captured. The next day, 'Jolly Greens' from the 37th ARRS made two attempts to pick up BAT 21B. Both times, they were driven off with heavy damage to their aircraft. Additionally, an OV-10, callsign NAIL 38, was hit and downed by an enemy missile. Its pilot, Captain Bill Henderson, was captured; its navigator, First Lieutenant Mark Clark (callsign NAIL 38 BRAVO), was able to hide and await rescue, like Lieutenant Colonel Hambleton.

The 20th TASS at Da Nang in the northern part of South Vietnam styled themselves the 'Highland Coveys'. Below, the pilot/controllers and observers of the squadron pose in front of the squadron 'hooch' in their party suits with an OV-10 and one of their black O-2s. At right, 20th TASS OV-10 pilot Chuck Corley sorts out his equipment before a mission. The battered SLR camera and binoculars mark his role as different to your average Vietnam 'fighter puke'.

***Left:* One of the 20th TASS's black O-2s, *Jeanie's Tiger* is seen at Pleiku in December 1969. Note the tiger stripes on the fin-tips. At least half-a-dozen of these night FACs were with the unit at one time. On a number of aircraft the cut-out door windows were painted over.**

***Right:* Leaving no doubt as to his job or whereabouts, the pilot of this O-2 flew with the 21st TASS at Phu Cat in 1969 in coordinated missions with AC-47 gunships.**

For two more days, rescue groups fought the weather and the enemy forces to try to rescue the two airmen. They could not get to them, so hundreds of airstrikes were put in to beat down the enemy gunners. On 6 April 1972, after 42 more air strikes, a rescue force of four HH-53s and six escorting A-1 'Sandy' aircraft launched to make another attempt to recover the two downed Americans. They were assisted by several FACs in O-2s and OV-10s, and numerous other support aircraft.

An HH-53C (JOLLY GREEN 67) was designated to make the rescue attempt, but as it came to a hover over BAT 21 BRAVO, it was raked by heavy enemy fire. The escorting 'Sandy' A-1s tried to engage the enemy guns, but they could not get them all – and they could see what the ground fire was doing to the helicopter, so several shouted for the crew to fly out of the area. The crew of JOLLY GREEN 67 aborted the rescue attempt and tried to manoeuvre their stricken aircraft to safety; the enemy fire continued, however, and the helicopter was so badly damaged that it crashed in a huge fireball a few kilometres south of the survivors. The fire was intense and lasted for several days. There was no indication of survivors.

***Above:* Some of the first OV-10 Broncos to arrive in Vietnam are seen being assembled at Bien Hoa in 1968. The aircraft had arrived knocked-down in open wooden crates.**

Bronco lost

The next day, another OV-10 (COVEY 282) supporting the rescue was shot down in the same area. The pilot, First Lieutenant Bruce Walker (COVEY 282 ALPHA), was on the ground and evading like the two earlier airmen. His crewman, US Marine First Lieutenant Larry Potts, was never heard from. With this news, General Abrams, the overall US commander in Saigon, directed that there would be no more helicopter rescue efforts for the three downed flyers. Instead, a ground team was formed to attempt to infiltrate through enemy lines and pick them up. It was planned and directed by US Marine Lieutenant Colonel Andy Anderson, and lead by US Navy SEAL Lieutenant Tom Norris. From 10-12 April, the team operated through enemy lines and rescued First Lieutenant Clark and Lieutenant Colonel Hambleton. They also intended to rescue First Lieutenant Walker; however, on 18 April, he was discovered by Viet Cong troops and killed. The rescues were over. Later, Lieutenant Tom Norris received the Medal of Honor for the mission.

The 'Bat 21' event was the largest sustained rescue operation of the war. Over 800 airstrikes, to include B-52s, were made in direct support. Numerous helicopters, A-1s and forward air controller aircraft were shot down or damaged. A total of 11 men was killed.

The spring offensive brought resumed bombing of North Vietnam, and some FAC operations north of the 17th Parallel. In the south, fighting remained fierce. A FAC mission in June 1972 by Captain Steven L. Bennett

***Above:* The OV-10 Forward Air Navigator's view of his pilot. The Bronco offered many advantages including reasonable armour protection, ejection seats and twin-engined safety.**

***Left:* A trio of Broncos from the 19th TASS fly in formation. The 19th were the first unit to fly the OV-10 in Vietnam, beginning with a 90-day evaluation with six aircraft in August 1968. The OV-10 soon proved its toughness when a 19th TASS aircraft returned safely after a collision with a tree.**

Cessna O-2A 23rd TASS, Nakhon Phanom RTAB, Thailand 1970

Crew
O-2 FACs were flown both solo and with an observer/artillery spotter, depending on the mission. Visibility was relatively poor compared to the O-1 with its narrow fuselage and tandem seating. A cut-out window on the starboard door slightly improved the view for a solo pilot who flew from the left seat.

Weapons
The primary offensive weapon (and target marking device) was the 2.75-inch Folding Fin Aircraft Rocket (FFAR). Up to 28 could be carried in four LAU-32 or LAU-59 launcher tubes. A pair of SUU-11A 7.62-mm gun pods with 1,500 rounds per gun could also be fitted to the wing pylons. A pair of M16 rifles could be carried strapped to the cabin sides for use by the crew in the event of a forced landing or, in some cases, to suppress enemy fire from the air.

The O-2A 'Super Skymaster' was a development of the 1966 version of Cessna's Model 337 light business and private aircraft. Cessna were willing to develop a narrow-cabin variant for the FAC role, but the USAF accepted a limited adaptation of the standard civillian aircraft fitted with hardpoints and extra radio equipment. The 'black FACs' of the 20th and 23rd TASS were used in conjunction with 'Spooky' gunships on 'Sleeptime' patrols along the Ho Chi Minh Trail and in other night actions. Some may have been flown by CIA FACs on clandestine missions over Laos.

Engines
The O-2A was fitted with two 210-hp (157 kW) Continental IO-360-D horizontally-opposed flat-six air-cooled piston engines. The direction of rotation for the McCauley variable-pitch propellers was the same, but because of their 'push-me-pull-you' layout, cancelled out each other's torque.The lack of propeller spinners is a reliable method of distinguishing an O-2 from a commercial model 337. A smoke generator on the rear engine could be used to help the 'fast-movers' spot the FAC's position.

Communications
Pilots referred to the O-2 as a 'flying radio set', equipped as it was with transceivers for communication with Air Force and Navy attack aircraft and friendly ground forces. This equipment included VHF (FM-622 and Wilcox 807) and UHF (AN/ARC-51BX) sets. An AN/APX-64 IFF unit was fitted as was TACAN and ADF for navigation.

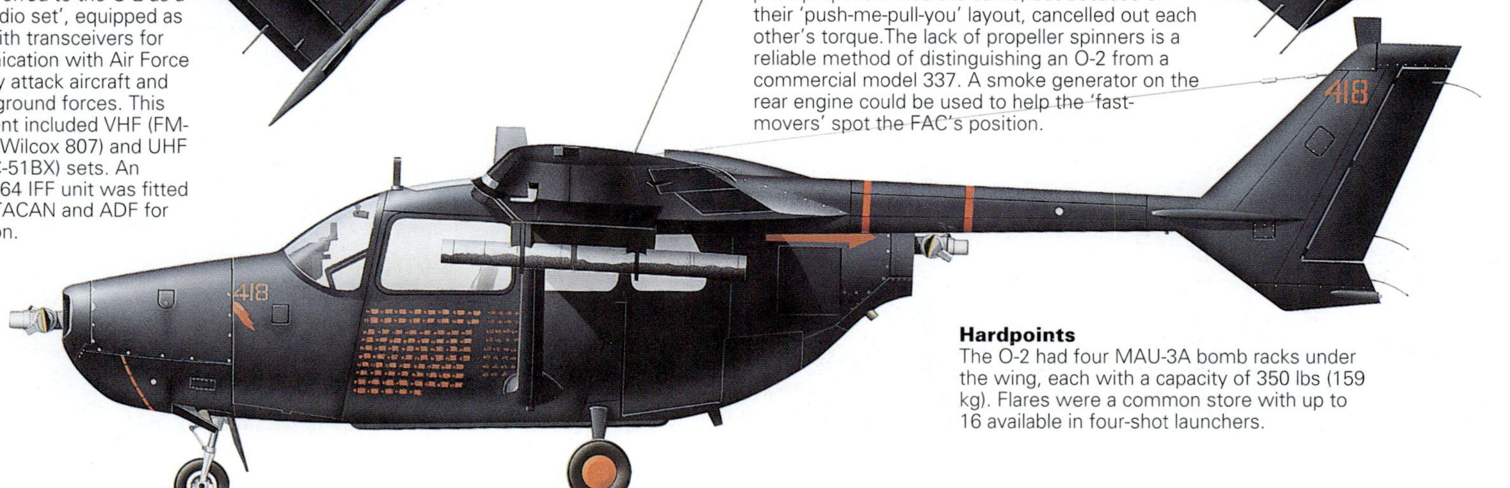

Hardpoints
The O-2 had four MAU-3A bomb racks under the wing, each with a capacity of 350 lbs (159 kg). Flares were a common store with up to 16 available in four-shot launchers.

The unusual angle adopted by this O-2A named* The Jefferson Airplane *of the 21st TASS at Phu Cat in November 1970 is not the result of a ground handling mishap, but a common field method of gaining access to the nosewheel for maintenance.

(COVEY 87) of the 23rd TASS turned into an unspeakable ordeal for the pilot and his backseat observer. Bennett was piloting an OV-10A Bronco (68-3804) on an artillery adjustment mission along a heavily defended route, where a large concentration of enemy troops was massing for an attack on a friendly unit. Bennett asked for tactical air support but was told it was unavailable. Artillery support was denied because friendly troops were too close to the target. Instead, Bennett strafed the hostile positions and completed four passes. On the fifth, however, his aircraft was struck by a surface-to-air missile, severely damaging the left engine and left main landing gear. He told his backseat observer to prepare for ejection, but the observer said his parachute had been shredded by the force of the missile.

Bennett had a good parachute, but he knew that if he ejected the observer would not survive. With Captain Darrel Whitcomb flying on his wing and giving visual reports, Bennett chose to ditch in the Gulf of Tonkin, even though no OV-10 pilot had ever survived a ditching. The impact of the water caused the aircraft to cartwheel and severely damaged the front cockpit, making escape for Bennett impossible. The observer made his way out and was rescued. Bennett was posthumously awarded the Medal of Honor, the second FAC to receive the medal. A US Navy ammunition ship was christened in Bennett's honour on 20 November 1997.

US Marine Corps Broncos

US Marine Corps' OV-10 Bronco operations in Southeast Asia began when its first combat-ready squadron, VMO-2, left the US in June 1968 and began combat operations on 6 July from the Marble Mountain air strip near Da Nang. VMO-1 became the second Marine squadron to operate the OV-10 in Vietnam in October 1968, and began operations in November. VMO-6 arrived soon afterward and operated from Quang Tri and Phu Bai, participating in Operation Dewey Canyon, a sweep of Viet Cong/NVA forces in the A Shau and Da Krong Valleys in April 1969. The unit was withdrawn in 1969.

The normal complement of each Marine squadron was 18 aircraft, and the aircraft operated from several locations – Da Nang, Chu Lai, Marble Mountain, Phu Bai, Quang Tri, and smaller air strips. Before the Marines withdrew the remaining OV-10 squadrons in late 1971, they utilised the OV-10A in almost every role for which it had been designed: forward air control, radio relay station, artillery spotter, helicopter escort, visual reconnaissance, convoy escort, and attack aircraft.

Marine Captain Ralph Tippe, who flew two tours in Vietnam, one in the OV-10, said, "The airplane is a 100 per cent improvement from nearly every viewpoint insofar as the air observer is concerned. We can cover many times the terrain, respond quickly to emergency situations. Before, the only firepower we had [in the Cessna O-1C Bird Dog] was strapped to our thighs. In the OV-10, we've got a brace of 7.62-mm machine-guns for suppressive fire. And it has a tough hide. One Bronco – not mine – took 15 50-calibre (12.7-mm) hits and came in with a smashed electrical panel and riddled aileron, and landed beautifully. No sweat. The ejection seats also give us a hell of a boost – in morale, and, literally, if we ever have to get out."

The Bronco would have been very useful sooner, but, nonetheless, to most people, the imperishable symbol of FAC operations will always be the Bird Dog. When the Vietnam armistice was signed in January 1973 and the last American and Allied personnel withdrew in April 1975, the forward air controllers had left behind an image of courage, improvisation, sacrifice and dedication.

FAC contribution

The contribution made by FACs in Vietnam is difficult to measure but is indisputably enormous, especially those who came in the early days when the OV-10 was still in the future and the Bird Dog was the only way to confront the Viet Cong. One way to gauge the significance of the FAC effort is to look at the price: 338 Air Force FACs lost their lives in the war. The Air Force lost 161 Bird Dogs in combat and another 150 in 'operational' mishaps, the latter strongly influenced by the gruelling conditions under which the men operated. About 45 per cent of the top awards for valour given to pilots in Vietnam went to forward air controllers.

The USMC developed their own version of the Bird Dog, the OE-2 (O-1C) 'Bird Dog II' in the mid-1950s. The aircraft featured the wing of the Cessna 180 with provision for rockets designed in from the outset. They were operated by VMO-2 and -6 (an aircraft of the latter unit is seen here in a 1968 photo) until replaced by OV-10s in 1969.

Left: The insignia of the 504th TIS (Theater Indoctrination School), as seen on the wall of the squadron's building at Nha Trang in October 1968. The Forward AIr Controllers' 'university' or 'FAC-U' as it was inevitably dubbed, was established here in September 1963.

The main Marine FAC aircraft was the O-1E, seen with 'Mud Marines' (left) near Hue in 1967 and over heavily-bombed jungle in 1968 (above).

Below: The OV-10 could take a far greater amount of battle damage than its predecessors and still return to base. The remains of an aircraft that didn't make it home, however, are seen in a forest near Bien Hoa in October 1968.

FAC units

34th Tactical Group

The 34th Tactical Group was the first USAF combat group in Southeast Asia, organised on 8 July 1963 and composed of two squadrons, the 19th TASS (O-1 Bird Dog) and the 1st Air Commando Squadron (A-1 Skyraider). On 1 August 1965, the 6250th Tactical Air Support Group (Provisional) was established, and on 8 November 1965 was redesignated the 505th Tactical Control Group.

505th Tactical Control Group

The organisation on 1 August 1965 of the 505th Tactical Control Group signalled a change in the structure of deployed tactical air control assets. The 505th took over all five TASS squadrons (19th through 23rd) as well as supporting communications and logistical units. Its first commander was Colonel Charles L. Daniel. Although the 505th oversaw an operational situation that remained little changed in the years that followed, this headquarters arrangement was inadequate and the commander recommended the formation of a numbered air division. His recommendation was rebuffed and, instead, the USAF moved to create an expanded combat group.

504th TASG

On 8 December 1966, the 504th Tactical Air Support Group was organised at Bien Hoa AB, South Vietnam. For an interim period of several weeks between September and December, this new combat group was identified by the provisional 6250th and 6253rd. All five tactical air support squadrons (TASSs, namely the 19th through 23rd) were assigned to the group. Previously, there had been no combat group at the top of the organisation chart for forward air controllers. As a practical matter, however, FACs often reported to ground combat commanders and rarely, if ever, had any business at 'Group HQ'. In a larger sense, the 'lone wolf' FAC pilot often was accountable to nobody but those with whom he fought. As Colonel Tom Cleland remembers, "Realistically, no one was in charge. FACs were a breed unto themselves and didn't bother much with the convoluted command structure."

With the drawdown of US forces in Vietnam, begun in August 1969 and accelerated in 1971-72, the TASS squadrons began to disband. On 15 March 1972, the 504th TASG

Above: An early 20th TASS Bronco pulls in tight for the camera giving a view of the back-seater's unoccupied LW-3B ejection seat.

Right: OV-10s of the 19th TASS at Bien Hoa in 1968 sit tucked into their revetments – which would seem to offer little real protection against enemy attack.

North American OV-10A Bronco

The twin-engined, twin-boom North American OV-10 Bronco was the result of an effort to develop a COIN (counter-insurgency) aircraft for the US Air Force and Marine Corps. Predating the FAC role in Southeast Asia, the OV-10 stems from a 1959 Marine Corps study which proposed an observation aircraft able to 'live' in the field with the troops it was to support. In 1961, the Air Force recognised the need for an aircraft suited to anti-guerrilla operations. The USAF envisioned an inexpensive aircraft, simple to maintain and easy to fly.

The Bronco's powerplant was two 600-shp (447-kW) Garrett T76-G-6/8 turboprop engines. Pilots initially considered it underpowered and, although improved engines became available over time, the Bronco was noted for long take-off runs in hot weather. Bigger and far more formidable than any other aircraft assigned to FAC work, the OV-10 had a 40-ft (12.19-m) wing span, maximum speed of about 288 mph (463 km/h) and a maximum take-off weight of 14,122 lb (6405 kg). The OV-10 had a perch for a second-seat FAN (forward air navigator) and, unlike the O-2, used it a great deal on operational missions.

A typical OV-10A combat sortie in Southeast Asia lasted 4.5 to 5 hours. Normal configuration included a 230-US gal (870-litre) fuel tank on the centreline, two LAU-59/A rocket pods with 2.75-in marking rockets on the weapon sponsons, and, if armed, 2,000 rounds of 7.62-mm ammunition for two M60 machine-guns.

The OV-10A pilot had at his disposal a complete radio kit including HF (HF-103), VHF (FM-622A), and UHF (AN/ARC-51) sets. Pilot and observer were protected by 268 lb (121 kg) of armour. The Bronco typically carried about 2,000 lb (907 kg) of ordnance, including numerous combinations of flares, smoke rockets, machine-guns, rockets, and light bombs.

In 1970, LTV Electrosystems modified 15 Broncos to the Pave Nail configuration to improve its night and precision strike capabilities. LORAN equipment was added to enhance navigation and target location, and a stabilised periscopic night scope was coupled to a combined laser rangefinder/target designator. The night scope and rangefinder/target designator were mounted in an underfuselage external pod mounted beneath the rear cockpit ejection seat. These systems were used for improved night reconnaissance and attack missions in conjunction with the early laser-guided bombs. The 23rd TASS is the only known unit to have operated this version of the Bronco. Surviving Pave Nail Broncos were reconfigured to standard OV-10As in 1974.

The OV-10A replaced the O-2A in TASS squadrons, the Navy's VAL-4 'Black Ponies', and the Marine Corps' VMO-1 and -2.

This 20th TASS OV-10A seen at Nakhon Phanom in 1969 carries a heavy load, including three rocket pods and two fuel tanks. The openings in the sponson for two of the four 7.62-mm M60C machine-guns (not fitted here) are also visible.

OV-10s were normally not as colourful as their predecessors, but* Lois Little II *of the 19th TASS sported a rare sharkmouth. Note the 'gull-wing' canopy arrangement.

While it is unlikely that the Viet Cong could read the sign in Lt Col Howie Pierson's OV-10, it provided a boost to squadron morale as combat operations began to wind down in 1972.

deactivated, at which time the three surviving TASS squadrons (20th, 21st and 23rd) were made subordinate to the commands in their assigned regions. These commands were, respectively, the 366th Tactical Fighter Wing at Da Nang, the 377th Air Base Wing at Tan Son Nhut, and the 56th Special Operations Wing at Nakhon Phanom.

19th TASS

The 19th TASS was activated on 17 June 1963 and organised on 8 July 1963 at Bien Hoa, with personnel arriving on base from July through October. Initial equipment consisted of 22 Cessna O-1F Bird Dogs. Authorised strength became 30 Bird Dogs. The squadron was deemed combat-ready on 15 September 1963. On 15 January 1971, the 19th TASS acquired the assets of the 22nd TASS, which went out of existence. On 19 January 1972, the 19th TASS was reassigned without personnel or equipment to Korea.

20th TASS

The 20th TASS (callsign COVEY for out-country operations; TRAIL for in-country work) FACs operated from Da Nang and numerous other locations, flying both in and out of South Vietnam, including missions into the adjacent area of North Vietnam known as Route Package I. The squadron operated O-1 Bird Dogs from 1964, O-2s from 1969, and OV-10s from 1971. On 27 March 1973, the 20th TASS was deactivated. All remaining OV-10 pilots were reassigned to the 23rd TASS at Nakhon Phanom.

21st TASS

The 21st TASS, responsible for II Corps and using callings CAGEY and RAGGED SCOOPER, operated from Pleiku and Nha Trang and, at the end of its life, Cam Ranh Bay. Like all squadrons it had detachments scattered about – including big ones at Cam Phouc, a Korean compound and Ban Me Thuot East, aka Camp Torres (504th TASG at Bien Hoa had 'administrative control' only; 21st TASS was at Nha Trang and moved to Cam Ranh but members of squadron were scattered all over II Corps with Americans, Vietnamese, Koreans) worked out of A-Camps along the tri-border Kontum area.

In 1967 alone, this squadron flew over 39,000 sorties while logging over 50,000 combat hours. On 21 February 1973, the 21st TASS was deactivated.

22nd TASS

The 22nd TASS was at Binh Thuy as the squadron supporting operations in IV Corps. It had several detachments and initially operated the Cessna O-1. On 15 January 1971, the 22nd TASS merged into the 19th TASS and deactivated.

23rd TASS

The 23rd TASS, or NAIL FACs, became the fifth such squadron in Southeast Asia when it was formed at Nakhon Phanom, Thailand in March 1966 with an initial strength of 30 O-1E Bird Dogs. The 'Nails' were charged with visual reconnaissance and air strike control in north and central Laos. In November 1967, the squadron converted to the Cessna O-2A Super Skymaster. By June 1969, the 23rd was flying a mixed fleet of O-2As and North American OV-10A Broncos. In 1971, the squadron began working up with the 'Pave Nail' modification.

The 23rd TASS was the last in action in Southeast Asia, still fighting at the time of the 27 January 1973 Vietnam ceasefire. The squadron fought in Cambodia until 15 August 1973. It remained in place and ready, and its crews flew in support of US forces during the *Mayaguez* incident of 1975. Shortly thereafter, the squadron was deactivated and all personnel and equipment returned to the US. The 23rd TASS reappeared at Davis-Monthan AFB,

Above: With the end of USAF FAC operations, it was (as always) time to party. Seen here in the 23rd TASS 'Nail Hooch' is Lt Col Howie Pierson with Air Force intelligence officer Capt. Christine Sienicki, now the wife of FAC Darrel Whitcomb. Pierson's 'party suit' proclaims him "Last FAC back across the Cambodia fence...15 August '73".

Below: This rare photograph shows the Pave Nail installation on a 23rd TASS OV-10. The stabilised designator/rangefinder pod was mounted beneath the rear instrument panel and could be swivelled by the back-seater to give a target azimuth. The forward part also rotated to give elevation changes.

***Above:** A USMC OV-10A with four 2.75-in (7-cm) rocket pods (two seven-shot and one 19-shot) flies off the South Vietnamese coast. VMO-1, VMO-2 and VMO-6 flew the Bronco in Vietnam.*

***Right:** Mixed weapon loads such as three rocket pods and a gun pod were often carried by USMC OV-10s. The Bronco impressed the Marine Corps with its ability to maintain 80 per cent reliability even during the monsoon.*

Arizona. and flew OA-10 'Warthogs' in Operation Desert Storm before being deactivated again in 1992.

Ravens

The FACs of the Steve Canyon/Project 404 programme, recruited for the secret war in Laos, were headquartered at the Long Tieng airfield – alias Lima Site 20A – where Hmong warlord General Vang Pao kept his own headquarters. Vang Pao officially commanded only his own ground troops, but unofficially he was also in charge of the Ravens, who also reported to the US ambassador in Laos – first G. McMurtrey Godley, then William Sullivan. Accused of being a motley, dishevelled, poorly disciplined private air force, the Ravens were in fact dedicated pilots and support personnel who had volunteered for remote and dangerous duty. They were scattered with their O-1 Bird Dogs in five military regions (MR): Luang Prabang (MR I), Long Tieng (MR II), Savannakhet (MR III), Pakse (MR IV) and Vientiane (MR V).

The Ravens were issued Cessna O-1F Bird Dogs with no national markings and used them to direct 'fast movers' and Hmong-piloted T-28s dropping ordnance on Pathet Lao, Viet Cong and North Vietnamese forces inside Laos. The T-28s were not procured for the FAC role, but the maverick Ravens never hesitated to appropriate them. One pilot flew more than 150 FAC sorties in a T-28D-5.

US Army

US Army forward air controllers belonged to the battalion, division or corps in their AOR (area of responsibility) and did not report to a headquarters group. As remembered by Steve 'Scurvydog' Harrison, of the 185th Reconnaissance Airplane Company 3rd Platoon 'Pterodactyls', "We really had no chain of command except to our ground commanders. [Our] organisation was very loose. Only on occasion, once a week or so, was a mission assigned. Mission assignments came from platoon HQ and usually came in the form of a 'who, what, when' to describe the mission, and contact radio freqs. Very little detail was given in pre-mission briefings, which were usually delivered in person (came to hooch before flight) by the platoon leader and were very informal."

US Marine Corps (VMO-1, 2 and 6)

Marine Bird Dog operations began with the first Shu Fly detachment of April 1962, when three OE-1s were deployed to provide FAC and observation for the first USMC helicopters deployed ashore to assist local forces. From early 1965 the mission expanded, and OE-1s and OE-2s were operated by VMO-1 and VMO-6.

The Marine Corps' first combat-ready OV-10 Bronco squadron was VMO-2, which began combat operations on 6 July 1968 from Marble Mountain, near Da Nang. VMO-1 was the second Bronco squadron in October 1968, followed by VMO-6, which operated from Quang Tri and Phu Bai. This unit was withdrawn to Futemma, Okinawa in October 1969. Normal squadron establishment was 18 aircraft.

Vietnamese Army/Air Force

The Vietnamese Army (ARVN) and Air Force (VNAF) performed some FAC duties during the Southeast Asia conflict but the army disposed of its fixed-wing assets at an early juncture, and after 1965 the FAC mission was formally assigned to US forces. The ARVN apparently operated a handful of Cessna O-1 Bird Dogs in about 1963-64, but they were later transferred to the VNAF, leaving the ARVN without fixed-wing aircraft.

The VNAF had nearly 300 liaison aircraft, mostly O-1s and U-17s, in service by 1972. Although not formally assigned the FAC mission, the VNAF often flew support missions for ground troops carrying an ARVN observer. The Vietnamese preferred using smoke grenades rather than smoke rockets, a risky technique which required more orbiting over the target. Although no photograph of one has survived to confirm it, the VNAF is shown on records as having acquired 35 Cessna O-2 Skymasters, augmenting two squadrons in I Corps. **Robert F. Dorr**

Australia and New Zealand contributed FAC pilots to the Vietnam conflict. The 'ANZAC' FACs were attached as individuals to regular USAF units as illustrated by the kangaroo insignia on this 19th TASS O-2A seen at Da Nang in 1968. The 14 RNZAF FAC pilots were active in the period 1968 to 1972, almost exclusively on OV-10s.

Bell Cobra Variants

P-39 Airacobra and P-63 Kingcobra

Many of the Airacobras and Kingcobras built for the US went directly to training units. The P-39D-1 and D-2 models, with their 20-mm cannon, were perceived as inferior by service units and were soon earmarked for training. In addition to novice fighter pilots, bomber crews also benefited from the P-39's use as a 'bounce ship' to simulate fighter attack. The unit to which this group of P-39D-1s belongs is unknown.

The P-39 Airacobra and P-63 Kingcobra were unique among production fighters of World War II for their mid-engine layout and tricycle undercarriage. Built to an exacting Air Corps specification, the P-39 proved ill-suited to the demands put on it in actual combat and was soon phased out. The all-new P-63 addressed these failings and in many ways was a superb fighter, but it never saw combat with the US forces. The Army and Bell, a small but always innovative company, tested many configurations and devices on the adaptable Cobra.

Pity the P-39. Unloved. Unwanted. Unrecognised. When a British pilot first flew a P-39C on 6 July 1941, he was 'dismayed' by the 359-mph (578-km/h) top speed. An American pilot spent much of 1941 fantasising about 'driving' a P-39 down the highway all the way from Tonopah, Nevada to Los Angeles, where he planned to use the menacing nose 37-mm cannon to stick up a grocery store. Half a century after World War II, men who were once young renew their friendships in annual meetings of pilots' associations for the P-38, P-40, P-47, and P-51, but no pilots' fraternity is thriving today for those who flew the P-39.

By the time Japan attacked Pearl Harbor on 7 December 1941, the Royal Air Force had already tested the Airacobra, flown it operationally, equipped a squadron, found the aircraft 'unsuitable', and retired it. The uncharitable attitude felt by many toward Bell's fighter was reflected in a 1 September 1942 letter to the factory by a company representative in the Pacific, who wrote:

"We frequently talk with the boys who have been in action against Zeros. Their big cry is, 'When in hell are the Brass Hats going to get wise to themselves and give us more H.P. [horsepower] motors?' In general they like the P-39, but its decided lack of power and performance is fast costing us...prestige."

One thing almost certain is that the manufacturer's house organ, the *Bellringer*, was wrong when it reported that on 8 January 1941 test pilot Andrew C. McDonough flew an Airacobra in a dive at a speed of 620 mph (997 km/h). Yet the Airacobra was a far more respectable warplane than British or American pilots often said it was. Even the P-39's maximum speed was respectable; in some regimes, it was faster than the Mitsubishi A6M Zero. It was also more heavily-armed than the

The Air Corps evaluated one XP-39 with and without a two-stage turbo supercharger, and 13 YP-39s without. Making a wildly optimistic assumption that aircraft weight would not grow in service and that performance would be improved without the supercharger's weight, the Airacobra was ordered into production without this equipment. The effect of this decision was to restrict the P-39's effectiveness to low altitudes, and thus blight its career. Seen here is the first of the YP-39s.

Despite their obvious similarities, the P-39 and P-63 shared no common components. The P-63A-1 in the foreground was approximately 12 per cent larger than the P-39Q-20 behind, with an empty weight 13 per cent greater and a maximum take-off weight up to 27 per cent greater. The P-63 had performance comparable to the P-51 Mustang, but by the time it was ready for combat service, the Army was no longer interested.

North American P-51 Mustang. The P-39 was nothing if not manoeuvrable. Using the common term for the Messerschmitt Bf 109 (ME. 109), a British test report in 1941 asserted, "the ME. 109 could not compete with the Airacobra in a turn and even if the ME. 109 were behind at the start the Airacobra should be able to outmanoeuvre and get on to the tail of the ME. 109 within two complete turns."

Design

The Bell P-39 Airacobra was unique among World War II fighters in its unorthodox powerplant installation. It was also the first US Army single-seat fighter with tricycle landing gear. The undercarriage was dictated, not chosen, because of the desire to mount heavy armament in the nose, reflecting the interest of all nations during the mid- and late 1930s in developing fighter aircraft with good forward firepower.

In early 1935, executives of the Bell Aircraft Corporation had been present at a demonstration of the American Armament Corporation's T-9 37-mm cannon (later built by Oldsmobile). Impressed by what they had seen, they instigated the design of a fighter which would include a T-9 cannon firing through the propeller hub. Bell was working also on the cannon-armed XFM-1 Airacuda twin-engined fighter, which became the company's first aircraft but never rated a production contract. In fact, while seeking to develop a high-altitude interceptor, Bell never seriously considered armament choices but was wedded from the start to the 37-mm weapon. This gun (which had 30 rounds, except on the YP-39 and P-39C where it had 15) became standard on all production models except the US Army P-39D-1 and the export P-400. Early Airacobras also had two 0.50-in (12.7-mm) Colt nose machine-guns with 270 rounds each and four 0.30-in (7.62-mm) Colt wing-mounted machine-guns with 1,000 rounds per gun.

The decision to locate the cannon to fire through the propeller hub meant that the engine had to be mounted within the fuselage, directly above the rear half of the low-set monoplane wing, with the propeller driven by an extension shaft which passed beneath the cockpit floor. Early Airacobra pilots were fearful of the damage the drive shaft might inflict if it should break loose or be damaged in combat. The arrangement proved as safe as any other, although one expert noted that it led to vibration as the aircraft got older.

With the engine situated far to the aft, a 10-ft (3-m) drive shaft was required to couple the engine and propeller reduction gearing. The result was an aircraft fuselage that was rigid both literally and figuratively: engineers had few choices about where to put key features and the orthodox, semi-monocoque aft fuselage was literally 'stiff'. The US Army gave Bell no choice about incorporating tricycle landing gear – including a nose wheel that added 128 lb (58 kg) to the preponderance of weight up front. Nor did the Army allow any choice about four 0.30-in (7.62-mm) Colt wing guns, which eventually remained standard until the P-39Q model, even though they involved a weight penalty that exceeded their benefit.

The Airacobra's retractable tricycle landing gear included a non-steering, self-castoring nose wheel that retracted straight up and aft into the forward fuselage. The pilot raised or lowered the gear using a toggle switch in the cockpit. All wheels were constructed of magnesium alloy and used tubed tyres of three types – treaded for ice or snow-packed fields, flat contour for desert or sandy fields, and smooth contour for normal operations. Contrary to myth, the tricycle configuration was no less robust than conventional undercarriage would have been. When First Lieutenant George A. Ziendowski ran out of fuel on a routine flight in early 1942, he had no difficulty landing on Highway 501 near Latta, South Carolina, a secondary highway just 20 ft (6 m) wide.

Powerplant

The Allison V-1710 was a 1,100- to 1,300-hp (820- to 970-kW) liquid-cooled, 12-cylinder Vee-type inline engine equipped with an integral single-stage, single-speed supercharger. Manufactured by the Allison Division of General Motors in Indianapolis, Indiana, this engine evolved from a powerplant once used on US Navy lighter-than-air craft, known as blimps. Like most inline powerplants, it made use of a liquid cooling system employing Prestone (ethylene glycol, usually referred to as glycol for short). By and large, the US Army still believed in the perceived advantages of a liquid-cooled engine over an air-cooled radial. A memo of the time spoke of "Much closer tolerances (you can't hear pistons 'slap' in a liquid-cooled engine), higher compression ratios, and much better horsepower per pound..." Each engine had a military designation with a number suffix (such as V-1710-35) and a manufacturer's designation with a letter-number suffix (such as V-1710-E4).

The V-1710 engine, which also propelled the Curtiss P-40 Hawk series, was generally well-received in the field, although pilots and maintainers never quite forgave Bell for deleting the turbo-supercharger on the Airacobra and thus hindering its higher-altitude performance. A 'secret' wartime report filed from hot-climate Henderson Field on Guadalcanal said: "Reports on the Allison engine are very similar to reports elsewhere. Pilots like the Allison engines' 'guts' and ability to take punishment when necessary. All P-39 and P-40 pilots would like better altitude performance. Allison engine installation in the P-39-type airplane is preferred by the ground crews because it is easier to maintain. The P-39 has a better daily 'status record' than either the P-40 or P-38."

Cockpit

The pilot of the P-39 Airacobra sat in a bucket-type, metal, non-adjustable seat. A Type B-11 Sutton safety harness was attached to the seat with a roller mechanism. Inertia-reel harnesses were not in use, and the pilot had to release the four-way clasp to lean forward for some tasks.

With its unique aluminium automobile-style doors on both sides of the cockpit, the Airacobra was more easy to get into than it appeared, but the cockpit was cramped and space was at a premium. The cabin was designed to accommodate a pilot 5 ft 8 in (1.72 m) in height and weighing no more than 200 lb (91 kg) with parachute. The doors were fitted with positive locks and catches to prevent them from being sucked out at high speed. Each door had a roll-down-type Plexiglass panel which could splinter if not wound full up or down when closing the door. Improperly secured, the door had a tendency to fly off in high-speed dives, and pilots somehow ignored a latch retro-fitted by Bell to prevent separation. Although the problem persisted throughout the

The 31st Pursuit Group at Selfridge Field was the first Airacobra unit, equipping with P-39Cs from early 1941. Due to production delays, many flew without armament in the short period before they were replaced by P-39Ds. Note how the exhaust staining on these 31st PG P-39Ds has half-obliterated the fuselage national insignia.

In the last few months of peace for the USA, a massive exercise known as the Carolina Maneuvers took place, covering much of the southeast of the country. Seen leaving in his P-39D for a night observation of the 'Blue' army is 2nd Lt John Robertson of the 39th PS, 31st PG. On 7 December 1941, five fighter groups were equipped with the P-39.

Airacobra's career, ironically, pilots also reported that the door was difficult to remove after a ditching at sea.

The Airacobra concept was deemed sound enough to win an order for a single Bell XP-39 (Model 12) prototype on 7 October 1937. This progenitor of 8,000 Airacobras flew on 6 April 1938. Twelve months later, following extensive evaluation by the US Army, 12 of the YP-39 pre-production version were ordered for a wider service test, plus a planned YP-39A that did not materialise.

While the Army's early Airacobra development proceeded, the US Navy evaluated the Bell XFL-1 Airabonita, with tailwheel-type landing gear, strengthened fuselage, and an arrester hook. First flown on 13 May 1940, the XFL-1 suffered from the beginning from weight and balance problems, and never displayed serious promise of becoming an operational, carrier-based fighter.

Following service evaluation of the XP-39, the National Advisory Committee for Aeronautics carried out a study of the prototype, recommending changes which included the provision of fairing doors for the mainwheel units, a lower-profile cockpit canopy, resiting of the engine air intake and coolant radiators, and deletion of the turbocharger. The Airacobra prototype was modified to this configuration under the designation XP-39B. As a result, the decision was taken to delete the turbocharger from all future aircraft.

First deliveries

At first designated P-45, the new fighter was ordered into production on 10 August 1939, the first contract being for 809 aircraft. Before the first of these was delivered, the designation reverted to P-39. The first 20 were completed to XP-39B standard but were designated P-39C (Model 13). Sixty more had armament changes and emerged as the P-39D (Model 15).

The US Army ordered 369 P-39Ds in September 1940, and initial deliveries began seven months later. The first operational squadron was the 39th Pursuit Squadron, 31st Pursuit Group, at Selfridge Field, Michigan, soon followed by the 40th and 41st. ('Pursuit' squadrons and groups became 'Fighter' squadrons and groups on 15 May 1942.)

At the same time, Bell began to turn out the first Airacobras ordered by the British Purchasing Commission, which followed up on an unfulfilled French order. Great Britain signed contracts for 675 Model 14 fighters (initially dubbed the Caribou, and later known in US parlance as the P-400). They were like the P-39D but with the 37-mm cannon replaced by one of 20-mm and the six 0.30-in. (7.62-mm) machine-guns replaced by an equal number of 0.303-in (7.7-mm) guns.

British Cobras

The United Kingdom began to receive its first Airacobras in July 1941. The first aircraft, a P-39C, arrived on 3 July and was flying three days later. An Airacobra was delivered to the Air Fighting Development Unit at Duxford on 30 July 1941 and was evaluated over a prolonged time – including comparisons with a captured Messerschmitt Bf 109E and with a Supermarine Spitfire Mk VB. Not surprisingly, the Airacobra was competitive against both fighters in speed and manoeuvrability at low altitude. The Airacobra out-turned and out-dived the Bf 109E in every encounter. But the mock dogfights were all conducted at 15,000 ft (4572 m) or lower, and British pilots found the Bell fighter "utterly useless" above 20,000 ft (6096 m).

In August of that year, No. 601 Squadron began to exchange its Hawker Hurricanes for Airacobras. A brief action was the subject of a November 1941 report from the US air attaché in London to the War Department in Washington:

"Permission was granted to take the first four Airacobras to RAF Manston, and from there to go to [occupied] France for trial against any enemy that might possibly be encountered. On 9 October 1941, the first two Airacobra airplanes fired their guns at a small trawler and at some men standing on the docks in a harbour of a French town. The following day some invasion barges were fired upon by an Airacobra which went to the French coast alone." The report noted that five Airacobras had crashed in RAF service and that "in each case the cause was determined 100 per cent pilot error".

The Bell company newspaper, the *Bellringer*, ran a two-page photo spread in December 1941 entitled 'Cobras Battle for Britain'. The subtitle read '"Airacobra Best Fighter in the World," says RAF.' In fact, nobody in the RAF was uttering any such sentiment.

RAF rejection

Royal Air Force officers immediately grasped the significance of the decision to delete the turbocharger. RAF pilots found that the Airacobra had inadequate climb and high-altitude performance. The fighter was simply unacceptable for the fighting conditions to be found in the European Theatre. Only about 80 of the aircraft in the original order actually entered RAF service, and only with No. 601 Squadron, which gladly gave them up for Supermarine Spitfires in March 1942. Britain eventually transferred a number of these aircraft to Russia and returned others to the USAAF. Some 212 of the Airacobra Mk Is originally ordered by the RAF were transferred to the USSR, although 54 of these were lost en route when the ships carrying them to Soviet ports were sunk. A few of these hapless P-400s ended up in American livery on Guadalcanal.

Although Bell incorporated changes in the P-39F, P-39J, P-39K and P-39L, the essential features of the Airacobras remained little different. Likewise, the P-39M, P-39N and

The first export customer for the Airacobra was Great Britain. Prior to delivery of its P-400s, which were originally named Caribou, three P-39Cs (DS173, 174 and 175) were shipped to the UK for trials. Unlike the Airacobra I, these aircraft had the 37-mm cannon and four nose guns of the USAAC's P-39Cs.

RAF experience with the Airacobra was neither extensive nor happy: only one squadron (No. 601) received the aircraft and then only flew three combat operations with it.* Skylark XIII *was AH601, the squadron CO's aircraft, and this view shows the Airacobra Mk I's long-barrelled 20-mm cannon and the 'Duxford fishtail' flame damper exhausts which were fitted after trials at Boscombe Down.

P-39Q – the latter two earmarked for the Soviet Union – had only minor changes.

On the day the US entered the war, the US Army had fielded a total of five pursuit groups equipped with 600 P-39D models: the 8th at Mitchell Field, New York; the 31st and 52nd at Selfridge, Michigan; the 36th in Puerto Rico; and the 53rd at MacDill Field, Florida.

Up to 100 Airacobras participated in the war games held in North Carolina and Louisiana in 1941. Company documents indicated that the Airacobras "established themselves as masters in the art of dealing death and destruction" while supposedly making life easy for maintenance crews. "Tie-ups for mechanical servicing were negligible. With a total of five squadrons on the line, 85 per cent of the planes were ready, willing, and able to let go at anybody at any time." Some of these Airacobras were slated for the Philippines, part of a build-up that was interrupted by the 8 December 1941 Japanese attack. None ever got there, but P-39s did reach Hawaii and found their way, thereafter, to New Guinea and Guadalcanal.

Combat

In 1942, the first year of US participation in World War II, Bell's Buffalo and Niagara Falls plants were receiving routine technical reports on P-39 performance from locations as distant as Iceland and the Panama Canal Zone, but most Airacobras were performing training duty in the US.

As part of Operation Bolero, the movement of an American expeditionary force to bases in England, the Army planned transatlantic ferry flights in early 1942 by the 31st Pursuit Group with P-39 Airacobras, together with a P-38 Lightning and B-17 Flying Fortress group. Eventually, P-39 participation in Bolero was cancelled and the 31st proceeded to Europe by sea, equipping with Spitfires on arrival.

Australia briefly employed 22 P-39D and P-39F Airacobras in its Nos 23, 24, 83 and 84 Squadrons, on home defence duties from April 1942. The Airacobra's time in the Royal Australian Air Force was brief and largely without notice.

The first combat mission by the Airacobra was flown by the 8th Fighter Group, which in March 1942 came to Australia, and thereafter to Port Moresby, New Guinea with D models. The report by Lieutenant Colonel Boyd D. 'Buzz' Wagner described the action against Mitsubishi A6M Zero fighters as follows:

"On [30 April 1942], 13 P-39Ds took off from Port Moresby on a ground strafing mission against Lae Airdrome, 180 miles [290 km] north. Approach was made on Lae from 50 miles [80 km] out to sea to avoid detection. When about 20 miles [32 km] out, four planes were sent ahead to engage the Japanese security patrol over Lae drome. Top cover drew enemy security patrol off to the east of the drome and

Above: The survivors of No. 601's Airacobras and all but a few of the others to reach the UK were supplied to the Soviet Union. Many others were supplied direct from Bell production. This posed view shows a VVS P-39 undergoing rearmament. Weapons servicing could be an extremely time-consuming affair, with cannon repairs involving removal of the entire propeller assembly and many other parts.

Below: This view of a USAAF Airacobra undergoing depot maintenance at Garbutt Field, Queensland, Australia gives a more realistic idea of the difficulties inherent in P-39 servicing. Despite the many removable panels on the P-39, engine maintenance was not easy. Some operations involved removing the rear canopy, head armour, the pilot's seat and one of the cockpit doors, as seen here.

By 1937, many in the Navy's Bureau of Aeronautics had come to believe that the radial engine was all but obsolete for fighter aircraft. Bell built a single Model 5 Airabonita and submitted it for a 1938 fighter competition. While the BuAer. was willing to consider a liquid-cooled engine, a tricycle undercarriage was a bit too radical a departure from convention and the XFL-1 (as the Navy called it) was the sole taildragger Cobra. The design lost out to Vought's XF4U-1 Corsair.

no resistance by air was encountered during the strafing. A line of 13 to 15 bombers was strafed on a sea approach in a three-three plane element. The planes in each element were disposed in echelon right. Our strafing planes were then attacked from above by several Zero fighters. Belly tanks were dropped immediately and throttles opened. Our formation began to pull away from the Zeros when the last four P-39s in the formation engaged in combat with three Zeros. In the meantime, more Zeros appeared and it is estimated that there were 12-13 altogether. The P-39s were hopelessly outnumbered so the entire formation turned back and a terrific dogfight ensued. All P-39s going down had been hit in the cooling system, as glycol spray could be seen streaming out behind, while all Zeros shot down went burning. All three P-39 pilots were safe upon landing, either bailing out or crash-landing on the beach." Wagner was credited with three Zeros and First Lieutenant George B. Greene, Jr with one.

First Airacobra 'ace'

The magazine for Bell employees sang the praises of pilot First Lieutenant Paul G. Brown, 'the first Airacobra ace', in an August 1942 article. (Brown is officially credited with three aerial victories.) Brown, the magazine reported, "has introduced a new technique in knocking out Jap Zeros. His is the simple method, backed by the sturdy structure of the Airacobra, of ramming 'em out of the sky.

"As he described the 'ramming' incident, he was flying over New Guinea with six companions on a scouting mission when they spotted six or seven Jap Zeros through a hole in the clouds. Going into action, each of the American fliers selected one enemy as his own special target.

"'I guess I was too eager to get close before using my cannon,' Lieutenant Brown said. 'In any event, my left wing caught the Jap's rudder and tore it off. The Zero plunged to the ground. I had hit him at 3,000 ft [914 m] and my plane dived to within 500 feet [152 m] before I was able to pull out of it. When I got back to my base, I found the edge of my left wing banged up, with pieces of the Zero imbedded in it. Some of the boys made me a match-box out of the pieces as a souvenir of the encounter.' On another mission, Brown made a forced landing by 'pancaking' on a beach in enemy territory. He managed to escape by digging sand from beneath the plane so he could release the landing gear."

The US air commander in the Southwest Pacific, Major General George H. Brett, was asked if US fighter pilots would give up their P-39s for Japanese Zeros. According to Brett, "The answer is definitely and almost unanimously in the negative. Such a trade would mean giving up the protection of armour, leak-proof gasoline tanks, and parachutes." Myths about the Mitsubishi fighter and its pilots died hard.

Dive-bomber Airacobra

At embattled Henderson Field on Guadalcanal, P-39D-2s and repossessed P-400s fought Japan's best, including the vaunted Mitsubishi A6M Zero. First Lieutenant Wallace L. Dinn, Jr of the 67th Fighter Squadron, 58th Fighter Group pioneered the use of the Airacobra as a dive-bomber to attack Japanese shipping, a role for which the P-39 had never been designed but at which – with proper technique and tactics – it excelled.

A 29 March 1943 report by an Army materiel officer visiting Guadalcanal described the

A53-20 was a P-39D-1, one of 22 D and F models that were allocated RAAF serials. Fifteen saw service with the RAAF between April 1942 and approximately October 1943. The aircraft were shuffled between four different squadrons before the survivors were returned to the USAAF.

In US service, the P-39 saw no combat in Europe and fairly little in North Africa. In the Pacific, the Airacobra, together with the P-40, was the primary Army fighter until well into 1944. These P-39Qs are seen on Makin Island in the Gilberts in 1943.

P-39 and P-63 production continued in parallel for some time to fulfil previous contracts. Seen here at Bell's Wheatfield factory at Niagara Falls, New York are some of the last Airacobras (P-39Q-30s – first, second, sixth and seventh rows from the right) and some early Kingcobras (P-63A-8s – third, fourth, fifth and eighth rows).

Below: The vast bulk of Kingcobra production went directly to the Soviet Union. Here, newly-built P-63A-10s await delivery by the Alsib (Alaska-Siberia) ferry route.

Airacobra in action:

"P-39K airplanes are...well liked by the pilots, especially since the arrival of P-38s on the island, which can give them high cover and allow them to operate in their own element. However, the P-39 and P-40 pilots resent their inability to fight at high altitude themselves and were very much impressed with reports [brought to them from stateside] on performance of the P-39N and P-63 airplanes.

"Army and Marine ground troops concede that victory at Guadalcanal would have been virtually impossible without the splendid work of the P-39s and P-40s in dive-bombing and ground strafing enemy strongpoints. The 37-mm cannon was particularly effective in this work. Its devastating firepower knocked out steel landing barges [and] anti-aircraft and machine-gun positions. In the last days of organised Jap resistance on the island, P-39s flew individual missions of dive-bombing and ground strafing from dawn until dusk. A shuttle service was in effect, with single P-39s landing for reloading and servicing every 5 to 10 minutes. One pilot reported flying 35 combat dive-bombing and strafing missions within four to five days."

The report continues by describing an action on 6 March 1943, only hours after P-39s arrived on Guadalcanal from Canton Island: "Two new pilots flew wing positions with two more experienced pilots on a routine search and familiarisation mission. The two new pilots had approximately six months' fighter experience at Canton Island following graduation from flying school. This was their first mission in the combat zone. They spotted 15 Japanese two-place dive-bombers returning from a mission. The four-ship flight was flying at approximately 4,000 ft [1219 m] and the bombers at 1,500 to 2,500 ft [457 to 762 m].

"The P-39s immediately attacked, all six machine-guns and cannons firing. After making their initial attack, they were in turn attacked by 40 Zero fighters, flying high cover. The enemy fighters overestimated their dive and missed them on the first pass. The P-39s dove for the wave tops, rolled all shutters tightly shut, and 'pushed everything to the firewall'. They easily outdistanced the Zeros and returned to Henderson Field unmarked. The Coast-watcher gave the flight credit for six dive-bombers which failed to return from the mission." Mindful of the need for feedback on cannon performance, the report concluded, "On personal inspection of the 37-mm brass, it was found that out of 12 shells fired without a jam on a single ship, three were slightly pinched by the lockframe closing on the forward edge of the casing. No jams occurred on any of the four ships' cannon." The quote contradicts other sources that say the cannon had a troublesome tendency to jam after firing a few shots.

Firepower

Another Army document noted that "pilots prefer the 37-mm to the 20-mm cannon because of the greater destructive power. Personal accounts of the pilots stated two instances of complete disintegration of Zero fighters when hit head-on with 37-mm shells. [There was] one instance of blowing off the entire tail assembly and part of the fuselage of a Japanese twin-engine bomber with 37-mm cannon fire."

In the last major air action at Guadalcanal on

Below: Major V. F. Sirotin of 17 IAP had 21 kills and some flamboyant nose art marked on his P-63 by early 1945. Although he was a Hero of the Soviet Union, this score was not enough to rank him among the 100 top Soviet aces of the war.

Below: A P-63C of an unidentified Soviet unit comes in to land. Underwing guns were deleted from Soviet P-39Qs and P-63s. Kingcobras were noted in service in the USSR as late as 1949.

Cobra Variants

Left: P-63Cs for France and the USSR are seen in this Bell publicity photo, together with a P-63A in USAAF markings.

Above: The P-63 was a far better performer at altitude than its predecessor, but was to be little used in the interceptor role.

17 June 1943, Airacobras tangled with dozens of Japanese bombers and fighters. Captain William D. Wells led a brace of Airacobras into a formation of 30 to 35 Aichi Type 99 carrier bombers and shot down four of them.

Although there were once plans to do so, no P-39 ever equipped a USAAF squadron in the British Isles. Typical of combat groups that had been scheduled to blood the Airacobra, the 31st Fighter Group ended up, instead, flying Spitfires after reaching the United Kingdom from Selfridge Field.

The Aleutians

The Aleutians were another story. On 14 September 1942, 14 P-39Ds and Fs of the 54th Fighter Group flew from a steel-planking Aleutian airstrip as part of a force, also including P-38s, B-24s, and a lone B-17, which made the first counter-strike on Japanese forces in the region. Airacobra pilots strafed anti-aircraft gun positions with their nose cannon, and shot down two floatplane fighters.

It is probably not true, as was claimed during the war, that First Lieutenant Clyde G. Rice shot down a Zero with a single 37-mm round high over the Aleutians. (Rice was said to have got several Airacobra victories in a 1942 article, though he is not officially credited with any.) However, First Lieutenant Gerald R. Johnson did rack up half a dozen Zero kills in the Aleutians at the controls of a P-39D Airacobra of the 42nd Fighter Squadron, 54th Fighter Group, before raising his total to 22 elsewhere.

P-39 and P-400 Airacobras found their way to US squadrons in North Africa. The American press gave some attention to the success of the Airacobra in prevailing over the Bf 109, and to the Bell fighter's role in knocking out tanks with its cannon – both almost certainly exaggeration. The USAAF decorated First Lieutenant Wallter J. Rivers for a setting afire a German destroyer in a P-39 strafing mission from North Africa. Wartime dispatches contained no dates, locations, units, etc. Rivers was said to have left the destroyer 'a roaring furnace' thanks to the firepower of his nose cannon. Both 20-mm and 37-mm nose armament was used in the theatre.

Most combat operations in the Airacobra were carried out by the Soviet air force in support of the Red Army. Intended primarily for close air support (including anti-tank work) but also employed in other roles including air-to-air combat, Airacobras equipped the 9th Guards Fighter Division and the 16th Guards Fighter Air Regiment.

On the Russian front

A glimpse of Airacobras at war on the Russian front, probably exaggerated, was provided by radio newsman Robert Magidoff on the NBC News Roundup on 25 May 1942: "I spent the day with a Russian squadron flying exclusively modern American fighters," Magidoff reported. "The squadron I visited brought down 86 enemy planes since the outbreak of the war; 29 of these laid down by flying Tommyhawks [a reference to the Curtiss Tomahawk], Kittyhawks, and Airacobras. 'Just look at these Cobras',' squadron leader Dimitro said to me, pointing at three fighters dashing across a rain-soaked runway. It took them but 20 seconds to take off. They circled above the field twice and then disappeared behind the horizon, on their way to patrol the skies over Moscow.

"'Yes, the Tommyhawk [*sic*] is a great plane,' said Dimitro, 'but the Kittyhawk is better and the Airacobra better still. You ought to see it in action.'" The broadcaster went on to proclaim that the Airacobra would be "the key to victory over Hitler in 1942."

Russian pilots often had opportunities to engage the Messerschmitt Bf 109 at low altitude, where the American-built fighter performed best. The 'Cobrastochka' (dear little Cobra) clearly performed better in Russian hands than American. Lieutenant Colonel Alexandr I. Pokryshkin became the Allies' second-ranking ace of the war with 59 aerial victories, 48 of them accomplished in his Airacobra. Eight other Soviet P-39 pilots reportedly racked up 20 or more aerial victories.

Among Russians praised in Bell documents were the brothers Glinka, Dmitri and Boris. Dmitri was reported to have flown 240 sorties and to have downed 39 German aircraft. Boris's score was listed as 26.

French forces received a total of 247 P-39K, P-39N, and P-39Q Airacobras. Free French pilots first received P-39 Airacobras at Maison Blanche in North Africa in May 1943 and a few days later claimed their first kill, a Dornier Do 217. Italy took delivery of 74 P-39Ns and 75

Most of the Army's P-63s went straight into training units, where they provided an economical alternative to P-47s and P-51s needed on the war fronts. These are P-63A-6s.

P-39Qs late in the war.

Although P-39 variants proliferated, all Airacobras were very similar. In one central Pacific squadron, US Army mechanics created an 'extra' Airacobra, nicknamed *Spare Parts*, from hulks and scrap. Painted black with a question mark on the fin in place of a serial number, this fighter flew night intercept missions.

Features in common to all models of the P-39 included a wing span of 34 ft (10.36 m) and length of 30 ft 2 in (9.19 m). All had a height, with a propeller blade vertical, of 11 ft 10 in (3.63 m), except the P-39Q of 12 ft 5 in (3.79 m). All models had the same ailerons, although several minor changes were made in the design of flaps on different Airacobra variants. All models had the same rudder area and movement, but there were minor changes in other tail features. Minor changes were found in export aircraft including those for France, Italy, and Australia.

Some 4,924 P-39s were sent to the Soviet Union, of which 4,758 reached their destinations. A total of 9,529 Airacobras was produced between 1939 and 1944. The US Army Air Forces reached a peak inventory of P-39 Airacobras in February 1944 with 2,105 aircraft. Production ended with assembly on 25 July 944 of the final P-39Q-30, aircraft 44-71504.

Airacobra units

The following Fighter Groups of the Air Corps/Air Force operated the P-39 between 1941 and 1945, although in some cases very briefly (squadrons in parentheses): the 8th FG (35th, 36th, 80th), 15th FG (12th, 15th, 36th), 18th FG (78th, 333rd), 20th FG (55th, 77th, 79th), 21st FG (531st), 31st FG (39th, 40th, 41st), 33rd FG (58th, 59th, 60th), 52nd FG (2nd, 4th), 53rd FG (13th, 14th and 15th), 54th FG (42nd, 56th, 57th), 56th FG (61st, 62nd, 63rd), 58th FG (67th, 68th, 69th), 318th FG (72nd), 332nd FG (99th, 100th, 301st, 302nd), 338th FG (305th, 306th, 312th), 343rd FG (18th), 347th FG (67th, 68th, 70th), 350th FG (345th, 346th, 347th), 354th (353rd, 355th, 356th), 357th FG (362nd, 363rd, 364th), 367th FG (392nd, 393rd, 394th), 372nd FG (407th, 408th, 409th), 473rd FG (451st, 452nd). P-39s were also used by the 342nd Composite Group (33rd), 59th Observation Group (488th, 489th, 490th), and the following bomber groups in the training role: 48th BG, 84th BG, 85th BG, 339th BG, 404th BG, 405th BG, 406th BG and the 478th BG.

Kingcobra

The Bell P-63 Kingcobra was very much a different aircraft – different in design, size, and performance – despite its misleading resemblance to, and commonality in certain respects with, the P-39 Airacobra. Common features included the general outward appearance, the engine behind the pilot driving a propeller through a long shaft, a nose cannon (albeit a different one), and tricycle landing gear. The principal difference, of course, was a wholly new, laminar-flow wing.

The Kingcobra is often described incorrectly as a larger and more powerful version of the XP-39E Airacobra for the air-to-ground role in close support and battlefield interdiction missions (while the XP-39E, itself, is often described incorrectly as having a laminar-flow wing). In fact, the XP-39E and P-63 were introduced at about the same time, in early 1941, as comparable but dissimilar approaches to the same problem, and both were initially expected to use the ill-fated Continental V-1430 engine. When it became evident that the V-1430 would not materialise, work on the Kingcobra proceeded based on the V-1710.

Above: In addition to training future fighter pilots, Kingcobras were used as 'jump ships' by bomber training units so that crews could practise defence against fighter attack. These aircraft were often painted in vivid colours.

Below: In order to increase the realism of bomber gunnery training, the extraordinary Project Pin Ball was devised. This involved armoured RP-63 Kingcobras being shot at with frangible bullets. This is the first RP-63G.

New design

On 27 June 1941, roughly coinciding with its decision to cancel the P-76, the US Army placed an order for two Bell XP-63 Kingcobra prototypes (41-19511/19512) to be powered by the 1,325-hp (988-kW) Allison V-1710-47 (E9) liquid-cooled engine in the same rear-mounted location as the Airacobra. The P-63 was in fact a new aircraft, capitalising on the P-39 layout. Most of its design features had been 'set in concrete' before Pearl Harbor, when the design looked as good as anything likely to fly in the near future.

Delays must have made it seem, for a time, that the P-63 Kingcobra programme was never going to get off the ground. Almost immediately in the early design stage, the 'lightweight' P-63 ballooned from 8,500 lb (3855 kg) to 10,000 lb (4536 kg). Conceived with four 0.50-in (12.7-mm) wing guns in addition to a nose cannon and two nose machine-guns (like the XP-39E), the evolving P-63 shed its wing armament to reduce weight, though wing guns were added later. The first aircraft flew on 7 December 1942 but was lost in an accident just weeks later. The second prototype flew on 5 February 1943 but crashed the following May.

Fortunately, a third prototype, the XP-63A, had been ordered in June 1942, and it flew on 26 April 1943. The XP-63A became an effective third prototype and test ship for the continuing development programme. It demonstrated a ruggedness that boded well for the harsh needs of the Soviet Union on the Eastern Front. A lightweight by the standard of most wartime fighters, the Kingcobra was to prove a sturdy machine that could absorb considerable battle damage.

On 29 September 1942, the US Army ordered production of the Kingcobra, which began in October 1943. The production P-63A, 1,725 of which were built in numerous sub-variants with minor changes in armament, armour and ordnance, was followed in 1943 by the P-63C with a 1,800-hp (1342-kW) Allison V-1710-117(E21) engine with water injection. The Royal Air Force tested one P-63A (42-68937) as the Kingcobra Mk I (FR408) and it is believed that a second machine, identity unknown, was also flown by British pilots.

One-off Kings

The P-63D was basically a P-63A with a bubble canopy, slightly greater (by 10 in/25 cm) wing span and a V-1710-109 engine.

Above right: The most radically modified P-63 was the Navy's swept-wing L-39. Two test aircraft gathered data on low-speed flight.

Left: The P-63F was essentially a P-63E with a taller fin and rudder. The 'X' markings signified its experimental category.

This Bell-modified P-63A was one of a number of tail configurations trialled by the manufacturer and the military on Kingcobra airframes.

The US Army examined the P-63A at Eglin Field, Florida, and concluded that it was not operationally suitable as a combat aircraft, even though pilots spoke well of it and performance was comparable to that of other fighters. The Army's reaction may have been due in part to the availability of newer types, including the P-51 Mustang. The Kingcobra remained an excellent candidate for use by the Soviet air arm, which had a need for a high-altitude fighter (where the P-39 Airacobra was deficient) which could also be employed in ground attack with the 37-mm gun.

The P-63C introduced a distinctive small ventral fin to improve lateral stability. Some 1,427 were manufactured. A Russian fighter pilot called this aircraft a "tank of the skies," reflecting the P-63 Kingcobra's survivability and potency against all sorts of ground targets, including main battle tanks.

P-63 variations

The sole, bubble-canopied P-63D was followed by the first of 13 P-63Es which retained the standard canopy. The P-63F introduced the V-1710-135(G4) powerplant and a taller vertical fin; one of two built survived the war to become H. L. Pemberton's mount in the 1947 Cleveland Air Races. This trio of improved Kingcobras, the P-63D, P-63E and P-63F – which warranted a new manufacturer's designation as the Bell Model 41 – came closest among Kingcobra variants to measuring up to the war's better-remembered fighter types, including the P-47 Thunderbolt and P-51 Mustang.

P-63s were ferried to Russia in seemingly endless numbers (beginning with the P-63A variant), pausing at way stations in Alaska and Iran. Years later, US veteran Wally Forman remembered the procedure. "Madison, Wisconsin was a stop-over for 39s and 63s bound for Russia. First leg was from Niagara Falls to Selfridge Field, then refuel. Second leg was Selfridge to Truax Field [in Madison]. The fighters were picked up by Russian female ferry pilots at Truax and flown to Edmonton, Anchorage and across.

"The Russian women were daredevil pilots, full of bravado. Not allowed to fraternise with GIs, but anxious to show their flying skill and bravery. One method of showing off was to pull up the wheels the second they had flying speed. Sometimes they pulled them up just *before* they had flying speed, resulting in settling back to the ground with those propeller blades beating a sickening tattoo on the concrete runways.

"Our GI barracks were right out in the field, where the runways made a big 'X'. If you were sleeping, the raucous noise of those beating propeller blades made you sit straight up in bed – sort of like a teacher using a piece of scratchy chalk on a blackboard. Don't believe there was any loss of life, but lots of plane repairs were necessary.

"Only fatality while I was there was in a 39. SOP [standard operating procedure] was to switch to the fullest fuel tank on final approach. One day a 39 did this, but the refueller at Selfridge had left the cap off one gas tank. When the pilot switched to that tank, it didn't even have fumes in it. Without an engine a 39 flew like a rock. He pancaked onto the highway that ran up the east side of the field, flipped and landed upside down. Kaput!"

Like the P-39, the P-63 in Soviet hands was short-changed again in terms of its reputation: though the Kingcobra, as noted, proved to be a potent ground attacker and tank-buster, it never received the 'press' of the Ilyushin Il-2 *Shturmovik*.

In Free French service, the P-63 had a more innocuous career. A total of 114 P-63C-5 Kingcobras reached the French beginning in

Racing Cobras

Above: Amid the many modified Cobras to appear on the racing scene in the immediate post-war years was Jim Harp's stock P-39L, seen at Cleveland in 1949.

Right: One of two P-63Fs was sold on the civilian market and raced for many years. A first place in the stock final at the Miami Air Races of 1979 was its last race to date.

N40A was built as a P-39Q-20 and converted to a TP-39Q two-seater. Reconverted to single-seat configuration, it appeared at Reno in 1972 and 1976, but never placed higher than eighth in the Consolation Race. Seen here at Orange County in 1959, it flies today with the Kalamazoo collection.

By 1970, stock Cobras were no longer competitive racers. Larry Havers took this ex-Thompson Trophy racer P-63C-5 (N9009, formerly N63231) and modified it almost beyond recognition. Havers had to bail out of the Cobra over Long Beach harbour after its engine failed on a 1972 test flight.

June 1945 (not 300 as often reported), too late for World War II action. In post-war years French 'Kings' were assigned to Sidi Ahmed in North Africa. In 1949, many were shipped to South Vietnam, where flying began at Tan Son Nhut airfield near Saigon in August. The 'Kings' moved to Hanoi and began flying strikes against Viet Minh forces in January 1951. The Kingcobra's brief role in the first Indochina war included several aircraft losses and concluded with a final mission flown on 30 April 1951.

The Kingcobra never served in combat with US forces. At one point in 1943, plans for the US IX Fighter Command in England called for 21 fighter groups of which five would be equipped with P-63 Kingcobras, the remainder with P-47s and P-51s. This plan never reached fruition, and Kingcobras retained stateside by the US Army were used primarily for training.

Flying targets

In 1945 and after, P-63 Kingcobras were used as flying targets, painted bright red ('Spanish orange'), piloted, and shot at by bomber crews using frangible bullets. As described in a Bell publication, "The frangible bullet, a Training Command invention, is a 0.30-in (7.62-mm) machine-gun slug made from a combination lead and plastic material hard enough to withstand being fired through a machine-gun but soft enough to splatter harmlessly into a fine powder on contact with the armoured plate surrounding vital parts of the target Kingcobra."

Project Pin Ball was a unique and peculiar way to achieve gunnery practice, but it worked. Combat equipment was removed and these 'robot' RP-63A, RP-63C, and RP-63G aircraft were insulated with a protective covering of Duralumin alloy, bullet-proof windshield and canopy glass, a steel grille over the engine air intake, steel guards for the exhaust stacks, and thick-walled, hollow propellers. When a hit was scored by another aircraft performing gunnery practice, a red light blinked to confirm impact – hence the project name, based on an arcade game machine.

Swept wings

A far more radical departure was the US Navy's first – and for many years, only – swept-wing aircraft. Two P-63 Kingcobras were rebuilt with swept-back wings and were test-flown under the non-standard designation L-39. The Navy was far behind US Army Air Forces in exploiting the swept-wing planform, developed in large part on the basis of captured German findings. The L-39 flew more than a year before the USAAF's XP-86 Sabre and provided valuable swept-wing data to all of the American armed forces.

At least two P-63s were modified to test a V-shaped tail configuration or 'butterfly' tail, more familiar as a feature of the Beech Bonanza. One (a P-63A-9) operated in a Bell programme at the factory while another (an RP-63G) was apparently converted by the Army. These V-tailed Kingcobras contributed to flight research even after Bell set aside early plans to include such an empennage on the XS-1 rocket-powered research aircraft.

When the National Air Races resumed in 1946, P-63 Kingcobras soon outnumbered Airacobras among the participants seeking the newly revived Thompson Trophy in Cleveland, Ohio. The P-63 was more powerful and heavier than the P-39 and had a larger wing with greater wing area – not an advantage, indeed not really needed, for pylon air racing. Nevertheless, 12 P-63s participated in the post-war races, as opposed to only three examples of the P-39.

The 'King' gave a good account for itself in the 1946 and 1947 Thompson Trophy races in Cleveland, Ohio and in the 1947 Tinnerman Trophy Race, a seven-lap event created especially for P-63 Kingcobras in the unfulfilled hope of producing a close race. The Kingcobra did less well in the 1946 and 1947 Bendix cross-country events, which began in California and terminated at Cleveland. 1947 was apparently the last year a Bell fighter flew in a cross-country event, though P-39s and P-63s appeared in pylon racing when it was restored in 1964.

Total Kingcobra production reached 3,303 airframes. Some 2,456 Kingcobras were delivered to Russia and, as noted, 114 P-63Cs went to France's Armée de l'Air. The Kingcobra was more than Bell's last big fighter success. It made a solid contribution and deserves to be remembered for it. In the post-war era, five P-63E-1 Kingcobras went to Honduras, where they fulfilled a military role only briefly; two later returned to the US in civilian registrations.

Robert F. Dorr

Bell P-39/P-63 Variants

Bell Model 3

The Bell Model 3 was a fighter proposal made by Bell Aircraft Corporation at its Buffalo, New York headquarters shortly after Larry Bell founded the company in 1935. The design was a response to Air Corps specification X-609 issued in early 1937. The proposal was displayed in crude mock-up form at Buffalo on 24 May 1937.

The Model 3 combined the sleek appearance of pre-war Greve or Thompson Trophy air racers with the tricycle gear, rear-mounted engine, and automobile-style pilot doors of the later Airacobra. On the Model 3, the pilot's cockpit was located completely behind the trailing edge of the wing, in the manner of the Curtiss XP-37. Unlike the Curtiss aircraft, the Bell design had tricycle landing gear because, with the wing blocking vision in front of and below the pilot, it would have been an extremely difficult aircraft to put down on a runway. Like the later Airacobra, it would have had a 1,150-hp (858-kW) Allison V-1710-C7 inline engine mounted in the fuselage behind the pilot, operated by a driveshaft extension running beneath the pilot's seat. Bell also offered rocket boosters to improve climb performance. The mock-up displayed provisions for a 25-mm nose cannon with 50 rounds of ammunition and two 0.50-in (12.7-mm) machine-guns with 200 rounds each.

The Model 3 would have been 27 ft 10.5 in (8.49 m) long with a wing span of 35 ft (10.67 m) and height of 9 ft 4.5 in (2.86 m). It was concurrent with, rather than a predecessor of, the design that became the Airacobra. Once the manufacturer moved ahead with the Model 4 instead, this project was terminated.

XP-39 (Bell Model 4)

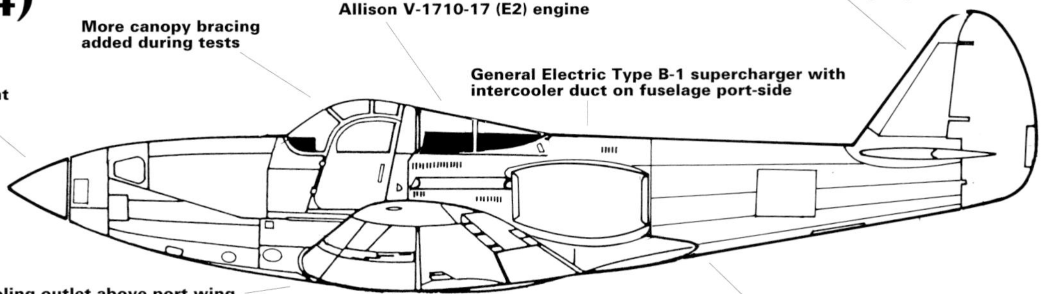

The XP-39 evolved after Bell engineers looked at several design concepts under the Model 4 rubric, also as a response to the 1937 specification X-609. The programme matured from drawing board to mock-up to actual aircraft with minor changes in cockpit and fin design. The prototype was powered by a 1,150-hp (858-kW) V-1710-17 (E2) engine and was fitted with a B-5 turbo-supercharger on the left side of its fuselage behind the exhaust stacks. It was the only Airacobra built with a second-stage turbo-supercharger. The decision to delete such a feature from the Airacobra in subsequent variants doomed this fighter to inadequate performance above 15,000 ft (4572 m), but it was competitive below that height.

The progenitor of the Airacobra series featured a three-bladed Curtiss-Wright propeller, and a radiator and oil cooler on its port side behind the exhaust outlets. The XP-39 went through minor changes, including the addition of braces on its cockpit, between roll-out and first flight.

The prototype for the Airacobra series took to the air for its maiden flight on 6 April 1939, flown by Bell test pilot James Taylor – not at Buffalo but at Wright Field, Ohio, to where it had been shipped by land. Taylor kept his records in a diary written in pencil, and his entry for that day consisted of just 29 words: "Flew airplane today. Everything went fine in the air. Experienced some oil cooler trouble. Also readjusted the idle setting getting 550 RPM to 2,600. Total flying time 20 minutes."

The XP-39 looked much like the shiny metal children's toys of the era – in a silver-painted finish with a dark anti-glare shield painted between the windscreen and the propeller. Red and white American stripes appeared horizontally on the rudder in the style typical of the late 1930s. This aircraft later became the XP-39B.

XP-39 serial (1): 38-326

The XP-39 had prominent intakes on the fuselage for the centre-mounted engine supercharger.

XP-39B (possibly designated Bell Model 4B)

First flown on 25 November 1939, the XP-39B was the original P-39 aircraft with many changes. Its improved Allison engine was now designated V-1710-37 (E5) and, most importantly, the turbo-supercharger was deleted.

Many of the changes occurred after NACA at Langley Field, Virginia conducted wind-tunnel tests on the prototype XP-39 and determined a need for numerous changes. They included streamlining the wheel doors, lowering and streamlining the canopy, moving the carburettor air scoop from the left side of the fuselage to behind the cockpit, and moving radiators from the fuselage sides to the central wingroot leading edges.

Removal of the turbo-supercharger was only one of the measures which defined the production Airacobra's configuration, but it may have doomed the P-39 to 'also ran' status among wartime fighters. This step reduced the P-39's high-altitude performance drastically, reflecting a by-then out-of-date doctrine which considered pursuit planes to be low-altitude, close-support craft for the ground infantryman.

The large fuselage side intakes were removed from the XP-39B, as was the supercharger and its underfuselage projections.

Among the changes made to the XP-39 to produce the XP-39B was a revised canopy structure, complete with tinted top panel.

Had it retained the turbo-supercharger, the Airacobra clearly would have played a more important role in the air-to-air arena.

The XP-39B suffered a belly landing during a demonstration at Wright Field, Ohio on 6 January 1940 at the hands of Army pilot Captain George E. Price (who refused an order by Larry Bell to bail out when an inflight emergency occurred). The aircraft survived and Captain Price later demonstrated it at Bolling Field in Washington, DC.

XP-39B serial (1 modified): 38-326

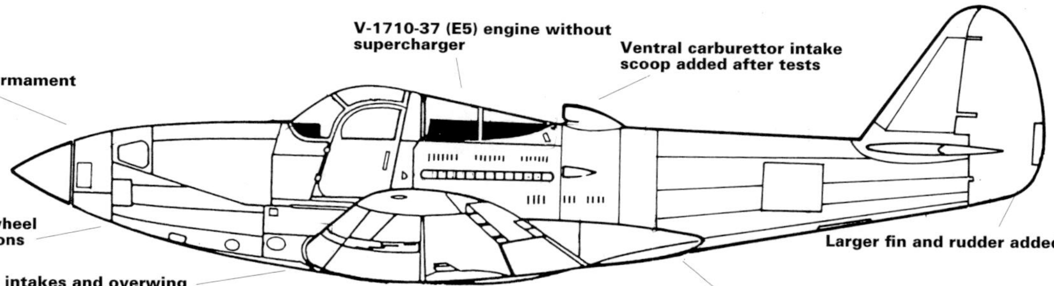

YP-39 (Model 12)

The YP-39 service-test model is best understood in its chronological context – after the XP-39B (above). The 'YP' incorporated design changes recommended by NACA (National Advisory Committee for Aeronautics) after its evaluation of the XP-39 prototype. The first YP-39 (40-27) went aloft on its maiden flight on 13 September 1940 – initially without armament installed. An order for 13 of these proof-of-concept Airacobras was placed on 27 April 1939. Delivery of the YP-39 aircraft (including one that had initially been planned as a YP-39A) was completed in December 1940.

Powerplant for the YP-39 was a 1,090-hp (813-kW) V-1710-37 (E5) engine with Curtiss-Electric propeller. Armament consisted of two 0.30-in (7.62-mm) Colt guns with 500 rounds per gun plus two 0.50-in (12.7-mm) Colt synchronised machine-guns with 200 rounds per gun, and the 37-mm cannon with 15 rounds (half the ammunition load for the cannon found on most Airacobras).

YP-39s were used in an exhaustive flight test programme which included high-speed dives and spin work. These service-test machines apparently never reached Army squadrons.

YP-39 serials (13): 40-027/039

The 13 YP-39 aircraft were effectively the service evaluation batch. The first aircraft were flown without armament (above), but the 37-mm cannon and four machine-guns were fitted to subsequent machines (below right).

Above: The wider-chord vertical fin was the main distinguishing feature of the YP-39. Some YP-39s were later issued to the first unit (31st Pursuit Group) along with P-39Cs to aid service entry, although most examples of both variants lacked armament at the time.

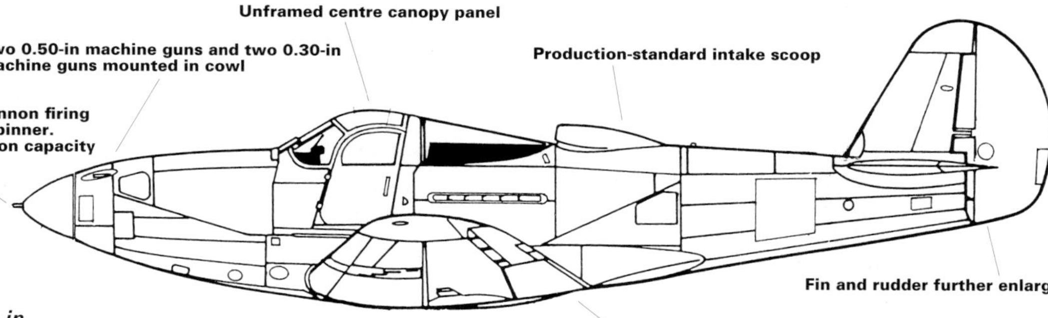

Below: YP-39s survived for some time, employed on various test programmes. Here, 40-34 is seen in October 1941 fitted with a propeller with large cuffs.

Below right: Another propeller test shows 40-34 in January 1943 with a four-bladed propeller. The rig is for calibrating the torque-meter.

YP-39A (Model 12)

This designation went to a planned service-test aircraft that was to have been converted from the YP-39. It would have had a V-1710-31(E2A) engine with the supercharger deleted. The project was cancelled and the aircraft intended for this modification was delivered as a YP-39.

P-39C (Model 12/P-45)

Three of the 20 P-39Cs built and delivered to the 31st Pursuit Group show off their lines for the official photographer, early in 1941.

The P-39C differed from all other Airacobras in having its 37-mm T-9 cannon with 15 rounds of ammunition plus two 0.30-in (7.65-mm) and two 0.50-in (12.7-mm) guns all in the nose, and no wing-mounted weapons. This variant was powered by a V-1710-35 (E4) engine and was initially designated P-45.

Apart from its armament, the C model was a production machine built to the standard of the XP-39B test ship with various revisions to the initial Airacobra design. Almost immediately, the Army decided that the P-39C was inadequately protected for its role as a ground-support aircraft and ordered substantial equipment changes, with the result that only 20 C models were built. By March 1941, all 20 P-39C fighters had been delivered to the 31st Pursuit Group at Selfridge Field, Michigan.

Three of these aircraft later went to England. The first underwent a test flight on 6 July 1941, and British officers were disappointed in the 359-mph (577-km/h) maximum speed attained during the flight. The aircraft used in this evaluation had tachometer problems and it was suggested at the time that the air speed might have been measured incorrectly. A November 1941 report by an American representative in the UK noted, "To try to explain the loss of 33 mph [53 km/h] is impossible. It was later admitted by the Bell company [that] an airplane weighing more than a ton less than British Aerocobras (*sic*) and highly polished was used for the publicity figure of 392 mph (631 km/h)."

P-39C serials (20): 40-2971/2990

The new Army fighters suffered from numerous teething problems, including overheated engines, burnt-out brakes and burst tyres.

This aircraft (DS173) was one of three P-39Cs sent to the UK for evaluation in advance of the arrival of the first Model 14 Airacobra Mk Is.

P-400 (Model 14) Airacobra Mk I

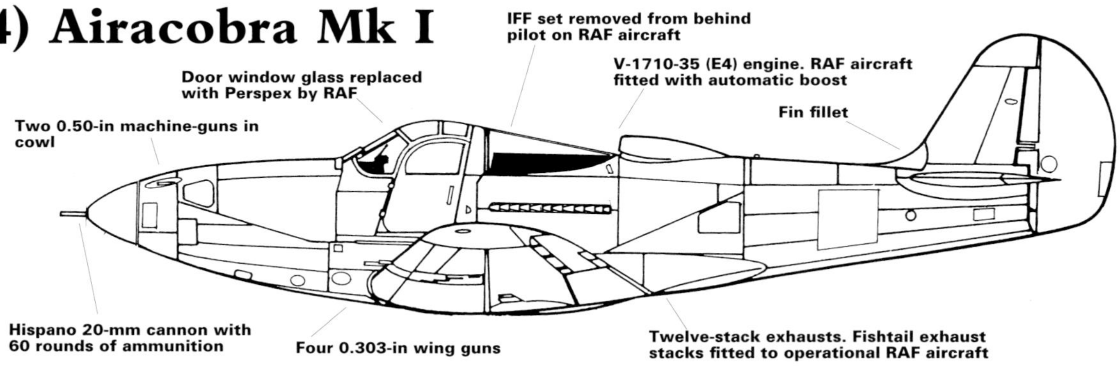

The P-400 Airacobra came into being when France ordered 170 pursuit ships. The type was similar to P-39C/D models but had a nose Hispano-Suiza Mk 404 20-mm cannon with 60 rounds of ammunition. The P-39D's six 0.30-in (7.62-mm) machine-guns were replaced by an equal number of Browning 0.303-in (7.7-mm) guns. An identifying feature of this model was the rectangular field of exhaust stacks located behind and below the pilot, which featured 12 stubs rather than the six that were found on P-39 fighters. When the aircraft entered service, it was modified with six fishtail exhaust stacks. It is unknown whether initial plans called for the use of French armament on these aircraft.

The French order was placed on 13 April 1940 but was taken over by the British two months later. Initially, the Royal Air Force intended to call this aircraft the Caribou, but in due course it decided to stick with the Airacobra name. The initial French contract for 170 aircraft was followed by two British contracts for 205 and 300 aircraft, respectively, for a total of 675 P-400s.

The Airacobra Mk I had a relatively brief RAF career, and only reached one front-line unit, No. 601 (County of London) Squadron. Around 400 were repossessed by the USAAF, and used under the P-400 designation, most still carrying their RAF serials.

RAF aircraft serials (675): AH570/739, AP264/384, BW100/183, BX135/174

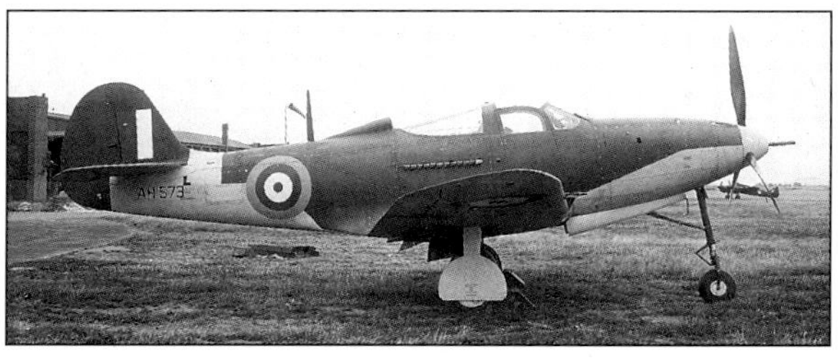

The first aircraft of the Airacobra Mk I batch were retained for trials in the US. The 10th Model 14 (right) has a US engine (with six exhaust stacks), not the 12-stacked export engine (above) of the fourth aircraft.

Left: Preceding the delivery of P-39Ds to the RAAF, BW114 was the solitary example of a P-400 delivered for familiarisation flights at Laverton.

Above: Several Airacobra airframes were operated in Portugal, including some interned during delivery flights to the USAAF in North Africa. This aircraft appears to be a P-400.

Above: No. 601 Sqn lines up for the camera, its Airacobra Mk Is displaying the fishtail exhaust stacks adopted for operations.

Right: An ex-RAF Airacobra I of the 67th FS, 347th FG on Guadalcanal. Such aircraft were redesignated P-400 and retained their RAF serials.

P-39D (Model 14A/15)

The **P-39D** model, which began to reach the US Army in April 1941, was identical to the XP-39B and P-39C but for different armament and a few minor internal changes. This first true production Airacobra had two 0.30-in (7.62-mm) nose guns deleted and four 0.30-in (7.62-mm) wing guns added. In addition, the ammunition for the 37-mm gun was increased to 30 rounds, and a centreline belly rack, self-sealing fuel tanks and a fillet on the vertical fin were added.

The D model differed from all others in having slightly smaller wing area of 213 sq ft (19.788 m²) as compared with 213.22 sq ft (19.808 m²) on all other models

Several aircraft in the P-39D series were used to evaluate centreline fuel tanks, meeting an Army requirement to be able to ferry the fighter from the West Coast to Hawaii. Real and mock-up tanks in sizes from 158 to 350 US gal (598 to 1324 litres) were flown on about half a dozen D model Airacobras.

P-39D serials (429): 40-2991/3050, 41-6722/7052, 41-7057/7058, 41-7080/7115

P-39D-1

The P-39D-1 (Model 14A) introduced a dorsal fillet to the vertical tail. Like the export P-400, it was armed with a Hispano-Suiza Mk 404 20-mm nose cannon with 60 rounds. However, the D-1 used 0.30-in (7.62-mm) wing guns in place of the British 0.303-in (7.7-mm) weapons.

P-39D-1 serials (336): 41-28257/28406, 42-38220/38404, 41-38563

P-39D-2

The P-39D-2 (Model 14A-1) Airacobra introduced minor changes, and also employed a 20-mm rather than a 37-mm nose cannon. It is likely that Airacobras armed with the 20-mm weapon were considered inferior by US Army pilots. At one juncture, when some P-39s were moved from Canton Island to Guadalcanal while others remained on Canton Island (where no fighting was taking place), the 333rd Fighter Squadron with D-2s was kept away from the combat zone, although a report noted that "guns and cannons [are] working very satisfactorily." Other Airacobras with 20-mm guns did, of course, reach the fighting, among them reclaimed P-400 export models.

P-39D-2 serials (158): 41-38405/38562

P-39D-3

Twenty-six aircraft were modified from other P-39D configurations to P-39D-3 standard, establishing a standard for photo-reconnaissance conversions. The P-39D-3 reconnaissance ships had K-24 and K-25 aerial cameras in the aft fuselage, plus armour added to protect oil and glycol coolers from ground fire.

P-39D-3 serials (26): 40-3025, 40-6730, 40-6767, 40-6773, 40-6780, 40-6791, 40-6818, 40-6965, 40-6985, 40-6990, 40-7002, 40-7011/7012, 40-7025, 40-7027, 40-7031, 40-7035, 40-7040, 40-7061/7062, 40-7065, 40-7068, 40-7073, 40-7075, 40-7094, 40-7097

P-39D-4

The P-39D-4 variant emerged when 11 aircraft were modified for photo-reconnaissance duty.

P-39D-4 serials (11 modified): 41-28281, 41-28288, 41-28340, 41-28367, 41-28370, 41-28375, 41-28400, 41-28402, 41-38296, 41-38301, 41-38315

This view clearly shows the armament of the P-39D-1: two nose guns, four wing guns and the long-barrelled Hispano 20-mm cannon in the nose. The purpose of the unusual framework under the nose of this aircraft, which was presumably undergoing an Army test programme, is unknown.

Above: In a manner similar to many fighter groups that later achieved fame over Europe, the 357th FG 'Yoxford Boys' worked up on P-39s before it was assigned to the combat theatre. This 363rd Fighter Squadron P-39D-1 was photographed on a training flight in 1943, a year in which the group changed bases four times. The death's head insignia seen on this aircraft was an unofficial squadron marking.

Above: This P-39D (no suffix) was one of 12 of this model and 10 Fs used by the RAAF between April 1942 and November 1943. A53-12 (41-6944) served with no fewer than four squadrons.

Above right: The 33rd FS had the unenviable job of the defence of Iceland. This is the first P-39 (a D) to arrive at Kaldadrnes in August 1942. The P-39s replaced P-40s, which had arrived a year before.

P-39D

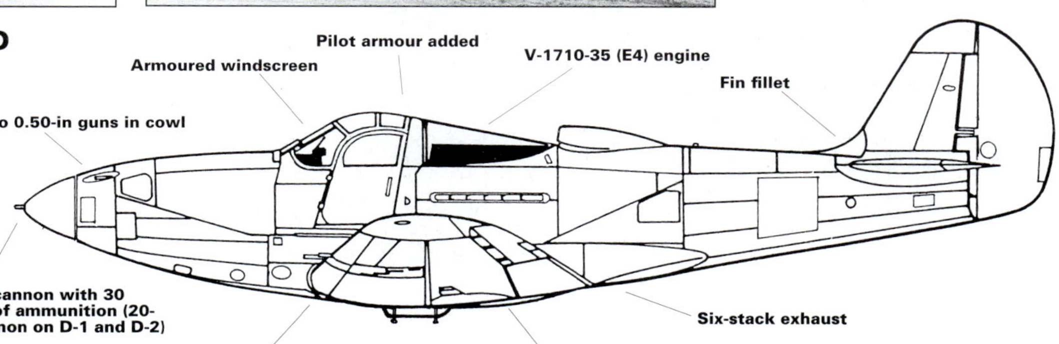

XP-39E (Model 23)

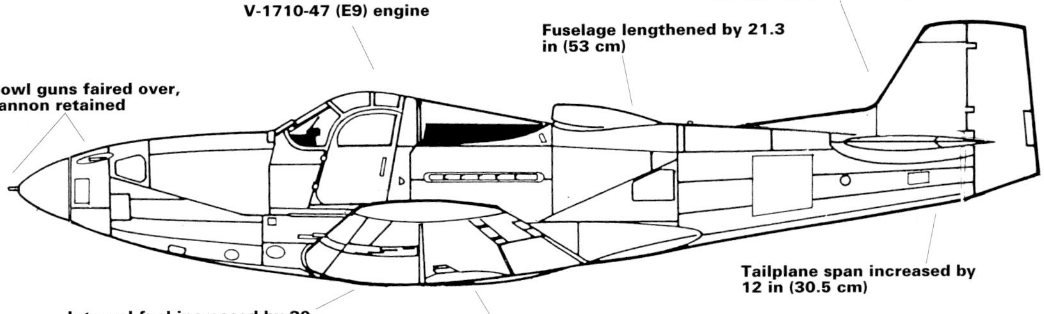

First flown on 26 February 1942 (one source says 21 February), the experimental XP-39E was a highly modified P-39D airframe which had originally been meant to undergo a major powerplant change, to the Continental V-1430 engine. When this powerplant became unavailable, the E model was flown with an Allison V-1710-47 (E9) engine with two-stage supercharger driving an Aeroproducts propeller.

The XP-39E fuselage was lengthened 1.75 ft (0.53 m) to accommodate the longer -47. The E model also had a slightly widened undercarriage. Its wing was larger than that of the standard P-39, and area was enlarged by 22 sq ft (2.04 m²) by increasing and slightly lengthening the root chord. Contrary to myth, the XP-39E did not have a laminar flow wing (which came later in the P-63 Kingcobra). It was distinguished in another respect, however. Vastly overweight at a maximum take-off weight of around 9,100 lb (4128 kg), the E model was by a considerable margin the heaviest Airacobra ever built.

Just three weeks after its maiden flight, the first XP-39E, dubbed the 'Green Hornet' by pilots, crashed while conducting spin tests on 26 March 1942. It was a dramatic moment. Test pilot Bob Stanley, who already had two emergency parachute jumps under his belt, pulled the wrong handle and jettisoned, rather than deploying, drag chutes designed to bring the aircraft out of a spin. With no choice but to escape, Stanley opened the car-style door, got out on the wing leading edge, and was observed for an extended time sitting there. The XP-39E completed about a dozen more spins with Stanley seated on the wing before the pilot finally leaped clear and parachuted successfully.

The second aircraft flew on 4 April 1942. Minor differences in wing and empennage shape and area were introduced with each of the three XP-39Es. Flight performance was impressive in many respects, including a maximum speed of 393 mph (632 km/h) at 24,000 ft (7315 m). Nevertheless, overall, the XP-39E was a disappointment and even though the aircraft's engine was optimised for high-altitude performance, Larry Bell found himself at one point recommending its production "as an attack airplane against invasion forces."

XP-39E serials (3): 41-19501/19502, 42-71464

P-39E (Model 23/ P-76/P-76A)

The P-39E designation applied to a planned production version of the XP-39E. These were initially identified as P-76 and P-76A. An order for 4,000 was cancelled.

The short fin and rudder of the first XP-39E was not adopted on the second aircraft. This P-51-like configuration and a much taller unit were tested.

The second XP-39E is seen at Wright Field. Following the loss of the first aircraft, the third (static test) example was brought up to flying condition.

P-39F (Model 15B)

The P-39F variant was similar to the P-39D but with an Aeroproducts 10-ft 4-in (3.14-m) propeller. The P-39F-2 sub-variant was a result of minor changes being made to 27 of these Airacobras. Reports that at least one P-39F variant was rebuilt as the proof-of-concept ship for an Airacobra two-seat transition trainer are not supported by any existing documentation today (see TP-39Q-5 entry).

P-39F serials (229 of which 27 modified as P-39F-2): 41-7116/7344
P-39F-2 serials (27): 41-7123, 41-7177, 41-7182/7183, 41-7226, 41-7230, 41-7248, 41-7266, 41-7270/7272, 41-7278, 41-7294/7295, 41-7299, 41-7302/7303, 41-7305, 41-7309/7310, 41-7312, 41-7318, 41-7325/7326, 41-7332, 41-7334, 41-7339

The 54th FG was another group assigned duty at the fringes of the war. This 57th FS P-39F is seen at Anchorage, Alaska in July 1942. The 54th returned to the US after six months in-theatre.

This P-39F was used by the Central Instructors School at Foster Field, Texas where "...crack pilots learn the latest techniques in blasting Axis planes."

P-39G (Model 26)

The P-39G designation was assigned at an early juncture to an aircraft intended to be identical to the P-39D-2 but with a different propeller. Before being cancelled, this designation initially applied to 1,800 fighter aircraft that were later produced as P-39K, L, M and N models.

P-39H

Designation not assigned.

P-39I

Designation not assigned.

Bell P-39K-1 Airacobra
40th FS, 35th FG
Port Moresby
New Guinea
February 1943

Undercarriage
The tricycle landing gear of the P-39 and P-63 made them unique among single-engined fighter aircraft of World War II, all others being of 'taildragger' configuration. This layout theoretically offered improved ground handling and safer landings, but in the rough combat conditions of the South West Pacific Area (SWPA), nosegear failures were a frequent cause of aircraft loss. Nevertheless, the Bell service representative on Guadalcanal in 1942 reported P-39s taking incredible punishment, operating from rough surfaces without apparent damage.

Armament
The P-39's primary armament was a 37-mm M4 cannon firing through the propeller hub, although the P-400 export model as supplied to the RAF and used by the USAAF in the SWPA used a Hispano 20-mm weapon. The 37-mm gun was one of the largest fitted to a production fighter aircraft during the war. It was 78 in (198 cm) in length and weighed 405 lb (184 kg) with ammunition, of which only 30 rounds were carried. Secondary armament consisted of a pair of 0.50-in machine-guns in the nose and four 0.30-in guns in the wings. A single 500-lb bomb could also be carried.

Pilot
This P-39 was flown by then-First Lieutenant William ('Mac') McDonough who scored two confirmed victories and one probable against Zeros on 6 February 1943 over Wau, in a battle in which 12 Japanese aircraft fell to his squadron, with a further five credited as probably destroyed. McDonough was promoted to major and scored twice more after converting to P-47s, but was killed when his parachute failed after an accident that occurred while he was awaiting transport home in April 1944.

The P-39K was a mid-production Airacobra and the first to be designated with block numbers, although the 'dash-one' was in fact the only model produced. Total production was 210 aircraft. The K differed from the previous production model (the P-39D) in having an Aeroproducts propeller. The P-39L (240 built) was basically identical but reverted to the Curtiss-Electric propeller with the same diameter of 10 ft 4.5 in (3.06 m).

40th FS 'The Fighting Fortieth'
Originally a part of the 31st FG, the first USAAC unit to receive the Airacobra, the 40th Pursuit Squadron (Interceptor) joined the 35th FG in January 1942 and was redesignated the 40th Fighter Squadron on 15 May, two weeks before arriving in New Guinea. The 40th was active in countering the Japanese landings at Buna in July 1942. By the end of 1943, when the 40th FS began conversion to the P-47, it had been credited with more than 50 kills.

Camouflage
The majority of P-39s delivered to the USAAF were finished in the basic scheme of olive drab over neutral grey. After mid-1942, medium green blotching was often applied to the edges of the flying surfaces as a measure of camouflage on the ground. P-400s serving in the Pacific usually retained the Bell-applied dark earth and dark green colours of the RAF.

P-39K

The P-39K series was the first of the fighters that had initially been designated P-39G. Bell manufactured 210 **P-39K-1** (Model 26A) aircraft with the V-1710-63 (E6) engine, of which six were modified to **P-39K-2** standard. One K model was modified to become the **P-39K-5** (prototype P-39N) with V-1710-85 (E19) engine, 11-ft 7-in (3.53-m) Aeroproducts propeller, carburettor air filter, new windshield, and other minor changes.

P-39K serials (210): 42-4244/4453
P-39K-2 serials (6): 42-4244, 42-4273, 42-4352, 42-4387, 42-4433, 42-4437

Above: A new engine variant and a new propeller distinguished the P-39K. This K-1 was seen at a depot in 1944 in an unusual paint scheme, similar to the RAF pattern.

Right: Various belly-tank variations were tested on P-39s. The 75-US gal (284-litre) type was unbaffled and caused unwanted trim changes as fuel sloshed around in flight.

P-39J (Model 15B)

The term P-39J identified 25 Airacobras that would have been the last P-39Fs but were delivered with an improved V-1710-59 (E12) engine with automatic manifold pressure regulator. This was deemed sufficient modification to justify a new designation.

P-39J serials (25): 41-7053/7056, 7059/7079

P-39L

Two hundred and fifty L model aircraft were built as the **P-39L-1** (Model 26B) and were like the P-39K-1 except for having a 10-ft 4-in (3.15-m) Curtiss Electric propeller. Eleven were modified to become **P-39L-2** photo-reconnaissance aircraft.

P-39L-1 serials (250): 42-4454/4703
P-39L-2 serials (11): 42-4457, 42-4461/4462, 42-4465/4466, 42-4470/4471, 42-4476, 42-4489, 42-4553, 42-4630

A P-39L-1 of the 81st Fighter Group in Tunisia in late 1943. The large IFF set behind the pilot's seat severely reduced rearward visibility.

Below: This P-39L-1 has covers on the wing guns but not on the nose cannon. If a cannon cover was fitted, the first shell out had to be ball ammunition – a high-explosive round might explode on firing and blow off the aircraft's nose.

P-39M

The term P-39M identified more Airacobras that began on the drawing board as the P-39G. Bell produced 240 **P-39M-1** (Model 26D) aircraft similar to P-39L-1, but powered by a V-1710-67 (E8) engine rated at 1,200 hp (895 kW) which gave poorer low-altitude performance but was 10 mph (16 km/h) faster at 15,000 ft (4570 m). Some M-1s employed the V-1710-83 (E18) engine either as a retrofit or a change mid-way along the production line.

The **P-39M-2** designation resulted from eight of these aircraft (of the 240) being modified to P-39M-2 standard for photo-reconnaissance, in similar manner to the P-39D-3.

P-39M serials (240): 42-4704/42-4943
P-39M-2 serials (8): 42-4704/4706, 42-4710, 42-4712, 42-4751, 42-4795, 42-4824

The P-39M was equipped with the Aeroproducts propeller and had improved medium-level performance.

A P-39M seen in Canada shows the cannon muzzle guard and ventral DF loop sometimes found on later P-39s.

P-39N (Model 26F)

In the P-39N series, a total of no fewer than 2,095 aircraft were manufactured, to say nothing of 205 more aircraft that were once assigned serials (42-19241/19445) but were not completed, these serials later being assigned to P-63E-1 Kingcobras. The first 500 of these had no suffix attached to the P-39M designator and were powered by the V-1710-85 (E19) engine driving a 10-ft 4-in

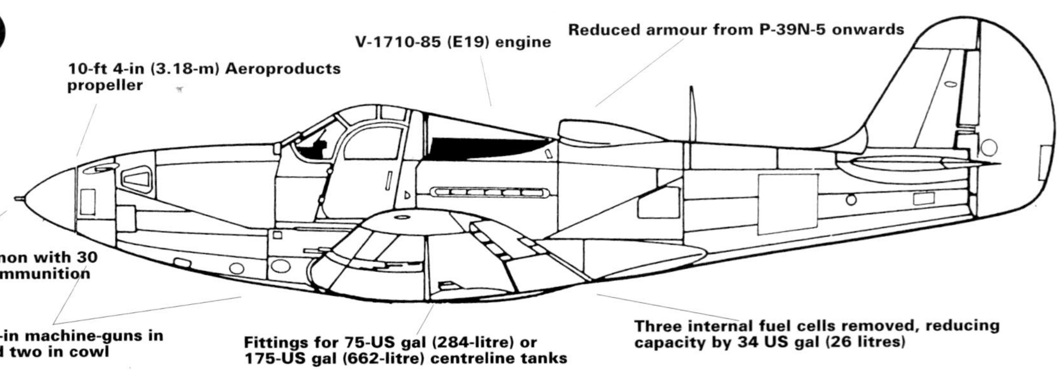

Although Airacobras from the P-39D onwards could carry bombs, this capability is rarely illustrated. These P-39Ns are from a training unit.

(3.18-m) Aeroproducts propeller. The first 166 of these had the same fuel capacity as earlier Airacobras, but thereafter Bell introduced a weight-saving measure by reducing internal fuel capacity from 120 to 86 US gal (454 to 325 litres) by removing three fuel cells. The P-39M and all sub-variants were able to accommodate 75- and 175-US gal (284- and 662-litre) belly tanks. The Airacobra was always somewhat short-legged, so kits were produced which made it possible for internal fuel cells to be field-fitted. P-39Ns went to French squadrons in North Africa from May 1943.

The **P-39N-1** (Model 26C) designation came next and identified 900 aircraft equipped with an enlarged 11-ft 7-in (3.51-m) Aeroproducts propeller. This model also differed in having an altered centre of gravity.

The **P-39N-2** was the photographic reconnaissance N model. The Army converted 128 P-39N-1s, following a familiar pattern that had begun with the P-39D-2.

The **P-39N-3** Airacobras were N-0 fighters modified for photo-reconnaissance in the manner of the P-39D-3. There were 35 examples of this version.

The **P-39N-5** (Model 26C-5) was like the P-39N-1 except for the installation of armour plate instead of bullet-proof glass behind the pilot's head in the cockpit. The N-5 also incorporated demand-type oxygen system and other minor changes. Bell built 695 P-39N-5s.

P-39N-0 serials (500): 42-4944/5043, 42-8727/9126
P-39N-1 serials (900): 42-9127/9726, 42-18246/18545
P-39N-2 serials (128): 42-9141, 42-9145, 42-9148, 42-9150, 42-9152, 42-9211, 42-9255, 42-9416, 42-9615, 42-9677, 42-9697/9712, 42-9714/9724, 42-9726, 42-18276/18285, 18287/18296, 42-18298/18300, 42-18302/18305, 42-18310, 42-18327, 42-18466, 42-18485/18545
P-39N-3 serials (35): 42-8808/8842
P-39N-5 serials (695): 42-18546/19240
P-39N-6 serials (84): 42-18676/18681, 42-18712/18725, 42-18768, 42-18818, 42-18829, 42-18831, 42-18841, 42-18857, 42-18870, 42-18876/18879, 42-18881/18882, 42-18884, 42-18887, 42-18889/18896, 42-18899/18907, 42-18909/18921, 42-18923/18925, 42-18927/18933, 42-18935/18941, 42-018947, 42-19043

This is a P-39N-2 photo ship with a pair of cameras in the rear fuselage and upgraded belly armour.

Italy's Co-belligerent Air Force received 149 P-39s, including 74 P-39s, in 1944. One of these, a war-weary N-1, is seen below. The Italian Airacobras initially equipped 4º Stormo, some serving until 1951.

P-39Q

The P-39Q family represented the final attempt to mould the Airacobra into a world-class fighting machine. Bell manufactured 4,905 before production ended. The Q model had a height of 12 ft 5 in (3.78 m).

The **P-39Q-1**, first of the sub-types in this series, retained the 86-US gal (325-litre) internal fuel capacity but restored armour plate weighing just over 231 lb (105 kg). With the exception of the armament changes, 150 P-39Q-1 fighters were otherwise similar to the P-39N-1 and were powered by the now-familiar V-1710-85 (E19) engine. Significantly, the Q-1 dispensed with four 0.30-in (7.62-mm) wing machine-guns, replacing them with one 0.50-in (12.7-mm) machine-gun added to each wing in an underwing pylon, with 300 rounds of ammunition per gun. This armament change was applauded by American pilots who considered the smaller-calibre weapon to be inadequate, but, ironically, virtually all Q models were flown by Russians, who were just as happy to dispense with the underwing machine-guns. The Soviets credited the Q model Airacobra with a maximum speed of 376 mph (605 km/h) as compared with 279 mph (449 km/h) for the LaGG-5.

Five **P-39Q-2** aircraft were created by modifying Q-1s to carry cameras for the photo-reconnaissance mission in the manner of the P-39D-3.

The **P-39Q-5** (Model 26Q-5) sub-variant was similar to the P-39Q-1 and used the same V-1710-85 (E19) powerplant, but had minor internal changes. Bell manufactured 950 of them with lighter armour and increased wing fuel capacity.

The **P-39Q-6** model (148 built) was brought about by modifying P-39Q-5s for photo-reconnaissance, again following the tradition of the P-39D-3.

The **P-39Q-10** (Model 26Q-10) designation applies to 705 Airacobras that were similar to the P-39Q-5 but had revised armour plate, additional winterisation of the oil system, rubber engine mounts, and various other minor changes. This model had its internal fuel capacity raised to 120 US gal (455 litres) and armour weighing 227 lb (103 kg). Bell turned out 705 Q-10 models but did not build 995 more that were assigned serials (42-21251/22245) and that later appeared on the books as P-63E-1 Kingcobra fighters.

Eight **P-39Q-11**s were modified from among the P-39Q-10 population for photo-reconnaissance use in yet another follow-up to the P-39D-3.

The **P-39Q-15** (Model 26Q-15) became a major sub-variant. Bell turned out exactly 1,000, similar to P-39Q-10 but with the oxygen system changed to two bottles instead of four, plus other minor alterations.

The **P-39Q-20** (Model 26Q-20) was similar to P-39Q-15 with numerous equipment changes. The US Army acquired an unknown number with wing gun pylons installed, but the majority went to Russia without the underwing gun pods. Free French forces also operated Q-20s. Bell built 891.

The second P-39Q-5 was tested with a 175-US gal (662-litre) conformal drop tank. Not surprisingly, the drag of the tank lessened the potential range improvement and adversely affected handling.

Some 109 **P-39Q-21** (Model 26Q-21) were built, similar to P-39Q-20, with a four-bladed Aeroproducts propeller. Wing guns were normally deleted on Russian aircraft.

Bell made 700 **P-39Q-25** (Model 26Q-25) fighters, which were similar to the P-39Q-20 but with a reinforced after-fuselage and horizontal stabiliser structure, and a four-bladed Aeroproducts propeller. The manufacturer deleted wing guns from these aircraft, which were exported to the Soviet Union.

The **P-39Q-30** (Model 27Q-30) was the final Airacobra and reverted to the proven three-bladed propeller. Bell built 400. The Q-30 was otherwise similar to the P-39Q-25, with minor changes, including wing guns deleted from those bound for Russia.

P-39Q-1 serials (150): 42-19446/19595
P-39Q-2 serials (5): 42-19479/19483
P-39Q-5 serials (950): 42-19596/20545
P-39Q-6 serials (148): 42-19608, 42-19610, 42-19612, 42-19614, 42-19616, 42-19624,

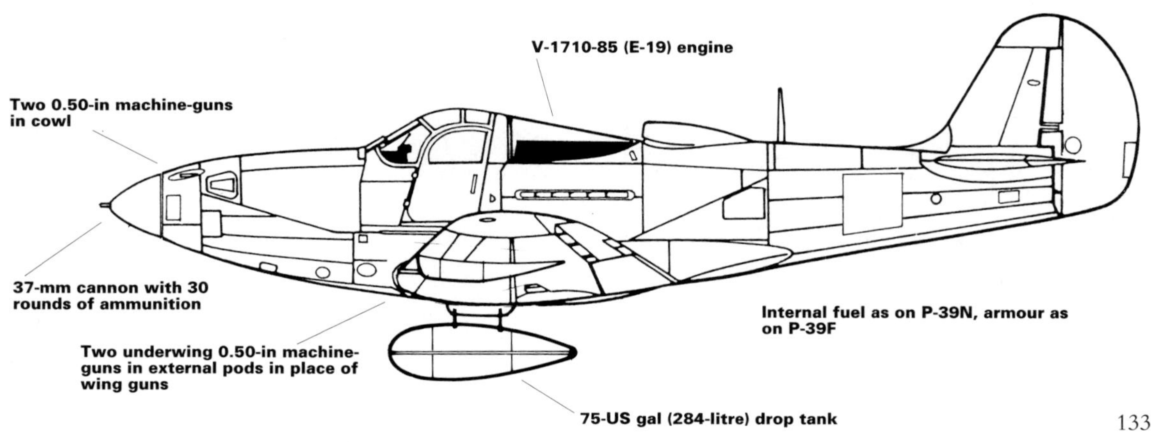

Little Rebel ***was a P-39Q-1 and the first Allied aircraft on Makin Island after its recapture, December 1943.***

42-19626, 42-19628, 42-19636, 42-19638, 42-19640, 42-19642, 42-19644/19646, all even numbers 42-16948/19694, all odd numbers 42-19697/19719, 42-19723, 42-19725, odd numbers 42-19927/19975, 42-19977/19979, 42-19981, 42-19983, 42-19985, 42-19987, all odd numbers 42-19989/20011, 42-20013/20015, 42-20017/20019, odd numbers 42-20021/20065, 42-20067/20069, odd numbers 42-20071/20093, 42-20095/20097, 42020099, 42-20101, 42-20103, 42-20105
P-39Q-10 serials (705): 42-20546/21250
P-39Q-15 serials (1,000): 44-2001/3000
P-39Q-20 serials (891): 44-3001/3940 (minus 49 aircraft, including 22 Q-22s)
P-39Q-25 serials (700): 44-32167/32666, 44-70905/71104
P-39Q-30 serials (400): 44-71105/71504

Below: The most distinctive new feature of the P-39Q was the underwing 0.50-in gun pods.

Most P-39Q-20s were built for the USSR and delivered without underwing guns; this example was destined for the USAAF and retained the guns.

TP-39Q-5 and RP-39Q-22 (Model 39)

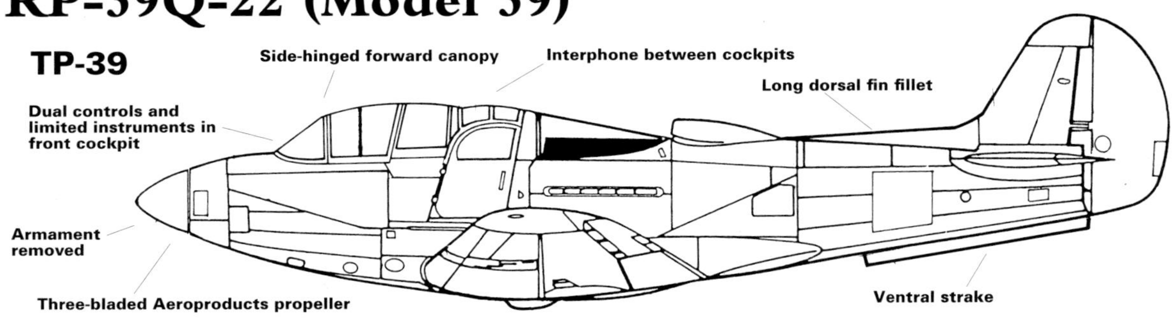

Although no fewer than six photos of it appeared in a Bell publication in November 1943 (and an image has been widely published with tail number and background touched out), the identity of the first TP-39 two-seat trainer modified by Bell was unclear until recently. The first Bell-modified two-seater is now known to be a **TP-39Q-5**, aircraft 42-20024. This aircraft is referred to, simply, as 'the TP-39' in manufacturer's literature and was apparently rolled out on 16 September 1943.

Fourth Air Force, the USAAF command responsible for tactical training, asked Arthur L. Fornoff of Bell's service division if a two-seater could be built "to handle just like the Cobra and, at the same time, carry an instructor to lend the student a guiding hand." Chief project engineer F. M. Salisbury headed the design team for the TP-39 and added a dorsal fin plus a small auxiliary ventral fin, both aimed at alleviating C of G changes. The work was done at Bell's Modification Center at Niagara Falls. Test pilot Jay Demming, and Norman Bethune of the service division, were apparently the first to fly the two-seater. This aircraft, in which they made a tour of the US West Coast in 1943, is described as follows:

"The space for the instructor in front of the standard cockpit was provided by removing the guns and cannon and the gun cowling, extending the cabin and adding a second set of controls and a simplified

This aircraft, designated TP-39Q-5, was the first two-seat Airacobra. From the start, it had an extended dorsal fin and ventral strake.

Seen wearing US markings before delivery to the VVS, this is one of the RP-39Q-22s converted by Bell.

Canopy variations and a short ventral strake distinguish this Soviet TP-39 from the Bell RP-39Q-22 batch.

This Soviet two-seater appears to be one of several two-seat P-39 conversions made by the VVS in addition to the aircraft supplied from the United States.

instrument panel. An inter-phone set allows conversation between the two pilots.

"The rear controls and instrument panel are identical with those of the production P-39 so that the student gets actual experience in the operation of the Airacobra."

The notion of having an instructor in front of his pupil might seem odd today, but Bell's Salisbury apparently saw no other way to do it. Several company employees, including president Larry Bell (who hated to fly), apparently received 'rides' in the TP-39.

The **RP-39Q-22** (Model 39) identifier was assigned to 12 two-seat fighter trainers converted from P-39Q-20s. These aircraft had armament removed, inter-phone added, and an additional fin area on the top and bottom of the rear fuselage. Changes included a ventral fin for stability, which was somewhat different in shape from the ventral fin on the first TP-39 built by Bell (see TP-39Q-5 entry). At least two of these two-seat Airacobras reached the Soviet Union and are identified by a Soviet source as TP-39Qs.

RP-39Q-22 serials (22): 44-3879, 44-3885/3887, 44-3889, 44-3895, 44-3897, 44-3905/3906, 44-3908, 44-3917/3918

RP-39Q-22

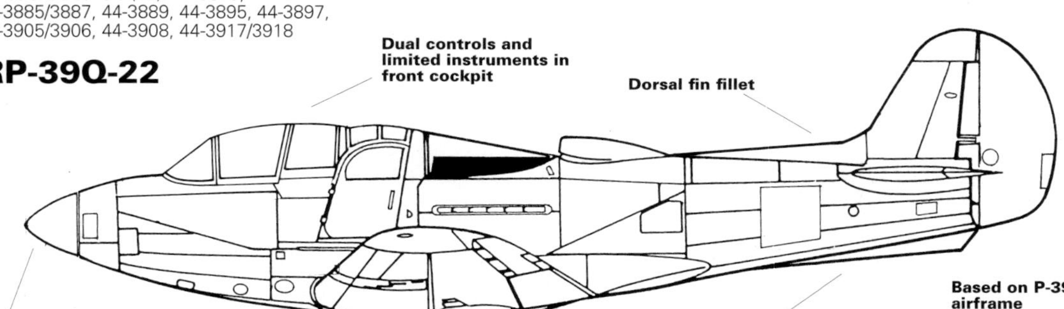

XFL-1 (Bell Model 5) Airabonita

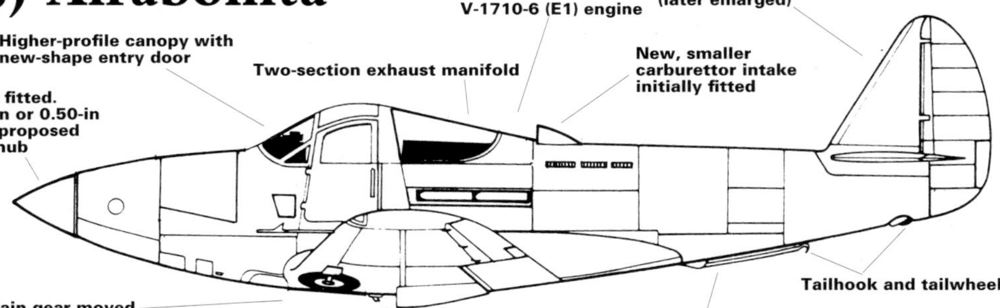

The XFL-1 Airabonita was the closest Bell ever came to producing a carrier-based fighter. In 1927, a US Navy edict banned the liquid-cooled piston engine from consideration in future aircraft. The service wanted to operate only aircraft with air-cooled radial engines, to be spared the burden of stocking aboard its ships the inflammable glycol used in liquid-cooling systems. Nevertheless, in November 1937 the Navy's Bureau of Aeronautics recommended procurement of an aircraft powered by the Allison V-1710 inline engine. Ultimately, the BuAer recommendation evolved into a design competition for which Bell – with no experience producing Navy warplanes – submitted a version of its Air Corps XP-39, powered by a V-1710-6 (E1) rated at 1,150 hp (858 kW).

The competition produced a contract for a fighter by Vought: the XF4U-1, soon named the Corsair. Months later, frustrated at its difficulty gaining access to XP-39 flight data, the Navy belatedly ordered a single XFL-1 aircraft from Bell.

The XFL-1 (this designation had previously been assigned to an abandoned Loening design of 1932) had a different windshield shape because of the need to deflect the barrier wire up and over the pilot during a carrier landing. The basic configuration with a tailwheel was part of Navy requirements, but was one of many factors that created enormous balance problems, exacerbated by the Navy's plan to use a 23-mm Madsen cannon in lieu of the XP-39's heavier 37-mm gun (though the plan was eventually abandoned).

First flight – actually a taxi test that evolved into an unplanned journey aloft – took place on 13 May 1940 with test pilot Brian Sparks flying the XFL-1. The US Navy began testing the XFL-1 in July 1940 at Naval Air Station Anacostia, in Washington, DC. Almost immediately, engine and balance problems forced a delay and testing at Anacostia was resumed during the period 7-29 April 1941. On 12 May 1941, the Navy officially determined the obvious, i.e., that the XFL-1 was "unsatisfactory for use as a carrier fighter." While the Corsair went on to glory, the XFL-1 basked at Patuxent River, Maryland for about another year before being scrapped.

The Airabonita was painted overall Navy grey, except for the upper wing surfaces which were chrome yellow. The XFL-1 was significantly different from the stock production Airacobra. Its wing span of 35 ft (10.66 m) was 12 in (30 cm) greater than that of the P-39. The wing had greater chord, and, at 29 ft 9.125 in (9.07 m), the fuselage of the Airabonita was shorter than the 30-ft 2-in (9.19-m) main body of the P-39. The Airabonita also had a taller canopy and the pilot sat higher in the cockpit.

XFL-1 BuNo. (1): 1588

The Airabonita was not just a tailwheel P-39. Other changes included an entirely new cooling system with large underwing scoops and overwing exhausts.

This view of the XFL-1 shows the shallow carburettor intake scoop behind the cockpit. Later this was replaced by a P-39-type unit. A larger fin was also fitted.

XTDL-1

The XTDL-1 designator was assigned to two target drone conversions by Bell of two P-39Q Airacobras for the Navy.

XTDL-1 BuNos (2): 91102/91103 (P-39Q-10 42-20807; P-39Q-5 42-19976)

XF2L-1K

The XF2L-1K designation was a change in Navy nomenclature for the XTDL-1.

42-20807 was the first of two XTDL-1 target drones for the Navy. They were delivered to NAS Cape May in February 1946 and used for test work, fitted with smoke generators.

P-39 racers

Cobra I
When the first post-war Thompson Trophy Race was undertaken, Bell test pilots Chalmers 'Slick' Goodlin, Alvin M. 'Tex' Johnston, and Jack Woolams prepared and entered two P-39 Airacobras. Jack Woolams was the driving force behind the scheme and flew *Cobra I*, a P-39Q-10 (42-20733). Tex Johnston flew *Cobra II*, a P-39Q-10 (42-20869). The two Airacobras were the aircraft that surrendered their three-bladed, 400-lb (181-kg) propellers for use by the two swept-wing L-39 Kingcobras, which were balanced too finely to use the four-bladed, 460-lb (209-kg) Kingcobra propeller. This left two Airacobra aircraft – which Bell had purchased for less than it would have been charged had it purchased only Airacobra propellers – plus two Kingcobra propellers at Bell's Niagara Falls factory, and thus the two Cobras were created. The aircraft swapped their V-1710-85 (E19) engines for the V-1710-135 (G4) powerplant also used on the RP-63G. Carburettor air scoop area was increased.

Cobra I never managed to see the finish line. Tragically, Woolams was killed in a flight from Bell's Niagara Falls factory in *Cobra I* and it was left to others to attempt to score in the National Air Races.

Cobra II
Flying *Cobra II*, a P-39Q-10 (42-20869/N92848), Johnston redeemed Woolams's loss by taking the 1946 Thompson Trophy race at an average speed of 373.908 mph (601.730 km/h). Jay Demming, one of Bell's first helicopter pilots, persuaded an entrepreneur to purchase *Cobra II*, and flew it to a third-place finish in the 1947 Thompson event at an average speed of 389.837 mph (627.365 km/h). With many modifications, including a change to the V-1710-143/145(G6) engine developed for the North American P-82 Twin Mustang, Allison test pilot Charles 'Chuck' Brown flew *Cobra KF-1*, as *Cobra II* was renamed, in the 1948 Thompson. Brown established a closed-course qualification record in this craft at 418 mph (673 km/h) but was forced to drop out without finishing. *Cobra KF-1* was abandoned for many years before being brought to Ed Maloney's museum in Claremont, California. The plane was purchased in 1969 by Mike Carroll, who intended to rename it *Cobra III*. This Airacobra was lost soon afterward in a mishap in which Carroll bailed out, was struck by the airframe, and lost his life.

***Cobra I** was prepared by **Bell** for the 1946 Thompson Trophy, but crashed with the sad loss of Jack Woolams before it could race.*

NX57521
A P-39Q-15 Airacobra (44-2433/NX57521) was flown in the 1946 National Air Races by Earl Ortman. This aircraft now belongs to the National Air & Space Museum at Silver Hill, Maryland and is displayed with the name *Galloping Gertie*.

***Below:** Bearing the name **Juba**, this is the P-39Q flown in the 1946 Nationals by Earl Ortman.*

***Above and below:** **Cobra II** was the aircraft flown by 'Tex' Johnston in the 1946 Thompson Trophy. It was later renamed **KF-1** when bought and raced by 'Chuck' Brown.*

XP-63 (Model 24)

The term XP-63 described two prototypes powered by the V-1710-47 (E9) engine with auxiliary supercharger. Armament consisted of a 37-mm cannon and two 0.50-in (12.7-mm) synchronised machine-guns in place of the six originally contemplated. After a troubled design process that was accompanied by a weight-reduction programme, Bell chief test pilot Robert M. Stanley took the first XP-63 (41-19511) for its maiden flight at Niagara Falls on 7 December 1942, the anniversary of the Pearl Harbor attack.

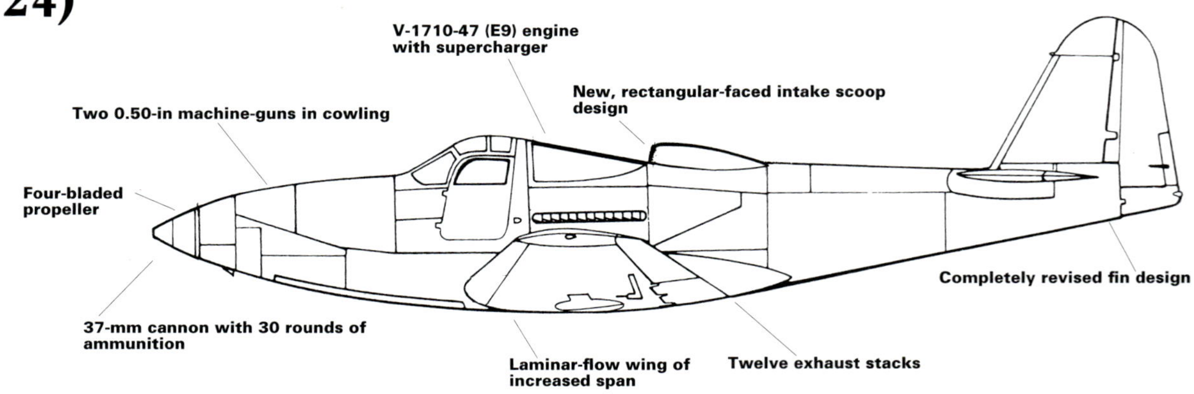

Pilot Jack Woolams ferried the prototype to the Material Command airfield at Muroc, near Los Angeles, in January 1943. On its first test flight there, Woolams encountered a landing gear universal joint problem that led to multiple difficulties and he bellied-in, damaging the aircraft beyond repair. It was later shipped to Wright Field and used for gun firing tests.

The second XP-63 (49-19512) flew on 5 February 1943. On 4 March 1943, on its 77th flight, it was lost when something disintegrated inside the big Allison engine, causing the cockpit to fill with smoke. Pilot Captain G. E. 'Gus' Lundquist parachuted to safety, but the Kingcobra programme – begun with the hope that it would make Bell a major contender in the wartime fighter business – was now without a flying aircraft. Fortunately, a third ship had already been ordered. It received the new designation XP-63A.

XP-63 serials (2): 41-19511/19512

The first of the XP-63s was wrecked at Muroc six weeks after its first flight. The new laminar-flow wing required much wind tunnel testing, which led to greater refinement of the overall design.

XP-63A (Model 24)

The XP-63A was a revised prototype with V-1710-93 (E11) engine rated at 1,500 hp (1119 kW) and with armament increased by two 0.50-in (12.7-mm) wing guns to a total of four, still short of the six originally planned. The XP-63A was, in fact, the third Kingcobra prototype, ordered in June 1942 and flown on 26 April 1943.

This XP-63A (42-78015) had been conceived as a Packard V-1650-5 Merlin engine testbed under the designation XP-63B but was never flown in that capacity because the few available Merlin engines were needed elsewhere for the North American Mustang. Powered instead by the proven V-1710-93 (E11), the XP-63A became a test ship for the continuing Kingcobra development programme.

The XP-63A was the fastest Kingcobra built, attaining 426 mph (686 km/h) on military power at 20,000 ft (6096 m). Air combat was not to be the Kingcobra's strong suit: the P-63 was envisioned for the ground attack role. Its nose armament of one 37-mm M10 cannon (an improved T-9) and two 0.50-in (12.7-mm) guns with a total of 900 rounds for all three guns, bolstered by additional wing guns in most models, was well suited for air-to-ground action. This Kingcobra also boasted 88 lb (40 kg) of armour, 100 US gal (378 litres) of internal fuel, and provision for a 500-lb (227-kg) bomb or 75-US gal (283-litre) drop tank beneath the fuselage. All of these features were to win the respect of the Soviet Union, which considered the Kingcobra to be the ideal supplement to its Airacobra force.

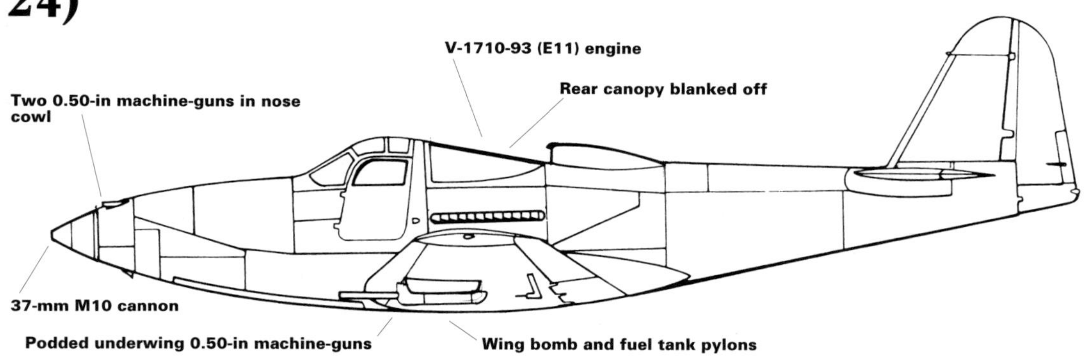

XP-63A serial (1): 42-78015

Following the loss of the two XP-63s, the XP-63A undertook most of the Kingcobra test programme. The rear canopy was faired over and test equipment installed behind the pilot – this was also done on the second XP-63. Armament, including underwing guns, was fitted.

P-63A (Model 33)

The P-63A model, with its 11 sub-variants, defined the shape and performance of the Kingcobra series. The A model achieved a maximum speed of 410 mph (660 km/h) at 25,000 ft (7620 m), cruising speed of 378 mph (608 km/h), service ceiling of 43,000 ft (13110 m), and range of 450 miles (724 km), all respectable figures that reveal the Kingcobra to be a better fighter than is often remembered.

Dimensions of the P-63A included wing span 38 ft 4 in (11.66 m), length 32 ft 8 in (9.98 m), height 12 ft 7 in (3.84 m) and wing area 248 sq ft (23.04 m^2). The aircraft weighed 6,375 lb (2892 kg) when empty, a figure which rose to a maximum take-off weight of 10,500 lb (4763 kg).

The **P-63A-1** was the first production version of the Kingcobra. It was armed with a Type M-4 37-mm cannon fed by a magazine containing 30 rounds (the same nose gun used on the P-63A-1 through

This was the first production P-63A, and is seen here heavily tufted during aerodynamic trials at Wright-Patterson in late 1943.

FR408 was one of two P-63As supplied under Lend-Lease to the UK for evaluation. They were both later used for laminar flow trials.

Surprisingly, given the Bell factory's location, there are few publicity shots like this one of a P-63A-9 over the American Falls with the city of Niagara Falls, NY behind.

The VVS took by far the lion's share of Kingcobra production. This is a P-63A-10 with M10 cannon. AN/APS-13 tail-warning radar was fitted to this and some other P-63s.

P-63A-8 models). In addition, it had two synchronised 0.50-in (12.7-mm) nose guns with 270 rounds per gun, two wing 0.50-in (12.7-mm) guns with 250 rounds per gun, and centreline rack for an auxiliary fuel tank (or a 500-lb/227-kg bomb).

P-63A-1 serials (50): 42-68861/68910

P-63A-5 (Model 33A-5)
The P-63A-5 model was similar to the P-63A-1 but with minor detail changes and different radios.

P-63A-5 serials (20): 42-68911/68930

P-63A-6 (Model 33A-6)
The P-63A-6 identifier was applied to 130 Kingcobras that were similar to the P-63A-5 but had provisions for a 64-US gal (242-litre) auxiliary fuel tank and 75-US gal (284-litre) wing drop tanks (or bombs).

P-63A-6 serials (130): 42-68931/69060

P-63A-7 (Model 33A-7)
The P-63A-7 Kingcobra was similar to the P-63A-6 but with modified 0.50-in (12.7-mm) nose gun mounts, elevator chord increased by 2 in (5 cm), and horizontal stabiliser and elevator redesign with span increased by 16 in (40 cm) to 14 ft 7 in (4.44 m).

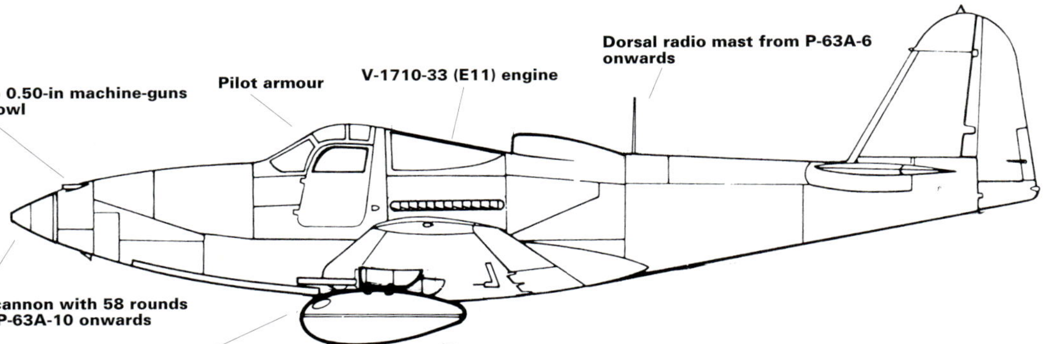

P-63A-7 serials (150): 42-69061/69210

P-63A-8 (Model 33A-8)
The P-63A-8 was the same aircraft as the P-63A-7 but offered greater speed with the addition of water injection, also found on all later versions of the Kingcobra. The A-8 introduced a Type N-6 gun camera. Ammunition for the two wing 0.50-in (12.7-mm) guns was reduced from 250 to 200 rounds.

P-63A-8 serials (200): 42-69211/69410

P-63A-9 (Model 33A-9)
The P-63A-9 sub-variant was identical to the P-63A-8 but with increased head and shoulder armour plate for the pilot. A P-63A-9 (42-69606) tested a Bell-developed Vee-tail configuration at the factory.

P-63A-9 serials (445): 42-69411/69646, 42-69648/69653, 42-65655/69768, 42-69770, 42-69772/69800, 42-69802/69860

P-63A-10 (Model 33A-10)
The P-63A-10 Kingcobra was the same as the P-63A-9 but introduced the M10 37-mm nose cannon with a 58-round magazine, the principal weapon that became standard with every subsequent model except the P-63D-1. This variant also introduced the Type N-9 electrical gun sight.

P-63A-10 serials (730): 42-69861/69879, 42-69975/70685

One of many NACA experiments with the Kingcobra involved an early P-63A-1 with a side-mounted intake.

This NACA P-63A was fitted with a P-51-style airscoop, possibly as part of the abandoned P-63B project.

XP-63B (Model 34)

The XP-63B designator went to a contract study for an aircraft that was never built. The B model was a proposed XP-63A with a Packard-built Rolls-Royce V-1650-5 Merlin, the same engine that powered, among others, all but the earliest P-51 Mustangs. The XP-63B would have had a revised coolant installation with a belly scoop.

P-63C (Model 33C)

P-63C-1 (Model 33C-1)
The P-63C-1 was similar to the P-63A-10 but with the engine changed to the V-1710-117 (E21) and wing span reduced by 10 in (25 cm) to 38 ft 4 in (11.68 m). A ventral fin was added as the result of a 'change order' and may not have been fitted to all aircraft. All C models had an internal fuel capacity of 107 US gal (405 litres) and 201 lb (91 kg) of armour.

P-63C-1 serials (215): 42-70686/70860, 43-10893/10932

Virtually all P-63Cs had a ventral fin added to improve directional stability. The C-5 was the most produced of any 'King' variant. France took over 100 P-63C-5s, although they did not arrive in time to see wartime service.

Bell P-63C-5 Kingcobra GC II/6 'Normandie-Niemen' Tan Son Nhut, Indochina, 1949

Performance
The P-63C with its 1,355-hp (1011-kW) water-injected V-1710-117 reached its maximum speed of 410 mph (660 km/h) at 25,000 ft (7620 m), compared to 357 mph (575 km/h) at 10,000 ft (3048 m) for the P-39Q with the 1,200-hp (895-kW) V-1710-85. The rated altitude of the P-63-5 was 25,000 ft (7620 m) compared to 15,500 ft (4724 m) for the P-39Q-30.

The P-63C was the last version of Bell's Cobra series produced in any quantity, with 1,427 produced, including 1,012 C-5s. Apart from engine variant, it was distinguishable from the P-63A by the underfin fairing, added to correct the 'unacceptable' stability characteristics of the first model Kingcobra.

Indochina
The P-63 saw service in Indochina with five Groupes de Chasse (GC): GC I/5, II/5, II/6, III/6, and I/9. The 'Kings' were employed in the ground attack role, using bombs and napalm against Viet Minh forces. Nearly 30 were lost to ground fire or wrecked in accidents between August 1949 and April 1951, when the type was retired.

Engine
Following tests of the XP-39E with the Allison V-1710-47 in place of the intended Continental V-1430, the USAAF ordered a new design, the XP-63, with this engine. This powerplant corrected the poor altitude performance of the P-39 by having a two-stage hydraulic turbocharger.

P-39 and P-63
Despite the obvious similarities, the P-39 and P-63 were completely different designs based around the same concepts of firepower, pilot visibility and ground handling. The most obvious visual difference was the four-bladed propeller on the P-63. The enlarged vertical fin was another recognition cue, but less obvious was the laminar-flow wing of the P-63, which was shallower in incidence with less dihedral and was 52 in (133 cm) greater in span.

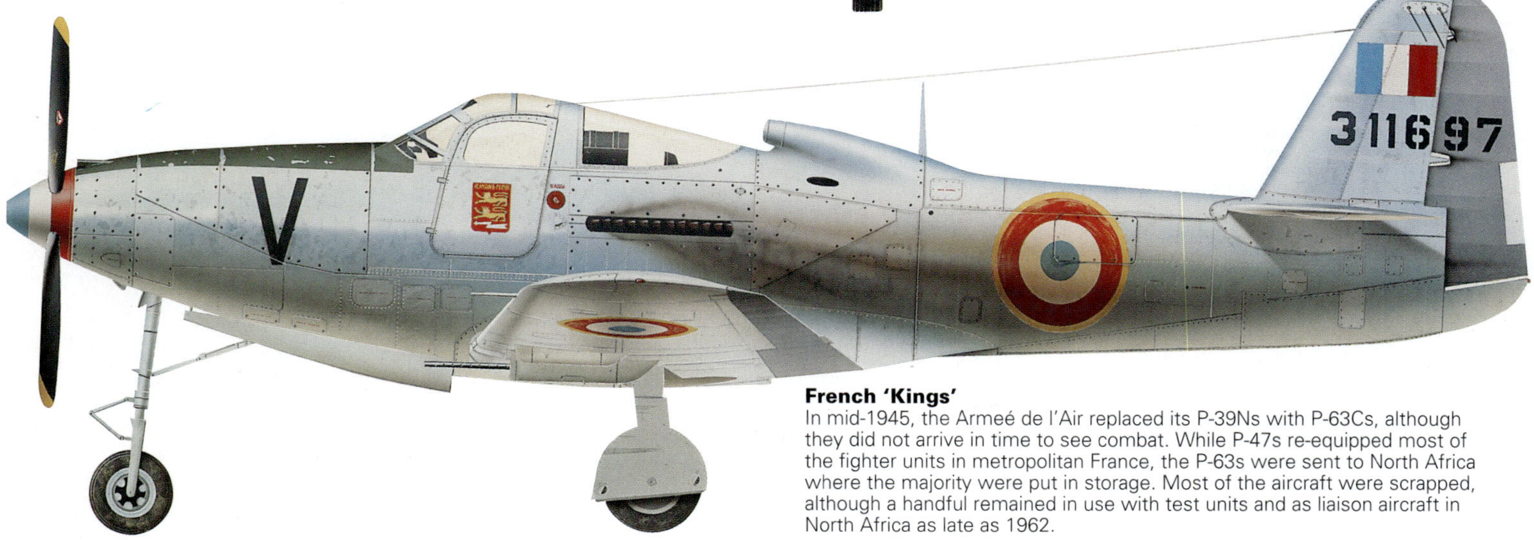

French 'Kings'
In mid-1945, the Armeé de l'Air replaced its P-39Ns with P-63Cs, although they did not arrive in time to see combat. While P-47s re-equipped most of the fighter units in metropolitan France, the P-63s were sent to North Africa where the majority were put in storage. Most of the aircraft were scrapped, although a handful remained in use with test units and as liaison aircraft in North Africa as late as 1962.

The majority of the P-63Cs built went to either France or the Soviet Union. This Soviet aircraft is a P-63C-1. The ventral fin was the major recognition feature of this variant.

This pre-delivery photograph depicts one of the French Lend-Lease aircraft. The bar was added either side of the roundel to aid identification.

P-63C-5 (Model 33C-5)
The P-63C-5 production Kingcobra was similar to the P-63C-1 model with ventral fin and minor changes. Bell manufactured 1,012 but did not complete 425 more (44-4676-5100) that later appeared on the books as unbuilt P-63E-1s.

P-63C-5 serials (1,012): 43-11133/11717, 44-4001/4427

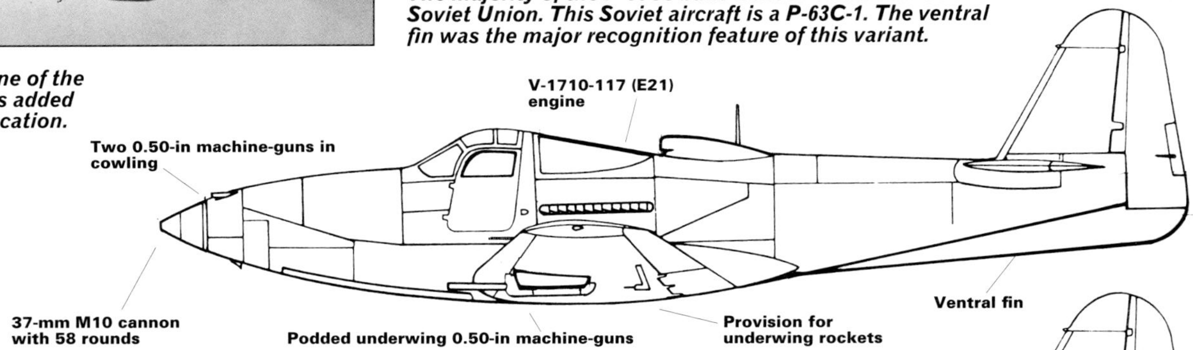

P-63D-1 (Model 37)

The P-63D-1 was a very different-looking Kingcobra with a distinctive, one-piece bubble canopy similar to that found on P-51D and late P-47D fighters. Powerplant was the V-1710-109 (E22). The P-63D-1 was the only Kingcobra to incorporate an M9E1 37-mm cannon with 48 rounds. Proposed as an alternate were an M10 37-mm cannon and a 20-mm cannon. The sole P-63D-1 was lost in a flight-test mishap that claimed the life of Bell test pilot Bob Borcherdt.

P-63D-1 serial (1): 43-11718

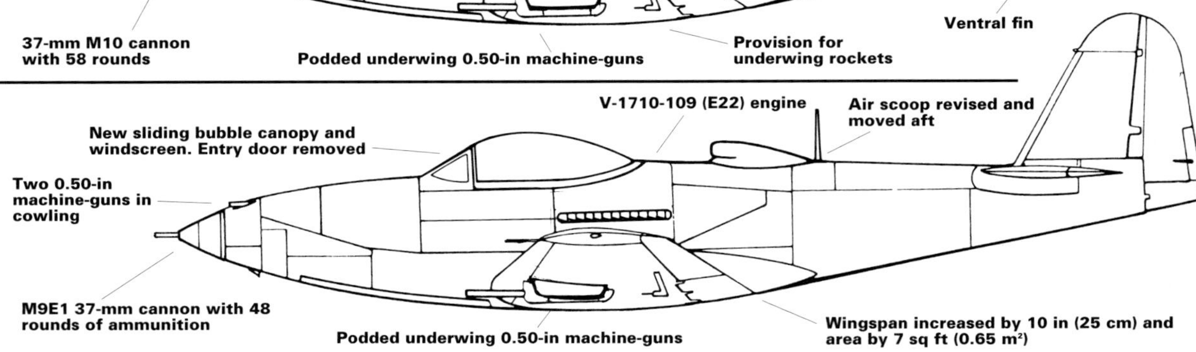

The P-63D tested the bubble canopy intended for the P-63E-5 fighter, which was also to have featured the tall fin of the P-63F. In the event, the E-5 aircraft was not built. A less obvious modification to the P-63D was the fitment of a wider-span wing (39 ft 2 in/11.94 m) adopted on the P-63E. The sole P-63D crashed, tragically taking Robert Borcherdt with it. The subsequent investigation discovered holes burned in the domes of two pistons, which had caused an engine fire.

P-63E (Model 41)

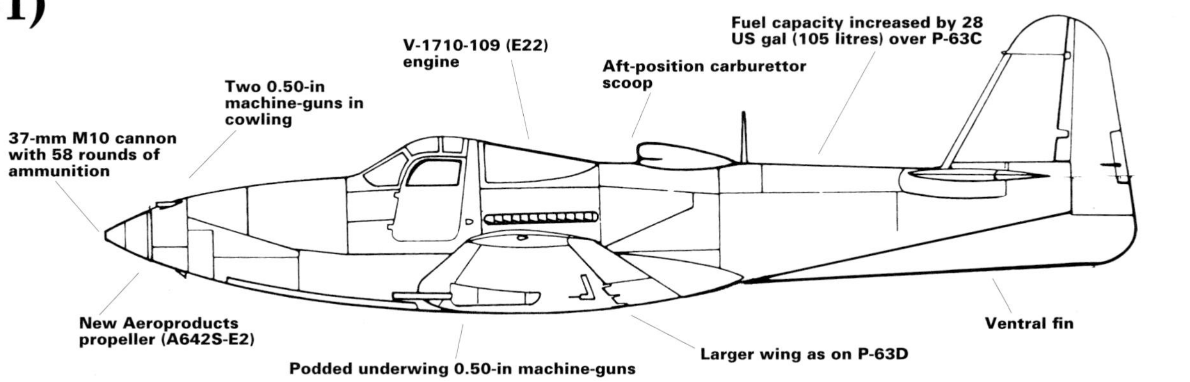

P-63E-1 (Model 41)
The P-63E-1 Kingcobra was similar to the P-63C-5 with V-1710-109 (E22) engine and M-10 37-mm cannon. It could have a 20-mm T-31 20-mm cannon with 175 rounds of ammunition as an alternate nose weapon. Early in the design stage, the P-63E series was expected to employ a Vee or 'butterfly' tail, but this idea never reached fruition.

Records indicate that orders for 1,557 P-63E-1 aircraft purchased for use by the Soviet Union were cancelled at the end of the war, consisting of 205 (42-19241/19445) that began on the order books as P-39N Airacobras, 995 (42-21251/22245) that began as P-39Q-10s, and 357 (43-11736/12092) that were designated P-63E-1 from the outset. Serial numbers were assigned to an additional 425 P-63E-1s (44-4676/5100) that began as P-63C-5 Kingcobras and for which a final contract had never been inked. Of the 13 ships built, the last five briefly appeared in a military role in Honduras in the late 1940s. One of the ex-Honduran aircraft (43-11727/N9003R) has been displayed for years at the Pima Air & Space Museum in Tucson, Arizona, initially in accurate Soviet markings and currently in US insignia.

P-63E-1 serials (13): 43-11720/11721, 43-11712/11735

P-63E-5 (Model 41A)
The P-63E-5 was to have been an improved P-63E-1 for the USSR, plans existing for the purchase of 1,674 for Lend-Lease supply to the Soviet Union. These aircraft were to have a revised instrument panel, and a bubble canopy similar to that of the P-63D-1. There would have been a revised cowling, larger wing fillets, strengthened rear fuselage, new vertical fin, and a 12-in (31-cm) ventral fin. The project was cancelled and none of these advanced Russian Kingcobras ever took to the air.

The P-63E-1 incorporated the larger wing of the P-63D, but returned to the original-style canopy.

The Fuerza Aérea Hondurena received five P-63E-1s (43-11727/11731 – FAH400-404) through MAP channels in the late 1940s. They served only briefly.

P-63F-1 (Model 43)

The P-63F-1 represented an effort by Bell to exploit a NACA study intended to enhance directional stability in the Kingcobra series. NACA studied several Kingcobras during the war, including one that was festooned with wool tufts apparently for inflight evaluations of P-63F-1 features. The F-1 fighter was similar to the P-63E-1 with V-1710-133 (E30) engine, a large dorsal fin, and a redesigned vertical fin. One survives today (see entry on racers).

P-63F-1 serials (2): 43-11719, 43-11722

It is not known whether the P-63F was ever intended for production, but it was used to test the tall vertical fin meant for the P-63E-5, which would have been built in large numbers for the Soviet Union had the war lasted.

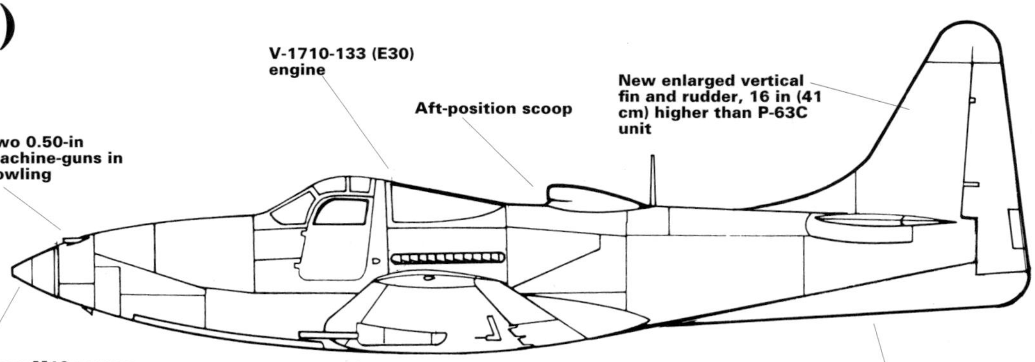

As befitted its experimental status, the P-63F-1 carried an 'X' on the fuselage, which was repeated above and below the wings.

RP-63

RP-63A-11 (Model 33A-11)
The RP-63A-11 Kingcobra was the prototype frangible bullet target aircraft, a fighter modified with a covering of armour plate to serve as an aerial target. This model was similar to the P-63A-9 but with no water injection, armament or external fuel tanks. The exterior of the aircraft was painted in Spanish orange. The aircraft became known popularly as 'Pinballs'.

RP-63A-11 serials (5): 42-69647, 42-69654, 42-69769, 42-69771, 42-69801

RP-63A-12 (Model 33A-12)
The RP-63A-12 was the production frangible bullet target aircraft. It was similar to the P-63A-10 model but was modified in the manner of the P-63A-11.

RP-63A-12 serials (95): 42-69880/69974

RP-63C-2 (Model 33C-2)
The RP-63C-2 was the second major

Left: **Pin Ball** *was the second RP-63A-11, featuring a low-profile airscoop. Sensors dispersed around the airframe recorded hits, which in turn illuminated lights mounted on the fuselage sides and in the propeller spinner.*

Above: This is an RP-63C-2, with a forward-facing airscoop. The RP-63s were principally used to train bomber gunners, using fighter tactics to 'attack' the bombers to give neophyte gunners realistic practice against fighter targets.

Bell P-39/P-63 Variants

The RP-63G had a simple slit airscoop on its back. Thirty-two were produced immediately after the war, but only had a brief career.

A sextet of RP-63s displays the orange colour scheme which was the most obvious feature of these piloted targets.

production Kingcobra intended to be a frangible bullet target aircraft. It was similar to the RP-63A-12 but had the V-1710-117 (E-21) engine and miscellaneous minor changes. The ventral fin was removed.

RP-63C-2 serials (200): 43-10933/11132

RP-63G-1 (Model 41G)
The RP-63G-1 was the third major production Kingcobra intended to be a frangible bullet target aircraft. This model was similar to the RP-63C-2 with V-1710-135 (G4) engine, no armament, and added armour plate. The project was deemed successful to the extent that the initial order for two RP-63Gs was modified on 30 June 1945 to call for the manufacture of 30 more.

For more than 40 years, an RP-63G (45-57295) has been on outdoor display at Lackland AFB, Texas, where enlisted airmen undergo basic training.

RP-63G serials: (32): 43-11723/11724, 45-57283/57312

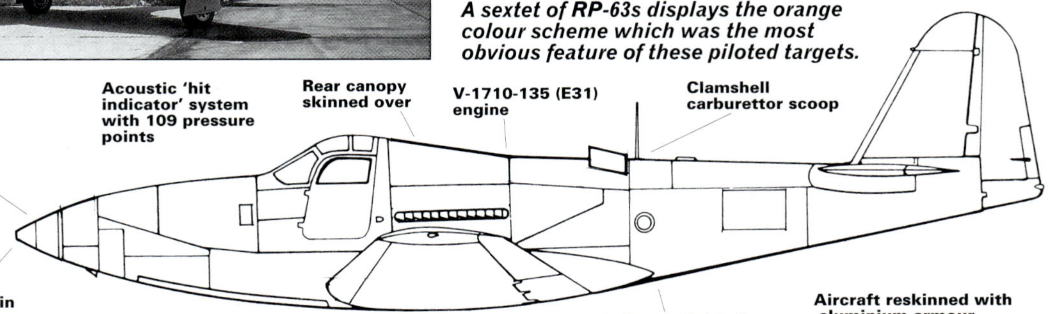

XP-63H (Model 45)

The XP-63H designator was assigned to a proposed testbed with an Allison V-1710-127 (E-27) Turbocompound engine.

TP-63

TP-63A-10 (Model 38)
The TP-63A-10 was a proposed two-seat Kingcobra that would have been brought about with a conversion kit for existing P-63A-10 fighters. It was inspired by the two-seat TP-39 Airacobra. The idea was not proceeded with and none was built at the factory, although at least three TP-63As (42-69304, 42-70503 and 43-11334) were completed in the Soviet Union.

P-63A-9 (Model 53)
Bell gave a new model number to a P-63A-9 modified as a two-seat company aircraft.

P-63E-1
Two P-63E-1s were modified with a second seat (for observer only) in the rear fuselage. They also had a probe extending through the spinner, and the radio equipment was moved forward to the armament bay.

This is the second of two P-63Es (registered NX41963 and NX41964) converted by Bell with a cockpit in the rear fuselage, necessitating some internal rearrangements.

Although it is not thought that Bell completed any TP-63s, this P-63A was converted to dual-control status in Russia, and is seen here during NII tests.

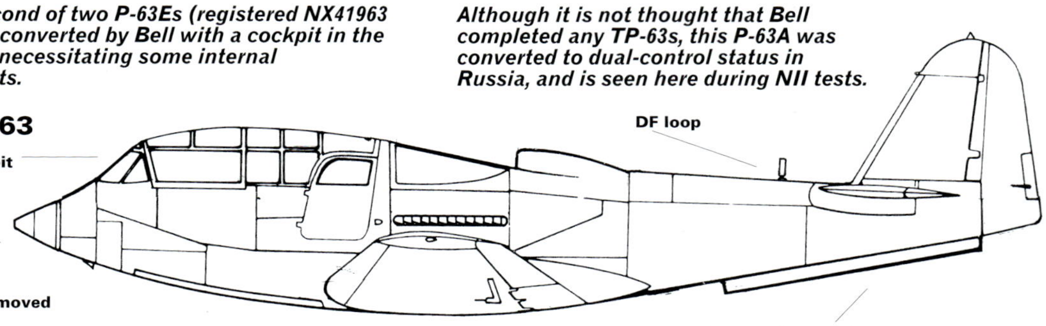

P-63 Vee-tail

Bell's Bob Stanley had been interested in Vee tails during the 1930s, and had built a sailplane to validate the concept. The idea remained in the back of his mind, and in late World War II he managed to sell the idea to Wright-Patterson, resulting in a P-63A-9 (42-69606) being fitted with a Vee-tail, preceded by a P-63A with a high-dihedral tailplane. In addition to the 'butterfly' tail, the aircraft also had extra keel area in the form of a ventral fin. A number of Bell pilots, including Stanley himself, flew the aircraft, and it showed mixed results. Some longitudinal stability problems were encountered at low speeds, while 'Tex' Johnston encountered unusual spinning characteristics. The aircraft flew only 12 flights for a total of 9½ hours.

The first 'butterfly' tail P-63 is seen taxiing for a test flight with 'Slick' Goodlin at the controls. Barely visible is the extra ventral fin area.

Equipped with a wing-mounted air data boom, this Air Force RP-63G tested Vee-tail arrangements for possible adoption by high-speed aircraft such as the X-1.

Renewed interest in Vee-tails, primarily for application to high-speed jet aircraft, resulted in a 1948 order from the newly-independent US Air Force for a further test aircraft. The machine was an RP-63G (45-57300), converted with a Vee-tail. Some reports suggest that the designation XP-63N was applied, but this designation has also been quoted in connection with the L-39. This aircraft tested 'butterfly' tails of 38° and 43° dihedral, and did not have the ventral fin. Results showed no major spinning or stability problems, but crosswind take-off and landing characteristics were poor, and the programme was dropped.

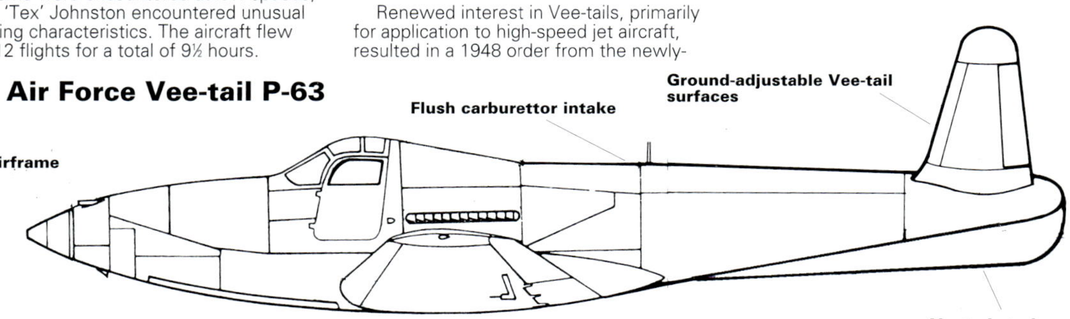

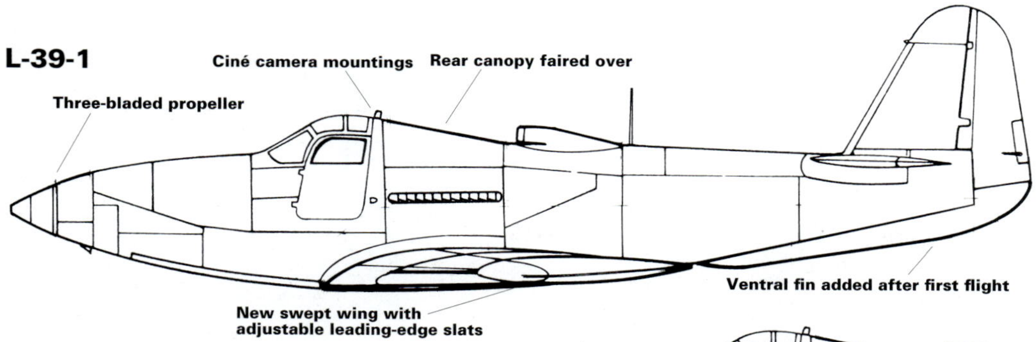

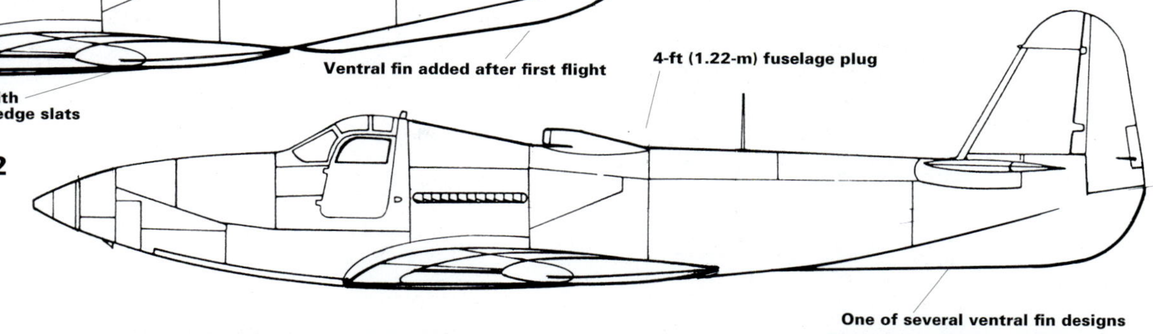

L-39

The L-39 was the first American aircraft with swept-back wings. This seemingly peculiar designation for a Navy aircraft was reached by using the Navy's manufacturer letter for Bell (L) together with the company's design number (39). Bell modified two P-63A-9 Kingcobras to L-39 configuration with a 35° swept wing (with a short inboard straight section) based on P-63E-1 outer wing panels. Because of centre of balance problems, Bell later purchased two P-39Q Airacobras because it needed the P-39 propellers for the L-39. The designation XP-63N was believed to have been applied unofficially.

The first L-39 flew on 23 April 1946, and after a few flights was modified with a rear fuselage plug which had the effect of reducing stabiliser incidence. At the same time a short-chord ventral fin was added. The second L-39 was completed with an even larger ventral fin, and had the extended rear fuselage from the outset. It was later fitted with a completely swept wing of a design planned for the X-2. Both aircraft tested a series of leading-edge slat designs of differing lengths. While L-39-2 remained at Bell in support of the X-2 programme, L-39-1 went to NACA at Langley for continuing test flights.

L-39 BuNos (2 modified): 90061/90062

Above: This is the L-39-1 with extended fuselage, ventral fin and mid-span leading-edge slats.

Right: The L-39-2 had a longer ventral fin, and is seen here testing nearly full-span slats.

P-63 racers

A P-63C Kingcobra (N62995, race no. 28) flown by Charles Tucker was entered in the 1946 Thompson race. Tucker purchased two P-63s for $1,000 each just after the war at Kingman, Arizona, hoping to excel in air racing. Tucker cropped off the wing of N62995, reducing its span from 38 ft 3 in (11.66 m) to 25 ft 9 in (7.85 m) and its wing area from 248 to 187 sq ft (23 to 17 m^2). Tucker also removed the ventral fin. He entered the 1946 races with an unmodified V-1710-117(E21) engine in N62995. Tucker sold this aircraft to Russ Hosler at the end of the 1948 races.

Tucker's second P-63C Kingcobra (44-4126/NX63231, race no. 30) was intended for the 1946 Bendix cross-country race, operated between Van Nuys, California and Cleveland over a distance of 2,048 miles (3296 km). This aircraft initially retained its wing size and was fitted with two wingtip drop tanks. In 1947, Tucker removed the tip tanks, cropped the wing span to about 28 ft 6 in (8.69 m), and flew the Tinnerman event which was for Kingcobras only. For the 1949 races, Tucker modified this ship further and painted it a brilliant purple. In 1949, he took third place in the Sohio Trophy Race and fifth place in the Thompson: the crash of Bill Odom's P-51 Mustang, *Beguine*, in the latter event marked the end of air racing in the US for a decade and a half, and Tucker remains on record as having wrung more speed from a Kingcobra than any other race pilot before or since. His qualifying speed in the 1949 Thompson was an enviable 393.328 mph (632.983 km/h).

A P-63C-5 Kingcobra (NX63941, race no. 72), *Lucky Jack*, was entered in the 1947 races by 'Lucky' Jack Singleton and flown by Raymond E. Eiche. It was lost in a pre-race mishap in which Eiche parachuted to safety.

A P-63C-5 (44-4393/NX62822, race no. 92) owned by Joseph M. Kinkella never finished the 1947 Bendix race, also Van Nuys-Cleveland. Kinkella was forced out at Pueblo, Colorado with engine troubles.

A P-63C-5 (44-4178/NX67115, race no. 47) piloted by Spiro 'Sammy' Diles dropped out of the 1946 Bendix event.

A P-63E-1 (NX69702, race no. 65) operated by Wilson V. 'Bill' Newhall appeared at the 1946 races but, because it was unmodified, probably was too heavy and had too much wing area to be a serious pylon-turning contender. Newhall returned in 1948.

A P-63A-7 (42-69063/NX69901, race no. 64 in 1946, 55 after 1947), modified with V-1710-133 (E-30) engine and revised intake duct, with an 11-ft 1-in (3.38-m) Aeroproducts three-bladed propeller, was flown in several post-war events. Bill Bour flew this aircraft in the 1947 Tinnerman but was unable to retract his landing gear and ended up in last place in a reduced field of five competitors. Bour also reached sixth place in this aircraft in the 1947 Thompson.

NX69901 returned in 1948 with a four-bladed propeller and the name *Spirit of Tick*, honouring pilot-owner Howard 'Tick' Lilly who was also a test pilot and was killed flying the Douglas D-558-I Skystreak at Muroc. Bob Eucker flew it to second place in the 1948 Tinnerman and to first place that year in the Sohio. With the Aeroproducts three-bladed propeller restored, Eucker flew it again in the 1949 Thompson.

A P-63C-5 (NX62797) was flown by Steve Wittman in 1946 and 1947 races, including the latter year's Tinnerman. It was essentially a stock aircraft without modifications.

A P-63C-5 (44-4181/NX73744, race no. 53) in natural metal finish was brought to the 1948 air races by Frank Singer. A year later, Singer returned with a P-63C-5 painted dark grey and trimmed in red. Decades later, it is not clear whether Singer had one Kingcobra or two. Reregistered N9009/ race no. 90, this ship was extensively modified and distinguished by a tiny bubble canopy when flown in the 1971 San Diego air races piloted by Larry Havens. This aircraft had a shortened wing, concave wingtips and a V-1710-135 (G-4) engine. Plans existed to convert the craft to a Merlin engine but, before they could materialise, it was lost on a trials flight on 7 September 1972, when Havens bailed out. The aircraft was salvaged and is being used by the Yankee Air Corps, Chino, California, to provide parts in the restoration of another ship (43-11117).

A P-63A-10 (42-70455/NX4699N, race no. 51) once slated for Free French Forces was the 1947 mount for Ken Knight, victor in that year's Tinnerman.

A P-63A-7 (42-69097/N52113, race no. 87) was flown by Alfred T. 'Al' Whiteside in the 1947 national races (with the name *Kismet*) and again in 1949 (without a name). The aircraft had a reduced wing span and squared-off wingtips. As G-BTWR, this ship returned to standard P-63 configuration and is listed today at the Fighter Collection at Duxford, England.

The sole surviving P-63F of two built (43-11719/NX1719, race no. 21) emerged in the post-war era as H. L. Pemberton's mount in the 1946 Cleveland Air Races, appearing again in 1949. No modifications were ever made to the F model and it was not a serious contender in the speed competition. This ship reappeared in the 1970s in bogus Soviet markings. It is active today (as N6763) with the Confederate Air Force, Midland, Texas.

A P-63C (44-4393/N62822, race no. 28) was flown in several post-1964 Reno air races by John Sandberg and Lefy Gardner. It was later part of the Fighter Collection at Duxford. This aircraft remained active until it was lost in a 4 June 1990 crash in France that killed pilot John Larcombe.

A P-63 (race no. 90) extensively modified and distinguished by a tiny bubble canopy flew in the 1971 San Diego air races, piloted by Larry Havens. This aircraft had a shortened wing, concave wingtips, and V-1710-135 (G-4) engine. Plans existed to convert the craft to a Merlin engine but, before they could materialise, it was lost on a trials flight and Havens bailed out.

Frank Singer's first Kingcobra was N73744, a P-63C-5 with slightly cropped wings and tailplanes with rounded-off tips.

A handful of P-63s had their wings brutally clipped for racing.* Kismet *flew in both the 1947 and 1949 National Air Races, and today is flying as a warbird in the UK.

P-39 in the USSR

Despite later downplaying of the contribution made by foreign aircraft, the P-39 was extremely popular with front-line units. Inscriptions on P-39s seem to have been relatively uncommon; that seen here reads 'Krasnoyarskii Komsomlets'.

The Bell P-39 Airacobra was the most numerous foreign fighter in the Soviet air force inventory. Under the Lend-Lease agreement the USSR received 5,578 Airacobras between December 1941 and February 1945. Some 4,952 of them actually saw service; the Red Army Air Force Import Directorate states that this accounts for 36 per cent of the fighters and 27 per cent of all aircraft supplied by the Allies. In Soviet service the Airacobra was operated mainly by Guards units. The famous ace A. I. Pokryshkin (one of three thrice-awarded Heroes of the Soviet Union – HSUs) and 11 of the 27 fighter pilots twice awarded the HSU title flew P-39s.

Soviet pilots had their first look at the Airacobra in Great Britain when a group of pilots was sent to No. 601 Sqn at RAF Duxford for training. After a brief period of negotiations, the British were only too glad to turn the disappointing P-400s over to the Russians. Some 212 of the 675 Airacobra Is originally ordered by the RAF were to be delivered to the USSR, instead, along with a number of Hurricanes. However, 54 of the Cobras were lost *en route* when the ships carrying them to Soviet ports were sunk

Crated Airacobras unloaded at Soviet northern ports travelled along several routes. Many aircraft arriving in Murmansk were reassembled there and delivered directly to units operating on the nearby Karelian front, or to the Northern Fleet's air arm. Most Cobras, however, went to Ivanovo, where the 22nd ZAP (Zapasnaya Aviapolk – Reserve Fighter Regiment) was based in late 1941. There, imported aircraft of all types arriving as knock-down kits were reassembled and test flown prior to being ferried to front-line bases. Destinations varied widely – from the Leningrad front up north to the Voronezh front in the south.

A small portion of imported fighters was assembled in Arkhangel'sk. To this end, an airfield with a wood-planked airstrip (!) was built in dense woods 25 km (15 miles) south of the city. Aircraft assembled there were flown to Ivanovo via Vologda.

The Soviet high command treated the Airacobra with much more trepidation than other imported aircraft which had seen service in the USSR. It is difficult to say now what the main reason was – the bad reputation the P-39 had earned in US and British service, the Airacobra's unconventional design or the great trouble involved in adapting the Spitfire and Hurricane to the Russian environment. Anyway, the first Cobras arrived in late December 1941 or early January 1942 but it was not until May that they became operational.

Service testing

Only a single Airacobra Mk I (AH718) of the initial batch of 20 was delivered to the 22nd ZAP in 1941. Soviet specialists were very strict when accepting the Cobras. NII VVS sent a special 'task force' to the regiment, which included lead engineer I. G. Rabkin, V. I. Usatov, P. S. Ivanov and V. F. Nikishin. Test pilot V. Ye. Golofastov was to try out the reassembled fighters.

"The very first days of service in January-February 1942 revealed a serious shortcoming in the Airacobra's oil system," Rabkin reminisced. "The engine oil could not be emptied fully. The oil left in the engine sump, reduction gearbox, oil cooler and certain oil lines would freeze, and all of these required lengthy warming-up with hot air before the engine could be started. We had to install de-oiling cocks in the oil lines and invent a special manifold which led hot air to all the necessary locations at once. This gadget was tested successfully and recommended for all units operating the type."

The pilots were in for a lot of surprises, too. Golofastov, who made the first taxi tests on a fighter with tricycle landing gear, praised the excellent view from the cockpit and the aircraft's ability to taxi at high speed over a snow-covered ramp with virtually no risk of standing on its nose. The first flight around the airfield went smoothly. Golofastov learned much about the aircraft in addition to what was in the American flight manual. However, on 18 January 1942, the Allison V-1710-E4 engine (c/n 4132) quit during a turn and Golofastov had to bail out. The accident investigating board ruled that an explosion had occurred in the intake manifold.

Despite this mishap, the Airacobra Mk I finished the NII VVS tests successfully. One of the

One of the very first of thousands of Bell fighters to see service in the Soviet Union was AH628, an ex-RAF Airacobra Mk I. Airacobra deliveries to the USSR came about as a result of a visit by Russian officers to Duxford on 8 November 1941, during the brief period of RAF operation of the type. AH628 was evaluated at Kol'tsovo, near Sverdlosk.

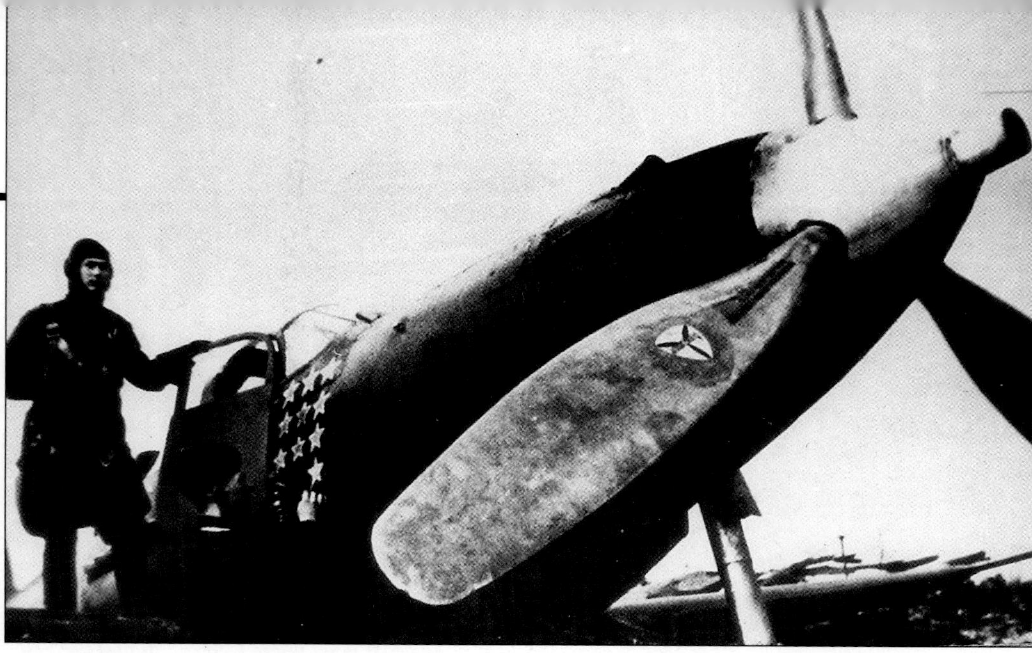

Striking a heroic pose for the official photographer, Captain I. Bochkov supervises the addition of another victory star to his Airacobra. Bochkov flew this aircraft with the 19th GvIAP in East Karelia in 1942. The aircraft is a P-39L model or later.

test aircraft (AH628) operated from Kol'tsovo air base near Sverdlovsk, another (AH644) was based at Chkalovskaya air base near Moscow. These two aircraft were flown by Colonel A. G. Kochetkov and Colonel Avtonomov respectively; A. G. Kubyshkin, I. Ye. Golofastov and A. F. Moshin also took part in the flying. The pilots reported that the Cobra was fairly nimble, with light control forces. The aircraft was stable during turns with normal C of G, shuddering and trying to straighten out if the stick was pulled too far back but showing no inclination to spin.

One aircraft became unserviceable when the supercharger disintegrated during tests. The test pilots were pleased by the Airacobra's handling and performance, and lead engineer Rabkin drew up a report when testing was finished. "At flight levels above 3000 m (9,840 ft), the Airacobra is superior to the Yak-1 and LaGG-3 fighters; it is one of the best aircraft as regards manoeuvrability in the horizontal plane." Airfield performance and range in economical cruise were also praised. The test team asserted that MiG-3 and LaGG-3 pilots would have no trouble converting to the Cobra. Excellent all-round visibility, especially in the rear hemisphere, enabled the P-39 to operate in poor weather.

Engine limits

On the minus side, the V-1710 lacked a constant-pressure valve regulating turbo pressure, so the engine could easily become overpressurised and disintegrate in low-level flight. The NII VVS team reminded that "the Airacobra demands correct treatment in service, and special attention has to be paid to knowing the engine's limits and the cockpit layout during conversion training."

The 145th IAP (Istrebitel'nyy Aviapolk – Fighter Regiment) was the first SovAF unit with which the Airacobra Mk I actually saw action. The unit took its training right on the front lines (without relocating temporarily into the rear area, as was the usual practice), using Russian-language manuals. The 145th IAP was not chosen randomly – on 4 April 1942, it was transformed into the 19th GvIAP, attaining Guards status for valour in combat on the Karelian front. In late April, 16 Airacobras arrived in crates at Afrikanda airfield; within the next month they were assembled under the supervision of the unit's engineer, Major P. Gol'tsev.

On 26 April 1942, Captain P. S. Kutakhov (who went on to become Marshal) made the first training flight on the first reassembled Cobra. A few more firsts: on 15 May 1942, Soviet air force Cobras had their first encounter with Luftwaffe aircraft, in which neither side scored any 'kills'. On the next day, Airacobra I AH660 engaged in a dogfight and was damaged, being declared a total loss after a forced landing. Luckily, the pilot, Lieutenant (sg) I. D. Gaidayenko, walked away. On 15 June it was first blood to the Cobras. Six P-400s took off from Murmashi airfield to intercept six Ju 88s intent on bombing Murmansk, with 16 Bf 110s flying top cover. The Soviet pilots reported nine enemy aircraft shot down; the Germans acknowledged the loss of one Ju 88A-4 coded 4D+DR (W.Nr. 0242) of III/KG 30, though at least three more German aircraft were damaged on that occasion.

Ramming attack

On his 96th sortie, Lieutenant Ye. A. Krivosheyev of the 19th GvIAP rammed a German fighter over Murmansk and was killed. He was posthumously awarded the HSU title.

Another Airacobra unit, the 20th GvIAP, also operated up north. The operations of the 19th and 20th GvIAPs were, of course, very important, but the 22nd ZAP under Colonel I. I. Shoomov remained the main unit handling the Cobra. By the time the P-400s started arriving, the 22nd ZAP had developed into a major training centre with a well-established training programme and good technical facilities. After a theory course, pilots would begin flying training, while trainee technicians participated in the unpacking and assembly of aircraft and repaired damaged machines. The unit had four assembly teams, one of which was tasked with assembling Cobras. [Note: an RAF team of 16, including one pilot, assisted this process in January 1942.]

Initially, three Airacobra Mk Is (AH610, AH653 and AH669) were used as trainers. After the trainees got their Airacobra type rating, fighter units would receive their Cobras, test-fly them and leave for the front.

The 508th IAP was the first unit to start Airacobra conversion training at the 22nd ZAP. However, on completing the training course the unit was ordered to convert again – this time to the LaGG-3. The reason behind this decision is hard to guess; probably the higher command decided the unit's personnel and commanders were not nearly experienced enough to fly the P-400.

The 153rd IAP was next, arriving in Ivanovo from the Leningrad front on 25 March 1942. The training was completed in 27 days, the pilots averaging 12 flying hours on the Cobra. On 14 July the unit left for the Voronezh front and arrived in Voronezh on 29 June under HSU Major S. I. Mironov. On the same date another Airacobra unit arrived – the 185th IAP under Lieutenant Colonel Vasin. As the two units were pressed into action they were included in the 3rd Strike Group (later 244th Air Division) under General L. A. Gorbatsevich. In addition to 40 Airacobras, the 244th operated 60 Douglas A-20 Boston bombers.

There was violent fighting on the Voronezh front, and the Cobra pilots joined the fray immediately. On 1 July alone, the P-400s flew 66 sorties. The intensity of the fighting mounted as the Wehrmacht began its summer offensive in southern Russia. Airacobra pilots claimed 16 'kills', including 11 Ju 88s. There were losses, too – two P-400s were shot down and one went missing. Eight more aircraft were damaged on the ground during a German air raid. Later, the *Stalinskiy Sokol* air force gazette ('Stalin's falcons' was the popular name given to wartime SovAF pilots) reported a successful dogfight in which Airacobras took part, publishing photos of the pilots: Major Mironov, Captain Kislyakov, Captain Kapin, Lieutenant (sg) Smirnov, Lieutenant (sg) Bezrodnyy, Lieutenant (sg) Amkoladze and others.

The fate of the two units was different. The 185th IAP flew Cobras only briefly; in August 1942 it was disbanded and the personnel moved

A number of the P-39s destined for the USSR were paid for by public subscription in the US. These P-39Q-25s (note the four-bladed propellers) wore the inscription 'East Aurora, NY Public Schools'.

These pictures show that the US-applied inscriptions on 'presentation' aircraft were retained on at least some P-39s in Soviet service. How many aircraft wore the Buffalo Belle marking or were provided by School 51 is unknown, but the aircraft above wears a similar badge to that shown at left being handed over to a Russian pilot on delivery from the USA.

to the 1st PAD (Peregonochnaya Aviadiveeziya – Ferry Air Division) under P. Mazurook. The 153rd IAP, on the other hand, moved to Lipetsk and continued operations until 25 September 1942. Its pilots flew 1,070 sorties on the Voronezh front, claiming the destruction of 64 German aircraft; eight Airacobras were shot down and three pilots killed in action, three more aircraft were lost and one pilot was killed in an accident. "The fact that combat losses are so few is due to the high skill of the pilots and the high performance of the Airacobra fighter," CO S. I. Mironov wrote in his report. After that, the 153rd IAP became the 28th GvIAP.

Aircraft shortage

Despite the initial combat success, Cobras were sparse on the Soviet-German front in 1942. By mid-November tactical units had a mere nine Airacobras in Karelia and 15 on the northwestern front, where the 28th GvIAP had relocated on 27 October after receiving new personnel and aircraft as attrition replacements. Nine more aircraft were operated by Moscow's 6th PVO (air defence) corps and 12 more (all but one in non-flying condition) in the Northern Fleet's air arm. The reasons were the painstaking (and thus slow) way in which Airacobra units were trained and the fact that only 193 Cobras were delivered in 1941-1942. They were mainly P-400s (Airacobra Mk Is), including some aircraft which had actually seen service with the RAF, but also some P-39Ds which the USSR had ordered directly.

Nearly all Airacobras delivered to the USSR at the time were armed with the reliable drum-fed 20-mm Hispano Mk 404 cannon instead of the 37-mm Oldsmobile cannon which equipped most USAF P-39s, and which was notoriously prone to jamming. In addition, Soviet Cobras had two synchronised 12.7-mm machine-guns in the nose and four 7.62-mm machine-guns in the wings.

High-level approval

In late 1942 the Soviet leaders (Stalin, Molotov, Mikoyan, etc.) were beginning to get reports of Soviet pilots' combat experience on foreign aircraft. For example, in late September engineer Lieutenant Colonel A. G. Kochetkov reported from the Karelian front where he was evaluating the combat capabilities of various US fighters: "The Airacobra clearly shows the best combat results. Even young pilots flying it successfully oppose Bf 109E and Bf 109F fighters." The Soviet air force top command voiced a complaint that was very much in line with this report: "The Americans produce the P-39 by the thousand, and all we get is a few aircraft." The air force command requested that deliveries of the Curtiss P-40B and P-40E Kittyhawk be reduced and deliveries of the Airacobra be increased instead.

On 7 October 1942 Stalin addressed Roosevelt accordingly: "I am told that delays in deliveries are caused mainly by the lack of capacity in freighters. To alleviate this problem, the Soviet government is prepared to agree to a reduction in deliveries of US war materials to the Soviet Union. We are prepared to temporarily do without deliveries of tanks, artillery, ammunition, handguns etc. However, we need an urgent increase in the deliveries of up-to-date fighter aircraft, notably the Airacobra." Stalin went on to request that deliveries of P-39s be increased to 500 aircraft per month.

Roosevelt replied that currently all Airacobras were delivered to front-line USAAF units straight off the production line. Nevertheless, he promised to increase P-39 production at the expense of other types and send some of the Cobras to the USSR. He was as good as his word: in 1943, Soviet air force units alone (i.e., not counting naval aviation units) received 2,627 Airacobras.

Pilot opinion

In the spring of 1943, a number of newly-formed regiments, most in southern Russia, were equipped with Airacobras. G. G. Golubev, who went on to become an HSU, recalls how the Soviet pilots reacted to the P-39: "The first impression was rather negative. The aircraft seemed too heavy and sluggish when compared to the nimble Polikarpov I-16. But when we retracted the undercarriage and entered the aerobatic zone we quickly found out that the first impression had been wrong. One thing we particularly liked was the radio. For the first time we could manoeuvre using ground control commands and not the flight leader's signals. The ground controller's voice directing us to the targets sounded like sweet music to us. Now we would give the 'mesers' the old what-for!

"Performing aerobatics on the Cobra called for a steady hand. At the slightest inaccuracy during a tight turn, a yo-yo manoeuvre or at the top of a loop the aircraft would go into a spin – often a flat spin (from which the P-39 could not recover). This was one of its main drawbacks."

The famous Soviet ace A. I. Pokryshkin, then holding the rank of captain and serving with the 16th IAP, related his judgement. "It was a shapely aircraft. One thing I particularly liked about the Airacobra was the armament. That was really something to shoot the enemy down with – a hard-hitting 37-mm cannon, two fast-firing heavy machine-guns and four normal calibre machine-guns. I wasn't put off when other pilots warned me that the Cobra was dangerously prone to spinning because of a C of G located well aft."

It should be noted that in early 1943 Soviet pilots tested the P-39's spinning characteristics.

Bell P-39Q Airacobra VoennoVozdushnyye Sily 1944-45

Armament
The first Russian Airacobras were P-400s originally intended for the RAF, and as such had Hispano 20-mm cannon in the nose. This weapon was preferred to the 37-mm by Russian pilots because of its greater reliability. Also, the trajectory of the shells more closely matched that of the 0.50-in guns, allowing a greater concentration of fire. Post-war, the nose gun was often replaced by a Soviet-made B-20 gun of the same calibre. The Soviets removed the wing gun pods from their P-39Qs or had the aircraft delivered without them, preferring better performance to extra firepower. In the fighter-bomber role, the P-39 could also carry 100-kg (220-lb) FAB-100 and 250-kg (551-lb) FAB-250 GP bombs.

Cockpit door
One of the more unusual features of the Bell Cobras was the car-type entry doors, a feature only found elsewhere among wartime fighter aircraft on early models of the Hawker Typhoon. The jettisonable door unit was much the same as that fitted to automobiles, with the normal opening handle and a winding handle for opening the window. The glass in the window was replaced with Perspex following RAF experience with the Airacobra.

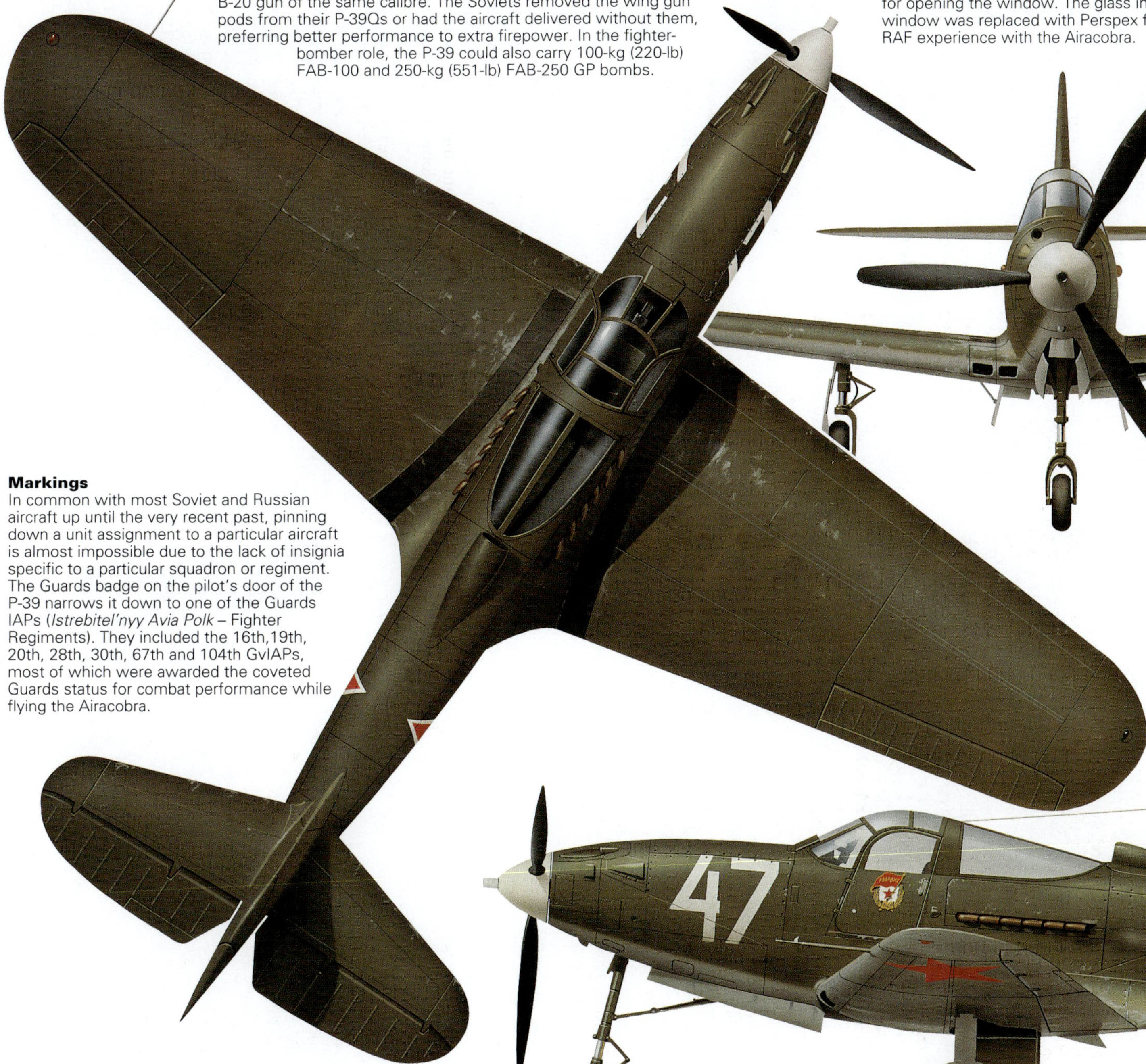

Markings
In common with most Soviet and Russian aircraft up until the very recent past, pinning down a unit assignment to a particular aircraft is almost impossible due to the lack of insignia specific to a particular squadron or regiment. The Guards badge on the pilot's door of the P-39 narrows it down to one of the Guards IAPs (*Istrebitel'nyy Avia Polk* – Fighter Regiments). They included the 16th,19th, 20th, 28th, 30th, 67th and 104th GvIAPs, most of which were awarded the coveted Guards status for combat performance while flying the Airacobra.

Airacobra aces
The top-scoring Cobra pilot of any nation, and the second-ranking Soviet ace of the war, was Alexsandr Pokryshkin of the 9th and 16th GvIAPs. His overall score was 59 enemy aircraft, 48 of them destroyed while flying Airacobras. The third-ranking ace, Grigori Rechkalov, scored many of his 58 kills on P-39s. One of the P-39 aces, Mikhail Baranov (total score 28), brought down a Bf 109 over Stalingrad by chopping its tail off with his propeller in a *Taran* or ramming attack, having expended all his ammunition on three others. Such attacks were relatively rare and not officially sanctioned.

Undercarriage
In the light of combat experience with the P-39, the nose undercarriage leg fork was strengthened, beginning with the P-39L model. This was a non-steerable, self-castoring unit. Undercarriage operation was electric, taking 28 seconds to extend. A 40-second pattern from the break (a half loop with gear down selected at the top) was popular among American units, but the slow extension time could cause trouble in an emergency.

NII VVS

New aircraft for the Soviet Air Force were tested at the NII VVS (State Scientific Institute of the Air Force). The Soviet Air Force was as concerned about the stability of the P-39 as was the USAAF. The P-39Q-10 at left was used for extensive tests in October 1943 and was fitted with a spin recovery parachute rig and the underwing 0.50-in gun packs usually deleted from Soviet Airacobras such as the PQ-39-20 seen above, also during NII trials. The 'star in circle' insignia did not appear on aircraft in regular Soviet service.

Test pilot V. Ye. Golofastov reported that, at C of G positions between 25.7 and 29 per cent MAC, the aircraft recovered quickly if the spin recovery manoeuvre was executed immediately after entering a spin. The US standard operational procedure for spin recovery was rejected as too complicated.

Kuban' clashes

The Airacobra made itself prominent during the fierce battles over the Kuban' region in late April 1943. Each day, 30 to 40 clashes with German aircraft would take place over the Myskhako peninsula and later over the *stanitsas* (Cossack villages) of Kiyevskaya and Moldovanskoye. On 9 March 1943, the 45th IAP under Lieutenant Colonel I. M. Dzoosov arrived at Krasnodar airfield and went into action immediately. Eighteen of the unit's 45 pilots had been in combat at the time of arrival. April 1943 was the most successful period for the unit, for the pilots and commanders had got to know the aircraft and tactics well. Within a month, Lieutenant I. I. Babak shot down 14 enemy aircraft, and Lieutenants (sg) D. B. Glinka and Sergeant N. D. Koodrya scored six 'kills' each.

However, the 45th IAP suffered losses, too. On 15 April alone, D. Glinka, V. l. Sap'yan, M. Petrov and I. Bezbabnov were shot down. As soon as fighting in the Kuban' region ceased, four 45th IAP pilots (B. B. Glinka, P. M. Berestenev, N. D. Koodrya and D. I. Koval', who had 15, 10, 11 and 10 'kills', respectively) became HSUs. The unit's CO was promoted to colonel and given command of the 9th GvIAD (ex-216th IAD). (The 45th IAP later became the 100th GvIAP.)

The 16th GvIAP had attained the prestigious Guards status even before converting to the P-39. Between 9 and 30 April, the unit flew 289 sorties on the Airacobra, claiming the destruction of 81 enemy aircraft, including 75 fighters. Within the same time frame, 18 P-39s were shot down or went missing, two more were written off in accidents and 11 pilots were killed. However, 19 new aircraft were delivered in the same month and the unit retained operational capability.

New tactics

The 16th GvIAP went on to become the most famous unit in the Soviet air force – or so it seems. The winning tactics employed by the unit were worked out over the Kuban'. This was the birthplace of the 'Kuban' ladder' – a multi-layer squadron formation in which the top pair flew 200-300 m (650-980 ft) above the bottom pair and each pair was placed farther away from the sun than the one flying below. This formation gave the pilots good all-round visibility and the ability to manoeuvre freely, and facilitated co-ordination between pairs in a dogfight. The man behind this tactic was A. I. Pokryshkin, who got his first HSU title on 24 May 1943, for scoring 13 'kills' plus six shared 'kills'. On the same day another ace, Captain V. I. Fadeyev, was awarded the HSU title – posthumously. He was one of the best fighter pilots of the 4th VA (Vozdooshnaya Armiya – Air Army), with 20 'kills' to his credit.

The 289th IAP, another Airacobra unit, was the most successful 'Hun hunter' in the Kuban' region. It entered action on 17 March 1943, operating from Korenovskaya airfield. Until 20 August the unit was in the thick of the action, making 1,625 sorties and downing 167 enemy aircraft – 112 of them during three tremendous battles staged between late April and early June. On 24 August the 289th IAP was transformed into the 104th GvIAP as a recognition of its combat success. The unit's CO, I. A. Taranenko, was awarded the HSU title and promoted; Major V. G. Semenishin, also HSU, took over as CO. The unit continued to fly the P-39, acting as part of the 9th GvIAD.

At the time, the proportion of Cobras in the Soviet tactical fighter inventory was still small. As of 1 July 1943, 27 P-39s were in action in Karelia, 30 on the Leningrad front, 45 in the Kuban' region, and 64 more were ready to counter the German offensive on the central front. By then, Airacobras made up about 5 per cent of the Soviet fighter force.

Soviet improvements

Earlier, the Airacobra I had been tested at NII VVS and found satisfactory. Then it was compared with the Yak-1 and LaGG-3, both powered by the Klimov M-105P, and the Bf 109F. However, in the year which followed, both Germany and the Allied forces had vastly improved their combat aircraft. The new Soviet La-5 and Yak-9 fighters were up against the Bf 109F-4, later joined by the Bf 109G-2 and Bf 109G-4. The Cobra compared poorly with these two types. Soviet specialists were well aware of this, and attempts to improve the P-400's performance were made as early as late 1942. One Airacobra I (BX382) was progressively lightened by removing the 7.62-mm wing guns and part of the armour, then the radio set, battery and oxygen bottles and, finally, reducing the fuel load by 100 kg (220 lb). The NII VVS test report recommended modifying the Airacobra I by removing the wing guns, half the armour plates and the lead ballast in the rear fuselage.

The Northern Fleet's air arm followed these recommendations and reduced the P-400's weight by 247 kg (544 lb). Test pilot A. G.

This P-39N is refuelled from a venerable Russian tanker during the summer of 1944. The Soviets relied heavily on obsolete equipment, including Hucks starters and other vehicles left over from World War I.

Left: A P-39Q of a Guards unit is seen at Poltava in the summer of 1944 during the period of Eighth Air Force shuttle missions to Russia. US and British aircraft in Russian service usually remained in the basic scheme in which they were delivered, although polished spinners were a common feature on Airacobras.

Below left: The Airacobra's wide-track main gear and tricycle configuration suited it to snowy and icy surfaces. The tail band on this aircraft suggests a naval unit.

Kochetkov, who was dispatched to the Northern Fleet's 2nd GvIAP in April 1943, reported that, even without wing guns, the Airacobra I had sufficient armament to shoot down enemy aircraft effectively. The time required to reach 5000 m (16,400 ft) and the practical ceiling was reduced by 1.3 minutes and 9 minutes, respectively; short-field performance was also improved. Still, most aircraft were delivered unmodified.

P-39L

Meanwhile, new models of the Airacobra were tested at NII VVS. In July 1943, engineer P. S. Opoprienko and test pilot V. Ye. Golofastov put P-39L-1 42-4666 through its paces. They reported that the aircraft was well equipped for bad-weather flying – it was fitted with the MN-26 DF set and had wing, tailplane and propeller blade de-icing.

The P-39L had other improvements, too. Combat reports had led to changes in armour protection (armour plate was added to the cockpit and removed from unimportant areas) and the introduction of a stiffened nosewheel fork. The cockpit, oil tank and armament bay were heated by air from the engine. The 1,150-hp (858-kW) Allison V-1710-35 (E4) powering early P-39 models was replaced by a V-1710-63 (E6) rated at 1,325 hp (988-kW) for take-off. As with most Airacobras delivered in 1943, the P-39L-1 had a 37-mm M-4 cannon firing through the propeller hub, two 12.7-mm Colt-Browning machine-guns in the nose and four 7.62-mm Colt-Browning machine-guns in the wings.

Unlike earlier and later Cobra tests at NII VVS, the aircraft was filled with US 100-octane avgas and performance in the take-off mode (i.e., at full military power with turbo pressure increased from 1,070 to 1,150 mm Hg) was also recorded. This boosted speed from 490 km/h (304 mph) to 530 km/h (329 mph) at ground level and from 554 km/h (344 mph) to 591 km/h (366 mph) at 3000 m (9,840 ft). At the time, high-octane fuel was nowhere to be found in front-line units, so pilots were advised against using full military power. In general, the test results were deemed satisfactory; the report indicated that at low and medium altitude, the P-39L-1 was almost equal in performance to the current Bf 109G-2 and Fw 190A-4.

Action on the Southern Front

The famous 9th GvIAP under I. A. Morozov was one of the units flying the P-39L-1. In August 1943, Soviet forces launched an offensive on the southern front, and the unit participated in the breaking-up of the German defences near Molochnaya river and in the liberation of Taganrog. Captain Amet-Khan Sultan, later twice HSU and test pilot, earned fame in these battles, downing two German bombers near Kalinovka on 20 August. On the next day, six P-39s flying combat air patrol cover in the region spotted 12 Ju 88s. The Soviet pilots came in head-on, sending the bombers scattering in all directions and making them drop the bombs prematurely, and shot down three of them – one of the 'kills' being scored by Amet-Khan. Hardly had this fight ended when a group of 15 He 111s put in an appearance. Again, the Soviet pilots attacked head-on; Amet-Khan downed one more bomber, which fell near Uspenskaya village.

Amet-Khan's group returned home safely. It so happened that General F. I. Tolbookhin, C-in-C of the southern front, had watched this battle from beginning to end. He immediately decorated Amet-Khan with the Order of the Combat Red Banner. During the nine most action-packed days, the 9th GvIAP's pilots flew 247 sorties on the Cobras, had 22 group dog-fights and destroyed 35 enemy aircraft.

Not all sorties ended well, however. In the spring of 1944, fierce battles started in the Crimea, culminating in the liberation of Sevastopol' and the whole peninsula on 12 May. During this period, the 9th GvIAP suffered heavy losses. Of the 39 Airacobras (including three in non-flying condition) it had at the start of the campaign, five were shot down by enemy aircraft and two by flak; two

A group of P-39s in temporary winter camouflage rests on a Russian airfield. The aircraft are either P-400s (Airacobra Mk Is) or P-39D-1/2s with the 20-mm cannon. Later P-39s for the USSR had winterisation features such as wing and tailplane de-icing boots.

Airacobra Aces

went missing; another two were lost in accidents.

In the second half of 1943, Airacobra deliveries to the USSR continued to grow. The aircraft were mostly ferried to the 22nd ZAP at Ivanovo via Fairbanks, Alaska, and to the 25th ZAP at Adjikabul' via Abadan (Iran). (Often they wore spurious markings, such as red stars superimposed on white roundels; these high-vis white portions were painted out as soon as the aircraft reached the conversion training units.)

New units

In 1943, 17 fighter regiments equipped with P-39s were formed, as compared to 14 in 1942. Later, the Soviet high command decided not to form any more new Airacobra units and to deliver new aircraft to existing units as attrition replacements. Cobra units were, if possible, grouped into fighter divisions, of which there were eight. Two of them – the 190th and 239th IADs (the latter became the 5th GvIAD) – constituted the 11th IAK under General G. A. Ivanov, the only all-Airacobra fighter corps in the Soviet air force.

In late 1943, new Cobra models started arriving: the P-39M, powered by the V-1710-83 and with slightly improved high-altitude performance, the P-39N, and P-39Q with the V-1710-85. The N and Q models were the most common in the SovAF. Both were tested at NII VVS, P-39N-0 42-8734 in July 1943 and P-39Q-10 42-20561 in October 1943. The aircraft differed only in detail: the P-39Q had the four 7.62-mm wing-mounted machine-guns of the earlier models replaced by 12.7-mm machine-guns in underwing pods. In overload configuration, the P-39Q-10 could carry a 530-kg (1,168-lb) drop tank or a 234-kg (516-lb) bomb on a centreline rack, though this noticeably affected the aircraft's stability. Another quirk of the Q was its increased sensitivity to elevator inputs during aerobatics. Pulling the stick back just a little too far was enough to send the aircraft into a spin.

US interest

In October 1943 US ambassador Averill Harryman remarked in a conversation with V. M. Molotov that "there is one aircraft type, namely the Airacobra, that the Soviet air force employs with considerable success. The

Despite the Airacobra's perceived failings in the fighter role among other Allied forces, the Soviets achieved much success with them against the Luftwaffe, finding them equal with the Bf 109 and Fw 190 at low level. Two of the top three Soviet aces, Pokryshkin and Rechlakov, flew P-39s for the bulk of their combat career. Alexsandr Ivanovich Pokryshkin (top, with flying helmet) was the first of two VVS pilots to be awarded the title Hero of the Soviet Union (HSU) three times. He served as commander of the 16th GvIAP and later the 9th GvIAP, amassing a final score of 59 enemy aircraft. Many lesser aces (by Soviet standards) scored highly with the P-39. Lt (sg) O. Zyuzin of the 11th GvIAP, part of the Black Sea Fleet (VVS ChF), was credited with at least 15 kills. His Airacobra (above) was marked in the traditional Soviet manner with red stars rather than German national insignia. Captain P.I. Chepinoga of the 508th IAP (seen here, right) has 21 victories marked on his P-39. Among the many medals he is wearing is the Golden Star of the Hero of the Soviet Union, the Order of Lenin (awarded simultaneously with the status of HSU) and the Order of the Red Banner.

P-39Ds or P-400s are seen in typically harsh winter conditions. While not perfect, the Soviets liked their 'Little Cobras' which were suited to the low-level combat environment and the short-range nature of most ground support sorties flown on the Eastern Front. Including P-63s, Bell products comprised 75 per cent of the American fighters supplied to the Soviets under Lend-Lease.

Russians seem to know how to use it even better than the Americans. It would make sense for Soviet pilots to share their experience with General Vandenberg (one of the top commanders of the USAAF)...This is why Vandenberg would like to visit the Soviet air force squadrons flying the Airacobra."

The Bell Aircraft Corporation expressed a similar request, and the Soviet leaders went along. General Vandenberg and company representatives visited the 6th ZAB (Zapasnaya Aviabrigada – Reserve Air Brigade) in Ivanovo, and the 67th and 30th GvIAPs. The Soviet pilots had some requests, e.g., they wanted an improvement in the ballistics and rate of fire of the 37-mm cannon. They claimed that late P-39Qs were much less stable than the early ...Cobras and that the armoured headrest introduced on this model impaired rearward visibility. (Despite this, one P-39Q flown by ace G. I. Rechkalov sported no fewer than 57 victory stars on the gun cowling.) Bell representatives said they would take this into account.

The US delegation's visit to the 6th ZAB was marred by the crash of a P-39Q-5 when the pilot became disorientated after recovering from a spin and had to bail out. It turned out that the spin had been caused by a too-far-aft centre of gravity.

Fatal spins

The Airacobra's propensity to spin caused many accidents, some fatal. Lieutenant Colonel I. M. Dzoosov recalled that some pilots even developed an uncontrollable fear of aerobatics. Three experienced NII VVS test pilots were killed when the P-39 spun in – K. A. Groozdev on 2 February 1943, K. A. Avtonomov on 3 January 1944, and K. I. Ovchinnikov on 27 April 1944.

In October 1943, P-39Q-10 42-20561 with underwing 12.7-mm machine-guns was tested at NII VVS specifically with a view to determining its spinning characteristics. Major V. Ye. Golofastov executed 115 spins, doing 180 turns all in all. The flights were made with five different C of G positions ranging from 28.4 to 30.9 per cent MAC and at weights of 3486 to 3578 kg (7,685 to 7,888 lb). The results were quite satisfactory – the report stated that "the spin manoeuvre on the P-39Q-series fighter is safe and recovery is possible within the usual C of G limits, provided the recovery manoeuvre is executed immediately and energetically, and the altitude is sufficient." The institute recommended that pilots study the recovery procedure once again and be careful about keeping the aircraft's C of G within its limits. Still, accidents continued.

Structural defects

When two fatal accidents, one non-fatal accident and one minor incident happened in the 11th IAK under General Ivanov, NII VVS lead engineer I. G. Rabkin and test pilots V. Ye. Golofastov and D. G. Pikulenko were sent to the corps' location on the northwestern front to investigate. Rabkin recalled that, on examining the wreckage of the Airacobras, he and the pilots discovered structural damage to the aft fuselage and cracks in the horizontal tail spars that were not caused by the impact.

An immediate inspection of all the unit's Airacobras was made. Fifteen aircraft were found to have structural damage at the same locations, which, if it grew any worse, could cause catastrophic failure. Tests conducted at TsAGI showed that US structural strength requirements were less stringent than the Soviet ones, and some aircraft could not withstand the stress when carrying bombs. After that, the 11th IAK Cobras were field-modified – the rear fuselage and tail unit were strengthened according to TsAGI recommendations.

In the US, a number of P-39Qs were converted to unarmed TP-39Q trainers by installing a second cockpit for the instructor with a conventional sideways-opening canopy in the gun bay forward of the original cockpit. A shallow ventral fin and sometimes a dorsal fillet were added to make up for the increased side area forward of the C of G. Since these were field-modified aircraft, the TP-39Qs had numerous detail differences. At least two TP-39Qs were delivered to the Soviet air force. Regrettably, accurate identification is impossible for the aircraft wore neither original USAF serials nor Soviet tactical codes. One aircraft had a dorsal fillet but the other did not; the shape of the ventral fin and the forward canopy frame was also different.

NII VVS maintained a close interest in the Airacobra throughout the war. The following test programmes were undertaken successfully in the second half of 1944 alone: spinning and aerobatics tests of P-39Q-10 43-2467, which showed that the Q spun more powerfully and irregularly than early P-39 models; tests of the same aircraft determining the maximum safe dive angles with 100-kg (220-lb) FAB-100 and 250-kg (551-lb) FAB-250 GP bombs, after which the Airacobra was deemed suitable for the fighter-bomber role; tests of P-39Q-30 44-71117 with the elevator trim tab locked in the neutral position; and spinning and aerobatics tests of P-39Q-15 44-29115 with altered C of G position and reinforced tail unit and rear fuselage.

The P-39 saw active service on the Soviet-German front until the end of the war. Eight fighter divisions and 25 regiments operated the type. As of 9 May 1945, the SovAF inventory included 1,178 Cobras, including 536 aircraft serving with the PVO, 478 in the naval air arm and 164 in tactical fighter units.

In the closing stage of the war, the Airacobras of A. I. Pokryshkin's unit operating from tactical airfields in Germany used the excellent German highways as landing strips. One photo depicting a P-39Q taking off from the Berlin-Breslau highway has been published often.

The P-39 stayed in Soviet service until the early 1950s. When the original US armament became unserviceable it was replaced by Soviet 20-mm B-20 cannon and 12.7-mm Berezin UBS machine-guns. In general, the Airacobra was a reliable aircraft which matched the requirements of contemporary warfare and was remembered with affection by Soviet pilots. In fact, it was the best-liked of all the Lend-Lease aircraft. **Yefim Gordon**

A number of P-39s were captured by the Finns in the later part of the war. These P-39Qs are shown in storage in 1947 and may be from the 19th IAP. Another aircraft, P-39Q-15 '26' (originally 44-2664), force-landed in Finland in 1944 and is now in storage for the Air Force Museum at Tikkakoski.

An Industry of Prototypes

Seagull

Supermarine's last seaplane

Type 381 Seagull ASR.Mk I prototype PA143 is seen aloft during the early months of flight testing. Supermarine's assertions that the aircraft was "the modern conception of a naval amphibian" and a "combination of Walrus and Spitfire experience" were difficult to dispute, but the days of the naval amphibian were numbered.

By 1939, Supermarine's exploits as a builder of seaplanes were legendary. Noel Pemberton Billing declared in 1913 his intention to build "boats that will fly, and not just aeroplanes with floats", registering 'Supermarine' as his telegraph address. His company built a variety of floatplanes, flying-boats and amphibians over the ensuing 30 years, many for military applications, the crowning glory of which was the RAF's victorious Schneider Trophy racers of the 1920s and early 1930s. Supermarine's seaplane-building days were destined to climax with the practical, high-performance Rolls-Royce Griffon-engined Seagull.

Supermarine's Seagull was one of a diverse group of late-war piston-engined designs destined never to enter military service. These aircraft were mostly overtaken by the rapid pace of aeronautical engineering development towards the end of World War II. Many succumbed in the face of the jet engine, while others, like the Seagull, were cancelled in favour of the helicopter, which was considered to be more suitable for their intended roles. That said, the Seagull combined innovative features in a uniquely 'clean' design that, had it entered service, would have proved to be one of the most versatile aircraft of its type. However, this was not to be, and the Seagull is remembered only as the last in a long line of Supermarine seaplane designs.

Built as an air-sea rescue aircraft, the Seagull did not start life as such. The original Air Ministry specification, S.12/40, called for an armed fleet reconnaissance amphibian for the Fleet Air Arm (FAA), able to be stowed aboard ship. An aircraft filling this requirement would replace two earlier Supermarine designs, the Walrus and Sea Otter, and in its submission Supermarine took a logical route, developing the proven basic configuration of these types, but with important changes. In fact, company proposals dated October 1940 suggested both biplane and monoplane versions of the new machine, each powered by either a Rolls-Royce Merlin 30 or a Bristol Taurus of unspecified mark. The Ministry accordingly convened a design conference the following April, at which proposals were considered.

RAE research

Meanwhile, the Royal Aircraft Establishment (RAE), Farnborough was in the throes of an aerodynamic research programme centred on the high-lift wing, an area that had been explored by Supermarine while working on

PA143 poses for a company photograph at the Supermarine factory at Woolston, near Southampton, sometime shortly after completion. The aircraft's retracted Handley-Page leading-edge slats are clearly discernible.

Above: Seagull prototype PA143 is seen at speed, about to get airborne. On-the-water testing was carried out off Southampton after initial ground-handling testing at Lee-on-Solent, while other test flying was carried out at Chilbolton, north of Southampton.

another prototype, to specification S.24/37. The aircraft built to this specification, the Type 322 torpedo-bomber/reconnaissance prototypes (nicknamed 'Dumbo'), failed to gain selection (being passed over in favour of Fairey's Barracuda), but featured a variable-incidence (v-i) wing that could be easily adapted for the monoplane S.12/40 design, Supermarine's Type 347. In short, the v-i wing offered a lift coefficient double that of a conventional wing – ideal for carrierborne aircraft. As sea trials would eventually demonstrate, the Seagull was able to get airborne from rest in just 900 ft (274 m). The RAE's tests had concerned full-span flaps and inset ailerons which were tested on a scale model of a Miles M.18 monoplane. Wind tunnel testing of a model Type 347 at Farnborough followed in 1942/43, examining stability characteristics at different wing incidence settings. Thus, with the fruits of Farnborough's research, Supermarine produced a wing with full-span, 40 per cent chord slotted flaps, inset ailerons and Handley Page full-span leading-edge slats.

Mounted above the fuselage on a single pylon, or 'trunk', which functioned in a similar way to a two-spar wing mounted vertically, the Seagull's v-i wing pivoted on hinges at the front wing spar root joints and was 'tilted' by two electrically-operated screw jacks operating on the auxiliary rear spar. In flight, the hinges and jacks also took all aerodynamic loads on the

Above: This view of one of the two Seagulls, from a seldom-photographed angle, clearly illustrates the design of the tailplane. During the RAE's wind tunnel testing in 1944, a conventional T-tail layout was proposed but rejected as it was less stable than the 'butterfly' tail. Also evident are the louvres fitted over the radiator outlet ducts either side of the wing pylon. They helped correct problems with retarded flow from these ducts when the duct flaps were open. The tendency of the starboard float to bury itself during deceleration after landing on water was addressed by lengthening the float struts.

Pre-war Seagulls

Supermarine built four main types of aircraft in the 50 or so years during which it was in business. These were single-engined, general-purpose amphibians; twin-engined flying-boats; monoplane racing seaplanes; and single-engined, single-seat fighters. It was of this first group that the Seagull was to be the final member, ending a line of like-named aircraft that stretched back to the 1920s. The first of them was the result of an Air Ministry Commercial Aircraft competition in 1920, in which Supermarine finished second (to the Vickers Viking III) and was originally named the Seal. The RAF, looking for an amphibian fleet spotter, tested the design shortly afterwards. Renamed Seagull, it was eventually ordered in small numbers by the Air Ministry, principally as a means of keeping the Supermarine company afloat during the depressed years after World War I. Seagull IIs (left) entered RAF service in 1923 with a fleet reconnaissance flight and later served aboard Royal Navy carriers. Others were delivered to the Royal Australian Air Force as Seagull IIIs. After the Seagull IV (a modified civil aircraft) came the entirely new Seagull V. Flown in prototype form (above) in 1933, it was built to a similar requirement to the earlier aircraft, initially for the RAAF. Royal Navy service followed (as the Walrus), but it was as an air-sea rescue aircraft during World War II that the Walrus was perhaps best known. The tractor-engined Sea Otter was an improved derivative of the Walrus.

Type 322 'Dumbo'

Two Type 322s were built in response to Specification S.24/37, which called for a shipborne torpedo dive-bomber and reconnaissance aircraft. Though Fairey's submission, which became the Barracuda, was selected, 'Dumbo' (as the Type 322s were known, thanks to their rather ungainly appearance) was a more advanced aircraft. Paradoxically, it was, in many ways, a simpler design. For example, with a variable-incidence wing, the air brakes or special flaps usually thought necessary for the dive-bombing role could be eliminated. If the specified performance could be achieved without retractable landing gear, fixed undercarriage would have equipped production aircraft as they did the two prototypes.

Above: A plan view of the Seagull illustrates the resemblance between wing shapes of the Type 322 and the Seagull. The v-i wing was easily adapted for use on the Seagull and used a very similar actuation system.

wing, as well as the weight of the hull. The wing itself was of Alclad throughout, with manual folding for stowage aboard carriers. Two longerons, chines and light alloy frames made up the hull which, like the wing, was skinned in flush-riveted Alclad sheet. Oil and coolant radiators for the engine were housed in the pylon supporting the wing, an arrangement that remained unchanged for the Taurus- and Griffon-engined versions. Finally, on the rear of the engine nacelle a Nash and Thomson turret with four 0.303-in (7.7-mm) Browning machine-guns was to be installed.

Monoplane preferred

Though Supermarine had included a biplane variant, with a lower top speed and a higher service ceiling, in its 1940 submission the company made its preference for the monoplane clear. It was, Supermarine said, "the modern conception of a naval amphibian" and a "combination of Walrus and Spitfire experience." On 9 April 1943 the Air Ministry issued Instructions to Proceed with the production of three monoplane aircraft to specification S.12/40, to be serialled PA143, PA147 and PA152.

Supermarine's experimental department at Hursley Park, near Winchester, England was chosen for the construction of the three hulls and final assembly of the three Seagulls. The wings were built at Castle Road, Salisbury, one of the dispersed Spitfire assembly plants. Tail units were built by Folland Aircraft at Hamble.

However, as production got under way, circumstances changed. Supermarine Sea Otter production had got off to a slow start; the company was overloaded with production contracts and responsibility for building this aircraft was handed to Saunders-Roe. By 1943 they were finally entering service, taking the pressure off its intended replacement, the Seagull. Some design requirements had also been relaxed, the Admiralty deciding that below-deck stowage aboard its older carriers was unnecessary. This meant that restrictions on span, folded dimensions, weight and height could all be lifted. With this decision came the replacement of the Merlin/Taurus powerplant alternatives with the larger Rolls-Royce Griffon, coinciding with a change in the Seagull's role.

New specification

Specification S.14/44 was drawn up on 27 November 1944 and covered an air-sea rescue (ASR) amphibian for operation from land or marine bases by day or night. Supermarine Type 381 (as the Seagull became) was essentially the original design altered to meet the new specification by removing the gun turret and fitting a 1,815-hp (1354-kW) Griffon 29. This engine had a two-speed, single-stage supercharger and fuel injection; the third prototype and production Seagulls were to be fitted with a 2,055-hp (1533-kW) Griffon (of unspecified mark, but with the Ministry of Aircraft Production rating RG.30SM) similar to the Griffon 57 with water-methanol injection, which boosted take-off power to 2,500 hp (1865 kW).

Finding a suitable propeller able to absorb the

In this view of the first Seagull ASR.Mk I, at rest on the Solent, the observer's standing-observation position in the rear of the pylon 'trunk' is clearly visible. Two transparent panels provided a good rearward and downward view for an observer. On the original S.12/40 design, a gun turret with four machine-guns was to be fitted. The 'butterfly' tail, with its considerable dihedral, would have allowed an excellent view and field of fire to the rear.

In this excellent colour shot by Charles Brown, prototype PA143 is seen in flight early in the test programme. Both aircraft were finished in standard FAA colours of the period – extra dark sea grey and white.

engine's power while meeting size constraints proved to be a challenge. As the Seagull was expected to occupy the same shipboard space as a Sea Otter, cropped versions of various existing airscrews were tested. However, the chosen design was a new Rotol contra-rotating, six-bladed, hydraulic type which, although it required modifications to the Griffon's reduction gear, allowed for a relatively small propeller diameter of 10 ft (3.05 m), and also eliminated take-off torque. The latter quality was much appreciated in operations from the confines of an aircraft-carrier deck. With these changes, production aircraft were expected to be capable of 260 mph (418 km/h) and have a range, with drop tanks, of 1,230 miles (1979 km).

Seagull ASR.Mk I

A type designation was also issued, the S.14/44 becoming the Seagull ASR.Mk I. Finally, on 14 July 1948, PA143 took to the air for the first time, flown by Lieutenant Commander Mike Lithgow, from Itchen near Supermarine's Woolston factory. Water taxi trials had begun in June and revealed a tendency to roll at slow speeds, and difficulty in keeping the aircraft straight. Longer float struts were introduced to correct a tendency of the starboard float to bury itself in the water during deceleration. Ground handling trials, water testing and test flying continued during 1948, the aircraft making an appearance at the Society of British Aircraft Constructors (SBAC) show at Farnborough on 11 September.

As with most new aircraft, test flying revealed a few aerodynamic 'snags' requiring attention. Buffeting and yawing were among criticisms levelled in flight test reports. While the former was cured with a few aerodynamic 'tweaks', the yaw problem demanded the fitting of a central tailfin and rudder. With these modifications PA143 was put through its paces once more, flights during the first eight months of 1949 proving the effectiveness of the changes. They also brought a positive spin-off in the reduction in the aircraft's stalling speed with flaps up and the wing at zero incidence.

As these tests came to an end the second Seagull, PA147, made its first flight, on 2

Above: In order to make the yellow 'P' (for prototype) marking more discernible against the white fuselage, the surrounding roundel was unusually 'filled in' with dark sea grey. The national roundel markings applied to PA143 were also unusual in that the red portion was smaller than on other FAA types of the period. This was corrected on PA147.

Right: In this view of the rear of the aircraft, the retractable combined tail wheel and water-rudder can be seen deployed. Above this, beneath the tailplane, a retractable arrester hook was installed prior to carrier trials aboard HMS **Illustrious*****. Note that the retracted undercarriage was not completely enclosed.***

PA143 gets a tow during the test programme in 1948. The leading-edge slats, seen here partly deployed, were connected to the 'outer flap' on the inside of the trailing edge and were controlled by an electric actuator. Among the modifications incorporated in '143 during 1948/49 was an anti-splash 'eyebrow' around the nose of the hull.

Left: Jettisonable windows either side of the fuselage, aft of the cockpit, were in line with the navigator's position on the port side of the aircraft. Above these were the intakes in the leading edge of the wing pylon: the small upper intake fed the carburettor, and the lower intake supplied the oil and coolant radiator.

Below: PA147 is seen at the 1949 SBAC show. The aerials fitted above and below each wingtip are believed to have been associated with the Rebecca IV search radar set installed in the aircraft. Wooden wingtips minimised radar interference.

September 1949. Within two weeks it made an appearance at that year's Farnborough SBAC show and shortly afterwards went to the RAE for arrester gear trials with Type 'G' ASR gear under its port wing, and a 15,430-lb (7000-kg) all-up weight. Deck-landing trials aboard HMS *Illustrious* followed in October. They explored the type's suitability for arrested landings and general deck handling of the type. In all, 54 landings were made aboard the carrier in various wind speeds and with varying wing incidence settings. Three Supermarine aircraft took part in these sea trials and returned favourable reports, though two service pilots from the Aeroplane & Armament Experimental Establishment (A&AEE), Boscombe Down had difficulties landing the aircraft, failing completely to pick up the arrester wires, and therefore being obliged to test the aircraft's overshoot capabilities!

Low minimum speed

Manoeuvrability in the water was addressed during tests with PA143 carried out by the Marine Aircraft Experimental Establishment (MAEE) at Felixstowe during December. Fin, rudder and water rudder modifications brought considerable improvement and also benefited handling in the air. Very slow speeds, as low as 35 mph (56 km/h), were achieved by Mike Lithgow – impressive for an aircraft weighing close to 7 tons.

Perhaps the highlight of the Seagull project came in 1950 when PA147 set a world 100-km (65-mile) closed-circuit air speed record for amphibians of 241.9 mph (389.3 km/h) in the hands of Leslie R. Colquhuon, on 22 July 1950.

Left: The Seagull's wing was variable in incidence between 2.5° and 12.5° and was actuated by a 1.5-hp (1.12-kW) electric motor powered by an 8-kVA alternator driven off the engine. This provided power for all onboard electrical systems, and was the first such use of AC current. In case of an electrical failure, the wing could be moved by a manual hand-operated jack in the observer's compartment in the wing pylon.

Below left: Operational Seagulls would have been able to carry two wing drop tanks, each of 60-Imp gal (273-litre) capacity. These supplemented internal wing tankage totalling 285 Imp gal (1296 litres), held in flexible fuel tanks forward of the main spar and rigid tanks aft of the spar. On internal fuel the Seagull had a range of 875 miles (1408 km); with the drop tanks this was increased to 1,230 miles (1979 km).

Below: This air-to-air photograph shows the way in which the aircraft's undercarriage was neatly stowed. Under the undercarriage hinge point, the U-shaped lock-down bracket can be seen. This held the lowered undercarriage in place. Also evident is the smaller of the centre tailfins fitted to correct instability problems.

Above: Though the size constraints imposed in the S.12/40 specification to allow stowage aboard the Royal Navy's older carriers were relaxed in S.14/44, wing folding remained a requirement. To this end, the wing's main spar was raked backwards to allow the wing to be folded in a single movement. Evident in this view of PA143 is one of the telescopic struts, fitted inside the wing float, used to secure the wing to the fuselage, once folded. Note also that the photograph appears to have been subject to wartime censorship which has, somewhat crudely, obliterated the background.

This mark had been set during the Air League Cup Race at Sherburn-in-Elmet, in which the aircraft finished fourth due to its handicap. Otherwise, flight tests with the two aircraft continued, including experiments with light alloy radiators and rocket-assisted take-off gear.

By then, however, there had been a policy change within the Ministry. Sikorsky Hoverfly Mk Is (R-4As and Bs) had entered FAA service in 1945; the helicopter was to be developed to meet the FAA's future ASR needs. Westland Dragonfly HR.Mk 1s (licence-built Sikorsky S-51s) of No. 705 Squadron were in service aboard Royal Navy carriers as 'plane guards' from 1950 and by 1952, Whirlwind HAR.Mk 21s (Sikorsky HRS-2s) were equipping the RN's first fully operational helicopter squadron, No. 848. This unit had a secondary ASR role. The third Seagull, PA152, was never completed and in 1952 was sold, with the two airworthy Seagulls, for scrap. So ended the life an excellent aircraft, another of the piston-engined 'might have beens'. **John Heathcott**

Specification

Crew: three (pilot, navigator and observer/sick-berth attendant)
Powerplant: one 1,815-hp (1353-kW) Rolls-Royce Griffon 29 (third prototype and production aircraft to be fitted with 2,055-hp (1533-kW) Griffon RG.30SM with 2,500-hp (1865-kW) take-off rating with water-methanol injection)
Performance: (estimated figures for production aircraft with Griffon RG.30SM) maximum speed 260 mph (418 km/h) at 11,800 ft (3599 m), 234 mph (377 km/h) at sea level; normal range 875 miles (1408 km) at 131 mph (211 km/h); normal endurance 6.5 hours; maximum rate of climb 1,430 ft/min (436 m/min) at 7,000 ft (2133 m) in MS gear; service ceiling 23,700 ft (7229 m); take-off run from deck 312 ft (96.7 m) in 31 mph (50 km/h) wind; take-off time from water in still air 16 seconds at 14,500 lb (6583 kg)
Weights: empty weight 10,510 lb (4770 kg); loaded weight 14,500 lb (6583 kg)
Dimensions: span 52 ft 6 in (16 m); maximum width wings folded 23 ft 6 in (7.17 m); length 44 ft 1.5 in (13.46 m); height (tail down) 15 ft 10.5 in (4.84 m); wing area 432 sq ft (40.13 m^2)

Right: Seen carrying race number '54', PA147 retracts its landing gear on take-off, possibly on the occasion of the 1950 Air League Cup Race. At this late stage in the Seagull programme, the various modifications made to the prototypes are evident, including the central tail fin (with dorsal fin fillet), modified nacelle and redesigned radiator outlet ducting.

Below: During trials at sea, PA143 needed to return ashore each night as it was too wide for the confines of the elevators aboard **Illustrious*****, and therefore could not be stowed in the carrier's hangar. Other Navy personnel took advantage of these flights; up to five people and their luggage could be accommodated in the aircraft.***

INDEX

Page numbers in **bold** refer to an illustration

INDEX

INDEX

Picture acknowledgments

Front cover: RCAF. **4:** Imperial War Museum, Bruce Robertson, RAF Museum, USAF. **5:** Imperial War Museum (two), RAF Museum, MoD, Aerospace. **6:** Aerospace (four), Imperial War Museum. **7:** Imperial War Museum (four). **8:** Imperial War Museum (three), MoD, Bruce Robertson. **9:** Imperial War Museum via Jim Winchester, Aerospace (three), ECPA, P. Laureau, MAP. **10:** Aerospace, MAP, Imperial War Museum (three). **11:** Aerospace, Imperial War Museum (four), MAP, ECPA. **12:** Imperial War Museum, Australian War Memorial, via A.J. Brown. **13:** USAF, Imperial War Museum (three), Aerospace (two), MAP. **14:** Imperial War Museum, Harry Gann Collection (two). **15:** MoD, Imperial War Museum, Bruce Robertson. **16:** Imperial War Museum (four), Aerospace (two). **17:** Andrew Thomas, Aerospace (two), Imperial War Museum (two). **18:** Imperial War Museum (two), Aerospace (two), US Navy. **19:** Warren Thompson, Aerospace (two), Francis K. Mason, Harry Gann Collection. **20:** Larry Davis Collection (three), Aerospace. **21:** Bruce Robertson, Aerospace (three). **22:** Aerospace, Harry Gann Collection, USAF (three). **23:** Imperial War Museum, Larry Davis Collection, Aerospace, USAF. **24-33:** SNCASO/Ouest Aviation/Sud Aviation (all). **34-35:** North American Aviation (NAA). **36:** Cliff Jolley via Larry Davis (LD), Lieutenant Colonel M. Van Gerpen via LD. **37:** NAA, R. Wainwright via LD, RCAF via Peter R. Foster. **38:** NAA, USAF Museum via LD, NAA via LD (two), Mac Blair via LD. **39:** NAA via LD (two), Harry Gann Collection. **40:** NAA via Warren M. Bodie, NAA via LD (three). **41:** R. Escola via LD, NAA via LD (two), USAF via LD, Brigadier General Robin Olds via LD. **42:** Peter Bowers via LD, USAF via LD, NAA via LD (two). **43:** NAA via LD (two), David Menard via LD, Dick Gilbert via LD. **44:** E. Martin via LD, Wm. J. Balogh via LD, Dick Gilbert via LD. **45:** NAA, NAA via LD (three), W. M. Jefferies via LD. **46:** Major General Stanley Newman via LD, Robert Lamprecht via LD, P. Paulsen via LD (two). **47:** NAA via LD (two), USAF via LD, Ron Picciani via LD. **48:** Lieutenant Colonel J. H. Meierdierck via LD, C. Williamson via LD, Aerospace, E. W. Quandt via LD. **49:** Joann Kilpack via LD, Warren M. Bodie, Flight Refuelling Ltd, NAA via LD. **50:** via Robert F. Dorr via LD, USAF via LD, via David Menard via LD. **51:** Ron Picciani via LD, R. B. Ochs via LD, Colonel R. B. Smith via LD, Dick Gilbert via LD. **52:** Robb Satterfield via LD, J. McCann via LD, USAF, NAA, Paul Barranger via LD. **53:** Ted W. Van Geffen, Aerospace, USAF via LD, USAF, Colonel F. Crain via LD. **54:** NAA via LD (two), Aerospace (three), Harry Gann, US Navy. **55:** USAF via LD, Stephen Miller via LD, Ozzie Neidermann via LD, R. C. Beitel via LD. **56:** Aerospace (two), Robert Mikesh, Hugh Muir via LD, via P. Laureau. **57:** USAF, USAF via LD, Aerospace (four). **58:** Harry Gann, NAA, USAF via LD, Warren M. Bodie (two). **59:** Paul Peterson via LD, NAA via LD, NAA (two), Al Schmidt via LD. **60:** Ron Picciani via LD, USAF via LD, NAA (two). **61:** Bruce Robertson (two), E. Schultz via LD. **62:** King Lotz via LD, David Menard via LD, Brigadier General Wm. Fairbrother via LD, Gordon Greer via LD. **63:** Major J. White via LD, Ivo Sešek via Dragiša Brašnović, David Menard via LD (two), Merle Olmsted via LD, Robert Mikesh. **64:** NAA, Aerospace, Luftwaffe, KLu. **65:** Aerospace (two), KLu, AAFCE, Jeff Ethell via LD. **66:** Brigadier General Ken Bell via LD, Lieutenant Colonel A. Bruder via LD, Ron Preciado via LD, Stephen Miller via LD. **67:** David Menard via LD, Doug Remington via LD, JEM Aviation Slide via LD, USAF via LD. **68:** Aerospace (two), Tom Brewer via LD, Bob Anderson via LD, Patrick Laureau, RAAF. **69:** Tom Brewer via LD, USAF via LD, KLu, R. McDonald via LD, Peter Steinemann. **70:** No. 92 Sqn/RAF, H. Sixma, Aerospace, Tom Brewer via LD, USAF,Dragiša Brašnović Collection, Ivo Sešek via Dragiša Brašnović. **75:** Sqn Ldr Eric Smith via LD, Irv Clark via LD, Jim Winchester/Aerospace, USAF via LD. **76:** Dave Wilder via LD, USAF Museum via LD, Jim Winchester/Aerospace, Aerospace, L. J. Vosloo, NAA via LD (three). **77:** L. J. Vosloo, RCAF, USAF via LD, NAA, KLu, USAF Museum via LD (two), David Menard via LD, NAA via LD. **78:** Al Schmidt via LD (two), NAA via LD (two). **80:** Lee Golwitzer via LD, Major General Fred Ascani via LD, Jim McLennan via LD, Mike Fox via LD. **81:** John Ludwig via LD, Stephen Miller via LD, Frosty Sheridan via LD, Lieutenant Colonel Stephen Pahs via LD. **82:** Bob Esposito via LD, Canadair (two), RCAF. **83:** NAA via LD, Canadair via T. Panopalis, Bristol, RAF Museum. **84:** RCAF (three), Canadair via T. Panopalis. **86:** Luftwaffe, Georg Fischbach via Warren M. Bodie, D. Eklund, Bruce Robertson, Robb Satterfield via LD, USAF Museum via LD. **87:** RCAF, Dragiša Brašnović Collection, EdA, Enzo Maio, NAA via LD, Canadair, Bruce Robertson, Aerospace, Werner Gysin via LD. **88:** Mike Fox via LD, CAC (two), Aerospace, N. M. Parnell, RAAF. **90:** Larry Davis, David Menard via LD, Marty Isham via LD, Christophe Donnet, Ron Picciani via LD, Chris Ryan, Peter R. Foster. **91:** P. Paulsen via LD, Warren M. Bodie, Robert Mikesh, Mike O'Conner via LD, Boeing, Harry Gann, David Donald (two). **92:** Aerospace (six), RAAF. **93:** Aerospace (two), RCAF via Peter R. Foster, David Menard via LD, Robb Satterfield via LD, Guido Buhlman via LD. **94:** Aerospace (three), David Menard via LD, USAF via LD, Colonel Jim Bassett via LD, Denis Hughes via LD. **95:** Canadair via T. Panopalis, Peter R. Foster, MAP, Claudio Toselli, David Menard via LD, Enzo Maio, Tom Brewer via LD. **96:** KLu, Aerospace (three), Lindsay Peacock, Marty Isham via LD, Harry Gann. **97:** USAF, Brigadier General J. Ralph via LD, David Menard via LD, via Jim Winchester, Aerospace, L. J. Vosloo, Herman Potgieter. **98:** USAF, Aerospace (three), via David Menard via LD, ROKAF, USAF via LD, Bob Hanes via LD. **99:** Robb Satterfield via LD, Bruce Robertson, Aerospace (two), M. J. Hooks, Harry Gann, Ivo Sešek via Dragiša Brašnović, Dragiša Brašnović Collection. **100:** USAF, Marty Isham Collection via Robert F. Dorr. **101:** USAF, Don Emigholz via Warren Thompson. **102:** Donal Whicker via Warren Thompson (two), George Nicholas via Robert F. Dorr. **103:** R. Pickett via Larry Davis, USAF via Larry Davis (three). **104:** via Robert F. Dorr, Warren Gustafson via Warren Thompson, Al Adcock via Robert F. Dorr, Thomas E. Cleland via Robert F. Dorr (two). **105:** Al Adcock via Larry Davis (two), USAF, Terry Love via Larry Davis, Larry Davis, Aerospace. **106:** USAF (two), via Larry Davis (two), David Menard via Larry Davis. **107:** Aerospace, USAF, Darrel Whitcomb via Robert F. Dorr, Marty Isham Collection via Robert F. Dorr, via Larry Davis. **108:** Larry Davis, Cessna, USAF, USAF via Larry Davis. **109:** via Robert F. Dorr, Norm Taylor via Robert F. Dorr, via Phil Chinnery, Chuck Corley via Robert F. Dorr (two). **110:** Marty Isham Collection via Robert F. Dorr, USAF via Larry Davis, Charles Fadden via Warren Thompson, Thomas E. Cleland via Robert F. Dorr, Chuck Corley via Robert F. Dorr. **112:** Norm Taylor via Robert F. Dorr, Peter B. Mersky Collection (three), via Warren Thompson. **113:** Charles Fadden via Warren Thompson (two), Chuck Corley via Robert F. Dorr, Larry Davis. **114:** USAF via Larry Davis, Darrel Whitcomb via Robert F. Dorr (three). **115:** Aerospace (two), USAF via Larry Davis. **116:** Aerospace, Bell. **117:** Bell, Larry Davis Collection. **118:** USAF, MoD. **119:** Aerospace (two), via Bruce Robertson. **120:** Bell, Aerospace, USAF. **121:** Bell, Aerospace, Yefim Gordon Archive (two). **122:** Aerospace (two), Bell. **123:** Aerospace, Bruce Robertson. **124:** Bell, Aerospace (two), Harry Gann Collection. **125:** Harry Gann (three), Chuck Aro. **126:** Bell, USAF via Bruce Robertson, Aerospace. **127:** Aerospace (two), Bell, NACA via Robert L. Burns (two). **128:** Bell, Aerospace (four), MoD. Bruce Robertson. **129:** Charles E. Brown, USAF via Harry Gann, Aerospace (two), via Harry Gann, via Andrew Thomas. **130:** Aerospace (two), via Harry Gann, USAF. **132:** Aerospace (two), Bruce Robertson, via Harry Gann (two), Bell. **133:** Aerospace (two), Bell (two). **134:** USAF, Bell, via Harry Gann, Aerospace, Yefim Gordon Archive. **135:** Yefim Gordon Archive (two), Aerospace (two). **136:** Aerospace (three), via Harry Gann, Charles Trask via David McClaren. **137:** David Ostrowski Collection. Bell, NACA via Robert L. Burns, MoD. **138:** Aerospace, Yefim Gordon Archive, NACA via Robert L. Burns (two), Larry Davis Collection. **140:** Aerospace, Yefim Gordon Archive, Bell. **141:** Aerospace (two), Bell (three), Bruce Robertson. **142:** Aerospace (two), USAF via Larry Davis, Yefim Gordon Archive, Bell, via Robert L. Burns. **143:** Aerospace (two), NACA, via Harry Gann. **144-151:** Yefim Gordon Archive. **152:** Vickers-Armstrongs (two). **153:** Vickers-Armstrongs, Aerospace, MoD (two). **154:** Aerospace (two), MoD. **155:** Charles E. Brown Collection/RAF Museum, MoD (three). **156:** Aerospace (four), Blackburn. **157:** Vickers-Armstrongs, Aerospace (two).